Articling Segment

PRINCIPLES OF APPRAISAL

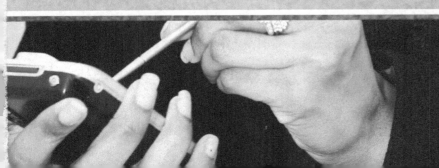

RE CO

Principles of Appraisal
© 2014 Real Estate Council of Ontario

DISCLAIMERS

This publication, including all third party material and all schedules, appendices, pre-printed forms, standard clauses, processes, facts, information and any other material contained therein (the "Publication"), is summary in nature and not intended to replace direct research of original source documents and expert advice. Real estate practitioners and consumers should seek appropriate counsel in matters relating to real estate. At all times, diligence and prudence should be uppermost as all real estate transactions are unique. This Publication is strictly intended for educational purposes only. RECO reserves the right to change or revise this Publication without notice, and will not be liable for any loss or damage incurred by you as a result of such changes or revisions.

RECO, the Ontario Real Estate Association (Designate), service providers and others associated with this Publication and offering of this program (collectively referred to as the "Program Providers") are not responsible for any deficiencies, defects, errors, omissions, or for the adequacy, sufficiency, completeness, suitability, accuracy, currency or applicability of the contents of this Publication. This disclaimer, and all that follow, applies regardless of whether this Publication is made available to you in paper or electronic form.

In the event that you access this Publication by means of the internet or other electronic transmission, you expressly agree that the Program Providers are not responsible for any damage to hardware or software, loss or corruption of data, or any other loss or damage, that may result from your use of this Publication or from your accessing any web site related to this Publication or utilizing any other means of electronic transmission owned or operated by, or on behalf of, the Program Providers. The Program Providers make no warranty or representation that any such web site, electronic document or electronic transmission will meet your requirements, will be uninter-rupted, timely, secure or error-free or that defects, if any, will be corrected.

The Program Providers disclaim all warranties of any kind, whether express or implied, including without limitation any warranties of merchantability or fitness for a particular purpose, related to this Publication. Further, the Program Providers are not liable for loss or damage, whether direct, indirect or consequential, and whether or not it was foreseeable, arising from the utilization of this Publication.

This Course Has Been Approved By The Registrar Under The *Real Estate And Business Brokers Act, 2002*.

Real Estate Council of Ontario
3300 Bloor Street West
Suite 1200, West Tower
Toronto, ON M8X 2X2

International Standard Book Number: 978-0-9780344-7-4
Content Development: Ontario Real Estate Association
Design and Graphics: Automation Plus Ltd.

Printing and Binding: MediaLinx Printing Group   Reprint: May, 2014

ROLE OF THE REGISTRAR UNDER REBBA 2002 IN EDUCATION

The Registrar under the *Real Estate and Business Brokers Act, 2002* (REBBA 2002) is responsible for setting the educational requirements for individuals who wish to obtain and maintain registration as a real estate salesperson or broker. In order to trade in real estate in Ontario, real estate salespersons, brokers and brokerages must be registered with the Real Estate Council of Ontario (RECO) under REBBA 2002. Before beginning a career as a real estate salesperson, individuals are required to complete the required pre-registration courses.

The Registrar, through an Educational Services Agreement, had designated the Ontario Real Estate Association as the organization authorized to provide the pre-registration, articling and broker educational program. All registration-related courses of study, including associated course content, must be approved by the Registrar prior to being offered to students.

DESIGNATE

The Ontario Real Estate Association, through its OREA Real Estate College, takes great pleasure in delivering this program on behalf of the Registrar pursuant to an Educational Services Agreement between the Real Estate Council of Ontario and the Ontario Real Estate Association.

The course curriculum supports the Real Estate Council of Ontario's mandate to protect the public interest through the development of skilled and educated real estate professionals by providing students with timely, comprehensive, accurate and up-to-date education that will allow them to succeed in the real estate marketplace. The OREA Real Estate College fulfills many of its responsibilities to the Registrar, the public of Ontario and the real estate profession by providing learning opportunities so that individuals, either contemplating registration or currently holding registration, can receive appropriate and timely training.

The real estate profession makes a valuable contribution to the economy of Canada and the welfare of its people. The Real Estate Council of Ontario and the Ontario Real Estate Association hope that the successful completion of *Principles of Appraisal* will inspire and motivate you to pursue advanced educational offerings throughout your career.

ACKNOWLEDGEMENTS

A course of this scope is only possible with the assistance of many dedicated professionals committed to the advancement of real estate skills and knowledge. A special note of thanks is owed to the Ontario Real Estate Association for its ongoing forty-year commitment to excellence in real estate education.

The terms REALTOR® and MLS® are identified as design marks in this publication. No attempt has been made to designate all words or terms in which proprietary rights might exist. The inclusion, definition, or description of a word or term is provided for general information purposes only and is not intended to affect any legal status associated with the word or term as a trademark, service mark or proprietary item.

HOW TO CONTACT OREA

Address	99 Duncan Mill Road Don Mills, ON M3B 1Z2
Instructor Support Line	(866) 444-5557 Clarification regarding *course content only*.
Missing Course Materials	(416) 391-6732 (866) 411-6732 Course Administration Services
College Education Centre	(866) 411-6732 (Toronto)

My OREA Community—Education Forums

OREA encourages the use of the Education Forums as a learning tool. This can be found on our website at **www.orea.com**. Log in to "My Portfolio" using your student ID and password. Once logged in, click on the *My OREA Community (Discussion Forum For Courses)* link. If you do not already have a "My Portfolio" password, please contact the College Education Centre. This positive exchange of content information with an expert who will answer posted questions can be practical and extensive. Participation in the forum is specific to each course and fellow students are encouraged to join the discussions. Privacy is protected.

PRINCIPLES OF APPRAISAL
CONTENTS AT A GLANCE

TABLE OF CONTENTS

TABLE OF CONTENTS (continued)

TABLE OF CONTENTS (continued)

TABLE OF CONTENTS (continued)

TABLE OF CONTENTS (continued)

APPENDIX

INTRODUCTION

LEARNING FEATURES

Chapter content summaries and **learning outcomes** detail the learning journey in each chapter.

Illustrations simplify and summarize complex topics. A picture is worth a thousand words. Detailed subject matter often requires visual enhancements to ensure complete understanding.

Curiosities offer novel ideas or explanatory details, while satisfying the inquisitive nature in us all. The element of discovery can expand awareness and consolidate subject matter.

Perspectives bring fresh outlooks and consolidate complex topics, usually using a story line. Everyday occurrences of real estate practitioners often complement the subject matter.

Cautions identify special concerns including situations where prudence is required and practices that can lead to dire consequences if pursued.

Market Memos are interspersed to bring reality to the subject matter. If a topic involves value, the memo may address new technologies that are revolutionizing the valuation process. If the topic details economic trends, the memo may highlight a specific indicator together with statistical data.

Each **Focus** concentrates on additional details for a particular topic. These informative descriptions bridge the gap between academic discussions and today's realities.

STUDY AIDS

Notables highlight key topics in each chapter to assist students with review and study efforts, along with a summary of key glossary terms.

A **Chapter Mini-Review** is provided with each chapter for personal review and assessment. The mini-review is a warm up for active learning exercises.

Active Learning Exercises are included at the end of each chapter. Various testing formats are used including multiple choice, fill-in-the-blanks and short answer exercises.

The **Appendix** contains *all* solutions (including solutions chapter mini-reviews and active learning exercises).

TIPS & GUIDELINES

Courses emphasize *learning by doing* through the mastery of practical real estate skills and knowledge. The course combines formal instruction, self evaluation and problem-solving with fictional characters and scenarios. Students must evaluate circumstances, make suggestions, correct errors and learn important lessons in preparation for the marketplace. Questions are posed that require introspection, strategic thinking, application of techniques and explanation of procedures.

HOW TO MAXIMIZE LEARNING

Make the Text Priority One	• Carefully review each chapter including every topic, illustration and example.
Follow the Learning Path	• Topics are logically sequenced by section and topics within chapters. • While creativity is encouraged, most students are advised to follow the pre-set order.
Complete all Questions/ Exercises	• Practice makes perfect. Complete all chapter mini-reviews and exercises. Solutions are provided in the *Appendix*. • Suggestion: Use a blank sheet of paper as an answer sheet where feasible, leaving the chapter mini-reviews and exercises blank for follow-up review.
Continuously Review	• When in doubt, review. Repeat readings, mini-reviews and active learning exercises as often as required. • Don't move forward without fully understanding all content. • Learning has a lot in common with building blocks. Start with a good foundation and a sound structure will emerge. • Remember, knowledge is cumulative. Don't skip any chapters.
Prepare for the Exam	• The examination tests subject matter covered in the primary text. No surprises…if you diligently study the materials. • Exam questions vary, but not the underlying purpose. Emphasis is on understanding concepts, techniques and procedures. • Don't expect a mere recital of facts.

PRINCIPLES OF APPRAISAL

ABOUT THIS TEXT

The *Principles of Appraisal* program builds on the fundamentals of valuation theory provided in Courses 1, 2 and 3, that included the concept of value and basic valuation principles. This course, concentrating on residential valuation, expands on that knowledge. Appraisal theory has been modified to address methodology that should be used by real estate practitioners in arriving at accurate estimates of value for listing and selling purposes.

Certain modifications and adjustments to appraisal methodology should be noted. In the cost approach, functional and locational obsolescence are discussed as causes of depreciation, but only physical deterioration is accounted for in the practical application of this approach. In the income approach, although mortgage/equity methods of capitalization are discussed, only the market method is applied.

Dollar amounts and other figures used in examples, exercises and case studies are not intended to relate to any specific market, but are provided for example purposes only. In appraisal practice, amounts or figures used must be obtained from the specific market on the date of valuation. Case studies are specifically structured to permit students to apply principles and approaches directly in the marketplace. Current acceptable appraisal theory has been used throughout this workbook, however the reader is cautioned that such premises and methodology are subject to revision.

CHAPTER 1

The Appraisal Profession

Introduction

The key issue for a salesperson is to accurately estimate the value of a property in order not only to obtain a listing, but also sell the property for a reasonable price in keeping with the client's needs. By studying and following the procedures and processes used by professional appraisers, the salesperson/broker will gain the knowledge and learn the techniques and disciplines necessary to arrive at an accurate valuation.

There is another reason to view appraising and appraisals through the eyes of the professional appraiser. Salespeople will certainly come into contact with a professional appraiser whether their client is buying, selling or refinancing property. Banks require appraisals and appraisers to value a property before providing the financing to close the sale. In short, whatever affects the valuation and appraisal of a property affects the salesperson, as valuing is a key component of the real estate business.

Before proceeding with the appraisal/valuation process, it is important to understand the key value concepts that will affect the valuation of a property from the moment an appraisal assignment is started to the time it is finished.

While most salespeople do not actually complete formal appraisal forms, the information contained within them is a great guide as to the necessary information that needs to be collected in order to do the valuation and be able to defend the estimated value outcomes.

Learning Outcomes

At the conclusion of this chapter, students will be able to:

- Define an appraisal and outline the different levels of appraising and appraisers.
- Identify and describe the different professional appraisal organizations active in Ontario.
- Outline the main trends and issues affecting the appraisal industry.
- Explain the different types of appraisal reports.
- Define and explain the different value concepts.
- Define and explain the main principles of value.

THE APPRAISAL

An appraisal is the act or process of estimating value. The resulting opinion of value derived from the appraisal may be informal, transmitted verbally, or it may be formal, presented in written form. Usually, it is a written statement setting forth an opinion of the value of an adequately described property as of a specified date, supported by the presentation and analysis of relevant data.

In effect, there are three levels of appraisers who get involved in estimating value:

Level 1—The public, meaning buyers and sellers.

Level 2—Salespeople and brokers.

Level 3—Professional appraisers, those with recognized accreditations.

NOTE: In Ontario, there is no requirement for a person to actually be licensed either by the Government or a particular organization in order to become an appraiser.

The Public

In a general sense, everyone is a real estate appraiser at some time. Anyone who has ever bought or sold a house, or who owns or has owned real estate, has formed an opinion about the value of a particular piece of real estate in order to reach a decision.

Salespeople and Brokers

This group of professionals requires a sufficient knowledge of real estate appraising in order to advise clients as to the value of a property when it comes to listing or buying a property. The REBBA 2002 Code of Ethics has the following to say about advising clients when it comes to the value of a property:

PROVIDING OPINIONS, ETC.   CODE

6.   (1) A registrant shall demonstrate reasonable knowledge, skill, judgment and competence in providing opinions, advice or information to any person in respect of a trade in real estate. O. Reg. 580/05, s. 6 (1).

(2) Without limiting the generality of subsection (1) or section 5,

(a) a brokerage shall not provide an opinion or advice about the value of real estate to any person unless the opinion or advice is provided on behalf of the brokerage by a broker or salesperson who has education or experience related to the valuation of real estate; and

(b) a broker or salesperson shall not provide an opinion or advice about the value of real estate to any person unless the broker or salesperson has education or experience related to the valuation of real estate. O. Reg. 580/05, s. 6 (2).

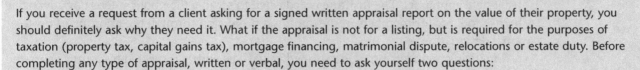

If you receive a request from a client asking for a signed written appraisal report on the value of their property, you should definitely ask why they need it. What if the appraisal is not for a listing, but is required for the purposes of taxation (property tax, capital gains tax), mortgage financing, matrimonial dispute, relocations or estate duty. Before completing any type of appraisal, written or verbal, you need to ask yourself two questions:

A. Do I have the appropriate education and/or the experience to provide an opinion of value or advice about the value of the subject property for the purpose requested?

B. Do I have errors and omissions insurance that will cover the type of appraisal being requested?

It is perfectly acceptable to tell a client that you do not have the education/experience or the insurance coverage to complete the opinion of value requested by your client. Your solution to a client's request for a signed written appraisal may be to refer them to an MVA, CRA or AACI.

Actually, the REBBA 2002 Code of Ethics is quite specific when it comes to the need to advise a client or customer to seek professional assistance from another person.

SERVICES FROM OTHERS   CODE

8. (1) A registrant shall advise a client or customer to obtain services from another person if the registrant is not able to provide the services with reasonable knowledge, skill, judgment and competence or is not authorized by law to provide the services. O. Reg. 580/05, s. 8 (1).

EXAMPLE

Jane Bloggs has been listing and selling residential real estate in Anycity for several years. A friend has asked Jane to value and complete an appraisal report on a commercial building in Smalltown for capital gains purposes. Jane turns down the request because:

- She has never valued a commercial building.
- She is not familiar with Smalltown.
- She has never prepared a formal appraisal report for capital gains tax purposes.
- Her errors and omissions insurance does not cover this type of appraisal assignment.

Jane instead refers her friend to Mike Appraiser who is an AACI practising in Smalltown.

Professional Appraisers

A professional appraiser is a researcher who has mastered the techniques and procedures to be applied in the appraisal of different types of property.

Professional appraisers can be found working in private practice (usually called fee appraisers) or as salaried employees of a corporation or one of the three levels of government. Professional appraisers provide values for a wide range of purposes including mortgage financing, tax assessments, investment decisions and compensation for expropriation.

Many professional appraisers have earned some form of designation from a creditable institution.

THE APPRAISAL INSTITUTE OF CANADA (AIC)

The Appraisal Institute of Canada, founded in 1938, is the national society of professional real estate appraisers. The Institute is dedicated to serving the public interest by advancing high standards for members of the appraisal profession through the granting of profess-ional designations.

Practising members provide reasoned valuations widely respected by courts, chartered banks, real estate corporations, trust companies, mortgage and lending institutions, all levels of government, and private individuals. Members are governed by the Canadian Uniform Standards of Professional Appraisal Practice that provide minimum performance standards for ethics, appraisal, review and consulting assignments. The Institute, in co-operation with the University of British Columbia, develops and maintains a Professional Program of Study leading to the Bachelor of Business in Real Estate and designation as an AACI, P.App or CRA.

The Appraisal Institute of Canada is the predominant appraisal organization in Canada and its designations are the most widely known/recognized. The AIC awards the Canadian Residential Appraiser (CRA) designation. The CRA denotes members who are qualified in the appraisal and valuation of individual, undeveloped residential dwelling sites and housing containing not more than four self-contained units.

The Institute grants the use of the CRA designation upon successful completion of required courses and other criteria established by the Institute. For complete details, visit their website at **www.aicanada.ca**. The national office of the Institute is located at 203–150 Isabella Street, Ottawa, ON K1S 1V7.

ACCREDITED APPRAISER CANADIAN INSTITUTE (AACI, P.APP)

The Appraisal Institute of Canada (AIC) awards the AACI, P.App designation. The AACI, P.App designation denotes fully accredited membership in the Institute and may be used by the holder for the appraisal of a full range of real property including residential, industrial, commercial and agricultural. Of course the AACI, P.App must be experienced in the type of property they are appraising. The "P.App" part of the designation means *Professional Appraiser*.

CANADIAN NATIONAL ASSOCIATION OF REAL ESTATE APPRAISERS (CNAREA)

CNAREA is a national, not for profit, independent association that certifies and regulates real property appraisers in Canada. It was established to provide an effective membership orientated organization of professional real estate appraisers based on their academic qualifications, training and practical experience.

In order to provide a higher level of professionalism, the Canadian National Association of Real Estate Appraisers maintains an active role with the Appraisal Foundation located in Washington DC, USA, and sits on the Appraisal Foundation Advisory Council (TAFAC). All certified designated members of the Canadian National Association of Real Estate Appraisers must abide by the Uniform Standards of Professional Appraisal Practice as promulgated by the Appraisal Standards Board of the Appraisal Foundation. CNAREA is located at Box 157 Qualicum Beach B.C. V9K 1S7. For further details, visit their website at **www.cnarea.ca**.

Designations

The CNAREA has a number of appraisal designations including:

DAR (Designated Appraiser Residential)

The DAR identifies a member who is qualified to perform appraisal and consultation assignments of residential type properties consisting of no more than four housing units, and non-complex commercial properties having a residential component.

DAC (Designated Appraiser Commercial)

The DAC identifies a member who is qualified to perform appraisal and consultation assignments of all types of real property including commercial, industrial and investment.

INSTITUTE OF MUNICIPAL ASSESSORS (IMA)

The IMA is the largest Canadian Professional Association representing members that practice in the field of Property Assessment and related Property Taxation functions.

The objects of the Institute are to promote the interests, education and professional efficiency of persons engaged in valuation of real property for the purposes of municipal assessment and taxation.

Designations

The M.I.M.A. designation is the Institute's highest standing and anyone attaining this designation is classified as an Accredited Member. The A.I.M.A. designation (Associate Member of the Institute of Municipal Assessors) must be attained before an individual can be considered for the M.I.M.A. designation. For complete details, visit their website at **www.assessorsinstitute.ca**. The institute is located at 10720 Yonge Street, Suite 206, Richmond Hill, ON L4C 3C9.

REAL ESTATE INSTITUTE OF CANADA (REIC)

In 1955, the Canadian Association of Real Estate Boards formed the Canadian Institute of REALTORS® to carry out its aims in the field of education. A three-year university course was prepared in co-operation with the University of Toronto. Successful students received a designation in real estate from the Institute.

In 1971, when the Canadian Association of Real Estate Boards became The Canadian Real Estate Association (CREA), the Canadian Institute of REALTORS® became a division of CREA. The name was subsequently changed to the Real Estate Institute of Canada and became a separate organization. Terry Barber, FRI, AACI, of Winnipeg was the first governor of the new Institute. The primary purpose of REIC was to act as the educational arm of CREA and to co-ordinate education courses on a national basis.

From seminars, to intense professional education, to the leading professional designations, all of REIC's programs serve its mission: establishing, maintaining, promoting and advancing professional standards of practice among those occupations concerned with real estate. REIC offers courses leading to the various designations including a specialized appraisal designation—the FRI (A). For complete details, go to **www.reic.ca**.

Designations
FRI (Fellow of the Real Estate Institute)

The FRI designation is awarded to licensed/registered individuals (i.e., salespeople/brokers) who have completed the Real Estate Institute of Canada (REIC) education program and who have demonstrated throughout the course of their careers, their dedication and determination to provide only the highest degree of real estate service and to adhere to FRI standards of practice.

FRI members who specialize in residential appraisals further their professional recognition with this accreditation. The FRI(A) denotes the Appraisal Specialist who has met the stringent and internationally accepted benchmark for the performance of residential appraisals and valuations of dwellings including a triplex and undeveloped building sites. FRI members, having a minimum of five years residential appraisal experience, may achieve the FRI(A) by completing advanced studies in economics, title searching and building construction.

For details regarding the FRI(A) program, contact the Real Estate Institute of Canada, 5407 Eglinton Avenue West, Suite 208, Etobicoke, ON M9C 5K6.

MVA-RESIDENTIAL DESIGNATION

This is a professional designation for REALTORS® who have demonstrated practical and current experience in the local real estate market ,and have completed a prescribed educational program in the field of residential appraisal.

Originally designed by the Ontario Real Estate Association (OREA) and the Canadian Real Estate Association (CREA), the MVA-Residential designation was later granted by provincial real estate associations in conjunction with the Alliance for Canadian Real Estate Education (ACRE).

This designation is no longer offered by OREA. Only current MVA designees as of July 31, 2007 will be able to continue to use the MVA credentials.

A real estate salesperson with an MVA-Residential designation may appraise residential dwellings with up to, and including, two units and may also appraise vacant land where the highest and best use would be a residential dwelling with no more than two units. The appraisals must be to estimate market value and an MVA-Residential appraiser cannot undertake an appraisal where the purpose is litigation, or where they are to be called as an expert witness.

TRENDS AND ISSUES

Automated Valuation Models

AVMs are software programs that can estimate the value of a property. They made their appearance in the 1970's, but became more commonly used in the 1990's with the appearance of electronic databases.

While automated valuation models are not new, they are being increasingly used for mortgage lending purposes and as a result, they compete for appraisal business. Indeed, AVMs have tended to reduce the need for appraisers when it comes to valuing a property for mortgage lending and mortgage insurance purposes. They provide information quickly and are cost effective. AVMs can reduce the appraisal part of the mortgage process from 2/3 days to 30 seconds. As a result, they expedite the process of home financing.

The reliability of AVMs can be affected by the nature of the area. AVMs work well when there is sufficient information on the property and area, there are lots of sales and the properties are all relatively similar. AVMs do not work well when there is a wide range of properties in the area (large and small—renovated/unrenovated) and relatively few sales.

Another major weakness of an AVM is a lack of a physical inspection of the property. AVMs cannot judge the condition of a property or neighbouring properties, or distinguish between a renovated or non-renovated property.

There is also some concern that the increased use of AVMs creates added opportunities for mortgage fraud. Where an AVM is being used, an appraiser no longer talks to the owner to get an appointment to inspect the property, all of which provides a better opportunity for people who do not own the property to apply for mortgages using false IDs or forged documents without the fear of being discovered.

Since AVMs are used in low risk transactions, they have reduced the need for professional appraisers when it comes to the more simple valuation assignments. Nevertheless, when the lending risk is high, appraisers are still being used. In essence, AVMs reduce the number of quick and low cost appraisal assignments, but leave the more complicated assignments and precision work for the professional appraiser.

NOTE: In general, the appraisal profession believes that standards for AVMs need to be created to safeguard the public, as well as the business community.

Automated Valuation Models (AVMs) — CURIOSITY

AVMs are a computer-based valuation methodology that derives a value estimate based on subject property attributes, recent sales and various trends compiled for neighbouring properties, as well as the local/regional markets. The appraiser here is the software program that collects and evaluates information, and then produces a value estimate.

AVMs are proving increasingly popular, particularly in assessment and mortgage financing sectors. Virtually instantaneous results occur from a web-based system by inputting a property address. The AVM database can track hundreds of property features for quick comparison between a subject property and recent comparable sales. Advanced systems not only provide an estimate (typically including a high/low range and confidence level regarding the estimate; e.g., low, medium or high level), but also key factors affecting the property's value.

The automated valuation model is typically driven by location-oriented data. In other words, the system groups properties within a defined neighbourhood affected by similar market trends and/or external influences. As with any system, the AVM is limited by the volume and accuracy of input data.

While originally designed strictly for valuation purposes, AVMs are being creatively linked to other spatially-defined data found in geographic information systems (GIS). For example, detailed reports can include a value estimate, together with demographics, local/regional price increase/decrease trends and other local/regional statistics all of which furnish a broad property profile. GISs are providing greatly enhanced information to complement existing data layers; e.g., physical property details (soil type, terrain, etc.), land registration data, survey details, structural descriptions, adjacent road systems, zoning and census data.

Appraisal Profession

Increased competition from AVMs has reduced the need for traditional residential appraisals; e.g., mortgage financing appraisals being completed by professional appraisers. This in turn has put downward pressure on appraisal fees and resulted in fewer members in appraisal organizations such as the AIC. There are, however, new opportunities which have developed for the professional appraisers that have remained in the industry.

To take advantage of these new opportunities, professional appraisers are moving away from the more traditional point in time mortgage appraisals to other types of assignments such as:

Valuation	Business valuation, expropriation, insurance cost estimating, mass appraisal.
Review	Appraisal review, arbitration/mediation, assessment review/appeal, due diligence assignments and expert witness.
Consulting	Pre-purchase advice, property sales—pre sale marketing, highest and best use studies, property development/land assembly/site selection and market forecasting.
Management	Property management, asset/portfolio management and administration functions related to real property.

Appraisal organizations such as the AIC have moved towards increased education, experience and exam requirements. With respect to the AIC, there is now a mandatory program of continuing education (re-certification) entitled *Continuing Professional Development*. It requires all AIC members (whether AACI, CRA or Candidates) to obtain 60 credits over a 5-year cycle.

One of the new requirements for obtaining a CRA or AACI designation is holding a university degree.

Technology

Technology has dramatically changed the way the professional appraiser completes an appraisal report. It has made the appraisal assignment easier, quicker and cheaper to complete. This technology change includes the introduction of digital cameras, appraisal software and the internet.

The internet enables information to be gathered far more quickly through portals such as the MLS®. It also provides for clients to send appraisal requests to appraisers and appraisers to send the completed report to the client electronically.

Digital cameras eliminate the cost and time of having to develop film and the photo files can quickly be downloaded into the form report.

The appraisal software allows the appraiser to quickly complete a report through copying and pasting, as well as downloading photos and maps straight into the form report.

So, while fees for mortgage financing assignments (for example) have come down or stayed the same over the past few years, the time and cost involved in completing an appraisal assignment has been correspondingly reduced.

Middlemen

The appraisal industry has, over the past few years, seen the emergence of Appraisal Management Companies (AMCs) or Vendor Management Companies (VMCs).

These companies have created relationships mostly with financial institutions and relocation companies so that much of the appraisal work for financing, power of sales and relocations is now ordered through them. The result of this is that there has been a moving away from personal service, where individual appraisers or small appraisal companies had relationships with financial institutions and relocation companies, towards all of the services being handled out of central locations through the AMCs. Many of these individual or small appraisal companies, who still wish to be involved in mortgage financing appraisal work or relocations, now take assignments from the AMC instead of directly from the financial/relocation institution. Of course the AMC takes a part of the appraisal fee. While, the appraiser now takes a lower fee, the benefits are that the appraiser no longer has to handle the relationship and administration, and can spend more time completing appraisal assignments as opposed to continuously marketing to current and potential clients. These appraisers are also given the use of sophisticated proprietary internet-based software owned by the AMC, without having to pay the costs associated with the software. For appraisers who have decided not to join the AMCs, they have moved away from the mortgage appraisal assignments and seek out high fee assignments instead; e.g., taxation, litigation appraisals, etc.

Mortgage Fraud	MARKET MEMO

There has over the past few years been a dramatic increase in fraud being committed by people transferring title electronically from the true owner into their name and then applying for a mortgage with title in their name (all without the knowledge of the true owner). The mortgage is usually relatively low compared to the value of property (e.g., $100,000 mortgage on a $300,000 home). For a low loan-to-value ratio, mortgage companies will usually use an AVM—this, of course, means no use of an appraiser.

In order to reduce this type of mortgage fraud, the suggestion coming out of the industry is that appraisers could be used to inspect the home, instead of just relying on AVMs. When inspecting the property, the appraiser would ask for photo id. It is felt that this would help expose possible mortgage fraud; e.g., when the real owner of the home answers the door to the appraiser and tells the appraiser that they have not applied for a mortgage, the appraiser would alert the mortgage company.

TYPES OF APPRAISAL REPORTS

There are two recognized types of appraisal reports to be found in the marketplace—the Form Report and the Narrative Report.

The Form Report

This report consists primarily of preprinted information that is checked off or details inserted where relevant. Space is provided for brief additional comments. The form report allows for a reasonably brief, but systematic and precise presentation of information and analysis.

There are many different form reports being used out in the marketplace, some specialized for mortgage financing, others specialized for relocations. The two appraisal form reports that will be used in this course are reproduced on the following pages. You should read through and become familiar with the information required.

The form report is generally used by appraisers for estimating the market value of single-family homes, duplexes, triplexes and fourplexes where the purpose of the appraisal would be for financing, relocation, capital gains tax, estate sales and matrimonial split ups where there will be an out of court settlement.

OREA Ontario Real Estate Association

Standard Appraisal Report
Single Family

Form 700
for use in the Province of Ontario

CLIENT: .... Client Ref No: ....

Client: Phone No: (............).. Fax No: (............).. E-mail: ....

Client's Customer: .... Appraiser: .... Appraiser's Ref No: ....

GENERAL APPRAISAL AND PROPERTY INFORMATION

Property Address: ....

Municipality: ....

Full Legal Description: ....

Owner: .... Assessment: Total .... Taxes $ .... Year ....

This Appraisal is to estimate **MARKET VALUE** for a: ☐ Sale ☐ Financing ☐ Other ....

Effective Date of Appraisal: .... Date of Inspection: ....

Highest and Best Use is: ☐ Current ☐ Other (*) ....

Zoning: .... Occupancy: ☐ Homeowner ☐ Tenant ☐ Vacant

SUBJECT & MARKET HISTORY

Subject Last Sold	**Subject Currently Listed**	**Property Values**	**Demand/Supply**
Date:	☐ Yes ☐ No	☐ Stable	☐ In Balance
Sale Price: $	Current List Price $	☐ Increasing	☐ Under Supply
Days on Market:	Days On Market	☐ Decreasing	☐ Over Supply

Typical Exposure Time Required for Properties to Sell in Subject Neighborhood is: ....

Typical Exposure Time Required for Properties to Sell on Subject Street is: ....

NEIGHBOURHOOD INFORMATION

Type		**Trend**	**Subject For Area is**	**Adjoining Homes**
☐ Rural	☐ Prestige	☐ Improving	☐ Comparable	☐ Comparable
☐ Residential	☐ Average	☐ Stable	☐ Superior *	☐ Superior
☐ Commercial	☐ Starter	☐ Declining	☐ Inferior	☐ Inferior
☐ Industrial				

Neighbourhood is: ....% Developed

Distance to

Elementary School	....	Age Range of Typical Property in Neighbourhood: .... to .... Years
Secondary School	....	Age Range of Typical Property on Subject Street: .... to .... Years
Public Transit	....	
Shopping	....	Price Range of Properties on Subject Street: $........................ to $........................
Downtown	....	
Recreational Facilities	....	Price Range of Properties in Neighbourhood: $........................ to $........................

Comments: (include any positive or negative factors that will have a measurable impact on the subject's marketability and value - items with an * should be discussed) ....

....

....

....

Form 700 Revised 2008 **Page 1 of 6**

Form 700   Standard Appraisal Report—Single Family, Page 2 of 6

SITE INFORMATION
Utilities & Services

Street
- ☐ Paved
- ☐ Municipal
- ☐ Sidewalks
- ☐ Street Lighting
- ☐ Underground Wiring
- ☐ Aboveground Wiring
- ☐ Gravel
- ☐ Private
- ☐ Curbs

Drainage
- ☐ Open Ditch
- ☐ Sanitary Sewer
- ☐ Other ....
- ☐ Storm Sewer
- ☐ Septic Tank

Water
- ☐ Municipal
- ☐ Cistern
- ☐ Other ....
- ☐ Private Well
- ☐ Shared Well

Utilities
- ☐ Hydro
- ☐ Gas
- ☐ Telephone
- ☐ Cable

Site Dimensions: ....   Encroachments: ☐ Yes* ☐ No

Total Site Area: ....   Easements: ☐ Yes* ☐ No

Site Shape: ....

Topography: Lot in relation to street grade: ☐ Even   ☐ Above   ☐ Below

Parking
Driveway
- ☐ Laneway
- ☐ Private
- ☐ Mutual
- ☐ Other ....
- ☐ None
- ☐ Paved
- ☐ Gravel

Garage (Indicate # of cars):
- ☐ Attached # ....
- ☐ Detached # ....
- ☐ Built In # ....
- ☐ Carport # ....

Site Appeal
- ☐ Excellent
- ☐ Good
- ☐ Average
- ☐ Fair*
- ☐ Poor*

Landscaping Includes: ....
....

Comments: (include any positive or negative factors that will have a measurable impact on the subject's marketability and value - items with an * should be discussed) ....
....

INFORMATION ON IMPROVEMENTS (BUILDINGS)
Building Type:
- ☐ Detached
- ☐ Semi-detached
- ☐ Attached Row
- ☐ Other ....
- ☐ High Ranch
- ☐ Apartment
- ☐ Split
- ☐ 1 Storey
- ☐ 1 1/2 Storey
- ☐ 2 Storey
- ☐ 3 Storey

Sq. Ft. (Above Grade)
Level 1 .... Level 4 ....
Level 2 .... Level 5 ....
Level 3 ....
Total ....

Actual Age ....Years   Effective Age ....Years   Total Economic Life ....Years

Exterior Finish
- ☐ Brick Veneer
- ☐ Solid Brick
- ☐ Stucco
- ☐ Alum. Siding
- ☐ Other ....
- ☐ Vinyl Siding
- ☐ Wood Siding
- ☐ Solid Stone
- ☐ Artificial Stone

Roof Material
- ☐ Asphalt Shingle
- ☐ Cedar Shake
- ☐ Metal
- ☐ Other ....
- ☐ Wood Shingle
- ☐ Slate
- ☐ Tar & Gravel

Foundation
- ☐ Poured Concrete
- ☐ Concrete Block
- ☐ Brick
- ☐ Stone
- ☐ Preserved Wood
- ☐ Other ....

Window Type
- ☐ Single
- ☐ Other: ....
- ☐ Thermal
- ☐ Wood Frame
- ☐ Aluminum
- ☐ Vinyl

Evidence of UFFI   ☐ Yes *   ☐ No

Construction Quality   ☐ Excellent   ☐ Good   ☐ Average   ☐ Fair   ☐ Poor*

Exterior Condition/Appeal   ☐ Excellent   ☐ Good   ☐ Average   ☐ Fair   ☐ Poor*

INFORMATION ON IMPROVEMENTS (INTERIOR)

Rooms	Living	Dining	Kitchen	Family	Beds	Bath	Wash	Rec	Other
Basement									
Main									
Second									
Third									

Room Sizes   ☐ Large   ☐ Medium   ☐ Small

Additional Information on Room Sizes (Optional): ....
....
....

Kitchen
☐ Modern
☐ Average
☐ Outdated

Bathrooms
☐ Modern
☐ Average
☐ Outdated

Closets/Storage
☐ Excellent
☐ Adequate
☐ Inadequate

Basement
☐ None
☐ Full
☐ Partial

☐ Crawl Space
% Finished ....

Floors
☐ Carpet
☐ Hardwood
☐ Vinyl Tile
☐ Ceramic
☐ Other ....

Walls/Ceilings
☐ Drywall
☐ Plaster
☐ Panelling
☐ Tile
☐ Other ....

Heating
☐ Forced Air
☐ Hot Water
☐ Baseboard
☐ Other ....

Fuel
☐ Gas
☐ Oil
☐ Electricity
☐ Other ....

Plumbing
☐ Copper
☐ Plastic
☐ Lead
☐ Galvanized
☐ Other ....

Electrical
☐ Fuses
☐ Circuit Breakers
Amps ....

Floor Plan
☐ Excellent   ☐ Good   ☐ Average   ☐ Fair   ☐ Poor*

Interior Condition
☐ Excellent   ☐ Good   ☐ Average   ☐ Fair   ☐ Poor*

Equipment/Built-Ins/Chattels Remaining With Property:
☐ HWT
☐ Central Air
☐ Heat Pump
☐ Stove
☐ Fireplace(s) ....
☐ Other: ....
....

☐ Fridge
☐ Washer
☐ Dryer
☐ Dishwasher

☐ Central Vac
☐ Humidifier
☐ Security System
☐ Dehumidifier

☐ Wood Stove
☐ Hood
☐ Oven
☐ Range

☐ Elect Air Cleaner
☐ Garburator
☐ Water Purifier/Filter
☐ Central Intercom

Equipment/Chattels Leased or Rented
....
....

Special Features
....
....

Comments: (include any positive or negative factors that will have a measurable impact on the subject's marketability and value - items with an * should be discussed) ....
....
....
....

Form 700   Standard Appraisal Report—Single Family, Page 4 of 6

COST APPROACH TO VALUE

Land Value .... $...................................

Improvements	Cost New	Depreciation	Current Value
Building	$.............................	$.............................	$.............................
Garage	$.............................	$.............................	$.............................
....	$.............................	$.............................	$.............................
....	$.............................	$.............................	$.............................
....	$.............................	$.............................	$.............................

Total Current Value of All Improvements $............................. $...................................

Indicated Value by the Cost Approach $...................................

Value Rounded to $...................................

DIRECT COMPARISON APPROACH
Competitive Listings

Item	Subject	Listing #1	Listing #2	Listing #3
Address				
Distance To Subject				
Original List Price				
Current List Price				
Original List Date				
Date Price Last Revised				
House Style				
Lot Size				
Building Size				
Age				
Condition				
Beds				
Baths				
Listing is: Inferior/Similar/Superior				

Comments:...
....
....
....

PRINCIPLES OF APPRAISAL

Sales Analysis

Item	Subject	Comparable 1	Comparable 2	Comparable 3
Address				
Distance To Subject				
Date Sold				
Sale Price				
Days On Market				
Time Adjustment				
Time Adjusted Price				
Location				
Lot Size				
House Style				
Age of House				
Total Sq. Footage				
Family Room				
Bedrooms				
Bathrooms				
Basement/% Finished				
Rec Room				
Garage/Parking				
Interior Condition				
Exterior Condition				
Total Adjustments				
Totally Adj. Sale Price				

Comments, Reconciliation And Estimate Of Value By The Direct Comparison Approach

....
....
....
....
....
....
....

Based on the above information and analysis, a value by the Direct Comparison Approach is estimated to be: ($...)

Form 700   Revised 2008   **Page 5 of 6**

Form 700   Standard Appraisal Report—Single Family, Page 6 of 6

FINAL RECONCILIATION, CERTIFICATION AND FINAL ESTIMATE OF VALUE

Given the nature of the subject property, the level and quality of information, the reliability of the necessary adjustments, and the actions of typical buyers

in the subject neighbourhood, most weight has been given to the value arrived at by the .... Approach.

- This valuation and report is subject to the attached assumptions and limiting conditions.
- This valuation and report has been completed in accordance with the Canadian Real Estate Association's Code of Ethics and Standard of Business Practice, as well as the Code of Ethics of the Real Estate and Business Brokers Act.
- I confirm that I personally inspected the subject property and that I have no current or contemplated interest or bias (positive or negative) towards the subject property.
- Unless otherwise detailed in writing within this report, I can confirm that I have no personal relationship or bias (positive or negative) towards any of the parties using or affected by this valuation and report.
- I can confirm that my being employed and paid to complete this valuation is not conditional on the amount of the valuation or on any specific information being included or excluded in this appraisal report.

Therefore, based on a .... day marketing period, a reasonable market value for the subject property as at

................................., 20.............. is estimated to be:

.... Dollars ($...)

Appraiser's Signature: ....   Date of Signature: ....

Appraiser's Name: ....   Company: ....
Appraiser's Address: ....   Phone No: ....
....   Fax No: ....
....   E-mail: ....

ATTACHMENTS

☐ Neighbourhood Map   ☐ Additional Information/Analysis: ....
☐ Copies of MLS Listing/Sales   ☐ Additional Assumptions/Limiting Conditions: ....
☐ Site/Building Sketch   ....
☐ Photos   ☐ Other: ....
☐ Survey

ASSUMPTIONS AND LIMITING CONDITIONS

1. This report may not be read or used by anyone other than the client without the written authorization of the appraiser. This report should only be used for the property and purpose identified within it. The appraiser accepts no responsibility or liability should the information contained within this report be used by anyone other than the client (or other authorized user) or for any other purpose or property other than that specified within this report.

2. Values are subject to varying and continual changes in market conditions and neighbourhood factors. Accordingly, the value presented in this report can only be relied on as the value estimated as of the effective date of appraisal specified in this report. Should the user of this report wish to know the value of the subject property as of another date, the appraiser will need to complete an update or a new appraisal report.

3. A search on title and ownership has not been performed. A good title with respect to the subject property has been assumed. Therefore, other than what is noted in this report, the appraiser assumes no responsibility for matters legal in nature that may affect the subject property's title, ownership, marketing or value.

4. Any sketches in this report are included solely for the purpose of assisting the reader in visualizing the property.

5. The appraiser has carried out a visual cosmetic inspection of the subject property only. This inspection and the ensuing appraisal report is not and should not be considered a structural, environmental or mechanical inspection and report. Accordingly, unless stated otherwise in this appraisal report, the appraiser is unaware of any hidden or not apparent structural, environmental or mechanical defects or problems and assumes for the purposes of this report and valuation that there are none. Therefore, should it subsequently become known that there is a structural, mechanical or environmental problem or defect, then the appraiser reserves the right to alter the value given in this appraisal report.

6. This appraisal has been based on the assumption that the subject property is in compliance with the applicable zoning, building codes, by-laws, and environmental regulations. Should this in fact turn out not to be so, the appraiser reserves the right to make any necessary changes to the final estimate of value.

7. This valuation has been based on the assumption that the information collected from industry recognized sources and professionals is in fact correct and can be relied upon for the purpose of this appraisal.

OREA Ontario Real Estate Association

Standard Appraisal Report
Condominium

Form 701
for use in the Province of Ontario

CLIENT: .... Client Ref No: ....

Client: Phone No: (............)................................... Fax No: (............)................................... E-mail: ....

Client's Customer: .... Appraiser: .... Appraiser's Ref No: ....

GENERAL APPRAISAL AND PROPERTY INFORMATION

Property Address: ....

Municipality: ....

Full Legal Description: ....

Owner: .... Assessment: Total .... Taxes $ .... Year ....

This Appraisal is to estimate **MARKET VALUE** for a: ☐ Sale ☐ Financing ☐ Other ....

Effective Date of Appraisal: .... Date of Inspection: ....

Highest and Best Use is: ☐ Current ☐ Other (*) ....

Zoning: .... Occupancy: ☐ Homeowner ☐ Tenant ☐ Vacant

SUBJECT & MARKET HISTORY

Subject Last Sold	**Subject Currently Listed**	**Property Values**	**Demand/Supply**
Date:	☐ Yes ☐ No	☐ Stable	☐ In Balance
Sale Price: $	Current List Price $	☐ Increasing	☐ Under Supply
Days on Market:	Days On Market	☐ Decreasing	☐ Over Supply

Typical Exposure Time Required for Properties to Sell in Subject Neighborhood is: ....

Typical Exposure Time Required for Properties to Sell in Subject Complex: ....

NEIGHBOURHOOD INFORMATION

Type

☐ Single Family Homes   ☐ Mixed Residential/Commercial

☐ Low Rise Rental Buildings   ☐ Mixed Residential/Industrial

☐ High Rise Rental Buildings   ☐ Prestige

☐ Town House Condos   ☐ Average

☐ Low Rise Condo Buildings   ☐ Starter

☐ High Rise Condo Buildings

Trend

☐ Improving

☐ Stable

☐ Declining*

For Area, Condo Building is

☐ Comparable

☐ Superior*

☐ Inferior

Distance to

Elementary School	....
Secondary School	....
Public Transit	....
Shopping	....
Downtown	....
Recreational Facilities	....

Neighbourhood is: ....% Developed

Price Range of Properties in Neighbourhood: $........................... to $...........................

Age Range of Typical Property in Neighbourhood: .... to .... Years

Comments: (include any positive or negative factors that will have a measurable impact on the subject's marketability and value - items with an * should be discussed) ....

....

....

Form 701   Standard Appraisal Report—Condominium, Page 2 of 6

GENERAL INFORMATION - SUBJECT CONDOMINIUM COMPLEX

Type of Condominium Complex

☐ Townhouse   ☐ Garden Home   ☐ Apartment Building

☐ Other ....   # Storeys ....   # Units in Complex ....

Age of Condominium Complex ....Years   Size of Units in Complex From .... to ....

Price Range of Units in Complex from $................................ to $................................

Complex Occupancy   Owner Occupied ....%   Rented ....%   Vacant ....%

Type of Parking	**Parking Space is**	**Storage/Locker Space**	**Storage/Locker Space is**
☐ Not Applicable	☐ Not Applicable	☐ Yes	☐ Exclusive Use/Common Element
☐ Underground Garage	☐ Exclusive Use/Common Element	☐ No	☐ Owned
☐ Aboveground w/Garage	☐ Owned	☐ # Lockers	☐ Assigned
☐ Aboveground w/o Garage	☐ Assigned	☐ Locker Size .... x	☐ Rented @ $ .... per Mth.
☐ Other	☐ Other		
Subject has .... Spaces	☐ Rented @ $ .... per Mth.		

Condition/Appeal of Interior Common Elements   ☐ Excellent   ☐ Good   ☐ Average   ☐ Fair   ☐ Poor*

Condition/Appeal of Exterior Common Elements   ☐ Excellent   ☐ Good   ☐ Average   ☐ Fair   ☐ Poor*

CONDOMINIUM FINANCIAL AND LEGAL INFORMATION

Subject Unit's Maintenance Fees Are: $ .... Per Month

Are Fees in Line with Other Similar Condominium Complexes?   ☐ Yes   ☐ No*

Maintenance Fees Include

☐ Maintenance of Common Elements	☐ Insurance	☐ Water	☐ Heat	☐ Hydro
☐ Garbage Collection	☐ Snow Removal	☐ Cable	☐ Lawn Care	

☐ Other ....

Is a Special Assessment Currently being levied?   ☐ Yes*   ☐ No

Are any Special Assessments Pending or Contemplated?   ☐ Yes*   ☐ No

As at the Date of Appraisal, the Reserve Fund contains: $ ....

Does the Property Management Company believe the Reserve Fund to be adequate?   ☐ Yes   ☐ No*

Are any Major Repairs/Improvements currently underway?   ☐ Yes*   ☐ No

Are any Major Repairs/Improvements Pending or Contemplated over the next two years?   ☐ Yes*   ☐ No

Are there any outstanding or anticipated legal actions?   ☐ Yes*   ☐ No

Has an independent reserve fund study been completed?   ☐ Yes   ☐ No

Date of last reserve fund study ....

Comments Regarding Condominium Complex: (include any positive or negative factors that will have a measurable impact on the subject's marketability and value - items with an * should be discussed)

....

....

....

....

....

SUBJECT UNIT INFORMATION

Form 701   Standard Appraisal Report—Condominium, Page 3 of 6

Type Of Unit
- ☐ Detached Townhouse
- ☐ Semi-detached Townhouse
- ☐ Attached Townhouse
- ☐ Apartment
- ☐ Other ....

Style Of Unit
- ☐ 1 Story
- ☐ 2 Storey
- ☐ 3 Storey
- ☐ Other ....

Sq. Ft. (Above Grade)
Level 1 ....   Level 4 ....
Level 2 ....   Level 5 ....
Level 3 ....
Total ....

Exterior Finish
- ☐ Brick Veneer
- ☐ Solid Brick
- ☐ Stucco
- ☐ Aluminum Siding
- ☐ Other ....
- ☐ Vinyl Siding
- ☐ Wood Siding
- ☐ Solid Stone
- ☐ Artificial Stone

Roof Material
- ☐ Asphalt Shingle
- ☐ Cedar Shake
- ☐ Metal
- ☐ Other ....
- ☐ Wood Shingle
- ☐ Slate
- ☐ Tar & Gravel

Foundation
- ☐ Poured Concrete
- ☐ Concrete Block
- ☐ Brick
- ☐ Stone
- ☐ Preserved Wood
- ☐ Other ....

Window Type
- ☐ Single
- ☐ Thermal
- ☐ Wood Frame
- ☐ Aluminum
- ☐ Vinyl
- ☐ Other ....

Evidence of UFFI   ☐ Yes*   ☐ No

Exterior Condition   ☐ Excellent   ☐ Good   ☐ Average   ☐ Fair   ☐ Poor*

Exterior Appeal   ☐ Excellent   ☐ Good   ☐ Average   ☐ Fair   ☐ Poor*

Rooms	Living	Dining	Kitchen	Family	Beds	Bath	Wash	Rec	Other
Basement									
Main									
Second									
Third									

Room Sizes   ☐ Large   ☐ Medium   ☐ Small

Additional Information on Room Sizes (Optional):
....
....
....

Kitchen
- ☐ Modern
- ☐ Average
- ☐ Outdated

Bathrooms
- ☐ Modern
- ☐ Average
- ☐ Outdated

Closets/Storage
- ☐ Excellent
- ☐ Adequate
- ☐ Inadequate

Basement
- ☐ None
- ☐ Full
- ☐ Partial
- ☐ Crawl Space
- % Finished ....

Floors
- ☐ Carpet
- ☐ Hardwood
- ☐ Vinyl Tile
- ☐ Ceramic
- ☐ Other ....

Walls/Ceilings
- ☐ Drywall
- ☐ Plaster
- ☐ Panelling
- ☐ Tile
- ☐ Other ....

Heating
- ☐ Forced Air
- ☐ Hot Water
- ☐ Baseboard
- ☐ Other ....
- ....

Fuel
- ☐ Gas
- ☐ Oil
- ☐ Electricity
- ☐ Other ....
- ....

Plumbing
- ☐ Copper
- ☐ Plastic
- ☐ Lead
- ☐ Galvanized
- ☐ Other ....

Electrical
- ☐ Fuses
- ☐ Circuit Breakers
- Amps ....

Floor Plan
- ☐ Excellent   ☐ Good   ☐ Average   ☐ Fair   ☐ Poor*

Interior Condition
- ☐ Excellent   ☐ Good   ☐ Average   ☐ Fair   ☐ Poor*

Equipment/Built-Ins/Chattels Remaining With Property:

Form 701   Standard Appraisal Report—Condominium, Page 4 of 6

☐ HWT	☐ Fridge	☐ Central Vac	☐ Wood Stove	☐ Elect Air Cleaner
☐ Central Air	☐ Washer	☐ Humidifier	☐ Hood	☐ Garburator
☐ Heat Pump	☐ Dryer	☐ Security System	☐ Oven	☐ Water Purifier/Filter
☐ Stove	☐ Dishwasher	☐ Dehumidifier	☐ Range	☐ Central Intercom
☐ Fireplace(s)				

Other: ....

....

Equipment/Chattels Leased or Rented

....

....

Special Features

....

....

Comments: (include any positive or negative factors that will have a measurable impact on the subject's marketability and value - items with an * should be discussed) ....

....

....

....

DIRECT COMPARISON APPROACH
Competitive Listings
Comments: ....

Item	Subject	Listing #1	Listing #2	Listing #3
Address				
Distance To Subject				
Original List Price				
Current List Price				
Original List Date				
Date Price Last Revised				
Unit Type/Style				
Size				
Age				
Location				
Exposure				
Condition				
Beds				
Baths				
Listing is: Inferior/Similar/Superior				

....

....

....

....

Sales Analysis

Comments, Reconciliation And Estimate Of Value By The Direct Comparison Approach

Item	Subject	Comparable 1		Comparable 2		Comparable 3	
Address							
Distance To Subject							
Date Sold							
Sale Price							
Days On Market							
Time Adjustment							
Time Adjusted Price							
Exposure							
Unit Type/Style							
Age of Unit							
Total Sq. Footage							
Family Room							
Bedrooms							
Bathrooms							
Basement/% Finished							
Rec Room							
Garage/Parking							
Unit Condition							
Exterior Condition							
Total Adjustments							
Totally Adj. Sale Price							

....
....
....
....
....
....

Based on the above information and analysis, a value by the Direct Comparison Approach is estimated to be: ($..)

Form 701   Standard Appraisal Report—Condominium, Page 6 of 6

CERTIFICATION AND FINAL ESTIMATE OF VALUE

- This valuation and report is subject to the attached assumptions and limiting conditions.
- This valuation and report has been completed in accordance with the Canadian Real Estate Association's Code of Ethics and Standard of Business Practice, as well as the Code of Ethics of the Real Estate and Business Brokers Act.
- I confirm that I personally inspected the subject property and that I have no current or contemplated interest or bias (positive or negative) towards the subject property.
- Unless otherwise detailed in writing within this report, I can confirm that I have no personal relationship or bias (positive or negative) towards any of the parties using or affected by this valuation and report.
- I can confirm that my being employed and paid to complete this valuation is not conditional on the amount of the valuation or on any specific information being included or excluded in this appraisal report.

Therefore, based on a .... day marketing period, a reasonable market value for the subject property as at

................................, 20.............. is estimated to be:

.... Dollars ($..)

Appraiser's Signature: ....   Date of Signature: ....

Appraiser's Name: ....   Company: ....
Appraiser's Address: ....   Phone No: ....
....   Fax No: ....
....   E-mail: ....

ATTACHMENTS

- ☐ Neighbourhood Map
- ☐ Copies of MLS Listing/Sales
- ☐ Site/Building Sketch
- ☐ Photos
- ☐ Survey

- ☐ Additional Information/Analysis: ....
- ☐ Additional Assumptions/Limiting Conditions: ....
    ....
- ☐ Other: ....
    ....

ASSUMPTIONS AND LIMITING CONDITIONS

1. This report may not be read or used by anyone other than the client without the written authorization of the appraiser. This report should only be used for the property and purpose identified within it. The appraiser accepts no responsibility or liability should the information contained within this report be used by anyone other than the client (or other authorized user) or for any other purpose or property other than that specified within this report.
2. Values are subject to varying and continual changes in market conditions and neighbourhood factors. Accordingly, the value presented in this report can only be relied on as the value estimated as of the effective date of appraisal specified in this report. Should the user of this report wish to know the value of the subject property as of another date, the appraiser will need to complete an update or a new appraisal report.
3. A search on title and ownership has not been performed. A good title with respect to the subject property has been assumed. Therefore, other than what is noted in this report, the appraiser assumes no responsibility for matters legal in nature that may affect the subject property's title, ownership, marketing or value.
4. Any sketches in this report are included solely for the purpose of assisting the reader in visualizing the property.
5. The appraiser has carried out a visual cosmetic inspection of the subject property only. This inspection and the ensuing appraisal report is not and should not be considered a structural, environmental or mechanical inspection and report. Accordingly, unless stated otherwise in this appraisal report, the appraiser is unaware of any hidden or not apparent structural, environmental or mechanical defects or problems and assumes for the purposes of this report and valuation that there are none. Therefore, should it subsequently become known that there is a structural, mechanical or environmental problem or defect, then the appraiser reserves the right to alter the value given in this appraisal report.
6. This appraisal has been based on the assumption that the subject property is in compliance with the applicable zoning, building codes, by-laws, environmental regulations and condominium by-laws and regulations. Should this in fact turn out not to be so, the appraiser reserves the right to make any necessary changes to the final estimate of value.
7. This valuation has been based on the assumption that the information collected from industry recognized sources and professionals is in fact correct and can be relied upon for the purpose of this appraisal.

Form 701   Revised 2008   **Page 6 of 6**

The Narrative Report

This report takes a logical, systematic and detailed approach by presenting in writing the theory, facts, analysis, application of methodology and finally conclusions. Narrative reports must be written in sufficient detail and in such a way that a reader will easily understand the appraiser's reasoning and justifications for the conclusions and estimates reached.

A narrative report can vary substantially in size based on the type of property and purpose of the appraisal. Narrative reports tend to be time consuming to prepare, with a commercial appraisal containing anywhere from 50, to in excess of, 100 pages.

This type of report is generally used by appraisers for estimating the market value of apartment buildings, office/commercial/industrial buildings and agricultural land for any purpose including financing, transfer of ownership, capital gains, etc. It is also used by appraisers to value single-family homes, duplexes, triplexes and fourplexes where the purpose would be for court/legal proceedings.

EXAMPLE   *Narrative Report*

Anne Appraiser is preparing a detailed narrative report on a residential property owned by Smith. Smith requires the appraisal for pending expropriation plans concerning new highway construction. Anne carefully details the main topic areas within the planned narrative report.

- Appraisal Summary *(important facts and conclusions)*
- Letter of Transmittal *(summary letter to the client)*
- Title Page
- Table of Contents
- Taxes and Assessment *(specific information regarding taxes on the property, taxation trends and impact on value)*
- Area and Neighbourhood Analysis *(description of external factors impacting value)*
- Site and Improvement Analysis *(exterior and interior description of the property)*
- Approaches to Value *(application of the market data, cost and income approaches to value)*
- Reconciliation *(details how the value estimate was determined)*
- Limiting Conditions *(information to client concerning assumptions and conditions underlying the report)*
- Exhibits *(documentary evidence including such things as maps, diagrams of the property and floor plans)*

Letter of Opinion   CAUTION

The *Letter of Opinion* is a brief, unsubstantiated statement of an appraiser's opinion of value or value range that is not recommended as a method of appraisal reporting.

Although only limited information is given in the letter of opinion, the individual providing such an opinion should understand that a complete appraisal process must still be conducted and all relevant data, analysis and conclusions kept within the appraiser's files. Indeed, completion of a full appraisal report may be required at some future date to substantiate the opinion.

While clients may expect a large reduction in the fee charged, a letter of opinion may not end up saving much more time than a form report or be particularly easier to complete. Also, given the vagueness of the letter of opinion, it often tends to create confusion and problems between the client and appraiser, resulting in both parties being dissatisfied. Letters of opinion are usually not accepted by lending institutions.

The *Residential Market Comparison Guide* is a form designed to show the owner of a property how his/her property ranks in competition with others that are now, or have been, on the market. Often referred to as a CMA (Comparative Market Analysis) in various jurisdictions in Canada, this guide is used to determine the probable asking price of the property. The form also contains additional lines to detail anticipated selling price, selling costs and ultimately estimated net proceeds to the seller.

OREA Ontario Real Estate Association

Residential Market Comparison Guide

Form 260
for use in the Province of Ontario

Subject Property:...

Prepared for:...

Prepared by:.. Date:..

COMPARABLES FOR SALE NOW:

Address	Price	Features/Comments

(Use back of form for additional features/comments if required)

COMPARABLES SOLD PAST 12 MONTHS:

Address	Price	Features/Comments

(Use back of form for additional features/comments if required)

COMPARABLES EXPIRED PAST 12 MONTHS:

Address	Price	Features/Comments

(Use back of form for additional features/comments if required)

ESTIMATED SELLING COSTS:

Brokerage Fee:	$ ....
Mortgage Payout Penalty	$ ....
Mortgage Discount	$ ....
Approximate Legal Costs	$ ....
Miscellaneous	$ ....
Total	$ ....

Recommendations: as of ....
I recommend a maximum list price of: $ ....
With estimated selling price of: $ ....
With estimated outstanding mortgage balance of $ ....
With estimated selling costs of: $ ....
Anticipated net proceeds would be: $ ....

Signature: ....

NB: The recipient of the above information acknowledges by reading, reviewing or receiving such information that the information may not be accurate or current or correct and agrees to indemnify, save harmless and release, the Brokerage, sales representative or broker by whom the information was prepared, from all manner of actions, causes of action, suits or claims of any kind whatsoever.

NB: The above information is the property of the Brokerage, sales representative or broker by whom it was prepared and is not to be shared, distributed, published, transmitted, assigned, communicated or transferred in any way whatsoever without the prior written consent of the Brokerage, sales representative or broker named above.

NB: The above information is NOT an appraisal and is to be used for marketing purposes only.

While it is true to say that most salespeople will complete a CMA as opposed to a form report, it is also true to say that a salesperson will benefit from being able to complete a form report. The form report contains much of the basic necessary information and steps/evaluations needed in order to be able to come up with a value for the subject property and therefore listing price needed to sell that property.

VALUE CONCEPTS

Value

Value is the quantity of one thing that can be obtained in exchange for another. Money is the common denominator by which real property value is usually measured. The utility of a commodity, such as property, is expressed in the amount of money that would be paid for its acquisition. Value is the present worth of future benefits arising out of ownership to typical users or investors and depends on the need for, and availability of, a commodity; i.e., supply and demand.

The Many Meanings of Value	MARKET MEMO

Value is the key word used in practically every segment of the real estate business. Its significance and importance would imply a precisely and clearly understood meaning. Unfortunately, this is not often the case. Value is a word for which there are as many definitions as there are types of value in everyday life. For example, the tax assessor usually thinks of value in terms of assessed value, the insurance agent in terms of insurable value, the accountant in terms of book value, the appraiser in terms of market value and the commercial practitioner in terms of both market value and investment value. Further, the banker or mortgagee is likely to equate value with lending value. A natural tendency exists to attach to the word value a variety of descriptive adjectives suggesting a specific kind of value: intrinsic value, sentimental value, salvage value, liquidation value and appraised value.

    A precise meaning has been a life-long study of many economic theorists. Most debates centre on objective versus subjective value. Objective value maintains that value is tied to the cost of reproduction. Subjective value states that value exists only in the minds of buyers and sellers.

    Further, one of the most important distinctions for real estate purposes is that value may have one value in exchange and quite a different value in use. A second important distinction arises from activities of commercial practitioners between market value (value based on the actions of typical buyers and sellers) and investment value (value of the subject property based on individual investor needs, goals and objectives).

Objective Value

Objective value is the value of a property based on the analysis of costs associated with the reproduction of that property (an exact replica) or one of equal utility (a replacement). Replacement cost is most commonly used given the ease of obtaining accurate information.

    Objective value plays a significant role in determining value by means of the cost approach. Essentially, two schools of thought have arisen over the concept of value. One school emphasizes the objective nature of value as it relates to the actual production cost of creating a property (the cost approach). The other, representing advocates of subjective value, believes that value exists only in the mind of potential buyers, sellers, owners and users of real estate (the direct comparison approach).

    In the residential appraisal process, both methods of valuation (Direct Comparison and Cost Approach) are used reflecting these schools of thought, but the direct comparison approach is more heavily relied upon.

Cost Approach	MARKET MEMO

It is worth pointing out that the cost approach can and does involve the use of both the objective concept of value and the subjective concept of value. Estimating the RCN (replacement/reproduction cost new) of a building using a cost services manual would be a good example of the use of the *objective* concept of value. Estimating the value of the site using the comparative sales method would be a good example of the use of the *subjective* concept of value in the cost approach.

Salesperson Lee is preparing an appraisal form report including both the direct comparison approach and the cost approach for a lender. Before completing the final report, Lee summarized his calculations concerning the cost approach as follows:

Estimated Value of Site		$77,000
Estimated Reproduction Cost New	117,550	
Estimated Amount of Accrued Depreciation:		
Physical Deterioration	21,200	
Functional Obsolescence	8,350	
Locational Obsolescence	3,600	
Total Depreciation—All Sources	−33,150	
Current Value of Improvements		+84,400
Market Value (Site + Depreciated Value)		**$161,400**

Subjective Value

This value is created and exists only in the minds of the potential buyers and sellers. Subjective value is the price that people will pay for a property, irrespective of its cost, as differentiated from objective value in which value is associated with the cost of production or cost of creating the property.

An appraiser uses subjective value in both the direct comparison approach and the income approach. In fact, the subjective value dominates real estate valuation. It can matter little what costs are associated with development of a property. Value is measured through the present worth of all the future benefits that likely will accrue through ownership. Future benefits do not necessarily indicate money; e.g., an income stream. Non-monetary benefits, in the case of residential property, may include subjective factors such as pleasurable living or amenities; e.g., being located next to a park or forest reserve.

Seller Smith is adamant about the price of his property. According to Smith's figures, a selling price of $169,000 is essential if he is to recapture his investment in the property and pay a commission and associated closing costs. Recent improvements to the house amounted to more than $30,000 and he purchased the lot and built the home for $135,000 one year ago.

Smith is arguing his position based on objective value; in other words, value is directly tied to the cost of the property and improvements.

Salesperson Lee, however, has completed a residential market comparison guide that clearly shows that comparable homes have been selling in the range of $150,000–$160,000. Lee's presentation is based on subjective value; the value that exists in the minds of potential buyers.

Value in Exchange

Value in exchange is the amount of goods and services that an informed buyer would offer in exchange for an economic good, under given market conditions. Value in exchange is relative, since there must be comparison with other economic goods and alternatives available from which the potential buyer may choose.

Value in exchange is best described as the probable price at which a commodity trades in a free, competitive and open market, and is synonymous with market value.

Market Value

There are a number of different definitions of market value. The definition that will be used in this course is as follows:

> *The highest price in terms of money, that the property will bring to a willing seller if exposed for sale on the open market; allowing a reasonable time to find a willing buyer, buying with the knowledge of all the uses to which it is adapted and for which it can be legally used, and with neither buyer or seller acting under necessity, compulsion nor peculiar or special circumstances*

Market value is not to be confused with market price; i.e., the amount paid, or to be paid, for a property in a particular transaction. Market price is an accomplished or historic fact. Market price tends to closely align with market value in an efficient market system involving willing, informed buyers and sellers acting rationally and prudently, given reasonable periods of time with no undue influences. Successive market prices in the sale of comparable homes form the basis of estimating the market value of a particular property.

Market value should not be confused with cost. Expending $150,000 in constructing a new home, plus $80,000 for the purchase of the land, in no way ensures a market value of $230,000. However, assuming a reasonably efficient market, the difference between actual cost and market value may be negligible, unless obsolescence was built into the property or intervening factors affect the marketplace, such as lack of housing supply, dynamic growth in a particular market or extremely depressed market conditions.

Let us take a look at some of the characteristics of market value:

Highest Price	This will clearly be based on selling the property for its highest and best use.
Open Market	This has generally come to be equated with selling on MLS®.
Reasonable Time	What is reasonable can only be assessed by looking at the average amount of time it is taking to sell properties within the subject neighbourhood.
Knowledge	It is assumed that both parties have equal knowledge. This should not be considered unusual as both parties will most likely be represented by a brokerage.
Necessity, Compulsion Nor Peculiar or Special Circumstances	It is assumed that neither party is under undue pressure or has a particular advantage/disadvantage that would be uncommon; e.g., the seller must sell the property quickly to avoid the property being taken away under power of sale or foreclosure; the buyer has access to 3% private financing, whereas most buyers would only be able to obtain mortgage financing at 6%.

When estimating the market value of a property using the above definition, it is important to select comparable sales where the conditions under which they sold are in keeping with the characteristics of market value; i.e., the comparables sold in a reasonable time, they sold in an open market, were sold on the basis of their highest and best use, and there were no special or unusual circumstances.

If a property seems to be a good comparable, but it sold at a price quite different from other comparable properties, further investigation will be needed. If it turns out that one or more of the characteristics of a market value sale have been violated, then that comparable sale should be discarded.

EXAMPLE   *Market Value*

Anne Appraiser is attempting to arrive at the market value of a property using the direct comparison approach. In completing a detailed form report, Anne has selected three comparable properties that sold within the immediate area for sale prices (market prices) of $179,000, $193,000 and $188,000. All three properties are similar to the subject property, were sold within the past four weeks and were arm's length transactions. Anne made various adjustments to the comparable properties and arrived at the following adjusted sale prices.

PROPERTY	SALE PRICE	TOTAL ADJUSTMENTS	ADJUSTED SALE PRICE
123 Main	$179,000	+$4,500	$183,500
123 Centre	$193,000	−$8,500	$184,500
141 Main	$188,000	−$2,000	$186,000

Based on these adjusted sale prices and other factors, Anne estimates that the market value of the home using the direct comparison approach is $185,000.

Market Price

Market price refers to the amount paid, or to be paid, for a property in a particular transaction. Market price is an accomplished or historic fact, as opposed to market value that remains an estimate until proven otherwise. Market price involves no assumption of prudent conduct by the buyer and/or seller and does not assume the absence of undue stimuli, reasonable exposure to the marketplace or any other condition basic to the market value concept. Under an efficient market system, where property is openly offered and promoted to well-informed, capable buyers, market price and market value closely approximate each other.

EXAMPLE   *Market Price*

Seller Smith decides to offer his property for sale, but does not want to involve a real estate brokerage. Based on his cursory review of the market, Smith determines that his home is worth approximately $140,000.

A neighbour, during casual conversation, mentions that friends of his, Mr. and Mrs. Jones, would probably be interested. Smith agrees to show them the property, but is adamant about the price. Mr. and Mrs. Jones purchase the property for $135,000, with a condition on financing. The appraiser, based on recent comparable sales in the immediate area, estimates the value of the property at $148,000. Accordingly, the lender approves the mortgage.

The buyers paid the market price; the appraiser estimated the market value.

Value In Use

Value in use is the value of an economic good to its owner/user or prospective buyer that is based on the productivity of the economic good to that specific individual. This usually consists of market value plus an increment that represents some extra value to the owner/user or prospective buyer.

THE OWNER/SELLER'S POINT OF VIEW

Value in Use here is the value given to a property by the owner who is using that property. The property would probably have been designed or used to suit the particular needs and enjoyment of the owner, and takes on a special significance that translates into an additional monetary value in the owner's opinion. This type of value is difficult to measure and is normally different in every case. It may often be higher than market value, since it is looked at from the owner's viewpoint only.

THE BUYER'S POINT OF VIEW

Value in Use here is the value given to a property from the perspective of a specific buyer rather than the average buyer. The property may have features that are particularly important to that buyer, but might not have the same significance to the average buyer; e.g., the property might have a lap pool and the buyer is an avid swimmer, the property might be located a block away from the buyer's office or aging parents. These features may add value to that specific buyer, but would not add value for the average buyer.

NOTE: Market value is looked at from the point of view of the average/typical buyer and not from the viewpoint of a specific buyer.

EXAMPLE   *Value in Use—Owner's Perspective*

Seller Smith, at retirement age, has installed an oversized swimming pool in the rear yard of his new two-bedroom, 940 square foot bungalow. As a former athlete, Smith prides himself in his physical prowess, uses the pool every day and conducts a rigorous exercise program. He took great pains to replicate a lap pool that he once used as a younger man in training for provincial competitions.

   For Smith, there is considerable value in use that probably exceeds the $38,000 price tag in terms of personal fitness and satisfaction. However, from the standpoint of the average buyer, the unusual shape and size of the pool may in fact add no particular value or, if it did, the value would be considerably less. If Smith elected to sell his home, undoubtedly he would think in terms of *value in use* as he attaches a high value to the pool. The buyer would negotiate in terms of *value in exchange* that would typically be a lower amount.

 # PRINCIPLES OF VALUE

The appraisal of real estate involves various principles that are either fundamental to understanding value or explain how various components of real estate contribute to value. These principles are isolated for discussion purposes but, in fact, are interrelated in the marketplace.

Principle of Anticipation

The principle of anticipation affirms that value is created by the anticipation of benefits, that is money or amenities, to be derived in the future. Value may be defined as the present worth of all rights of future benefits. When buying a home, buyers anticipate that certain benefits will accrue in future years, and the purchase price is based on the present worth of those anticipated future benefits.

Principle of Balance

The principle of balance holds that value is created and maintained in proportion to the equilibrium attained in the amount and location of essential uses of real estate. The degree of value of a property is governed by the balance of apportionment of the *factors of production*. Loss in value will result if there are less services and agencies than a neighbourhood needs or more services than a neighbourhood can support. For example, where there are too many drugstores in a community, either some will be successful at the expense of the others or none will yield an adequate return on the investment they represent.

With an individual property, the agents or factors in production (labour, coordination, capital and land) must be in proper balance in order to maintain maximum value. Too much or too little of any one of the factors, in proportion to the services rendered by the others, tends to reduce value, for example, having two building custodians where only one is needed will result in less net income, which in turn translates into less value when income is capitalized in the appraisal process.

Principle of Change

The principle of change states that economic and social forces are constantly at work and that changes caused by these forces affect real property. Accordingly, the appraiser views real property and its environment as in transition, observing evidence of trends that may affect the property in the future. The principle of change is fundamentally the law of cause and effect. The principle of change illustrates the fact that a value estimate provided by an appraiser is only valid as of a specific time. This principle is a constant consideration when estimating value and the effective date of an appraisal is always clearly identified in the report.

> **EXAMPLE**   *Principles of Value—Change*
>
> Anne Appraiser is hired to estimate the value of a property at 123 Main Street. This two-storey residence occupied by the Smith family is zoned single-family residential. Mr. Smith requires the appraisal as he is placing a first mortgage on the property with a new lending institution. Anne completes the lender's standard form report and states in writing that the property is worth $240,000 as of November 30th, 20xx. One week following the appraisal and before the bank issued a commitment letter on the mortgage, the major employer in the community, in a totally unexpected move, files for bankruptcy leaving more than two thousand workers, one-fifth of the total work force in the town, unemployed. Real estate inventory swells immediately with supply far outpacing demand. Within sixty days, a noticeable downturn in prices occurs. The lender, now more cautious, calls for a second opinion from another appraiser. The second appraisal, impacted by economic factors not present earlier, is $195,000.

Principle of Competition

The principle of competition, in terms of appraisal theory, stating that excessive profits will tend to breed competition that, in turn, has a negative impact on profits; or as often heard and simply put: *excess profit breeds ruinous competition.*

> **EXAMPLE**   *Principles of Value—Competition*
>
> Smith anticipates and initially receives high returns from a *You Store It (Anycity) Inc.* facility on the east side of the city. His forecasted demand proves correct and, although lacking any market data to suggest a larger facility, he confidently starts a second phase, effectively doubling the number of storage units. However, various large tracts of land are zoned for similar facilities and within months, three competing firms have increased the supply of units by 500%. Smith, as well as the competitors, are subsequently drawn into a price war to capture the finite market for this type of service. The value of the real estate is affected given lower levels of income.

Principle of Conformity

The principle of conformity states that land must be utilized to reasonably conform with the existing standards of the area in order to maintain maximum value. The word *reasonable* denotes the degree of conformity. Too much conformity results in monotony that could be as detrimental to value as not having conformity at all. In residential areas, variety in building styles of the same quality presents a more pleasing appearance than rows of identical houses. Zoning regulations protect a neighbourhood from conversion to or intrusion of inharmonious uses and generally support the principle of conformity. This principle is useful in detailing a neighbourhood analysis.

Principle of Progression

The principle of progression is an extension of the principle of conformity and states that in the case of properties that are dissimilar, the value of the poorer property will be affected positively by the presence of the property of higher value.

EXAMPLE   *Principles of Value—Progression*

Buyer Jones has often heard the old adage about buying the worst house on the street. However, he is now experiencing the reality of the statement. Jones is looking for a three-bedroom home with a single-car garage, while seeking the advantage of the principle of progression. Through a buyer representative, he has located three properties that are roughly comparable in terms of size, condition and overall appearance:

	ADDRESS	LISTED PRICE
Property 1	42 Main Street	$168,500
Property 2	233 West Street	$172,000
Property 3	136 The Ridge	$215,000

Properties 1 and 2 are located in single-family residential areas where the majority of homes are priced between $155,000 and $175,000. Property 3, however, is the smallest home on *The Ridge*. Homes adjacent to the property and in the immediate area sell between $240,000 and $350,000. Jones is particularly attracted to Property 3, but doesn't want to pay the higher price. The salesperson explains to his client that the higher value for Property 3 is as a result of it being surrounded by higher priced homes. The principle of progression is at work.

Principle of Regression

This principal is an extension of the principle of conformity which states that to maintain maximum value, land must be utilized to reasonably conform with the existing standards of the area. The principle of regression extends that concept by stating that between dissimilar properties, the value of the better property will be affected adversely by the presence of the property of lesser value.

EXAMPLE   *Principles of Value—Regression*

Buyer Jones understands the advantages of acquiring the worst home on the street and benefiting from the principle of progression; i.e., the value of the lower priced property will be positively impacted by the presence of properties of greater value. However, he is about to experience the opposite effect, known as the *principle of regression*.

Jones acquired an attractive bungalow with a single-car garage without regard to adjacent older properties. The home is obviously the best property in the general area. When Jones listed the property, many buyers were impressed, but no offer was forthcoming. The listing salesperson provided three comparable sales that were almost identical to Jones' property in terms of size, condition and overall appearance, but located in better neighbourhoods:

	ADDRESS	SALE PRICE
Property 1	402 Main Street	$214,500
Property 2	321 West Street	$205,000
Property 3	136 The Ridge	$215,000

Despite the listing salesperson's recommendation to market the property at $195,900, Jones could see no appreciable differences (except for the neighbourhood) and listed at $215,900. After two months with no offers, he reduced the price to $199,900 and the property sold for $194,500. As the listing salesperson explained, the value of Jones' property was directly impacted by lower priced properties in the immediate area.

PRINCIPLES OF APPRAISAL

Principle of Consistent Use

The principle of consistent use states that when improved land is in transition to another highest and best use, it cannot be appraised with one use allocated to the land and another to the building or other improvements. If an appraiser is estimating the market value of a parcel of land improved with an old house, and estimates that the highest and best use is for an office building development, then the appraisal should not accord any value to the house over that of the land. Adding value for the old house would be inconsistent as its worth in the market is overshadowed by the commercial value of the land and cannot be additive to it. In dealing with compensation for expropriated property, this theory is referred to as *double recovery*.

Principle of Contribution

The principle of contribution is a valuation principle stating that the value of any component of a property is measured by how much it adds to the net income (or market value; i.e., the subject property is non-income producing, such as a residential house) by reason of its presence, or detracts from the net income (or market value), by reason of its absence. Therefore, the value of any factor in production depends upon its contribution to net income or value and not upon its cost. The principle of contribution is sometimes known as the *principle of marginal productivity*.

> **EXAMPLE**   *Principles of Value—Contribution*
>
> Buyer Jones is attempting to justify the cost of new bathroom installation amounting to $18,000 in a townhouse valued at $169,000. While the true cost is $18,000, the market value may only be increased by $5,500. Based on the principal of contribution, the new bathroom is said to have a contributory value of $5,500. The addition of this bathroom would constitute an over improvement (superadequacy) and would not normally be justified.

Principle of External Factors

The principle of external factors (sometimes referred to as *externalities* by appraisers) involves a broad array of situations that can impact the value of property. External factors can include circumstances or situations near the property, or more distant influences that nevertheless impact value. In the case of adjacent factors, value may be enhanced by the existence and proximity of services provided to the property. On a more general perspective, overall economic conditions within the immediate area, the region as a whole, or for that matter, the country, can impact the value of real estate. Real estate is vulnerable to economic prosperity, as well as economic slowdowns. Real estate can also be impacted by government regulations and requirements that affect the marketability of real estate.

> **EXAMPLE**   *Principles of Value—External Factors*
>
> Buyer Smith acquired a residential bungalow in East Ridge, a suburb of Anycity, approximately two years ago. At the time of acquisition, the property was valued at $159,000. Since that time, Anycity has lost three major employers resulting in double-digit unemployment figures. To compound matters, significant improvements to various municipal services have resulted in a dramatic increase in property tax. These two external factors have affected property values. Local real estate brokerages report that residential properties are being sold for approximately 10% less than two years ago. Smith has had his property appraised and the market value is currently estimated at $143,000.

Principle of Highest and Best Use

The highest and best use is the use which, at the time of the appraisal, is most likely to produce the greatest net return in money or amenities to the land over a given period of time.

Highest and best use is analyzed from two perspectives: the value of the land as though vacant or as improved. The "as though vacant" approach establishes how the land can best be utilized, not necessarily how it is currently used. The "as improved" approach provides an indication of value based on the current structure, but with regard to the highest and best use for that structure. Consequently, highest and best use analysis can arrive at differing values based on assumptions made. This subject will be taken up in much greater detail in a later chapter.

Principle of Increasing and Decreasing Returns

This is a valuation principle stating that when successive increments of one or more factors of production are added to fixed amounts of the other factors, an initial enhancement of income in dollars, benefits or amenities occurs, to a point of maximum return (the point of diminishing returns), followed by a relative decrease in incremental value in relation to the value of the added factor(s). This principle is also referred to as the *principle of diminishing returns* or the *principle of variable proportions*.

EXAMPLE   *Principles of Value—Increasing and Decreasing Returns*

Example 1

Builder Anderson discovers an amazing fact about house construction in Anycity. While a 1,200 square foot bungalow with a single-garage commands $125,000, the same bungalow with a double garage (costing $15,000 more) adds $25,000, bringing the value to $150,000. Several sales at this level confirm his theory. Anderson then concludes that the addition of a third garage (at a cost of $15,000) will produce a similar increase raising the market value to $175,000. However, after constructing a bungalow with the triple car garage, the property remained unsold for six months and ultimately sold for $157,500. Anderson has experienced the law of increasing and decreasing returns. While the two-car garage added value beyond its cost to the builder, the successive addition of more garages does not incrementally increase market value.

Example 2

Smith operates a manufacturing plant that produces electrical appliances. Owing to an increased administrative workload, he is unable to effectively manage the 20 employees on a daily basis. Consequently, worker efficiency and production quality have suffered. Smith, based on the advice of a consultant, hires a full-time manager to oversee the day-to-day operation. As a result, overall efficiency leaped 15 percent, with customer returns of defective equipment dropping by 50 percent over three months. Corporate profits rose by 10% after paying the manager's salary.

Seeing the impressive results, Smith reasoned that two managers could achieve even better results and hires a second person. In the next three months, no appreciable difference was evident and, in fact, profits dipped slightly. Smith experienced the principle of increasing and decreasing returns. The addition of management expertise is only effective to a point after which the incremental value of that additional factor of production (in this case, labour) becomes proportionately less and less effective.

Principle of Substitution

A principle stating that a prudent buyer would pay no more for real property than the cost of acquiring an equally desirable substitute in the marketplace. This principle presumes that buyers will consider the alternatives available to them, that they will act rationally and prudently on the basis of information about those alternatives, and that time is not a significant factor, i.e., the substitute property can be acquired without unreasonable delay.

> **EXAMPLE**   *Principles of Value—Substitution*
>
> Buyer Jones is seriously considering two properties: a one-year-old, resale bungalow offered at $179,900 and a new unoccupied bungalow built by the same builder on an adjacent street priced at $179,500 (including GST). After inspecting both properties, Jones discovered the following differences. The resale property, while showing minor wear and tear, was fully decorated. In addition, all landscaping was completed and the driveway was paved.
>
> Jones, in making his ultimate decision, is unwittingly using the principle of substitution. He is carefully weighing out alternatives in terms of desirability and cost. His ultimate conclusion will be rationally based on differences noted between the two properties assuming that both can be acquired for approximately the same price.

Principle of Supply and Demand

The principle of supply and demand states that market value is determined by the interaction of the forces of supply and demand as of the date of the appraisal. According to this principle, if the supply increases but the demand remains constant, the price will decrease. If the demand increases but the supply remains constant, the price will increase. If both supply and demand increase or decrease proportionately, price will remain relatively stable. The value of real estate tends to be set by the relationship between supply and demand at the time of valuation.

> **EXAMPLE**   *Principles of Value—Supply and Demand*
>
> The importance of this principle is obvious. Consider the effect on house prices if a large corporation moves its head office and employees from City "A" to City "B." In City "A", prices will fall because of oversupply, while in City "B" prices will rise due to increased demand (assuming that supply and demand were previously equal in both cities).
>
> As another example, if construction of new homes exceeds demand, the resulting over-supply will ultimately impact prices.

Principle of Surplus Productivity

This is a principle relating to the net income remaining after all expenses necessary to the operation have been paid and the capital invested in improvements has been satisfied. This remaining net income is imputable to the land and tends to fix the value of the property. As a result, the land is valuable according to the surplus productivity imputable to it.

In the operation of an income producing property, three levels of return are necessary, while the fourth (the land) can command only the residual income with no fixed or necessary rate of return. These four levels are called the factors in production and must be satisfied in order of labour, coordination, capital and land. Surplus attributable to land largely determines its value and with well-developed real estate, the land should yield a reasonable return, based on its current realistic value.

EXAMPLE   *Principles of Value—Surplus Productivity*

Salesperson Jamieson is applying the principle of surplus productivity to arrive at the value of land. The improvements on the subject property have an estimated value of $150,000 and a forecasted net operating income of $27,000. Market research indicates that a discount (return) rate of 10% applies and that the remaining economic life of the building is 40 years. The income is capitalized based on the return rate (10%), plus the recapture rate of 2.5% (100 ÷ 40 or 2.5% per year).

Net Operating Income	$27,000
Income Earned by the Building *(150,000 x (.10 + .025)*	$18,750
Residual (Surplus) Income Attributable to the Land	$8,250
Value of the Land *($8,250 ÷ .10)*	$82,500

NOTE: Given that the real estate industry uses both metric and imperial measurements, this course will switch backwards and forwards between the two to give the learner a flavour for both. In reality, the theories and practices work equally well in both standards of measurement.

KNOWLEDGE INTEGRATION

Notables

- There are three levels of appraisers.

- It is necessary for a salesperson to consider his/her experience, education and whether he/she is covered by insurance before accepting an appraisal assignment.

- There are a number of different professional appraisal organizations and they incorporate standards of practice that cover what can and cannot be done by the designated appraiser.

- There are a number of different trends and issues that are affecting the real estate appraisal industry at present; e.g., AVMs, technology, fraud, etc.

- Form Reports and Narrative Reports are the predominant types of appraisal reports that are used in the appraisal industry. Letters of opinion should only be used with caution.

- There are many types of value which are used and apply in appraising properties and they need to be understood; e.g., market value, value in use, etc.

- Principles of value assist in the understanding and explanation of how real estate values are affected and how properties should be valued.

Web Links

Web links are included for general interest regarding selected chapter topics.

Appraisal Institute of Canada	www.aicanada.ca
Canadian National Association of Real Estate Appraisers	www.cnarea.ca
Institute of Municipal Assessors	www.assessorsinstitute.ca
Real Estate Institute of Canada	www.reic.ca

Chapter Mini-Review

Solutions are located in the Appendix.

1. An appraisal is an estimate of value which must be presented in written form.

   ◯ True   ◯ False

2. In Ontario, there is no requirement for an appraiser to actually be licensed by either the government or any particular organization.

   ◯ True   ◯ False

3. It is not a problem for a salesperson to give advice about the value of a property that is listed in an area where the salesperson has no expertise or knowledge.

   ◯ True   ◯ False

4. An appraiser with a CRA designation is qualified to appraise an office building.

   ◯ True   ◯ False

5. AVMs compete with professional appraisers for appraisal business especially when it comes to valuations for mortgage lending purposes.

   ◯ True   ◯ False

6. A form report would be used by an appraiser when estimating the market value of an office building.

   ◯ True   ◯ False

7. An appraisal completed by a letter of opinion does not require the same research, analysis and conclusions as does a valuation completed on a form report.

   ◯ True   ◯ False

8. Subjective value states that value exists in the minds of buyers and sellers.

   ◯ True   ◯ False

9. The subjective concept of value dominates in real estate valuation.

   ◯ True   ◯ False

10. Market price and market value would always be the same.

    ◯ True   ◯ False

11. John is thinking of paying $10,000 more for 123 Main Street than for 125 Main Street because it has a fireplace and central air conditioning not found in 125 Main Street. This is an example of the principle of anticipation.

    ◯ True   ◯ False

12. The definition of highest and best use is *"that use which at the time of the appraisal is most likely to produce the greatest net return in money or amenities to the building over a given period of time."*

    ◯ True   ◯ False

Active Learning Exercises

Solutions are located in the Appendix.

■ Exercise 1

List the main characteristics of *market value*.

■ Exercise 2

Market value, subjective value, objective value and value in use. Which of these types of value best describes the following scenarios?

2.1   The buyer paid $30,000 more than was paid for similar properties in the neigh-bourhood because it was located next door to her elderly parents.

2.2   The buyers' salesperson showed them several MLS® comparable sales that indicated that the subject property's worth was $250,000–260,000. The buyer paid $255,000 for the property.

2.3   The seller wanted to list the property based on the cost of the building and the land.

2.4   The buyer was only willing to pay $400,000 for the property, although the cost of the building and the land was over $425,000.

◼ Exercise 3

Explain the difference between *Market Value* and *Market Price*.

◼ Exercise 4

What is the difference between the *Objective Concept of Value* and the *Subjective Concept of Value?*

◼ Exercise 5

Why would the value in use of a property be greater than the market value of a property?

◼ Exercise 6   Multiple Choice

6.1   Which of the following would assist in providing a necessary level of conformity within a neighbourhood?

   a.   Easements
   b.   Zoning
   c.   Encroachments
   d.   Profits

6.2   Mike Smith is a salesperson who has been listing and selling single-family homes for several years in Anycity. He has been asked by one of his clients to value a condominium apartment unit in Anycity for capital gains tax purposes. Mike's training and experience is strictly limited to listing and selling single-family homes. What should he do?

   a.   Advise his client of his lack of training and experience, but proceed to complete the appraisal if the client still wishes.

   b.   Use his knowledge and experience of single-family homes to assist him in valuing the condominium.

   c.   Turn down the client's request because of his lack of training and experience with respect to this type of property and assignment.

   d.   Complete the appraisal, but ensure that a limiting condition is put in the appraisal that outlines his lack of training and experience.

6.3   Which of the following statements accurately reflects the principle of regression?

   a.   The value of the better property will be affected positively by the presence of the property of lesser value.

   b.   The property of lesser value will be negatively affected by the presence of the property of greater value.

   c.   The value of the better property will be affected adversely by the presence of the property of lesser value.

   d.   The property of lesser value would not be positively or negatively affected by the presence of the property of greater value.

6.4   An appraiser with a CRA designation is qualified to appraise a residential home containing up to a maximum of:

   a.   6 self-contained units.

   b.   2 self-contained units.

   c.   10 self-contained units.

   d.   4 self-contained units.

6.5   For what type of appraisal would a form report not be used? The valuation of a:

   a.   60-unit apartment building for mortgage financing purposes.

   b.   duplex for transfer or ownership purposes.

   c.   single-family home for estate purposes.

   d.   single-family home for capital gains taxes.

6.6   Which of the following scenarios incorporates one of the main characteristics of market value?

   a.   The property was marketed for a reasonable length of time before it sold.

   b.   The property was located next to similar properties.

   c.   Supply and demand in the neighbourhood was balanced.

   d.   Each additional bathroom cost $5,000, but increased value by $7,000.

6.7   Which of the following situations would be the most likely to cause the market value of a property to be different from its market price?

a.   The property was being sold on MLS®.

b.   The property sold within a reasonable amount of time.

c.   The seller needed to sell quickly because of financial difficulties.

d.   The buyer and seller negotiated with both having equal and adequate knowledge.

6.8   Which principle would explain why an appraisal report would always include the effective date of the appraisal?

a.   Highest and Best Use

b.   Change

c.   Anticipation

d.   Consistent Use

6.9   24 Main Street is a 25-year-old, detached 1,900 square foot bungalow surrounded by 3,200 square feet detached 2-storey 5-year-old homes. Describe what impact the above scenario would likely have on the value of 24 Main Street.

a.   There would be a negative impact on the value of 24 Main Street.

b.   There would be a positive impact on the value of 24 Main Street.

c.   There would be no impact on the value of 24 Main Street.

d.   There could be either a positive and negative impact on the value of 24 Main Street.

6.10   In valuing properties, it is important to keep in mind that:

a.   a prudent buyer will pay no more for a property than the cost of acquiring an equally desirable substitute in the market place.

b.   an appraiser, in estimating market value, must only consider the current use of the property as being the highest and best use.

c.   the value of a property will continue to increase as more and more amenities and features are added to it.

d.   excessive profits will tend to decrease competition, which in turn will have a negative impact on value.

CHAPTER 2

Accepting a Request for an Appraisal

Introduction

Before valuing a property for a client, it is important for the appraiser to understand the reasons for the valuation and what the client will do with it. There are many reasons for valuing a property (e.g., listing and sale; mortgage financing; capital gains tax; divorce settlement, etc.). The appraiser needs to know what he/she is getting him/herself into. As a salesperson, you may not have the experience, education or insurance coverage to complete a valuation for anything other than for listing purposes. Asking a series of questions and requiring certain information from a prospective client before agreeing to an appraisal assignment is important—appraisers refer to this as *Defining the Problem*.

Once the appraisal assignment has been agreed to, collecting information on the subject's listing and selling history and zoning before you leave the office will help in understanding

what the highest and best use of the property may likely be, and will assist in determining the type of comparables that will be needed as a result.

Time is well spent estimating the highest and best use of a property as a proper valuation cannot be conducted without understanding what a property can be used for and what it would likely be bought for. For example, it would be a mistake to value a property as a bungalow, if the bungalow would be bought by a developer to be knocked down to make way for a high-rise condominium. Here the land value would be appropriately tied to it's potential development as a condominium complex.

Learning Outcomes

At the conclusion of this chapter, students will be able to:

- List and explain the questions that need to be asked and answered in *Defining the Problem*; i.e., the information needed by the appraiser before he/she will agree to take on an appraisal assignment.
- Outline what needs to be included in any agreement to complete an appraisal assignment.
- Describe the preliminary work an appraiser will want to do before going out and completing the inspections and field work.
- Explain what factors determine the estimate of highest and best use of a property.
- Describe what factors are looked at in forecasting.

FIRST CONTACT

When an appraiser/salesperson is first contacted and asked to complete a valuation on a property, the appraiser/salesperson needs to be able to ask a number of questions in order to be able to understand what it is they are being asked to do. In the appraisal industry, those series of questions are referred to as *defining the problem* (the essential questions). Once an appraiser has a good idea of what it is they are being asked to do, they can decide whether they want to proceed with the valuation assignment and how much they want to charge the client for it.

Defining the Problem

The following is a list of questions that will need to be asked in order to understand the *terms of reference* (what is required) with respect to the appraisal assignment:

1) WHAT IS THE IDENTITY OF THE PROPERTY TO BE APPRAISED?

It is essential that a complete and accurate identification of the subject property be provided. This identification is achieved by obtaining not only the municipal address, but also the full legal description of the property. The municipal address alone is not sufficient, as a street may appear a number of times in a town or city. In addition, the legal description not only accurately identifies the unique location of the property, but it also establishes the boundaries within which the property is located.

2) WHAT ARE THE PROPERTY RIGHTS BEING APPRAISED?

There are many different types of interests in land. The appraiser needs to find out what type of estate/interest they are being asked to value. There are estates such as fee simple, future estate, leasehold estate and life estate. There are interests in land that can impact these estates, such as easements and covenants. This course will deal with the fee simple estate and easements/covenants.

Fee Simple

Fee simple is the highest estate or absolute right in real property. Fee simple provides the most rights with the fewest limitations and is generally considered absolute ownership. However, this bundle of rights (the right to use, sell, lease, enter, give away or refrain from any of these rights in regard to property) is subject to various restrictions imposed by laws of governing bodies.

3) WHAT IS THE PURPOSE OF THE APPRAISAL?

The purpose of the appraisal refers to the use that will be made of the value estimate. Five major purposes or reasons are outlined for which an appraisal may be required.

A. Transfer of Ownership	Involves the buying, selling and exchanging of real estate.
B. Extension of Credit	Normally relates to mortgage lending or other financing and an estimate of value to establish the loan amount.
C. Compensation for Damage or Loss	Usually involves insurance claims or expropriation.
D. Taxation	Includes municipal assessment for property taxes and income tax on capital gains.

E. Land Use Studies or Feasibility Studies	Largely carried out for developers and investors interested in establishing the highest and best use of a particular parcel of land. This process typically involves a number of estimates of value for different forms of development; e.g., freehold detached homes, as compared to condominium townhouses.

It is essential that the purpose be established at the very beginning of the assignment and be clearly stated in the appraisal report. It will determine what type of value will be required for that appraisal assignment. An appraisal for an insurance claim will require insurance value (land not included), as opposed to market value for transfer of ownership purposes.

4) WHAT TYPE OF VALUE IS REQUIRED?

As previously mentioned, there are many different types of value; e.g., market value, value in use, insurance value, lending value, assessment value, etc. As a result, it is important to know what type of value is required. This will of course depend on the purpose of the appraisal and the intention of the client. It is important that the client understand what type of value is being used and the best way of doing that is to define the value to the client, so that there is no confusion or complication down the road.

EXAMPLE   *Defining Value*

The owner of 123 Main Street has asked Anne Appraiser to value her property for sale purposes (transfer of ownership). Anne will use market value in her appraisal assignment. Part of the definition of market value is "...*a reasonable time to find a willing buyer...*". A reasonable time in the subject neighbourhood would be 90 days. The owner is in financial difficulty and would like to know the value of the property based on a 30 day marketing period. This would be a special condition and should be noted when defining the value being used.

5) WHAT IS THE EFFECTIVE DATE OF THE APPRAISAL?

Every estimate of value is valid only under specific market conditions. This applies whether it is market value, insurable value, investment value, lending value or any other specific value that is to be estimated. Value is the result of the interaction of the forces of market supply and demand. When these conditions change, the value estimate based upon them will also change. Therefore, every appraisal must be made as of a specific date to identify the prevailing market forces and conditions in terms of which value is estimated. This is the effective date of the appraisal, often referred to as *the date on which the appraisal applies* or the *as of* date.

When it comes to valuing a property for a transfer of ownership or extension of credit, the effective date of the appraisal will be the same date as the date of the inspection of the property. However, there are situations where the effective date would not be the same as the date of inspection of the property. The inspection date might be today, but the valuation needs to be as of some date in the past.

Retroactive appraisals might include the following:

- Valuation for Capital Gains Tax.
- A valuation for probating a will and selling an estate—here the effective date would be the date of death.
- A value for expropriation where the valuation date would likely be the date of the taking or registration of the expropriation.

- A valuation to settle a fire insurance claim where the effective date would be the date on which the fire occurred.
- A valuation for a marriage separation where the effective date might be the date of separation.

NOTE: It is important to note that it is not the appraiser's job to decide the effective date—that should come from the client or their lawyer/accountant.

EXAMPLE   *Effective Dates*

John owned and lived at 123 Main Street until September 3rd, 1995 when he rented the home to tenants and relocated to France for his job. John returned from France on April 16th, 1998 at which time he moved back into the house. His accountant asked Anne Appraiser to inspect the property today (no changes having occurred to the property over the years), but to value it as of September 3rd, 1995 and April 16th, 1998. Any increase in estimated value between these dates might attract capital gains tax as it would have been considered an investment property during that period.

Valuations In The Past   **CURIOSITY**

Of course, there are challenges when it comes to inspecting a property today for a valuation some time in the past. The questions that need to be asked are:

- What changes have occurred and what did the property look like on the effective date?
- What forces and factors were at work at the time of the effective date?
- What sales/listings are available from the effective date? This would be more of a challenge the further back the valuation date is.

6) WHAT ASSUMPTIONS AND LIMITING CONDITIONS ARE NEEDED FOR THE APPRAISAL ASSIGNMENT?

Assumptions and limiting conditions are a series of qualifying statements and assumptions commonly associated with appraisal reports in which the appraiser sets out items that define, limit and/or restrict the scope of the appraisal and inform the client accordingly. Limiting conditions are usually grouped under *Assumptions and Limiting Conditions* that may be included in a letter of transmittal, but more commonly at the end of the appraisal report.

Limiting conditions normally relate to such issues as legal title (no warranty by the appraiser concerning title validity), the appraiser's reliance on information furnished by others is deemed to be correct, the improvements on the property are assumed to be confined within the property boundaries, a disclaimer that the appraiser does not have expertise concerning the existence of hazardous materials or their impact on value, and other matters that the appraiser feels should be specifically highlighted to the person requesting the report.

The standard assumptions and limiting conditions for an appraisal assignment, together with a more thorough discussion of this subject, are described in Chapter 8. Appraisers will vary the scope of the assumptions and limiting conditions based on circumstances; e.g., the appraiser is unable to inspect the whole house due to tenancy; water damage is seen in the basement—however, the extent and nature of the problem cannot be determined as of the effective date of the appraisal.

In summary, every client needs to know what the appraiser did or did not do; is responsible for or not responsible for; and is assuming or not assuming in connection with the valuation of their property.

Other Questions	MARKET MEMO

While not considered a formal part of "Defining the Problem", appraisers would normally want to ask additional questions before agreeing to complete an appraisal assignment. The answers to these questions will help the appraiser decide whether they will want to proceed with the assignment, how much to charge and how long it will take to complete the assignment. Typical questions might be as follows:

- What type of property is the appraiser being asked to appraise; e.g., vacant land, detached two-storey single-family home, office building, retail store etc?
- What is the zoning; e.g., residential, commercial, industrial or mixed?

AGREEING TO COMPLETE AN APPRAISAL ASSIGNMENT

A request for an appraisal is generally received either by phone, fax, e-mail or directly by completing an application form online.

When the appraiser is dealing with a regular client and the fee is to be relatively small, the appraiser will complete the assignment based on a relatively informal request and will invoice/bill the client afterwards. Of course, the informal request will still need to detail the necessary information; i.e., *define the problem* for the appraiser to understand what is being asked of him/her and for him/her to be able to agree to the assignment.

For a client that is not well known to the appraiser (e.g., a house owner) and where the fee is relatively small, the appraiser may well ask for payment up front before the assignment is started.

For large fee assignments, (even if the client is well known), an appraiser may have the person requesting the appraisal assignment sign a letter of agreement prepared by the appraiser. In addition, part of the fee may be payable up front. The content of this letter of agreement should include:

- Identification of the property (address and legal description).
- Purpose of the appraisal and the type of value required (including a definition of value required).
- The effective date of the appraisal and date by which the appraisal report must be completed and delivered.
- The appraisal fee and the terms of payment.
- The ability to alter the fee should the property or assignment turn out to be different than that set out by the client during the initial conversations/correspondence.

Once the appraisal assignment has been agreed on, the appraiser will want to start on some preliminary work.

Preliminary Work

Before going out to do the inspection of the neighbourhood, subject property and comparables, you will want to do some preliminary work in the office which will include looking at some of the following:

- When the subject last sold or was listed for sale.
- The property's tax assessment.
- The zoning.
- The *Highest and Best Use* of the subject (your view of the highest and best use of a property may change as you move forward through the many stages of the appraisal assignment).
- Demand and supply. Understanding the state of the supply and demand in the area will give you a good indication of whether property values are increasing, stable or decreasing in the subject neighbourhood.
- Comparable sales and listings you may use in the value assignment (this is only possible if you have prior knowledge of the subject from either previous listings/visits or from details given to you by the owner/purchaser). Obviously having good comparables ready before you go out may save you time with respect to a second visit to the area. Time spent researching and trying to find good comparable sales is invaluable. The accuracy of an appraisal assignment will depend on finding good comparable sales that require few, or relatively few, adjustments.

MLS® HISTORY OF THE PROPERTY

By looking back at the subject property in terms of its marketing and sale history, you will have a preliminary guide as to how the subject is perceived by the marketplace. This research may take on extra importance especially when there is a lack of good current comparable sales/listings from which to estimate value.

TAX ASSESSMENT INFORMATION

It is always important to look at the taxes of the subject compared to those of the comparables. Lower taxes can be an attractive feature for a property. However, if the subject has taxes that are substantially higher than the other comparable properties in the neighbourhood and there is no reasonable explanation for it, then it is possible that those taxes could be appealed and reduced, resulting in no need for a value adjustment between the subject and comparables for the tax difference.

Some MLS® systems contain assessment information. If this information is not available in the office, then it is essential to obtain it from the seller at the time of inspection. As a last resort, a visit to the local municipal office will provide accurate assessment information.

NOTE: If the subject property has significantly different taxes than that of the properties chosen as comparables, then that may be a warning that those properties may not be truly comparable.

ZONING AND MUNICIPAL INFORMATION

Zoning and the presence or lack of a building permit can have an impact on the value of a property. Therefore, it is important to make some initial enquiries to see if the subject property conforms to zoning or is legal non-conforming. This can be done by reference to zoning maps or by making a call to the local municipal zoning/building departments.

EXAMPLE   *Zoning Impacts*

Scenario 1

Properties A and B are both 50 x 125 feet lots developed with 1,200 square foot bungalows. These two properties are located three streets apart in the same neighbourhood. There is a large demand in the area to knock down the bungalows and build 4,000–5,000 square foot two-storey homes. Property A is zoned R2 Z1.0, which allows for the building of up to a 6,250 square foot house. Property B is zoned R2 Z0.5, which would allow for the building of only up to a 3,125 square foot house.

   Clearly, in this case, the demand for 4,000–5,000 square foot houses would result in Property A being more valuable than B because of the zoning.

Scenario 2

Properties A and B are both 60 by 150 feet lots developed with 4,500 square feet homes. These two properties are located 2 streets apart in the same neighbourhood. Property A is zoned R2 Z1.0 and B is zoned R2 Z0.5 The zoning allows for a 9,000 square foot house to be built on Property A, but only a 4,500 square foot home on B. There is no demand in the area for more than a 4,500 square foot house.

   Clearly, the difference in zoning here would have no perceptible impact on value between the two properties, as there is no demand to take advantage of the differences.

EXAMPLE   *Building Permits*

You are valuing a 60-year-old house with a 1-year-old family room extension. When enquiring about zoning, you discover that no permits have been issued on the property for the past 10 years. This should be of concern and requires a discussion with the owner and client. In this scenario, you will need an instruction from the client as to how to proceed; i.e., do they want you to proceed on the basis that the owner will be able to get the requisite permits, the problem can be title insured or do they want the value of the family room to be removed in the valuation. It could also be that a client who is a mortgage lender may not want to proceed with the valuation and financing. It will be the client who should instruct as to how to proceed—make sure you are covered by attaching the requisite Assumption and Limiting Condition.

Zoning Conformity/Legality	CAUTION

Only a lawyer can really give an opinion on title as to whether a property does or does not conform to zoning, or whether the subject property has had the requisite permits issued and signed off for building, renovations or floor plan changes. However you need to identify the zoning and make sure that the client is aware of any concerns you may have, leaving it to them as to whether they want to investigate further.

HIGHEST AND BEST USE

All properties must be valued based on their highest and best use. In other words, your estimate of value is directly related to what a typical buyer with a reasonable knowledge of the market and property would use or do with the property. It is natural that the amount of money that a buyer would pay is based on the use and enjoyment (income or profit) that he/she would derive from the property.

   There are two situations that the appraiser may come across when appraising a property.

- Situation 1—The property is a vacant site (the site is undeveloped).
- Situation 2—The property is an improved site (the site is developed with buildings/improvements).

SITUATION 1

When an appraiser is looking at a vacant site, there are several general factors that he/she must consider in estimating the highest and best use. These general factors would include:

A. The Zoning   What is or is not allowed to be built on the site? The appraiser should estimate a highest and best use that is in conformity with the zoning, unless there is a probable and imminent prospect the zoning will change or be amended to accommodate a highest and best use estimate that currently is not legal.

B. Is the use being proposed physically possible? This physical possibility is related to factors such as the size/shape of the lot, the soil/drainage, etc.

C. Is there a demand for this use being proposed? Would the use be economically and financially feasible? There is not much point in estimating a highest and best use for which there is little demand or which would cost more to develop than it would return in value/income.

SITUATION 2

When an appraiser is looking at a site that is improved with buildings, then the appraiser's first job is to decide whether this current use is actually the highest and best use. The appraiser needs to ask several questions in order to confirm whether the current use is the highest and best use. These questions would revolve around the following:

A. Do the improvements conform to the zoning or are they legal non-conforming?

B. Do the improvements conform to the other homes in the area?

C. Do the improvements add value to the land; i.e., would a typical purchaser pay for the buildings over and above what they would pay for the land?

If the answer to all three questions is YES, then the current use is most likely the highest and best use of the land. If the answer to one or all of the questions is NO, then the appraiser may need to consider that the value of the site should be based on an alternative (different) highest and best use. In considering that another use may be the highest and best use, the appraiser is in effect looking at the site as if it is vacant (undeveloped).

Given the time, effort and cost of developing and or redeveloping a property, the appraiser will need fairly strong evidence to draw the conclusion that another use of a property (different to the current one) is indeed a higher and better use.

Highest and Best Use   CURIOSITY

In the overwhelming majority of cases, properties are already developed to their highest and best use. The typical buyer/owner will use a property to its best advantage whether for enjoyment or profit. This is not only because of natural human nature, but also because of economic pressures to do so.

EXAMPLE   *Highest and Best Use*

Scenario 1: A Change In Use

The subject property is a 1,500 square foot, 45-year-old bungalow sitting on a lot that is 300 x 400 feet. The zoning is commercial. This property is located on a street now completely developed with 40 to 60-storey office buildings. The economy is currently booming. The typical buyer of the subject would likely develop it as a high-rise office building. That, therefore, is its highest and best use and should be valued as such, and not as a residential bungalow.

Scenario 2: Current Use

The subject property is a residential detached two-storey 45-year-old building located on a main road. The zoning is commercial/retail. There is very little pedestrian traffic and all the other properties located on this main road are similar detached homes that have remained residential despite the commercial/retail that has been in place for 10 years. The typical buyer of the subject would continue to use it as a residence. Clearly therefore, the highest and best use remains residential despite the zoning and main road location.

Impacting Value   PERSPECTIVE

Alice Carpenter, an appraiser, and Janet Fields, a property owner, sit down together and talk about the information in the Subject and Market History section of the Appraisal Form. Here are some of the questions and answers that come about in their conversation.

JANET   What is forecasting and how does it apply to valuing a property for listing purposes?

ALICE   When I do a valuation for listing purposes, I price the property so that it will sell in a reasonable time. In your neighbourhood, a reasonable marketing time appears to be from 45–75 days. Accordingly, in your case, forecasting is about looking at what is likely to happen over the next 75 days or so and then making sure the value I have given you reflects an analysis of that time period. Until recently, many appraisers thought it was sufficient to give a client a value for listing purposes that was good only for the day on which it was given. The fact is, most properties do not sell on the day the valuation is given. They sell perhaps 30, 60, 90 or 120 days later and this needs to be taken into account.

Supply and demand forces, both on the day of the valuation and anticipated over the following months, are the dominant factors in forecasting. Other things to keep in mind are as follows:

- What has the price trend been over the previous few months? If prices have been declining, will that continue or what possible factors might stop or reverse that trend?

- Are there any seasonal factors to take into account? For example, sales may slow down significantly at the end of November or the beginning of December because of the onset of winter and the approaching Christmas period.

- It is important to carefully analyze competitive listings and find out what is happening to them. Find out if their listing prices are being or have been reduced? Are showings increasing or declining? What offers have there been and if so, at what price?

- An appraiser/salesperson should listen to his/her buyers and sellers. What are they saying? Has some piece of news made the buyers anxious about buying or eager to purchase? Has something happened to make sellers hold off selling or want to sell more quickly?

The answers to all of the above will help provide a more complete picture of what is likely to happen within the near future. After all, today's prospective buyers are the buyers of tomorrow and the foreseeable future. Let's look at the following example to help in getting a clearer picture of forecasting.

continued...

Impacting Value   **PERSPECTIVE**

EXAMPLE

You have been asked to value the subject property for listing and sale purposes. It is March 23, 20xx, and the client wants to be out of the property within three months. A typical property is taking 30–60 days to sell.

Based on the comparable sales you have used and without considering the factors involved in forecasting, you feel that the subject's value ranges from $268,000–283,000 and are looking at a final value of $280,000. You suddenly realize that you have not done any forecasting in coming up with your value for listing purposes. You now gather the following information which you feel is connected to the forecasting:

- Over the past couple of weeks, a number of large companies within the subject area have announced major layoffs. In addition, mortgage rates have just increased by ½%.

- Properties A and B which are very comparable to the subject and may even be superior have had their listing prices reduced within the past two weeks from $289,000 to 279,000 and from $299,900 to 278,900 respectively. Property A was originally listed on January 3, 20xx, and Property B came on the market on January 5, 20xx.

- You find out that both properties had offers over the past few days. Both offers fell through.

- You have noticed that an unusually high number of listings have been reduced in price over the past few weeks. Buyers are now talking about being concerned about their jobs and perhaps putting off buying.

- The local Real Estate Board has reported a significant drop in the number of sales to listings over the past two weeks.

Clearly, all the above factors should be leading you to forecast a softening in prices and perhaps an increase in the number of days to sell. When you take all this into account it would be much more prudent if you revised your final estimate of value from $280,000 so that it sits closer to the lower end of your original value range at $270,000.

JANET   What is the relevance of knowing the typical exposure time for properties in a neighbourhood?

ALICE   The typical exposure time for properties to sell tells you the state of the neighbourhood market in terms of its activity. Most homes are valued based on their being marketed or being exposed on the market for a reasonable length of time. That reasonable length of time is the typical exposure time required for properties to sell within the subject neighbourhood. As a result, this information is important to know. You should preferably choose comparables that sold within the typical exposure time. Let's look at the following example to help in getting a clearer picture of the relevance of knowing typical exposure times.

EXAMPLE

You are valuing the subject property in a neighbourhood where the typical exposure time is 60–90 days. You have chosen a comparable that is almost identical to the subject. It sold for $240,000 after being on the market for 180 days. Given the length of time on the market, you decide to investigate further. It turns out that the comparable had been poorly marketed and overpriced. For the first 160 days this comparable had been listed at $289,900, for the last 20 days it had a listing price of $249,900. After 160 days the property had become stale and the owner was becoming a little desperate to sell.

Your research shows that as a result of the above, the comparable sold below the expected market value. In this case, you will need to either discard the comparable, or make an appropriate adjustment to take care of the comparables lower sale value due to length of exposure/marketing time. Of course, if your research had shown that the length of exposure time had not impacted on the comparable's final selling price, then no adjustment would be necessary.

continued...

Impacting Value   PERSPECTIVE

JANET   How does knowing about the subject's previous listing and sale help in the valuation of the subject?

ALICE   Firstly, the subject's previous listing and sale can indicate to you if it is going to be difficult to market and sell for whatever reason. Let's look at a couple of examples that will help explain this in more detail.

EXAMPLE 1

The subject property sold in January, 4 years ago, after 190 days on the market. It resold in May, 2 years later, after being listed for 200 days. During both of the above time frames, the average days on market for a typical home in the subject market was between 30–60 days. Clearly, this should indicate to you right away that something might be wrong with the subject. In this case, it turns out that the subject's floor plan is not common for the area and is unpopular. Naturally, you will need to adjust the market value of the subject for this. Secondly, the previous sale price may help you determine the current value range within which the subject sits.

EXAMPLE 2

The subject property is a detached two-storey home that sold in August, 5 years ago, for $210,000 and then in September, 2 years later, for $229,000. Other detached two-storey homes that sold in August, 5 years ago, for between $205,000 and 215,000 and in September, 2 years later, for between $220,000 and 240,000, are now selling for between $275,000 and 300,000. Clearly, the above will help you establish the price range (i.e., $275,000–300,000) within which you may want to start your search for good comparable sales.

This is particularly helpful information when you are uncertain of the price range within which the subject sits because there is a lack of highly similar properties, and you are having to extend your search for comparables in terms of location, time and physical differences.

JANET   How can the current listing price of the subject impact on your valuation?

ALICE   The current listing price of the subject property will in all likelihood set its upper limit of value. Let's look at an example that will help explain this in more detail.

EXAMPLE

The subject property has been listed at a price of $199,900 for the last 30 days. The market has been fairly active, but stable, and properties are selling within 15–30 days if well priced. The above should tell you that the subject is worth something less than $199,900. So, if you feel that you have comparables that indicate that the subject is worth $205,000, then you have either chosen the wrong comparables or the adjustments/analysis has been somewhat faulty.

KNOWLEDGE INTEGRATION

Notables

- An appraiser needs to understand why a client needs an appraisal and what will be done with it. The questions asked by the appraiser form part of *Defining the Problem*.

- When an appraiser decides to undertake an appraisal assignment, there may be an informal or formal agreement completed with the client. This is dependant on the type of assignment being requested.

- There is a certain amount of research that an appraiser completes before leaving the office to complete an inspection of the subject property and the other field work; e.g., subject listing and sale history.

- All properties must be valued based on their highest and best use.

- The highest and best use of a property may be estimated in circumstances where:
  - the property is a vacant site.
  - the property is an improved site.
  - the property's current improvements are not the highest and best use, and there is an alternative use which would be the highest and best use.

- Forecasting may be incorporated into a value estimate for sale purposes because properties do not sell on the date their value is estimated.

Chapter Mini-Review

Solutions are located in the Appendix.

1. The purpose of *Defining the Problem* is to understand what it is the appraiser is being asked to do in the appraisal assignment.

   ◯ True   ◯ False

2. One of the purposes for which an appraisal would be required would be to estimate market value.

   ◯ True   ◯ False

3. Market value is the only type of value used by appraisers.

   ◯ True   ◯ False

4. One purpose for which an appraisal might be required is for a land use study.

   ◯ True   ◯ False

5. The effective date of an appraisal would be the date the appraisal report was completed.

   ◯ True   ◯ False

6. The zoning of a property would not have an impact on the value of a property.

   ◯ True   ◯ False

7. The date of inspection and the effective date would not be the same when it comes to valuing a property for the purpose of a marriage separation.

   ○ True   ○ False

8. When completing the preliminary work in an appraisal assignment, the appraiser would want to establish if the subject property contained any functional obsolescence.

   ○ True   ○ False

9. The highest and best use of a property does not change over a period of time.

   ○ True   ○ False

10. The accuracy of the Direct Comparison Approach will depend on being able to locate good comparable sales that require few or relatively few adjustments.

    ○ True   ○ False

11. Assumptions and limiting conditions tell a client what an appraiser did or did not do as well as what the appraiser is or is not responsible for in the valuation of their property.

    ○ True   ○ False

12. The property is developed with a detached two-storey building containing a store and apartment. If, after careful consideration, it is determined that this is not the highest and best use of the property, the highest and best use of the property would now be determined by looking at the property as if it were a vacant site, because the store and apartment would not add value to the land.

    ○ True   ○ False

Active Learning Exercises

Solutions are located in the Appendix.

■ Exercise 1

1.1   You arrive at a property and find that the site has been developed with a 4,100 square foot single-family home. What are you looking for and what sort of question do you ask in order to confirm that the subject property is in its highest and best use?

1.2   If the subject site had been vacant (i.e., there was no house sitting on the site), what would you look for and what kind of questions would you ask in order to confirm the subject's highest and best use?

■ Exercise 2

Why would the effective date of appraisal be different from the date of inspection?

Exercise 3

Where would you obtain the information for the General Appraisal and Property Information as well as Subject and Market History sections of the *Standard Appraisal Report—Single Family* (OREA Form 700)?

Exercise 4

Tarquin Trust has asked you to value 23 Asquith Road. This property is a vacant site with zoning that will allow for the construction of a 2,500 square foot house.

4.1   The owner of the site tells you that he can get rezoning for the site that would allow for the construction of a 3,500 square foot home. This would make the site more valuable. The owner tells you to value the property based on this rezoning. What do you do?

4.2   Would it have made any difference to your answer above if the valuation was being done for potential buyers of 23 Asquith Road who wanted the appraisal done to show what the value of the property would be if rezoning did in fact take place?

▦ Exercise 5

What is the relevance of knowing the typical exposure time for properties on the subject street and neighbourhood?

▦ Exercise 6

How does knowing the subject property's previous listing and selling price help in the valuation of the subject?

▦ Exercise 7

How can the current listing price of the subject property impact the valuation?

▦ Exercise 8   Multiple Choice

8.1   The type of value required for an appraisal assignment will depend on the:

    a.   zoning of the property.

    b.   effective date of the appraisal.

    c.   highest and best use of the property.

    d.   purpose of the appraisal.

8.2   Jim has appraised 123 Main Street and estimated a value of $324,000 as of May 21st, 20xx. For what period of time would that value be valid?

    a.   The value would be valid for 30 days after the effective date.

    b.   The value would be valid for a 45 to 60 day marketing period.

    c.   There is no specific time period for which a value would be valid.

    d.   It would only be valid as of the effective date of the appraisal.

8.3   Provide a circumstance in which the effective date and the date of inspection would not be the same.

    a.   A trustee needs an appraisal for probating a will.

    b.   A buyer needs an appraisal for mortgage financing.

    c.   A seller needs an appraisal for listing purposes.

    d.   A buyer needs an appraisal for the purpose of making an offer.

8.4   What is the purpose of assumptions and limiting conditions?

    a.   They outline the circumstances and conditions under which an appraisal was completed.

    b.   They prevent a client from being able to sue the appraiser for negligent mistakes made during the valuation.

    c.   It is the certification of the appraiser's ability to appraise the client's property without limitations.

    d.   They outline the problems in the client's property and what will be done to correct those problems.

8.5   One of the factors that would be looked at in estimating the highest and best use of a vacant site would be the:

    a.   zoning of the property.

    b.   purpose of the appraisal.

    c.   tax value of the property.

    d.   type of value required.

8.6   Jim is appraising 123 Manin Road (a vacant site) for a bank for mortgage financing. He believes that the highest and best use of the site would be a six-storey 80-unit apartment building. There is demand for this use and it is physically possible. However, the current zoning only allows for a three-storey 40-unit apartment building. Under what circumstances would this property's highest and best use still be estimated as a six-storey 80-unit apartment building?

    a.   If a change to the zoning were possible and an application had been made.

    b.   If the owner of the subject property had given Jim permission to do so.

    c.   Under no circumstances could Jim do that, unless permission was given by the zoning department.

    d.   If a change in zoning for the subject property was probable and imminent.

8.7 What would be one of the factors that an appraiser would look at in confirming that the current improvements of a site are its highest and best use?

a. The typical number of days it takes to sell a property in the neighbourhood.

b. Whether the improvements conform to the other properties in the area.

c. The change in prices experienced in the area over the past 12 months.

d. Value of the subject site as compared to the other sites in the area.

8.8 The property is developed with a single-family home on a main road. The zoning allows for a five-storey office building and the lot could easily physically accommodate that type of improvement. The cost of putting up the office building would be $2,000,000 and it would add $1,700,000 in value to the subject site. Would the 5-storey office building in fact be the highest and best use of the land?

a. No, because the current use is always the best use of the property.

b. Yes, the zoning allows for it and it is physically possible.

c. No, because it would not be financially viable.

d. Yes, because it would add much more value to the land than the single-family house.

8.9 You are appraising the market value of a property for sale purposes. You have estimated that a reasonable time to sell a property would be 60 days. How would you have come up with the 60 days?

a. The number of days it had taken to sell the subject property in previous years.

b. The average number of days that current listings had been on the market for.

c. The typical exposure time needed to sell similar properties in the neighbourhood.

d. The average number of days that expired listings had been on the market for.

8.10 What piece or pieces of information that you would note on an appraisal could help you identify if a specific property was going to be difficult to market and sell as compared to other similar properties?

a. The previous listing and sale history of the property itself.

b. The assumptions and limiting conditions outlined in the appraisal report.

c. How many times the property had sold over the past several years.

d. The supply and demand of comparable properties in the area.

8.11 The subject property has been listed at $222,000 for 70 days. It is a very active market, but there have been no offers on the property. The typical exposure time for similar properties in the neighbourhood is 60 days. How does the listing price assist you in valuing the property?

a. The current listing price sets the lower limit of value.

b. The current listing price sets the upper limit of value.

c. It would tell you what the property is worth.

d. It would not tell you anything, as it is just a listing.

CHAPTER 3

Neighbourhood Analysis

Introduction

The value of a property is going to be directly affected by the factors and forces at work in the neighbourhood within which it is located. Therefore, it is important for the appraiser to know what is going on in the neighbourhood and how that impacts the value of the properties located there.

Factors and forces can impact in a positive or negative way, or actually have a neutral impact. There are a number of tools at the appraiser's disposal in order for him/her to confirm the impact of a factor or force and its dollar value. Those tools require information to be collected from the market place—that information for the most part comes in the form of listings and sales.

In essence, at any stage of the appraisal, the appraiser needs to collect information, analyze it, come up with a conclusion and prove that the conclusion is correct by using hard market data.

Learning Outcomes

At the conclusion of this chapter, students will be able to:

- Describe what defines a neighbourhood and its boundaries.
- Discuss the factors and forces at work in a neighbourhood and how they influence values.
- Describe a trend and the impact that it can have on value.
- Describe the stages in the life cycle of a neighbourhood and explain how to identify the stage of the neighbourhood at the time of valuation.
- Define conformity and outline the impact it can have on the values within the neighbourhood.
- Discuss how and from where to collect the information and data on the factors and forces at work within the neighbourhood.
- Explain the need to measure the impact of the forces and factors at work within a neighbourhood.
- Outline the role that value ranges within a neighbourhood play on the value of the subject property.

THE NEIGHBOURHOOD

A property's value is most directly affected by what is going on in the neighbourhood in which it is located.

The simplest definition of a neighbourhood is a part of a city, a smaller segment within a larger segment. While it is common practice to describe a neighbourhood by its physical appearance (building types, condition, street layouts and amenities), it is actually the people who live in the neighbourhood that determine and shape the nature and character of the area. Of course, any changes to the economic, political, social values, resources and outlook of the people in the neighbourhood will ultimately have an influence on the physical appearance and character of the neighbourhood.

The Influence People Can Have On Neighbourhoods	MARKET MEMO

Carrot Town is a 100-year-old neighbourhood. The neighbourhood was originally inhabited by wealthy income earners who built and maintained large, expensive homes serviced by high-end quality amenities. For various reasons, over the past 10 years the upper income families have moved out making way for low-income families. The low-income families do not have the spending power to either maintain and or improve the homes as needed or sustain high-end retail/commercial businesses. The result of all this is that:

- The homes have started to look neglected and rather dated.
- Many of the homes have been converted into duplexes, triplexes, fourplexes and rooming houses.
- Many of the fine retail shops have now either been replaced with low-end retail/commercial businesses or are vacant and showing signs of disrepair.
- Residential selling prices have declined relative to other neighbourhoods and the city is collecting much lower taxes here.
- The streetscapes and parks do not seem to show the same pride and care of maintenance as in the past.

BOUNDARIES OF A NEIGHBOURHOOD

While people determine the nature and character of the neighbourhood, it is still important to identify the boundaries of the area. One important reason in noting the boundaries is to use comparable sales that are influenced by the same factors and forces as the subject—because they are located within the same neighbourhood.

Boundaries can be divided into three types as shown below:

Natural	*e.g., rivers, lakes, hills, mountains and ravines.*
Political	*e.g., municipal boundaries or city limits, land use or zoning changes, and school areas.*
Man-Made	*e.g., railroad tracks, major highways or roads, and rights-of-way for public utilities.*

NEIGHBOURHOOD FACTORS

A neighbourhood can be affected by a number of factors. These factors are generally grouped under the following headings:

Physical	Location in relation to services and amenities.
Economic	Stability of uses, property values, vacancies and sale price trends.
Political	Legislative impact such as taxation, local improvements and official plan restrictions.
Social	Population growth/decline, crime rates and age groupings.

EXAMPLE   *Analysis—Single-Family*

Salesperson Ward has been asked to provide an appraisal for a single-family home in a low density neighbourhood. Ward describes the neighbourhood in terms of four factors:

Physical   Poor location can offset many other factors that would otherwise enhance its value. Within the neighbourhood, Salesperson Ward will consider proximity of public transportation, parks, schools, churches, retail and service outlets, topography, landscape, and availability/ quality of utilities. Her checklist also includes nuisances or hazards such as smoke, noise, pollution and heavy traffic.

Economic   Ward will also give regard to stability of uses, property values, vacancies, new construction, personal and family income levels, degree of maintenance (pride of ownership), stage in the neighbourhood age (life) cycle, amount of undeveloped land available, mortgage lending policies, interest rates, sale price trends and rate of turnover.

Political or Governmental   Ward must be aware of legal factors affecting low density residential values, such as zoning regulations, building codes, property taxes, local improvement taxes, official plans, site plan control agreements and deed restrictions.

Social   Significant social factors include population trends with respect to growth or decline, trends to larger/smaller family sizes, harmony or lack of harmony of ethnic or economic groupings, educational attitudes, level of prestige, crime rates, age groupings and population densities.

TREND ANALYSIS

It would be impossible to value a property without understanding what trends in a neighbourhood were affecting its value. It is also important to understand that trends can change over time, so it is important for an appraiser/salesperson to be informed about the current trends in the area that they practice real estate in. A trend is defined as a series of related changes brought about by a chain of causes and effects. A trend possesses the four distinct features as illustrated below.

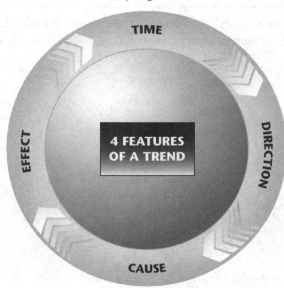

Analyzing Trends

Examples of trends would include:

- changes in floor plans—kitchen/family room and kitchen/dining room combination;
- smaller families—less need for the larger homes;
- aging population—movement away from single-family homes into condominiums;
- lower mortgage rates—increased demand for homes; and
- high unemployment—less demand for homes.

EXAMPLE   *The Impact of Trends on Value*

Over the past few years (time), mortgage rates have declined (direction) due to low inflation (cause), resulting in more buyers looking for homes and pushing up property prices (effect).

Scenario 1

Jill is valuing a home that has been carpeted, but has no hardwood floors. She researches the trends that have been occurring in the area and finds that the subject property is in a neighbourhood where new or renovated homes have, over the past few years, been finished or refinished with hardwood floors. This trend leads Jill to conclude that the subject might be less valuable because it has carpeting, whereas it is the presence of hardwood floors that is popular. Based on this information and analysis, Jill goes to the marketplace and tests the value difference between homes that have sold with carpeting and those that have sold with hardwood floors. Jill finds that homes with hardwood floors sell for $10,000 more than similar homes with carpeting.

Scenario 2

John is an appraiser who doesn't seem to understand the importance of trends and never bothers to research them. He has been asked to appraise a detached two-storey house. Prices in the subject neighbourhood have declined by 10% over the past three months. John has chosen three comparable sales which are very similar to the subject. However, they sold three to four months ago for $210,000, $212,000 and $214,000 respectively. Current sale prices are closer to $200,000. John is ignorant of the downward price trend, does not analyze competitive listings and estimates the subject's value at $212,000. In ignoring the downward price trend, he has arrived at an overpriced estimate of value.

 # NEIGHBOURHOOD LIFE CYCLE PHASES

One trend that needs to be assessed by an appraiser is the life cycle phase of a neighbourhood. In other words, what phase is the neighbourhood going through at the time of the appraisal.

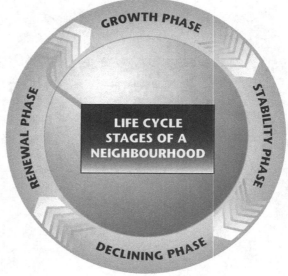

All neighbourhoods, whether catering to the low or upper income areas, will eventually go through each of the phases to one degree or another. In some areas it will be more obvious than in others. Actually some neighbourhoods, especially the older inner city ones, will have already gone through the cycle once or maybe even twice.

GROWTH PHASE

This phase is the period during which a neighbourhood is first being developed; e.g., a new subdivision. It is becoming popular and building construction is replacing much of the vacant land. New construction includes not only residential housing, but the development of a full range of amenities such as schools, plazas, parks, etc., which has either just been completed or is ongoing.

STABILITY PHASE

This phase is the period during which the neighbourhood has been completely built up, has reached the height of its popularity and values are at their highest in comparison to other similar neighbourhoods. A full range of amenities would be present for the population.

DECLINING PHASE

This phase is the period during which a fully developed neighbourhood is losing its appeal and popularity. Properties tend to look less well-maintained. Retail/Commercial businesses are either closing or moving away, leaving higher than usual vacancies. Property values tend to decline as compared to other similar neighbourhoods. This phase may be caused by the growth of other neighbourhoods.

RENEWAL PHASE

This is the period during which a neighbourhood is rebounding from a period of neglect or decline and finding itself popular and in demand again. New construction, property renovation and a renewed interest from retail/commercial enterprises is evident; e.g., high profile retailers are starting to move back into the area.

EXAMPLE   *Detecting The Life Cycle Stage*

Scenario 1

Carrot Town was built for and became popular with lower income families during the early 1890's. The housing stock was composed of attached and semi-detached Victorian homes. It flourished until after the Second World War, when many families moved out to the then newly developed suburbs offering detached bungalows with large lots. As a result, many homes in Carrot Town became tenant-occupied or were converted into rooming houses. Over the next few decades (50's, 60's, 70's), the homes displayed a lack of care and maintenance and required renovation. During this time, a high number of the retail stores and shops along the main street went out of business or became vacant. During the late 70's and early 80's, the attractive architectural nature of the Victorian homes, the mature treelined streets, the proximity to parks, the downtown core and jobs resulted in middle to high income families moving back into the area. Substantial improvement occurred with respect to many of the homes being attractively renovated/restored. New retail stores and businesses opened up to cater to these middle to upper income families. This improvement has accelerated and been sustained over the past 20 years.

Clearly the above indicates that Carrot Town has gone through all four stages of the neighbourhood life cycle; i.e., growth, stability, decline and finally renewal.

continued...

EXAMPLE   *Detecting The Life Cycle Stage (continued)*

Scenario 2

Neighbourhoods A and B were very similar areas developed 60 years ago with 1,500–2,500 square foot detached bungalows and two-storey homes. Five years ago, the prices in both neighbourhoods ranged from $150,000 to 200,000. Today, selling prices in Neighbourhood A are in the $175,000 to 225,000 range, while properties in Neighbourhood B now sell for between $225,000 and $275,000. Your investigation of this emerging value difference reveals that Neighbourhood A has been going through some decline, whereas Neighbourhood B has been enjoying a period of renewal.

CONFORMITY

It is always important to look at a neighbourhood in terms of whether it has a certain level of conformity with respect to the type, quality and size (and ultimately the value) of homes. The level of conformity (regression and progression) can certainly impact property values quite significantly in the immediate area. Very often, the larger the disparity between homes in a neighbourhood, the larger the value impact.

Just because one property is twice the size of another does not necessarily mean it is worth twice as much. It is common for owners of the largest or highest quality properties in a neighbourhood to point to the value of similar homes in a superior area and claim the value of their property to be the same. They are often unwilling to accept the fact that the inferior homes surrounding their house are having a locational impact.

EXAMPLE   *Impact of the Surrounding Properties on the Subject—Regression*

In Neighbourhood A, 1% of the homes are detached two-storey with sizes ranging from 2,400–2,800 square feet and the other 99% of properties are semi-detached ranging from 1,500–2,000 square feet. Your investigation reveals that the smaller semi-detached homes sell for between $185,000 and 200,000, while the larger detached properties sell from $280,000 to 290,000. The same larger detached homes in Neighbourhood B (where 80% of the homes are detached 2,400–2,800 square feet) sell for between $380,000 and 390,000.

From the information being provided, the value of the larger detached homes in Neighbourhood A are being pulled down by the value of the overwhelming number of much smaller semi-detached properties.

COLLECTING INFORMATION

In order to value a property, you have to understand the factors and forces that are at work within a neighbourhood and be able to assess and finally measure their impact on marketability and value. This obviously requires that you collect the information that you will need to use in your valuation.

There are many different ways and places from which information can be gathered. The following table list a few examples:

Stats Canada	Make-up and size of families; population and age make-up; income levels and types of jobs.
Municipal Offices	Property assessments; zoning and planned construction; housing starts; business employment opportunities; economic forecasts.
Real Estate Boards	Sales information; price levels; supply and demand.
Newspapers	The economy; local developments and trends, whether positive or negative in nature.
CMHC	The economy, mortgage rates, consumer expenditure (home improvements and renovations).

The above sources are excellent. However, a physical inspection of the neighbourhood which includes talking to local residents and salespeople/appraisers will provide you with a wealth of information, and confirm with your own eyes and ears information you have gathered from other sources. This information includes pride of ownership, the appeal of the housing stock and the streets, and the availability and proximity of facilities such as shopping, transportation, schools, parks, etc.

Of course, the Internet has over the past few years become an important source of information. Most governmental offices, newspapers and real estate boards have web sites from which you can gather the information from the comfort of your office/home. There are also commercial web sites which provide detailed, specific neighbourhood information on everything from theatres to community centres to job opportunities. Maps of locations are very often included.

Don't Just Collect Information—Analyze It FOCUS

It is not enough just to collect the data on the forces and factors at work within a neighbourhood. The information needs to be analyzed and interpreted as to its impact on the value for the subject. Whatever conclusion is arrived at must also be supported by direct evidence from the marketplace.

> **EXAMPLE**   *Analysis Backed by Data*
>
> An appraiser's research shows that interest rates have increased by 1½% over the past three months. Accordingly, this appraiser believes that she will find that properties have become more expensive to purchase, with the result that there has been less buying activity and a decrease in demand as compared to supply over the past three month period. The appraiser also thinks that she will find lower property prices, as compared to three months ago. The appraiser now researches the market place to see if her interpretation, analysis and conclusion in this case is correct. The direct evidence from the market shows that:
>
> • Over the past three months, the ratio of sales to listings has actually declined.
>
> • The sale prices of homes today are lower than the sale price of similar homes three months ago.
>
> Clearly the appraiser's analysis and conclusions are supported by the market and can be used in her valuation.

MEASURING IMPACT ON VALUE

As previously mentioned, it is important, when collecting information on a neighbourhood, that you also analyze and measure the impact on value for each factor and force. In order to measure the impact on value, you will need to look at either one or both of the following:

- The sales, listings and expired listings that have occurred in the subject neighbourhood over a given period of time during which the factors and forces under analysis were or were not present.

- The sales, listings and expired listings that have occurred over a given period of time in other similar neighbourhoods, which have or have not been subject to the same forces and factors as under analysis in the subject area.

It is the accumulation of all the factors and forces at work that will eventually set the prices being received by homes in the neighbourhood. Obviously, the prices and the price range of homes in the area will determine the value and price that the subject will eventually receive when sold.

> **EXAMPLE**   *Factors and Forces at Work in a Neighbourhood*
>
> Scenario 1
> Neighbourhood A is very similar to Neighbourhood B except that there is some heavy industrial development within ½ a mile of Neighbourhood A, whereas the closest industrial development to Neighbourhood B is about five miles away.
> New detached two-storey 2,000 square feet homes in Neighbourhood A sell for $210,000. The same new homes in Neighbourhood B sell for $230,000. With no other real differences between the neighbourhoods, it is clear that the proximity of industry to Neighbourhood A has had a significant measurable negative impact on value.
>
> Scenario 2
> Six months ago, the prices of homes in a small community north of Anycity ranged from $150,000 to 200,000. The subject property is typical for the area and is estimated to be worth $170,000. All of a sudden, two businesses in the community employing 50% of the workforce shut down. As a result, the homes in the area today sell for between $125,000 and 150,000.
> With no other significant changes having taken place over the past 6 months, it is clear that the business closures have had a significant negative impact on value. This impact has also left its mark on the subject property where the value has fallen in line with the new lower price range and is now estimated to be worth $135,000.

Alice Carpenter, an appraiser, and Janet Fields, a property owner, sit down together and talk about the information in the Neighbourhood sections of the *Standard Appraisal Report—Single Family* (OREA Form 700). Here are some of the questions and answers that come about in their conversation.

JANET   In the comments section on page 1 of the form, you have rated the neighbourhood in terms of its appeal as good to excellent. How do you go about determining the rating?

ALICE   I would look at and compare the subject neighbourhood's facilities with other similar areas that would appeal to the same type of buyer/home owner. Let me explain this with the following scenarios:

> *Scenario 1*
> People in Neighbourhood A have to travel two miles to the nearest shopping mall/plaza. Property owners in other, but similar areas, enjoy the presence of extensive shopping facilities immediately within their neighbourhoods. This would suggest to me that Neighbourhood A has a fair to poor rating when it comes to proximity to shopping.

> *Scenario 2*
> Neighbourhood A enjoys the presence of 6 schools catering to most of the children living within the neighbourhood. The majority of other similar neighbourhoods only have the use of two schools, resulting in many of the children having to travel out of the area for schooling. This would suggest a good to excellent rating in terms of schools for Neighbourhood A.

JANET   How can you tell if a neighbourhood is improving, stable or declining?

ALICE   I do this by observation and investigating the answers to the following questions:

- How well are the homes being maintained and what level of renovation or new construction is taking place?
- What are the income levels of people moving in and out of the area?
- Are prices staying stable, improving or declining in terms of comparison with other neighbourhoods?

Let's look at an example to see how this works in reality:

> **EXAMPLE**
> You are valuing a home in an area where a lot of renovation and new construction is starting to take place. You observe that many of the lower income families living as tenants are now moving out of the neighbourhood as the homes are being sold and are being replaced with higher income families moving in to occupy the homes they have just bought. In addition, homes are beginning to be sold faster and at a higher price than in what used to be comparable neighbourhoods. All of this should suggest to you that the neighbourhood is in an improving trend.

JANET   In your appraisal report, the value range of properties in the neighbourhood is $250,000 to 650,000. What is the importance of this information with respect to the subject?

ALICE   The subject's value is going to be determined by the prices being obtained by comparable properties being sold in the neighbourhood. Accordingly, it is important to know what those prices are. Let's look at an example to see how this works in practice.

continued...

PRINCIPLES OF APPRAISAL

Analyzing A Neighbourhood—The Issues   **PERSPECTIVE**

EXAMPLE

Properties in your neighbourhood are selling from $250,000 for the small frame bungalows to $650,000 for the large modern detached two-storey homes. Given that the subject is an older detached brick bungalow, its value will sit within the above range, although clearly closer to the lower end than to the upper end. This range serves as an important starting reference point for the appraiser/salesperson and can be used to deal with an owner who perhaps initially believes that his/her bungalow is worth $700,000.

JANET   On page 1 of the appraisal form, there is a comparison of the price range of properties on the subject street, as compared the price range of properties in the neighbourhood. Why is this?

ALICE   It will help in determining how the subject street is regarded within the neighbourhood. In other words is the subject street a good, average or poor location? This will help identify whether an adjustment will be required when using comparable sales from other streets in the area. Let's look at an example to explain this further.

EXAMPLE

The price range of properties in the neighbourhood goes from $450,000 to $750,000. On the subject street, the prices range from $650,000 to $750,000. On another street in the area, 123 Everly Gardens, the prices range from $500,000 to $600,000. Clearly, the subject street is a more prestigious street than Everly Gardens. It may be that there are bigger homes, newer homes or just a more attractive location given that it located close to a park. This is important to know when analyzing the need for adjustments to a comparable on Everly Gardens, as opposed to the subject street.

KNOWLEDGE INTEGRATION

Notables

- At any one time, there are physical, social, economic and political forces at work in a neighbourhood that can impact the value of properties within that neighbourhood.

- There are 4 distinct features of a trend. Trends must be considered in order to be able to accurately value a property.

- There are 4 possible stages that a neighbourhood can go through in terms of its life cycle. Each stage will have a different impact on value.

- The level of conformity of properties within a neighbourhood can have an impact on the value of the property being appraised.

- There are many sources from which an appraiser can collect necessary information on the neighbourhood.

- Information needs to be collected and analyzed, and then conclusions must be supported by market data.

- Sales and listings are the sources from which the dollar impact of neighbourhood factors can be measured.

Chapter Mini-Review

Solutions are located in the Appendix.

1. A typical example of a neighbour-hood boundary would be a ravine or a major highway.

   ○ True   ○ False

2. A neighbourhood with easy access to transportation will be negatively affected.

   ○ True   ○ False

3. The four distinct features of a trend are: growth, stability, decline and renewal.

   ○ True   ○ False

4. A trend in a neighbourhood can have an impact on the value of the subject property.

   ○ True   ○ False

5. A neighbourhood goes through 2 distinct phases of a life cycle.

   ○ True   ○ False

6. The subject's value is going to be determined by the prices being obtained by comparable properties in the neighbourhood.

   ○ True   ○ False

7. For a neighbourhood in decline you are more likely to see people of higher income levels moving into the area.

   ○ True   ○ False

8. The growth phase of a neighbour-hood occurs when a neighbourhood is first being developed.

   ○ True   ○ False

9. If the price range of properties on the subject street is at the high end of the price range for the neighbour-hood, then the subject street will be considered as having one of the infer-ior locations in the neighbourhood.

   ○ True   ○ False

10. The amount of time to sell a property in a neighbourhood that was in a renewal phase will likely be longer than if the neighbourhood were in decline.

    ○ True   ○ False

Active Learning Exercises

Solutions are located in the Appendix.

▣ Exercise 1

You are valuing a subject property that is much larger and of a higher quality than the majority of the other homes in the neighbourhood.

1.1   What would the likely impact be on the subject's value with respect to being surrounded by smaller homes of lower quality?

1.2   What principle is involved here?

1.3   How would you go about supporting your conclusion?

■ **Exercise 2**

In trying to establish what stage of the life cycle a neighbourhood is in, what information would you be looking for?

■ **Exercise 3   Multiple Choice**

3.1   Ignoring neighbourhood trends in an appraisal assignment could result in an appraiser:

    a.   overvaluing or undervaluing the final value of the subject property.

    b.   arriving at a more accurate final value for the subject property.

    c.   being able to more easily establish the life cycle stage that a neighbourhood is going through.

    d.   less easily able to identify the sources of the information that needs to be collected.

In the course of valuing a property, you collect the following information:

- Over the past five years, many of the homes in Neighbourhood A have started to appear run down and in many instances pride of ownership has disappeared.

- Five years ago, 90% of the homes were owner occupied and the average family income was $75,000. Today, about 50% of the homes are tenanted and the average family income in the area is down to $45,000.

- Five years ago, selling prices in Neighbourhood A ranged from $200,000 to 225,000. At the same time, prices in Neighbourhood B (a very similar area located two miles from Neighbourhood A) ranged from $195,000 to 230,000.

- Over the past five years, Neighbourhood B has enjoyed a period of stability, with very little change to its character and appearance. Selling prices today range from $250,000 to 295,000.

- Today, selling prices in Neighbourhood A range from $215,000 to 245,000.

- Within the province, property prices have generally risen 15–30% over the past five years due to economic improvement and inflation.

3.2 What stage of the life cycle has Neighbourhood A been going through during the past five year period?

   a. Stability

   b. Growth

   c. Decline

   d. Renewal

3.3 What market data given in the case study would confirm the stage of the life cycle that Neighbourhood A had been going through over the past 5 years?

   a. Prices in Neighbourhood A ranged from $200,000 to $225,000, while prices in Neighbourhood B ranged from $195,000 to $230,000 5 years ago.

   b. Prices in Neighbourhood A have risen by less than 10% over the past 5 years, while prices in Neighbourhood B have risen by between 25 and 30%.

   c. Prices in Neighbourhood A have risen by between 25 and 30% over the past 5 years while prices in Neighbourhood B have gone up by less than 10%.

   d. Within the province, property prices have generally risen 15–30% over the past five years due to economic improvement and inflation.

CASE STUDY FOR QUESTIONS 3.4 AND 3.5

In the course of valuing a property, you collect the following information:

- The subject property is a 1,000 square foot bungalow located in Neighbourhood A.
- 98% of the properties in Neighbourhood A are 2,000–2,500 square foot two-storey homes.
- These 2,000–2,500 square foot homes sell for between $190,000 and 210,000.
- The few 1,000 square foot houses that are available in Neighbourhood A, sell for approximately $160,000.
- Neighbourhood B is located next to Neighbourhood A. Neighbourhood B is predominantly made up of 1,000 square foot bungalows very similar to the subject property. These bungalows sell for approximately $130,000.
- The only difference between Neighbourhood A and B is related to the size of the majority of homes in each area.

3.4   What is the impact on the value of the subject property as a result of it being surrounded by much larger homes?

   a.   The subject's value has been positively impacted.

   b.   There has been no impact on the subject's value.

   c.   The subject's value has been negatively impacted.

   d.   The impact will have been both positive and negative.

3.5   What market data would confirm the impact on the value of the subject?

   a.   1,000 square foot bungalows in Neighbourhood A sell for $160,000, while they sell for $130,000 in Neighbourhood B.

   b.   The fact that Neighbourhood B is located next door to Neighbourhood A would confirm the impact.

   c.   The only difference between Neighbourhood A and B is related to the size of the majority of homes in each area.

   d.   2,000–2,500 square foot homes in Neighbourhood A sell for between $190,000 and 210,000.

CASE STUDY FOR QUESTIONS 3.6 AND 3.7

In the course of valuing a property, you collect the following information:

- Neighbourhood A is developed with older detached 2,000–2,500 square foot, two-storey homes ranging in value from $150,000 to $175,000.

- This neighbourhood benefits from the presence of two modern theatres and more than a dozen restaurants, and it appeals to middle income families.

- Neighbourhood B is a very similar neighbourhood, but is located three miles away. It is also developed with older detached 2,000–2,500 square foot, two-storey homes and again appeals to the middle income segment of the population.

- Neighbourhood B lacks the presence of theatres and only has a couple of restaurants along the main street. Prices here range from $140,000 to $165,000.

- There are no significant differences between the two neighbourhoods, other than the theatres and restaurants.

3.6 What impact does the presence of two theatres and over a dozen restaurants have on Neighbourhood A?

   a. It has a negative impact on value.

   b. It has no impact on value.

   c. It has a positive impact on value.

   d. It has both a positive and negative impact.

3.7 What market data would confirm the impact on value within Neighbourhood A?

   a. The fact that Neighbourhood A is located 3 miles away from Neighbourhood B.

   b. Neighbourhood A is developed with older detached 2,000 to 2,500 square foot homes.

   c. House prices in Neighbourhood A are up to $10,000 more than in Neighbourhood B.

   d. Both neighbourhoods appeal to the middle income segment of the population.

3.8 A residential neighbourhood could be negatively affected by:

   a. declining family income levels.

   b. increasing job opportunities.

   c. low interest rates.

   d. a wide range of amenities.

3.9 A residential neighbourhood could be positively affected by:

   a. a lack of schools in the area.

   b. a growth in population.

   c. a high crime rate.

   d. a lack of tree-lined streets.

3.10 Describe what you would expect to see in a neighbourhood that is in a declining phase.

   a. The neighbourhood would be increasing in popularity.
   b. Lots of new construction in the neighbourhood.
   c. Property prices would be rising faster than before.
   d. Properties becoming less well maintained than before.

3.11 2% of the homes in the neighbourhood are 70-year-old, 1,200 square foot bungalows sitting on 30 by 140 foot lots. 98% of the homes in the area are more expensive 70-year-old, detached 2-storey 2,500 square foot homes sitting on 50 by 150 foot lots. What impact would this scenario have on the bungalows?

   a. It would tend to drive down the prices of the bungalows.
   b. It would make the bungalows appear less appealing.
   c. It would make the bungalows the same value as the detached two-storey homes.
   d. It would tend to drive up the prices of the bungalows.

CHAPTER 4

Site Analysis

Introduction

There are three basic components to a property:

- *The Site*   A site is a piece of land that is ready to be built on; i.e., it is land that is zoned, graded, drained, has road access and any necessary services. Site and lot are words that are often used as interchangeable.
- *Improvements to the Site*   Generally, this is considered as landscaping, but for the purposes of this course, we shall include items such as fences, detached garages and sheds as part of improvements to the site.
- *Improvements on the Site*   Generally refers to the house that sits on the lot. It will become apparent during the Cost Approach to Value why a property is divided into three separate sections. For this chapter, we shall be looking at the information you need to collect on the site and all the other improvements, except the main house, which will be analyzed in the next chapter.

In this chapter, we concentrate on the site and those improvements to the site. The physical inspection of the site requires the appraiser to be looking for anything that has a positive or negative impact on value. Anything different about the site that is not standard for the area, should be followed up on to see if it is having either a positive or negative impact; e.g., the site is pie-shaped, whereas most of the sites in the area are rectangular. The appraiser may believe from experience that something about the site will detract from its value, however he/she will need to look at data from the market place to either prove or disprove those beliefs. The market data usually involves looking at and comparing sales and listings.

The information collected on the site needs to be sufficient to be able to complete the appraisal of the property either through the Cost Approach or the Direct Comparison Approach.

Learning Outcomes

At the conclusion of this chapter, students will be able to:

- Outline the technical difference between land and site.
- Describe the physical, economic, environmental, legal and location factors that affect the value of a site.
- Explain assemblage, plottage and excess land.
- Describe the impact that easements and encroachments have on value and explain how to estimate the dollar impact.
- Describe the various environmental issues that an appraiser should be aware of.
- Describe the impact of a stigma on value.
- Describe the various sources and means of collecting the necessary information.
- Explain the difference between the physical and functional condition of the site.
- Identify when to call in outside experts.

LAND VERSUS SITE

There are technical appraisal differences between the words *land* and *site*.

Land includes the surface of the earth, supra-surface air space and sub-surface area and is typically referred to as raw acreage, raw land or unimproved land because it is unused or in a natural state.

A site, on the other hand, is a parcel of land that has been subdivided and serviced to some degree so that it can be used for some purpose, usually as a building site. Generally, the land will have been cleared, graded for drainage and provided with access to a street or road, together with storm and sanitary sewers, gas, water, electricity, and telephone service. Usually, arrangements have been made to ensure that the intended use is legally permitted.

Having said that, there is a technical difference between the words land and site. You will find that this course uses the word *land* to mean the same thing as *site*—in other words they are used interchangeably. As a result, vacant land and vacant site will both refer to land that is ready to be built upon, but that has no man-made improvements on it; e.g., landscaping, house, etc.

Factors Affecting the Value of the Site

In order to be able to value a property, it is important to understand what kind of factors could impact the value of that site. These factors can be summarized under the following four headings:

• Locational Factors	• Physical Factors
• Legal-Governmental Factors	• Economic Factors

LOCATIONAL FACTORS

The location of a particular site must be viewed in terms of its relationship to surrounding facilities and conditions impacting the value of that property. The assessment of locational factors forms part of the overall process of site analysis when appraising property.

Examples of common locational factors include such things as patterns of land use surrounding the subject site; availability of utilities; access from the site to transportation, stores and recreational amenities; hazards and nuisances close to or adjacent to the site, and traffic flows on the subject street.

EXAMPLE   *Locational Factors*

Seller Smith is having his residential property appraised for mortgage purposes. The appraiser is particularly interested in locational factors affecting value. Smith inquires about just what types of locational factors might impact his property. The appraiser provides the following explanation:

> *Location is always expressed in terms of the relationship of the site to surrounding and nearby facilities and nuisances. In looking at your property, I will probably consider the following four major factors.*
>
> ***1. Land Use Pattern in the Area***
>
> *The location of various types of land uses within a city or neighbourhood is not determined at random. Uses come about in response to market demand and are effectively controlled by zoning by-laws. Your home is not adversely affected as most properties in the area are similar in size, structure and overall condition.*
>
> ***2. Access***
>
> *Proximity to desired facilities such as schools, shopping centres, workplaces, recreational centres and other civic facilities is a plus factor. While your home is located somewhat distant from the main shopping areas, a small shopping complex is only two blocks away. Public transportation facilities are just down the street, as is a small park. Overall, these locational factors are a positive force in establishing your value.*
>
> ***3. Corner Influence***
>
> *The effect of a corner location on value depends on the type of land use. Commercial corners provide the site with additional access and exposure for advertising purposes. Corners for single-family residential properties may have an adverse effect on value. Residential corners often lack private rear yards, an amenity usually sought by the buyer. Corner properties may also cause the owner additional maintenance; e.g., snow removal and side yard upkeep. The fact that your home is located on a corner will have a negative impact on the value.*
>
> ***4. Hazards and Nuisances***
>
> *The existence of nearby hazards and nuisances such as non-conforming land uses, noise, odour and traffic have a detrimental effect. There are no such deficiencies impacting your property or its value.*

PHYSICAL FACTORS

Physical factors are the portion of a site analysis within the appraisal process where the appraiser evaluates the site in terms of such things as overall dimensions, soils, topography, actual site services and utilities, landscaping, plottage, excess land and assembly. For the purposes of this chapter, we will include an analysis of improvements to the site such as landscaping, wells, septic systems, swimming pools, etc. Improvements on the site (buildings) will be dealt with in the next chapter.

Site Dimensions

The frontage, depth and width of a parcel of land. Site dimensions and resulting shape and area create the ultimate desirability, utility and value of any site. Frontage is that side of a site that abuts a public street or highway. Depth is the distance(s) between the front and rear lot lines. Width is the distance between the side lines of a lot. The shape of a site is determined by its frontage, depth and width. Area is the size of the site measured in square metres, square feet, hectares, acres, etc. One of the questions that needs to be asked by the appraiser is *Are the site dimensions standard for the area? If they are not, what impact will this have on the subject's value?*.

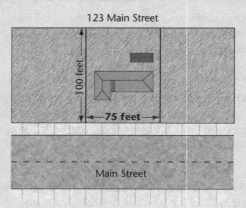

EXAMPLE   *Frontage*

Salesperson Lane, of ABC Realty Inc. has just listed a property at 123 Main Street, Anycity, with a frontage of 75 feet (22.86 metres) on Main Street and a depth of 100 feet (30.48 metres).

Assemblage

Assemblage is the combining of two or more abutting parcels of land into one ownership or use for the purpose of greater utility. The assembly of land is most commonly associated with suburban developments in which large tracts of land are acquired and merged for residential sub-divisions. However, assemblage is an ongoing process in a variety of locations as existing residential neighbourhoods are redeveloped. Smaller parcels of land are combined to form the basis for new commercial ventures, and downtown core areas undergo transformations from small buildings to larger structures requiring greater land areas.

Practitioners occasionally confuse assemblage with plottage value. Plottage value refers to an incremental value owing to the merging process. Assemblage is merely the process of combining properties and could result in either an increase in value (plottage value), or a decrease in unit value owing to the creation of excess land. Presumably, most assembly activities proceed on the basis that plottage value will occur.

EXAMPLE   *Assemblage*

Seller Smith wishes to acquire the extra lot abutting his residential site for the purpose of building a larger, irregular shaped swimming pool at the same time his new home is being constructed. The increased pool size will not add substantial value. In fact, the merged property will create excess land, with no economic benefit as a whole. This form of assemblage is referred to as *excess land*. If the owner had acquired the adjacent property to build a larger home, the value of the entire lot and house, as a total entity, might well increase and the assemblage can be referred to as *plottage*.

Plottage

Plottage refers to a value increment resulting from the assembly of two or more sites, when the combined utility is proportionately greater than the sum of the individual utilities.

> **EXAMPLE**   *Plottage*
>
> Seller Smith currently has a vacant residential lot measuring 50' x 160' in an area zoned for single and multiple family residential. As a lot for a single-detached home, the property is estimated to be worth about $90,000. Under current zoning by-laws, multiple units are not considered by the municipal council, unless the total ground area exceeds 10,000 square feet. Recently, an adjacent vacant piece of property came on the market at $95,000. This property is also limited under the current by-law to single-family usage, owing to its 51' x 160' size. Smith is considering the purchase of the adjacent lot, as that acquisition could potentially increase the value of the combined properties well beyond the sum of the two values ($90,000 + $95,000), if rezoning is granted and a building permit issued for a multi-unit structure.

Excess Land

A site that is larger than standard, where the additional size does not provide proportional utility or proportional increase in value.

> **EXAMPLE**   *Excess Land*
>
> As a basic illustration of the concept, consider two lots zoned for single-detached homes both with 40' frontages. Lot A, which is 120' deep, is usual to the area and lot B is 145' deep. The two properties sell for $45,000 and $47,800 respectively, as the additional depth does not proportionately add to value and is therefore viewed as excess land from a valuation point of view. To more accurately quantify the excess nature of this land, consider the square footage of both lots in relation to their value. Lot A has a total of 4,800 square feet, while Lot B is approximately 21% larger with a square footage of 5,800. However, the price for Lot B is approximately 6% higher.

LEGAL-GOVERNMENTAL FACTORS

These factors could include easements, encroachments, zoning and private deed restrictions.

Private Restrictions

Private restrictions generally contained in a deed have varying effects on value. Developers often include deed restrictions or restrictive covenants for the protection and interest of other owners. For example, developers may include restrictions on such things as colour of siding, types of fencing and minimum size of dwelling. This may have a positive impact on value since it provides for a certain level of conformity.

On the other hand, a deed may have a private restriction in it that prevents a property from being developed to its highest and best use. This could have a negative impact on the value of the site given that the site cannot achieve its highest and best use.

Easements

The impact on value of an easement (right-of-way) depends on the nature, scope and extent of the easement. In other words, how much enjoyment or use does the easement add or take away from the ownership of the property. In many cases, an easement will have a positive impact on one property (the dominant tenement), but a negative impact on the other property (the servient tenement). In other cases, the easement may be so minor that it will have no impact on any of the properties involved.

EXAMPLE   *Finding the Dollar Value of an Easement*

Scenario 1

You are valuing a detached two-storey home on a property that has a utility easement that allows hydro, cable and the telephone company to enter the property to make repairs and maintain the lines located at the back of the property. This is a very common easement in the subject neighbourhood. The easement extends across the rear of the backyard and is 10' wide. The lot is 150' long and grass covers the easement (this would be typical landscaping for the area). The easement was last used four years ago by the hydro company for maintenance purposes and they were on the property for about an hour.

Your investigation reveals that detached two-storey properties with a similar utility easement in the subject neighbourhood sell within 90 days for $150,000–$155,000. Identical or very comparable detached two-storey properties without the easement in the same neighbourhood also sell within 90 days for $150,000–155,000.

Based on the above information, it is clear that the subject property's utility easement is very minor in nature and is unlikely to have any significant impact on marketing or value. There has been very little disturbance to the owner's quiet enjoyment of the property (1 hour, 4 years ago) and the easement has not prevented the owner from developing the site to suit her purposes; i.e., the easement is covered with grass which would be standard in the neighbourhood for this part of the lot.

Scenario 2

You are valuing a property (the subject) with lot dimensions of 40' x 100'. It is subject to an easement 12' wide that runs down the whole length of the east side of the lot and then across the rear of the site. The easement is used by the owner of the neighbouring property and allows her to drive a car across the subject property in order to park at the rear of her own property. Without this easement, the neighbouring property would have no access to on-site parking.

Your investigation into the neighbourhood turns up the sale five months ago of a detached bungalow known as Property C. This property had an easement similar to the subject running across it. Property C's lot is 42' x 107' and sold for $160,000. You note that other detached bungalows in the neighbourhood that were very similar to Property C, but without the easement, were selling for $170,000–$175,000 five months ago.

With no other significant differences between Property C and the other detached bungalow sales other than the easement, it is clear that this type of easement on a relatively small lot, will have a significant negative impact on the value and marketing of the subject. This negative impact indicated by the market appears to be logical. A large part of the subject property is being used and enjoyed by someone else. The owner is being restricted from using that part of the lot covered by the easement for his/her own enjoyment; e.g., he/she would not be able to put a fence, swimming pool or deck on the easement. The owners of the subject property would also suffer from a lack of privacy.

Scenario 3

Properties A and B are located next door to each other in the heart of cottage country. Property A has a 10-foot easement (right-of-way) over Property B. This allows the owner of Property A to walk across the lot of Property B in order to gain access to the beach along the shore of Lake Victoria. Without this easement, Property A would have no access to the beach, lake and swimming.

Your investigation reveals the sale nine months ago of Property C, a 1,500 square foot cottage with an identical right-of-way over Property B allowing it to have the same beach access as Property A. Property C sold for $270,000. You are also able to find two 1,500 square foot cottages (properties D and E), similar to Property C and located close by, but which did not enjoy access to the beach because they lacked the use of a right-of-way (easement). Properties D and E sold nine months ago for $245,000 and $250,000 respectively. There are no real differences between properties C, D and E, other than the right-of-way.

continued...

PRINCIPLES OF APPRAISAL

Encroachments

The salesperson/appraiser should watch for encroachments, given that the value of a property can be affected by the presence of one. The value impact will of course depend on the nature and extent of the encroachment, and whether it will be allowed to remain or will likely be required to be removed.

An up-to-date survey will likely reveal the presence of an encroachment whether on the subject property or by the subject property onto a neighbouring site. In a number of cases you will probably need to consult a lawyer in order to ascertain the legal issues surrounding the encroachment (i.e., what is the likelihood that it can remain or will need to be removed—will an encroachment agreement or title insurance solve the problem?). In addition, you may need to talk to a contractor in order to estimate the costs of removal or remedy. In order to assess the impact on value and marketing, you will need to look at the sale prices of similar properties that sold with and without the type of encroachment you are faced with.

EXAMPLE   *Finding the Dollar Value of Encroachments*

You are valuing the subject property (Property A) which has a 12' x 20' detached garage. Almost one third of the garage is, however, sitting on the neighbour's property that has the lot dimensions of 30' x 105'. There is an encroachment agreement, but it allows for the neighbour to retain the right to ask that the garage be removed at any time. While the current owner is not likely to ask to have it removed, there is no way of knowing what a buyer of that neighbouring property would do. It would cost a few thousand dollars to have the garage moved fully onto the subject lot.

Your investigation reveals the recent sale in the subject neighbourhood of Property C that also had a similar encroachment of the garage on a neighbouring property with a relatively small lot of 32' x 108'. Property C sold for $170,000 after 200 days. You discover that other properties in the neighbourhood identical to Property C, but without the encroachment,, were selling at the same time for between $175,000 and $176,000 in less than 100 days.

Given the relatively small size of the lot being encroached upon, there appears to be a risk here to any potential purchaser of the subject property; i.e., the current or future owner of the neighbouring property may ask for the garage to be removed. If the garage does have to be removed, then there will be a cost in terms of money, time and aggravation. Clearly, the market recognizes this risk and accordingly the encroachment is likely to have a negative impact on value in the order of $5,000 to $6,000 and on marketing in terms of the number of days to sell.

ECONOMIC FACTORS

Most economic factors operate at the neighbourhood level. Nevertheless, there are certain elements definitely related to site analysis which may be measured in dollars.

Examples of economic factors could include prices of comparable sites, tax burden, utility costs and service costs.

Tax Burden

The level of assessments, taxes and special assessments for utilities or streets is an important ingredient in the cost of owning the site or property. An important consideration is the comparative treatment of the subject site in relation to other comparable sites in the same area. The method of payment of taxes and special assessments can also constitute a burden on the landowner and should be investigated.

Sale of Comparable Sites

The selling prices of comparable sites will tend to set the range within which the value of the subject site is most likely to be found.

ENVIRONMENTAL ISSUES

There are a number of environmental issues that could be faced when inspecting the subject site. These are related to the contamination of the soil and ground water from such materials as lead, PCBs and gasoline, etc. This could have occurred as a result of the presence of industry, underground storage tanks, dumping of hazardous waste or spills. While you are not being asked to be an expert in environmental issues, a clear understanding of the history of the property and how it has been used over the years is necessary. This information can come from the owner's documents, registry office or city and provincial records. In addition, do a vigilant physical inspection of the site; e.g., site backs onto a paint factory or you notice the tip of a pipe jutting out of the ground. Soil contamination requires you to find out the nature, cause, extent of the contamination (if any), and obtain a recommendation as to the necessary remedial action together with the costs. This will likely require hiring an expert to perform an environmental audit.

Environmental Audits		MARKET MEMO

Environmental audits are broadly grouped under three levels of analysis, referred to as phases. A brief overview of each is provided:

PHASE 1
Visual inspection combined with a review of owner documents, registry information, ministry/ department records and certificates, and other relevant environmental records. A Phase 1 audit determines if reasons exist to believe that a property may have some form of environmental contamination.

PHASE 2
More costly investigation involving various tests, hazardous waste assessment/analysis and soil/ water sampling. A Phase 2 audit determines the scope of environmental problems, along with recommendations for remedial action.

PHASE 3
The final phase involves detailed remedial steps and costs associated with circumstances identified in Phase 2.

In order to measure the impact of environmental problems, assess the sales or listings of properties with these concerns and compare their prices to similar properties without the environmental problems. It is preferable to compare recent sales within the subject neighbourhood, but if there are none, it is quite acceptable to look in other neighbourhoods that would appeal to the same kind of buyer.

| Stigma | MARKET MEMO |

It is important to note that even if the contamination of a site is thoroughly cleaned up, a stigma may still be attached to the property resulting in the continuation to some degree of a negative impact on marketing and value. This stigma may persist as future liability or health risks and hidden clean-up costs may still exist.

> **EXAMPLE**   *Finding the Dollar Value of Stigma*
>
> A property sold 6 months ago for $350,000. Three months ago you were asked to value the property for refinancing purposes. The property is a residential site containing a 3,000 square foot home built 20 years ago. Your investigation of the history of the site shows that a paint factory existed on the site 45 years ago. You share this information with the owner and the bank. An environmental audit is done by an expert resulting in the need for an extensive clean-up of the site at a cost of $100,000. The owner decides to sell the property in *As Is* condition and leave the clean-up to a prospective purchaser. The property finally sold a few weeks ago for $175,000. There has been no change in market conditions or prices over the past six months. Based on the calculation below, there appears to be a stigma of $75,000 attached to the property's contamination. It is quite probable that this stigma will continue into the near future even after a complete clean-up has occurred.

Value Before Contamination Was Known	$350,000
Value After Contamination Discovered	−175,000
Loss In Value	**$175,000**
Less: Cost of Clean-Up	−100,000
Cost of Stigma	**$75,000**

COLLECTING INFORMATION

In order to estimate a value on the subject property, you will need to collect as much relevant information as you can on the site. It is important to stress that collecting information, while very important in itself, is only one part of the process of being able to estimate value. You also need to analyze the information, come to a conclusion as to its impact and then support that conclusion by obtaining evidence from the marketplace; i.e., sales, listings and expired listings. The needed information is collected in two ways:

- *from written and verbal sources; and*
- *through observation from a physical inspection.*

Written and Verbal Sources

There are, in most cases, people who have either inspected the property before you or have lived in or known the property for years. These people can be invaluable resources and include the owner.

Have the owner complete a *Seller Property Information Statement*. The owner is required to answer such questions as:

- Is the lot subject to flooding?
- Are you aware of any problems re: quantity and quality of water?
- Are you aware of any problems with the septic system?

The answers to these questions are important. If there are problems with the quality and quantity of water being produced by a well, then there is going to be a negative impact on value as compared to a property that has a well which is producing potable water with an adequate flow rate. A property with a drainage or inadequate septic system is clearly not going to be as valuable as one where the system is adequate for the needs of the house and is working properly. The point here is that because a physical inspection, no matter how careful, may not reveal these problems, it is important to have the owner complete the Seller Property Information Statement and sign it.

SPIS Is Only a Starting Point   FOCUS

It is important that you do not feel restricted or constrained by the content or format of a Seller Property Information Statement (SPIS) that is not able to cover every conceivable situation, fact or circumstance. However, as you go through the inspection of a site, keep asking questions such as: are there any problems here? How old is the component or item (e.g., deck or fence)? When was work or repairs done? What type of repairs were carried out? If the answers on the statement or from the owner conflict with what you are seeing, it is important that you investigate until you are satisfied.

Previous Inspection Reports
This is a report that can help identify problem areas or components for you. Accordingly, it is a good idea to read any completed inspection reports on the site prior to your physical inspection. As you go through the site, check those items outlined as problems or concerns in the inspection report to see if they have been corrected. Again, be prepared to discuss any problems and repairs with the owner or even ask if you can talk to the author of the report if the owner is uncertain of something.

Previous Listings
Very often a previous listing will mention the special features of a site such as landscaping or location backing to a park. Conversely, the listing may describe a problem such as the presence of an easement. As you carry out your physical inspection, it will be important to check what you see against what is written in the listing. If in doubt, discuss the issues with the owner and only move on when you are satisfied with what you are seeing or hearing.

Neighbours
Neighbours can very often be a great source of information. They may be able to tell you about something that happened to the subject site that either the owner forgot to mention, was not aware of or occurred when a previous owner lived there; e.g., every spring with the melting of snow and the water runoff from other properties, the subject site is prone to flooding—this is related to the topography of the site and the drainage qualities of the soil. Again, it is important that you check what you hear from the neighbour with what you see during your physical inspection. Do not be put off from discussing your observations or concerns with the owner—they may be able to resolve your questions easily and quickly.

Other Sources
Surveys; e.g., encroachments, shape and dimensions of the site. Title deeds; e.g., easements and dimensions of the site. Invoices and bills; e.g., repairs, installations and site upgrades.

Physical Inspection

This is a very important part of the valuation process. The inspection needs to be done in a methodical manner, and should not be rushed. During the inspection, you should look at each part and component of the site in terms of both its physical and functional contribution to the property.

When you look at an item or component physically, you are comparing the condition of the item as you see it on the date of inspection as compared to the condition of that item when it was brand new. Man-made components of the site such as decks, walkways, fences and pools will of course start to physically deteriorate from the time they are constructed. On the other hand natural components of the site such as sod, grass, trees, flowers may often improve over a period of time.

When you look at an item or component of a site functionally, you are comparing the performance, quality, appeal and or style of the component to the components that you would commonly expect to see in sites such as the subject as at the date of appraisal. It is very important to understand the difference between inspecting a site to gauge the physical condition, as opposed to functional condition.

EXAMPLE   *The Difference Between Physical and Functional Value*

A brand new swimming pool was installed 3 weeks ago. Swimming pools are not popular in the area and very few properties have a pool. Physically, the pool is in great condition (brand new)—however, functionally, it can be considered poor, given that it doesn't offer much appeal and is unpopular. As a result, the pool could have cost $40,000, but may add nothing to the value of the property or could even have a negative impact.

A new septic system was installed a month ago. Unfortunately, the holding tank was not large enough to handle the number of occupants and bathroom fixtures on the property. The physical condition of the septic system might be great, but it does not provide the necessary performance. Accordingly, it can be considered as functionally poor.

Artificial grass was installed in the front and back yard 3 months ago. Most homes in the area have natural grass and artificial grass is not appealing or popular. Clearly, the physical condition is good, however, functionally it can be considered poor given its lack of appeal.

A property has a large 10-year-old wood deck at the back of the house. Decks are very popular in the area. The deck is, however, sagging and large chunks of wood are missing or splintered. While the deck is clearly functionally popular and appealing, this is offset by its poor condition. As a result, the deck may add no value to the property or may even have a negative impact.

Something is Wrong—Don't Guess   CAUTION

If, during the physical inspection, you notice a problem or suspect something is wrong, it is important that you are able to identify the cause and extent of the problem, as well as the impact on value that the problem is going to have whether it is corrected or left as is. Of course you, as a salesperson, are not a trained engineer or inspector and it is crucial that you do not guess the cause, nature and extent of a suspected problem. In most instances where you suspect something is wrong, you should recommend the owner call in an expert. You will want a report on what the problem is, what is causing it, what damage or further damage it can do, the solution to the problem, and the cost of the solution so that you can identify and measure the possible impact on value.

Suppose, as an example, you are inspecting a property where the water supply comes from a drilled well, which is located on-site. You suspect that the water is contaminated or of poor quality (your suspicions could come as a result of odours, discolourization of water, strange taste of water, repeated sickness within the family, build-up of mineral scales or proximity to industry or an old landfill site).

There are many types of chemical or bacterial contaminants that could be present in the well that could result in the suspected contamination or poor quality water, all with very different consequences and costs. The answer for you is simple—do not guess. Guessing could result in legal and financial problems for you. Instead, get an expert to carry out an investigation for you and the owner. The solution to the suspected problem could be as inexpensive and simple as disinfection by chlorinating (shocking the well) or the installation of a water softener. On the other hand, the solution could be as expensive as installing a sophisticated water treatment system or even having to drill a new well.

How do you ensure that you have the necessary information required to accurately estimate the value of a property? The only way of ensuring you have the necessary information is by asking the right questions. What are the right questions? Let's take a look at some examples below:

Situation—The subject property is located within a flood plain zone.

Questions to ask:

- What is the likelihood of flooding over the next 25 years?
- What restrictions are placed on developing or redeveloping the site or adding to the existing buildings?
- What has been done on the subject property to protect the home from being flooded?
- What kind of insurance coverage has the owner been able to get on the property?
- Has the subject sold before and how does its selling price and marketing time compare to similar properties that sold at the same time and were not in the flood plain zone?
- Is there a difference in selling price and marketing time between other homes that sold in the flood plain zone and similar/identical homes that sold outside of the zone?

Situation—In terms of site dimensions, the subject property has a 40-foot frontage, 140-foot depth and 10-foot rear width. In other words, the subject has a reverse pie-shaped lot.

Questions to ask:

- Is this shape common for the area?
- Does this pie shape limit the owner's enjoyment of the property as compared to other more typical sites?
- Does the shape prevent the owner from developing or redeveloping the site in a way that would be typical or expected for the area; e.g., additions, landscaping, swimming pool?
- Is there a difference in selling price and marketing time between homes that have sold with this pie shape and similar/identical homes that sold with the more typical rectangular lot shapes?

Situation—The subject property's water is supplied by a well.

Questions to ask:

- What is the flow rate of the well and is it adequate for the property?
- What is the cost of maintenance?
- Is the well water clear of contamination and when was the last water testing done?
- Are wells the typical water supply source for properties in the neighbourhood?
- Assuming the well water is uncontaminated and provides adequate flow rate, is there a difference in selling price and marketing time between properties that use a well and similar properties in the area that are on municipal water?

Situation—The subject property has a 7-foot wide mutual drive for parking on-site.

Questions to ask:

- Is this common for the neighbourhood and is the driveway wide enough for a modern car?
- Given the width of the mutual drive, is there any use or value to this type of driveway and parking?
- Is there a possibility of front yard/pad parking?
- What would the cost be of applying and putting in front yard parking?
- What do properties with this type and width of driveway sell for as compared to properties with a wide mutual driveway, no driveway or wide private driveway? Is there a difference in marketing time required?

Discussing Site Factors That May Impact Value   PERSPECTIVE

JANET Although my property is not affected by any encroachments, I was just wondering whether encroachments always have a significant negative impact on value.

ALICE No, not always. The impact on value will depend on the nature and extent of the encroachment as well as the likelihood that a cost is going to be incurred. The following is an encroachment example where there Is no real impact on marketing or value.

> **EXAMPLE**
>
> You are valuing a property where four of the steps to the front door of the house encroach on city property that has been reserved for possible road widening in the future. This part of the city property is currently part of the front yard of the subject and is landscaped with grass and flower beds. There is an encroachment agreement with respect to the steps, but it allows for the city to retain the right to request that the steps be removed should there be need for road widening. It would appear to be a very remote probability that the city in fact would start road widening within the foreseeable future. In addition, this type of easement seems to be very common for the area.
>
> Your investigation into the neighbourhood reveals that currently detached 1,200 square foot bungalows with step encroachments onto city property are selling for between $160,000 and 165,000 within 90 days. Identical detached 1,200 square foot bungalows without the encroachment are also selling for between $160,000 and 165,000 within 90 days. The subject property's encroachment is common and unlikely to involve the owner or potential purchaser in any costs within the foreseeable future. In other words, there is a very low risk factor here. The market appears to confirm this by indicating that there is no perceptible negative impact on value or marketing time.

JANET In the Comments Section of the Appraisal Form you note that my site is standard for the area. What are you looking for when considering whether the site is standard or non-conforming?

ALICE My investigation and research to uncover information is always done with a view to assessing the impact of the facts on marketing and value. In terms of a site being standard or non-conforming, I am looking at its size, dimensions, shape, topography, soil and drainage, and comparing it to what I will find in the majority of other sites in the neighbourhood. If the subject site is similar to most of the other sites in the area, then a valuation of the subject is probably going to be a relatively simple exercise, given an active market. On the contrary, if the subject site is non-conforming (i.e., different to the majority of sites), then a much more complex investigation will be needed to see why and how the difference impacts on value and marketing, as compared to the standard sites. The following example may help explain this further:

> **EXAMPLE**
>
> You have been asked to value a detached two-storey property (Property A) with an extremely steep sloping site. The site slopes downward from the back of the lot to the street. In order to get to the front door, you have to climb 20 steps from the side walk at the front of the property. The landscaping of the backyard has been kept fairly basic and there is no swimming pool because of the extra costs involved as a result of the steepness of the site. Property A is currently listed for sale and has been on the market for 190 days. In a discussion with the listing agent, you discover that prospective purchasers have made the following comments: too many stairs to climb especially in the winter; I would like to put in a swimming pool and further landscape the backyard, but it will be costly; I am concerned about flooding of the basement in the spring. The majority of properties in the area have standard sites which slope very gently back up from the sidewalk and as a result many of them enjoy a much higher level of landscaping, including the use of an in-ground pool.
>
> *continued...*

EXAMPLE *(continued)*

Your investigation into the neighbourhood reveals the sale of a detached two-storey home, Property B. This property has a very steep sloping site similar to Property A, lacks the use of a swimming pool and only has some very basic landscaping. Property B sold two months ago for $225,000 after being on the market for over 140 days. During your investigation into the neighbourhood, you also find two sales of Property C and D, which are identical to Property B except for the use of a very gently sloping site. These two properties sold for $232,000 and $233,000 respectively two months ago after less than 90 days on the market. Clearly, there are problems associated with the steepness of Property A's site and these have been outlined by prospective purchasers. It would appear that these problems will result in a negative impact on value and marketing. This conclusion is well supported by Property A's own extended marketing time and by the sale of Property B, after more than 140 days marketing period for $7,000 to $8,000 less than the highly comparable Properties C and D, which needed less than 90 days marketing.

JANET   I have a private drive. Is that considered better than a mutual drive?

ALICE   All things being equal, a private drive is generally considered better than a mutual drive. The expectation, perception and reality is that having the exclusive use of something is better than having to share. Sharing can often lead to disputes and arguments. However, the level of impact on value and marketing of either a private drive or mutual drive will depend on a number of factors including the width of the drive, accessibility to the drive, the condition of the drive, etc. The following two scenarios may help explain this further:

SCENARIO 1

You are valuing the subject property (Property A) which shares the use of a 12' wide mutual drive with Property B. The owner of Property B often leaves his car in the mutual driveway and has refused to resurface his portion of the driveway. Your investigation into the neighbourhood reveals the sale four months ago of Properties C and D for $180,000 and $185,000 respectively. These two properties are identical to each other in all respects except that Property C has a 13' wide mutual driveway and Property D has a 13' wide private driveway. Clearly, having a mutual driveway has not been a great experience for the owner of Property A and this kind of experience is not uncommon. Accordingly, it can generally be expected that this less attractive type of driveway is going to have a negative impact when compared to a private driveway. This conclusion is supported by the fact that Property C sold for $5,000 less than identical Property D as a result of the use of a mutual as opposed to private driveway.

SCENARIO 2

Property A is a detached two-storey property with an 8' wide private drive that is cracked and uneven. It is so narrow that only a small car can use the drive and even then the owner has to be careful not to scrape the side of the car. This property sold six months ago for $158,000. Property B is located in the same neighbourhood and is almost identical to Property A, except it shares a 15' wide mutual drive with a neighbouring home. This mutual driveway has recently been resurfaced and is in excellent condition. Property B also sold about six months ago for $158,000. While a private drive is more desirable than a mutual drive, the inferior size and condition of Property A's private drive appears to be offset by the size and condition of Property B's mutual drive. The selling price of both properties seems to confirm this conclusion.

KNOWLEDGE INTEGRATION

Notables

- At any one time, there are physical, locational, economic and legal-governmental forces at work that can impact the value of a site.

- Covenants, easements and encroachments must be investigated to determine whether they are having an impact on the value of a property. That impact may be negative, positive or neutral.

- There are many sources from which an appraiser can collect necessary information on a site.

- Information needs to be collected and analyzed and then conclusions must be supported by market data.

- Sales and listings are the sources from which the dollar impact of site factors can be measured.

- An inspection of a site and the improvements to the site must be looked at from both a physical and functional point of view.

- If the appraiser has concerns about the integrity of a site, he/she needs to recommend that experts be hired to carry out necessary inspections.

Chapter Mini-Review

Solutions are located in the Appendix.

1. Plottage occurs when assembled land creates a property with a highest and best use that is better than the highest and best use of the individual sites.

    ⚪ True   ⚪ False

2. An easement can have either a positive or negative impact on the value of a property.

    ⚪ True   ⚪ False

3. If properties with and without a particular easement sell for roughly the same price, it is an indication that the easement is having a negative impact on value.

    ⚪ True   ⚪ False

4. In order to measure the impact of an environmental problem on a site, compare the selling prices of properties with the same environmental problem to the selling prices of properties without the environmental problem.

    ⚪ True   ⚪ False

5. There are only two types of factors that can have an impact on the value of a site; i.e., economic and locational.

    ⚪ True   ⚪ False

6. Once the soil contamination present in a site has been cleaned up, the stigma associated with the contamination will disappear.

    ⚪ True   ⚪ False

7. A vacant site refers to a site that is improved with buildings.

   ◯ True   ◯ False

8. A corner lot is generally associated as being a negative influence on value when it comes to a residential property, but a positive influence when it comes to a commercial property.

   ◯ True   ◯ False

9. If an old landfill site is located next to or near the subject site, you would want to know whether the subject has been exposed to any contamination.

   ◯ True   ◯ False

10. Inspecting a site to gather information on its functionality would involve looking at the condition of the site and its improvements.

   ◯ True   ◯ False

Active Learning Exercises

Solutions are located in the Appendix.

■ Exercise 1

Elaine Smith is a real estate salesperson who has been asked to price the subject property (Property A) for listing purposes. Property A is a detached two-storey, 2,500 square foot home on a 50' x 400' lot. It enjoys the use of a pool and deck with the back 200 feet being landscaped only with grass.

The overwhelming majority of lots in the neighbourhood range from 40' x 150' to 50' x 200' and are developed with similar 2,000–2,500 square foot homes. Many of these homes are landscaped with a pool and deck. On the whole, selling prices of these properties extend from $250,000–300,000. The zoning of a 40' x 150' and 50' x 200' lot would allow for a 4,000 and 5,000 square foot house respectively.

The owner of the subject property, John Bloggs, believes his property is worth $400,000 as the lot is twice the size of most other properties in the neighbourhood and there is so much a prospective purchaser could do with it. Mr. Bloggs has lived in the property for three years and there have been two other owners of the subject property over the past 12 years.

Elaine Smith thinks that the property is worth much less, because she feels that the extra 200 foot depth is really excess land and adds very little extra to the appeal and value. During Elaine's investigation and research, she uncovers the sale of Property B for $305,000. This property sold eight months ago and enjoys a lot size of 50' x 395' and it is developed with a 2,450 square-foot house. Elaine also finds two eight-month-old sales (Properties C and D) with lot sizes of 50' x 195' and 50' x 200' respectively. Both properties C and D are developed with 2,450 square-foot houses. Apart from the difference in lot sizes, Properties B, C and D are almost identical to each other. Property C sold for $298,000 and D sold for $300,000. 50' x 200' lots in the area sell for about $100,000.

1.1   Do you agree with Elaine Smith's assessment of the subject site. What information
provided supports your analysis?

1.2   What market data supports your conclusion?

■ Exercise 2

You have been asked to value the subject property (Property A) in order to determine a listing price for the sale of the property. The property is a detached 1,500 square foot bungalow located on Pleasant Boulevard, a four lane road with a high traffic flow. From your knowledge of the street and conversations with the owner and neighbours, you are well aware of the complaints about noise, pollution, lack of privacy and difficulty in getting cars out of the driveway, especially during rush hour.

Your investigation into the neighbourhood reveals that over the past six months, the 1,300–1,600 square-foot detached homes on Pleasant Boulevard have sold in the $160,000 to 180,000 range after being on the market for 180–210 days. You also notice over the same time frame that identical 1,300–1,600 detached homes located on the quiet side streets behind Pleasant Boulevard have been selling for between $175,000 and $195,000 and in only 60–90 days.

2.1   What kind of impact do you think the subject property's location on Pleasant Blvd. will have on its marketing and value?

2.2   What market data supports your conclusions?

▣ Exercise 3

Name four sources for collecting information on the subject site. Describe what information these sources might reveal.

▣ Exercise 4

For each of the following statements, list the concerns and questions you would have, together with the actions you might want to take.

4.1   A very recent survey shows 3 feet of the subject property's 20' x 15' family room addition encroaches on the neighbour's site.

4.2   A 10-foot utility easement runs across the east side of the subject property.

4.3   You notice that an old landfill site is located a short distance from the subject property.

4.4   The subject site has a very steep sloping topography.

■ Exercise 5   Multiple Choice

CASE STUDY FOR QUESTIONS 5.1 AND 5.2

There are two multiple choice questions (5.1 & 5.2) at the end of this case study. The questions are based on the information provided here:

Scenario

You have been asked to value the subject property that has a 15' x 30' in-ground swimming pool. Unfortunately, 2' x 30' of the pool encroaches onto a 20-foot hydro easement at the rear of the property.

The hydro company is aware of this encroachment and there is in fact an encroachment agreement. The agreement does, however, allow the hydro company to ask for the removal of the pool from the easement at any time, should it so require. The encroachment agreement has been in place for eight years.

You have talked to a lawyer who believes that the chances of the hydro company requiring the swimming pool be removed are remote. In addition, for a few hundred dollars, it will be possible to obtain title insurance to cover the possible cost and consequences of this problem.

Your investigation of the neighbourhood reveals the sale three months ago of Property A that is a detached two-storey 1,500 square foot bungalow with a 60' x 200' lot that sold for $195,000 after 70 days on the market. Property A also has a swimming pool that encroaches three feet onto a hydro easement and there is a similar encroachment agreement covering this situation. Properties almost identical to A, but without the encroachment, have over the past six months been selling for between $194,000 and $196,000 in under 90 days of being on the market.

5.1   Based on the information provided above, is the encroachment likely to have a negative impact on value?

   a.   Yes. The hydro company could request that the pool be removed once they find out about the encroachment. This will result in a cost as well as a loss in value due to the removal of the swimming pool.

   b.   No. There is an encroachment agreement in place and over the past 5 years, there has been no request to remove the swimming pool. In addition, title insurance could cover any costs and consequences of this encroachment.

   c.   No. The pool sits within the subject lot and as a result the owner can ask the hydro company to remove its easement because it interferes with the enjoyment of the swimming pool. The cost of removing the easement would be borne by the hydro company.

   d.   Yes. The presence of the encroachment agreement and the need for title insurance will alert a potential purchaser to the problem and will actually make the property difficult to sell.

5.2   What market data would confirm the dollar impact on value of the encroachment on the subject property?

   a.   The subject property has a 15' x 30' in-ground swimming where 2' x 30' of the pool encroaches onto a 20-foot hydro easement at the rear of the property.

   b.   Property A had a similar encroachment and yet sold for the same price and within the same time frame as properties without the encroachment.

   c.   Property A is a detached two-storey 1,500 square foot bungalow with a 60' x 200' lot. It has a similar encroachment.

   d.   The hydro company has an encroachment agreement which allows the company to ask for the removal of the pool from the easement at any time, should it so require.

CASE STUDY FOR QUESTIONS 5.3 AND 5.4

There are two multiple choice questions (5.3 & 5.4) at the end of this case study. The questions are based on the information provided here:

Scenario

You have been asked to value the subject property (Property A) in order to determine a listing price for the sale of the property. Property A is a detached 2,000 square-foot, two-storey house on a 40' x 120' lot. It has a deck in the backyard, but no swimming pool. The subject property's lot and house is fairly standard for the neighbourhood. However, there is a 12-foot municipal easement that runs down the east side and back across the rear of the site. Apart from the deck, the site is landscaped with grass. Most properties in the neighbourhood enjoy the use of both a deck and swimming pool. However, given the size of the lot, the presence of the easement has prevented the owner of the subject property from installing a swimming pool.

Your investigation into the neighbourhood has revealed the sale five months ago of Property B for $190,000. This detached two-storey 2,200 square foot house sits on a 41' x 118' lot with an 11' municipal easement similar to the subject. Property B has a deck, but no swimming pool, again because of the easement. It took 150 days to sell. You also discover the sale five months ago of Properties C and D that are almost identical to Property B, but are not subject to the municipal easement. These properties sold for $193,000 and $194,000 respectively in less than 100 days.

5.3   Do you think the easement will have any impact on the subject property's value and marketing?

    a.   Yes. The easement has resulted in only a detached 2,000 square foot house being placed on the property.

    b.   No. The easement has not prevented the owner from enjoying the use of the property; e.g., it has a deck.

    c.   Yes. The easement is preventing the owner from installing a pool which is popular in the area.

    d.   No. The subject lot is fairly standard for the neighbourhood and therefore the easement will have no impact at all.

5.4   What market data can be used to confirm the dollar impact of the easement on the subject property's value?

    a.   Property B has an 11 foot easement similar to the subject and it has a deck, but no swimming pool.

    b.   Properties C and D are almost identical to Property B, but are not subject to the municipal easement.

    c.   Property B took much longer to sell and sold for $3,000 to $4,000 less than Properties C and D.

    d.   Property A is a detached 2,000 square-foot, two-storey house on a 40' x 120' lot with a deck, but no swimming pool.

5.5   You are appraising a property with a pie-shaped lot and would like to know what dollar impact this would have on the value of the subject. How would you be able to determine the dollar impact?

a.   By looking at the marketing time needed to sell properties with a pie-shaped lots, as compared to the marketing time of similar properties with standard shaped lots.

b.   By looking at the listing prices of properties with a pie-shaped lot, as compared to the listing prices of similar properties with standard shaped lots.

c.   By looking at the selling prices of properties with a pie-shaped lot, as compared to the selling prices of similar properties with standard shaped lots.

d.   By looking at the cost of constructing a home on pie-shaped lots, as compared to the cost of constructing the same type of home on standard lots.

5.6   The subject property has a brand new swimming pool. Swimming pools are unpopular in the area with very few houses having one. As a result, the pool can be seen to be:

a.   in poor physical condition, but functionally good.

b.   both physically and functionally in good condition.

c.   both physically and functionally in poor condition.

d.   in good physical condition, but functionally poor.

5.7   Which of the following is an example of plottage?

a.   123 Main Street is a vacant site worth $175,000 and 125 Main Street is a vacant site worth $200,000. If the two sites were assembled, the assembled site would be worth $475,000.

b.   123 Main Street is a vacant site worth $175,000 and 125 Main Street is a vacant site worth $200,000. If the two sites were assembled, the assembled site would be worth $375,000.

c.   123 Main Street is a vacant site worth $175,000 and 125 Main Street is a vacant site worth $200,000. If the two sites were assembled, the assembled site would be worth less than $375,000.

d.   123 Main Street is a vacant site worth $175,000 and 125 Main Street is a vacant site worth $200,000. If the two sites were assembled, the assembled site would be worth between $175,000 and $200,000.

5.8   123 Main Street is a vacant site with a lot size of 40' x 150'. It sold for $250,000. 190 Main Street is an identical vacant site, except that it has a lot size of 40' x 300'. It sold for $258,000. 190 Main Street would be considered to:

a.   be an example of plottage because it has a larger lot and is more valuable than 123 Main Street.

b.   have excess land because it is 200% larger in size, but worth only 3.2% more than 123 Main Street.

c.   have excess land because its value per front foot is greater than the front foot value of 123 Main Street.

d.   be an example of plottage because its value per front foot is greater than the front foot value of 123 Main Street.

5.9   Describe a physical factor that could have an influence on the value of a site.

    a.   The topography of the site.

    b.   The site's tax assessment.

    c.   The site located on a corner.

    d.   The zoning of the site.

5.10   123 Main Street and 125 Main Street are sites with 30 foot frontages. They are both worth $60,000 per front foot. If these two lots were assembled, the price per front foot:

    a.   might stay the same, increase or decrease depending on the utility of the assembled land.

    b.   would increase as assembled land provides greater utility than is present in the individual lots.

    c.   would decrease as there is an inverse relationship between price and the site frontage.

    d.   might increase as a result of excess land being created by the assemblage of the sites.

CHAPTER 5

Building Analysis

Introduction

Accurate information on the condition and functionality of the main residence building is essential for a proper valuation during the Cost and Direct Comparison Approach. Should the appraiser see something in or about the house that is unusual for the area, he/she must investigate further to find out whether there will be a value impact. Only the market place can confirm whether there has been a value impact and usually that requires a study of the sales and listings in the area.

If the appraiser sees or suspects a problem with the structure, it is important that he/she requests additional information or asks for an expert (home inspector or engineer) to be brought in to carry out an assessment.

Whatever information has been collected on the subject property should be collected on the comparables used in either the Cost or Direct Comparison Approach. Of course, additional information needs to be collected on the comparables used; e.g., sale price and date, chattels included in sale, any unusual motivation or financing, etc.

Learning Outcomes

At the conclusion of this chapter, students will be able to:

- Describe what information needs to be collected on the subject building.
- Discuss the requirements for measuring the size of a house.
- Describe the economic life, remaining economic life and effective age of a building and explain how they are arrived at.
- Define *over improvement* and describe its impact on value.
- Describe the various sources and means of collecting the necessary information.
- Outline what needs to be looked at during a physical inspection of the buildings and explain the difference between a physical and functional view of the improvements.
- Describe the various environmental and building construction issues that can arise.
- Outline the steps in dealing with and assessing the nature, extent and cost of environmental or building construction issues and problems.
- Explain the possible impacts of environmental and building construction problems on value and explain how dollar values are assigned to the impact.
- Discuss the need for collecting information on comparable properties.
- Explain the impact of chattels on value.

INFORMATION

In order to estimate a value on the subject property, you will need to collect as much relevant information as you can on the subject building (i.e., improvements on the site as opposed to improvements to the site). It is important to stress that collecting information, while very important in itself, is only one part of the process of being able to estimate value. You also need to analyze the information, come to a conclusion as to its impact and then support that conclusion by obtaining evidence from the marketplace; i.e., sales, listings and expired listings.

 # INFORMATION TO CONSIDER

The following categories of information need to be considered when doing the inspection and report on a residential building.

GENERAL DATA	CONSTRUCTION DATA
Relates to such items as the chronological age of the structure, its square footage (exterior measurements), type and style of building, general condition, etc.	Considers a block foundation versus a poured concrete foundation, wood framing versus steel framing, brick veneer versus siding, asphalt shingles versus other kinds of roofing (e.g., steel, concrete or cedar shake), etc.

EQUIPMENT AND SYSTEMS DATA	FUNCTIONAL CRITERIA
Relates to the electrical, plumbing, heating, ventilation, air conditioning, built-in vacuum, built-in intercom, built-in security systems, water treatment systems, sprinkler systems, cable, telephone, smart wiring systems and any other systems that may be in the structure.	Relates to the appeal, utility, popularity and performance of the building and its components, as compared to other buildings and their components; e.g., the floor plan, ensuite in master bedroom as opposed to no ensuite, hardwood floors as opposed to carpeting, combined kitchen/family room as opposed to a kitchen with eat-in area, old octopus furnace as opposed to a high efficiency furnace.

BUILDING AREA/SIZE

For appraisal purposes, the measurement of the size/area of the subject and comparable buildings should be calculated from the dimensions of the exterior, and for only those areas that are completely finished and are 100% above ground level. Living areas above ground that are not finished should still be measured, but need to be separated out from the final measurement of the house size.

In practice, you will measure the ground floor from the exterior and then multiply by the number of levels above ground.

In some cases, and depending on local custom or the type of building, you may need to deviate from the above instructions. If you do deviate, then make sure that you measure the subject building and the comparable buildings in the same way and make notes in the appraisal as to how you calculated the building size; i.e., how you measured and what was, and was not, included.

ECONOMIC LIFE OF A BUILDING

The period over which the improvements to a site contributes to the value of the property as a whole. The economic life of a structure refers to the amount of time that a structure (from the day it is built) would be useful or habitable given no renovation, updating or modernization over that time period. Most appraisers would use 50 to 60 years as a rule of thumb for physical economic life. In reality, economic life is estimated by looking at/researching how long buildings similar to the subject in the same neighbourhood have remained liveable/useful/valuable before they have had to be renovated/modernized or demolished.

> **EXAMPLE**   *The Economic Life of a Building*
>
> 123 Main Street was built in 1950. Nothing was done to this property (except cleaning and general maintenance). By 2008, it had become unlivable and added no value to the property. A builder purchased it that year and it was demolished to make way for a new house. The economic life for this building appears to have been about 58 years.
>
> 160 Main Street was built in 1946. Nothing was done to this property (except cleaning and general maintenance). By 2008, it had become unlivable and added no value to the property. A builder purchased it that year and it was totally renovated and modernized. The economic life for this building appears to have been about 62 years.
>
> Based on this evidence, one could estimate the economic life of these kinds of buildings to be 60 years.

REMAINING ECONOMIC LIFE

The estimated number of years remaining in the economic life of a building as from the effective date of the appraisal. You can extend the remaining life of a building (without changing the economic life) by renovating/modernizing it.

> **EXAMPLE**   *Remaining Economic Life*
>
> 123 Main Street was built in 1967 in a neighbourhood where homes have always had an economic life of 60 years. By 2007, after just receiving general maintenance and cleaning, the house was felt to have an effective age of 40 years and was seen to have a remaining life of 20 years. That year it was totally renovated and modernized. As a result, it was estimated that this property's effective age in 2007 was reduced to 5 years and its remaining economic life was increased to 55 years (remember the economic life remains 60 years—therefore 60 − 5 = 55).
>
> If this home continues to be renovated every 40 years, its effective age will continue to be reduced and in theory its remaining economic life can be extended indefinitely, all the while the building's economic life remains at 60 years.

ACTUAL AGE

The actual number of years that have passed since a structure was built; also referred to as the *chronological age*. The actual age of a structure must be differentiated from its effective age for appraisal purposes.

EFFECTIVE AGE

The estimated age in years based on the amount of care and attention a building has received. Care and attention could include renovation and modernization.

If a building has had better than average maintenance, its effective age may be less than its actual age. If there has been inadequate maintenance, it may be greater. A 40-year-old building may have an effective age of 20 years due to rehabilitation or modernization.

continued...

EFFECTIVE AGE (continued)

EXAMPLE   *Effective Age*

Buyer Jones is acquiring Smith's home, built 20 years ago. For this type of building in this neigh-bourhood, the economic life has been estimated at 50 years. The appraiser is attempting to establish the value of the property for lending purposes and is preparing a form report. Based on the condition of the property, the appraiser estimates that Smith's home has an effective age of only 15 years. The lower effective age is due to various improvements that Smith has put into the property; e.g., new kitchen cupboards, new carpeting and updated décor in most rooms.

The illustration below visually demonstrates this effective age in relation to economic life and actual age. You will note that the effective age of a building, together with its remaining economic life, equals the total economic life of a building.

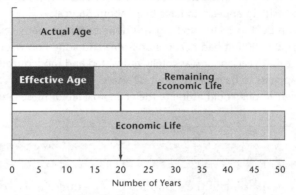

OVER IMPROVEMENT

The placement of improvements on a property that are excessive and consequently inconsistent with the overall size, quality or appearance of other improvements within the general vicinity. An example would be the construction of a large expensive home within a neighbourhood consisting almost exclusively of small, detached, older bungalows. The cost of the over-improved property may not be reflected in market value as determined by an average buyer ready, willing and able to acquire the property.

The following example illustrates the extent to which value is affected when over improvements are involved in renovations to a structure.

EXAMPLE   *Over Improvements*

Salesperson Lee is attempting to explain the concept of over improvement to a potential seller/client. The owner, Mr. Wilson, recently renovated his home, not realizing that a corporate transfer was in the future. Wilson's home was originally an 1,100 square foot bungalow with a garage. Most of the properties in the area are roughly the same size and general range of value. Wilson just completed a sizeable addition, costing approximately $55,000, on the rear of the house. The addition added a main level family room, laundry room and a three-piece bath.

Lee demonstrated with a comparative market analysis that most homes in the immediate area sell for between $160,000 and $175,000. However, two properties in the neighbourhood had also undergone significant additions and both recently sold for less than $200,000. Lee, while sympathetic to Wilson's significant cash outlay, estimated that the property would probably realize approximately $200,000. Had the home been left in its original condition, the market value would have been around $170,000. Effectively, Wilson's investment of $55,000 has a market value of approximately $30,000.

Recap of Formulas for Economic Life

The following formulas apply when calculating economic life:

Economic Life = Effective Age + Remaining Economic Life

Effective Age = Economic Life − Remaining Economic Life

Remaining Economic Life = Economic Life − Effective Age

While in real life the economic life of a building can change, it is usually the one constant in the equation at any given time.

COLLECTING INFORMATION

The information needed to complete a valuation is collected in two ways:

- from written and verbal sources; e.g., owners and a completed SPIS, previous inspection reports, previous listings, neighbours, surveys, architectural drawings, etc.
- observation from a physical inspection.

In Chapter 4, we looked at collecting information on the site. However, we are now looking at the interior and exterior of a building, and not the site and its exterior improvements. With respect to using the Seller Property Information Statement, the owner is expected to answer such questions as:

- Have you made any renovations, additions or improvements to the property and was a building permit obtained?
- Is the fireplace in working order?
- Are you aware of any problems with the plumbing system?

The answers to these questions are important. If the fireplace is not working, then there may be a negative impact on value as compared to a comparable house where the fireplace is working. Equally, if renovations were done to the subject property, but the necessary permits were not obtained, this may result in the subject not being as valuable as a comparable property with the same renovations, but with a permit having been obtained. The point here is that because a physical inspection, no matter how careful, may not reveal this information, it is important to have the owner complete the statement and sign it. Previous listings may indicate the presence of UFFI and neighbours may know about basement flooding, roof damage, insect or rodent infestation, or UFFI insulation.

PHYSICAL INSPECTION

This is a very important part of the valuation process. The inspection needs to be done in a methodical manner, and should not be rushed. During the inspection, look at each part and component of the building in terms of both its physical and functional contribution to the property.

When looking at an item or component physically, you are comparing the condition of the item as seen on the date of inspection, as compared to the condition of that item when it was brand new. For example, suppose that on the date of inspection you find a four-year-old vinyl tile kitchen flooring has deteriorated with cracks, holes and general fading. Clearly, this deterioration is physical and would not have been present when it was installed new. Based on this observation, the physical condition of the vinyl will probably be rated as poor.

When looking at an item of a home functionally, you are comparing the performance, quality, appeal and/or style of the component to components commonly seen in houses as at the date of appraisal. Suppose that on the date of inspection the subject has an old gravity furnace, however, the majority of similar homes in the area have high efficiency gas furnaces. Clearly, the octopus furnace would be rated as functionally poor even if it is in excellent physical condition. It is important to understand the difference between the physical condition of a home as opposed to the functional condition.

> **EXAMPLE**   *Physical Versus Functional*
>
> You have just inspected a home and found that the owner had, the previous day, installed a new 60-amp electrical service. Clearly, when you look at this component from a physical point of view (comparing the component to when it was new), its condition and performance is excellent. After all, it is a new 60-amp service just installed that morning. However, when you look at the service from a functional point of view, it would be attributed a poor rating given its performance capabilities as compared to the electrical services (more than likely 100 to 200-amp service) that would be found in similar homes today.

Asking Questions   CURIOSITY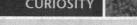

How do you ensure that you have the necessary information required to accurately estimate the value of a property? The only way of ensuring you have the necessary information is by asking the right questions. What are the right questions? Let's take a look at some examples below:

Situation—Three years ago the subject property had a 300 square foot family room extension added without a permit.
Questions to ask:

- Does the extension comply with building and zoning regulations?
- How easy will it be to get a permit and how much will it cost?
- What are the chances that the city might require that the extension be removed if it does not comply or that the city might require costly work be done in order for the property to comply?
- If the extension does not comply with building and zoning regulations, what will be the impact on buyer reaction and value if the extension has to be demolished or at least some work is required to ensure its compliance?

Situation—The subject property's furnace is leased and not owned.
Questions to ask:

- Is leasing a furnace common for the area?
- What are the lease terms?
- If it is common, what is the value impact and buyer reaction to a furnace being leased as opposed to owned?
- If it is not common, what is the value impact and buyer reaction to a furnace being leased as opposed to owned?

Situation—The subject property's electrical system has aluminum wiring.
Questions to ask:

- What is the condition of the wiring?
- Have any special components (i.e., connectors, receptacles, circuit breakers) designated CUAL or CO/ALR been installed?
- Is there a stigma attached to the presence of aluminum wiring?
- Even if the wiring is safe, what will be the value impact and buyer reaction to the presence of this wiring in the subject?

Knowing When to Get Professional Help Reality Check — CAUTION

If during the physical inspection you notice a problem or suspect something is wrong, it is important to identify the cause and extent of the problem, as well as the impact on value that the problem is going to have whether it is corrected or left as is.

Appraisers/salespeople are not trained building/home inspectors and it is crucial not guess the cause, nature and extent of a suspected problem. Always advise the owner to seek professional assistance such as a home inspector or structural engineer, depending on the problem. Request a report on what the problem is, what is its cause, what damage or further damage it can do, the solution to the problem and the cost of the solution. This information will assist in identifying and measuring the possible impact on value.

EXAMPLE

You are inspecting a home and notice a small pool of water in the basement. It was raining the night before and the water is located below a window close to the laundry tubs. The owner has informed you that water appears every so often, but does not know where it originated. The following are some possibilities.

- A leak in the window.
- A leak in the laundry tub.
- A leak through the foundation due to poor grading or lack of drainage.
- A damaged municipal water line under the floor of the basement.
- A crack in the foundation wall.

These five possibilities have very different consequences and costs. Do not guess. Guessing could result in legal and financial problems for any practitioner. Instead, get a professional home inspector or engineer to carry out an investigation. It might be as simple as water through the window or as expensive as lack of proper drainage and grading, or even a structural fault.

Common Concerns/Problems — CURIOSITY

There are a number of environmental and building construction issues that the salesperson may face including: UFFI, cedar shakes, termites, pyrite, electromagnetic fields (hydro lines), lead, radon, PCBs, etc.

This text is not intended to delve into the detail of cause and effect of potential problems. However, practitioners need to keep abreast of the many common issues affecting properties today. Keeping up-to-date enables salespeople to know when to seek additional and/or expert advice and also be equipped with the skills to assess what impact a particular problem might have on the marketing and value of the subject.

Unfortunately, even if problems have been addressed and rectified, a stigma may still remain with the property, possibly resulting in a continuation to some degree of the negative impact on value. For example, a residential home might be situated on the former site of a gas station. Even though the storage tanks have been removed and environmental assessments showing no residual contamination have been carried out, buyers may still react negatively to the perceived stigma. Another example might be a residential property having been insulated with UFFI during the mid-70's. The UFFI has since been removed, but buyers may still react negatively to the perceived stigma.

In order to measure the impact of environmental or structural concerns, the salesperson needs to look at the sales or listings of homes with these issues and compare their prices to similar homes without the environmental or structural problems. It is preferable to look at and compare recent sales within the subject neighbourhood, however, in the absence of such sales, it is quite acceptable to look in other neighbourhoods that would appeal to the same buyer.

continued...

Common Concerns/Problems

CURIOSITY

EXAMPLE   *The Dollar Value of UFFI*

You are valuing a subject property that is insulated with UFFI and need to determine the impact on the value. After a thorough investigation, you are unable to locate any recent or past sales in the subject neighbourhood that had been insulated with UFFI. However, a recent sale of a semi-detached two-storey home insulated with UFFI in a very comparable neighbourhood five miles away has been discovered. This comparable neighbourhood was found to appeal to the same type of buyer as the subject neighbourhood. The comparable sold for $200,000, whereas other more or less identical semis without UFFI were selling in the neighbourhood for $220,000. This information suggests (with no other major differences between the properties) that homes with UFFI might sell for 9% less.

Comparable Sales Data

MARKET MEMO

Whatever information is collected on the subject building, comparable sales data must be collected in order to value the subject by both the Direct Comparison Approach and by the Cost Approach. The following additional information will also need to be collected on comparable sales.

Date of Sale
The date that the terms of the sale were negotiated and agreed to by both parties.

Date of Closing
The date that title passed from the seller to the buyer and the money transferred from the buyer to the seller. The amount of time agreed to between the sale date and closing date can have an influence on the price paid for the comparable. A faster than normal closing for the area (e.g., within 7 days of negotiations) may suggest that a lower price was negotiated because the seller would receive the funds and the buyer would have to raise the money fairly quickly. Of course the opposite may be true if the closing after negotiations was much longer than average (e.g., six months). Naturally, the salesperson would have to support any such conclusions by gathering evidence from the marketplace to see if the comparable sold for more or less money than other similar homes at the time and confirm whether this could be attributable to the length of the closing.

Sale Price
Including any special conditions or financing attached to the sale. An example could be a seller take back mortgage at below current market mortgage rates. This might inflate the price paid for the building as a result of the seller losing money on a lower return and the buyer getting a monetary advantage not available on other properties.

Motivation of the Parties
For example, was the sale a result of financial pressure or the need to relocate quickly by the seller, or did the buyer just *have to have* that property because it backed onto the property of his/her elderly parents? This is very difficult to establish and does require talking to the parties involved in the comparable sale.

Chattels Involved in the Sale
If the seller had a relatively new fridge, stove, dryer, washer and dishwasher, this could add up to several thousand dollars for the buyer.

Improvements	PERSPECTIVE

Alice and Janet sit down together and talk about the Information on Improvements section of the Appraisal Form. Following are some highlights from their discussion.

JANET You have included chattels in your valuation of my home. I thought only fixtures were counted as part of the property.

ALICE The purpose of buying a home is to live in and enjoy its amenities. In order to live in a house, you need facilities such as a kitchen and bathroom. A kitchen would not be terribly functional without a fridge and stove, and not as enjoyable if there were no dishwasher. In addition, chattels such as a central vacuum, water purifier, washer and dryer add to the enjoyment, just as cathedral ceilings, fireplace and skylights. What I am basically saying is that most chattels can be seen as an integral part of the home, especially if they are common for homes in the subject neighbourhood. For years the argument has been that chattels do not add or subtract from value, but are part of negotiations (e.g., used to close a deal). This argument is very misleading because everything in a house (i.e., from the size to the number of bedrooms) is negotiable in terms of the price to be paid. Therefore, chattels are an important part of negotiations and, as a result, are part of the price paid. This means that there must be a value attributable to the chattels. Let's take a look at an example to help clarify this further.

> **EXAMPLE**
> The Petersons are buyers who have been negotiating an offer through their agent to buy 176 Main Street. Their last offer was at $216,000 and they have told the sellers that that is the final offer. The last counter by the sellers was at $218,000 and they have refused to come down any further. They are only $2,000 apart, but there is a stalemate. The Petersons do want to buy the property and the sellers do wish to sell. The offer includes a fridge and stove but the dishwasher, washer and dryer have been excluded by the sellers. The Petersons tell their agent that they would be willing to pay the $218,000 if the sellers agree to include the dishwasher, washer and dryer in the sale. The sellers eventually agree to this and the property is sold. What has really happened here is that the buyers have effectively paid $2,000 for the three chattels. In other words, the chattels added $2,000 value to the property.

JANET The house was built in 1947. How did you come up with an effective age of 25 years for my home?

ALICE The effective age of a building is based on the observed condition. In other words, never mind when the building was constructed, how old does the home look and perform in terms of its condition and functionality. This is obviously not an exact science since, to a great degree, it relies on the subjective judgment of the salesperson/appraiser. What I did with respect to your home was to take into account that some modernization and updating had taken place since it was built in 1947. When I compared your building (in terms of its condition, functionality and performance) to 25-year-old homes, I found a great deal of similarity. Accordingly, I estimated the effective age of your home as being 25 years old.

JANET My neighbour told me about a friend who built a house that was an over improvement for the area. The friend spent a fortune on the home and will never see his money back when he sells. Can you explain this to me?

ALICE An over improvement occurs where a property is much larger or of a much higher quality than the majority of homes in the neighbourhood. The principle of conformity (regression) is involved here and, as a result, the value of the over improved property is pushed downwards to the point where it sits close to, although perhaps slightly above, the general value range of the majority of smaller/less quality homes in the neighbourhood. Accordingly, while a home may be 100% larger than the other homes in the area, its value may only be 10% higher. Again, it is the marketplace that will decide whether a property has been over improved or not. Let's take a look at an example to help clarify this further.

continued...

EXAMPLE

Suppose I am appraising a detached two-storey, 3,000 square foot, 50-year-old house with a 2-year-old 500 square foot family room addition in a neighbourhood where the majority of homes are similar 2,000–2,500 square foot properties, without the family room.

During my research, I find two detached two-storey 50-year-old homes that sold within the past 3 months. The first property is a typical 2,500 square foot house without the family room, while the second property is a 3,050 square foot house with a one-year-old 600 square foot family room addition that cost $60,000 to build. It turns out that property #1 sold for $310,000 and property #2 sold for $330,000.

With no other differences between the properties, except for the additional size in the family room, I could reasonably conclude that the $60,000 family room addition was an over improvement affected by the principle of regression. This conclusion would then suggest that the property I was appraising is also suffering from the same over improvement and value impact. Had property #2 sold for $370,000, then it would be possible to conclude that the family room addition was in fact not an over improvement.

KNOWLEDGE INTEGRATION

Notables

- There are a number of different categories of information that need to be collected on a building; e.g., general data, construction data, etc.

- It is important to be able to estimate the economic life and effective age of a building.

- An inspection of a building requires the appraiser to consider both its physical condition and functionality.

- The appraiser needs to be aware of environmental and construction issues/concerns that can affect the appeal and value of a property.

- Information must not only be collected on the subject property, but also on the comparables to be used in each of the approaches to value.

- Chattels may also need to be considered in the valuation of a property.

- A property can be over improved in terms of the size and quality of those improvements, and this has implications for its value.

- There are a number of sources from which information can be obtained with respect to the subject building.

Chapter Mini-Review

Solutions are located in the Appendix.

1. An example of functional data to be collected on a house would be the chronological age of the structure.

   ◯ True   ◯ False

2. Any component (e.g., a furnace) in a house can be in physically good condition, but functionally poor.

   ◯ True   ◯ False

3. For appraisal purposes, any room that is partially above grade is included in the size of the house.

   ◯ True   ◯ False

4. If you suspect a house has a problem, then you need to find out what the problem is, what the cause of it is, what damage or further damage can be done, the solution to the problem and the cost of the solution.

   ◯ True   ◯ False

5. The effective age of a building could be the same, greater or less than its actual age depending on the care and maintenance it has received.

   ◯ True   ◯ False

6. If you add the effective age of a building to its economic life you will arrive at the remaining life of a building.

   ◯ True   ◯ False

7. If a building no longer adds value to a property, it has come to the end of its economic life.

   ◯ True   ◯ False

8. An over improvement can occur where a property is much larger or of a much higher quality than the other homes in the neighbourhood.

   ◯ True   ◯ False

9. A seller take back mortgage at below current market mortgage rates might deflate the price paid for the building.

   ◯ True   ◯ False

10. The rational for a building being an over improvement is explained by the principle of conformity.

    ◯ True   ◯ False

Active Learning Exercises

Solutions are located in the Appendix.

■ Exercise 1

During a conversation with a friend, you are given the following information: John Smith, a builder, bought a vacant site in Neighbourhood A for $70,000 six months ago. He built a 2,300 square foot house on the site and plans to sell it for $100 per square foot. The $100 per square foot represents high quality materials and workmanship. Site values in Neighbourhood A generally range from $60,000–75,000. Property values in Neighbourhood A generally range from $150,000–250,000, with a few exceptions. This neighbourhood has 1,500–2,300 square foot homes of average quality. Most homes here are built for between $60 and $75 per square foot.

John believes he will be able to sell his property for $310,000–330,000. Five months ago, there was the sale in Neighbourhood A of an exceptional 2,200 square foot home for $270,000. This property was sold by another builder who had bought the site six months earlier for $75,000, built a house on it at a cost of $100 per square foot and had expected to sell the completed property for $295,000. There has been no change in market conditions or the character of the neighbourhoods over the past 12 months.

Please note that the costs quoted include a profit margin for the builder; i.e., it would be the costs charged by a builder to a customer.

1.1   Do you think John will be able to sell his property for more than $300,000? Explain, describing the forces at work affecting the value of John's property.

1.2   What specific market data supports your answer and conclusions?

■ Exercise 2

You have been asked to value a property that is being sold with a dishwasher, fridge, stove, dryer and microwave. These chattels are all under two years old and would cost about $6,000 new. You notice that three months ago two very similar one-year-old properties sold in the neighbourhood for $160,000 and $164,000. The property that sold for $164,000 included a dishwasher, fridge, stove, dryer and microwave. The property that sold for $160,000 did not include any chattels at all. Apart from the chattels, there are no other significant differences between the two sold properties.

2.1   What impact, if any, do you believe that the inclusion of chattels will have on the selling price; i.e., value of the subject property? Give reasoning for your answer.

2.2   What market data provided supports your analysis and conclusions?

■ **Exercise 3**

You are valuing a 25-year-old detached two-storey 2,500 square feet home and have just started to collect information on the building. Name 5 sources for collecting information on this building. Describe what information these sources might reveal.

■ **Exercise 4**

List the concerns and questions you would have given the following circumstances.

4.1   The subject property's furnace is leased and not owned.

4.2   The subject property has crawl space instead of a full basement.

4.3   The subject property is a detached two-storey home with a two bedroom floor plan.

■ Exercise 5   Multiple Choice

CASE STUDY FOR QUESTIONS 5.1 AND 5.2	
You are inspecting a 60-year-old subject property where brand new earth-tone shag carpeting was installed a week ago.	• Over 20 years ago earth-tone shag carpeting was very popular in the subject neighbourhood. Today, very few of the older homes and none of the new homes under construction are being laid with this type and colour of carpeting. • Your investigation of the neighbourhood reveals two very similar 60-year-old homes that sold in the past three months. The only significant difference is that one property sold for $250,000 with earth-tone shag carpeting in excellent condition, while the other property sold for $255,000 with a standard beige pile carpeting of similar quality and condition.

5.1   How do you rate the physical condition and functional appeal of the subject property's flooring?

    a.   The physical condition of the shag carpeting is poor, its functional appeal is excellent.

    b.   The physical condition of the shag carpeting is poor, its functional appeal is poor.

    c.   The physical condition of the shag carpeting is excellent, its functional appeal is excellent.

    d.   The physical condition of the shag carpeting is excellent, its functional appeal is poor.

5.2   What value impact will the presence of earth-tone carpeting have on the subject property and what market data supports your conclusion?

    a.   The presence of the earth-tone shag carpeting will have no value impact. Over 20 years ago earth tone shag carpeting was very popular in the subject neighbourhood.

    b.   The presence of the earth-tone shag carpeting will have a negative value impact. The property with the shag carpeting sold for $5,000 less than the property with a standard beige pile carpeting.

    c.   The presence of the earth-tone shag carpeting will have a positive value impact. The property with the shag carpeting sold for only $5,000 less than the property with a standard beige pile carpeting.

    d.   The presence of the earth-tone shag carpeting will have a positive value impact. Over 20 years ago earth tone shag carpeting was very popular in the subject neighbourhood.

5.3   The building is actually 30 years old, the effective age is 10 years. What could you possibly deduce from this information?

    a.   The building has probably been very poorly maintained and is most unlikely to have received any measure of modernization/renovation.

    b.   The building has an economic life of 30 years and a remaining economic life of 10 years.

    c.   The building has been very well maintained and has most likely received a good deal of modernization/renovation.

    d.   The building has an economic life of 40 years and a remaining economic life of 30 years.

5.4   The building is actually 30 years old, the effective age is 40 years. What could you possibly deduce from this information?

    a.   The building has received less than average care and maintenance.

    b.   The building has received well above average care and maintenance.

    c.   The building has an economic life of 70 years and a remaining life of 30 years.

    d.   The building has an economic life of 70 years and a remaining life of 40 years.

5.5   A home inspection of 123 Main Street reveals the presence of UFFI. How would you go about measuring the dollar impact of the presence of UFFI in the home?

    a.   Compare the listing prices of homes with UFFI to the listing prices of similar homes without UFFI.

    b.   Compare the selling prices of homes with UFFI to the selling prices of similar homes without UFFI.

    c.   Find out what the cost of removing all of the UFFI from 123 Main Street is going to be.

    d.   Compare the listing prices of homes with UFFI to the selling prices of similar homes without UFFI.

PRINCIPLES OF APPRAISAL

5.6   The economic life of a building refers to:

    a.   the estimated total period of time remaining from the date of the appraisal that a building would be expected to continue to contribute to the value of a property given no renovations, updating or modernization.

    b.   the estimated total period of time during which a brand new building would be expected to contribute to the value of a property given no renovations, updating or modernization.

    c.   the estimated total period of time during which a brand new building would be expected to contribute to the value of a property, given that appropriate renovations, updating and modernization takes place.

    d.   the estimated total period of time remaining from the date of the appraisal that a building would be expected to continue to contribute to the value of a property, given that appropriate renovations, updating and modernization take place.

5.7   The actual age of the building is 50 years, the effective age is 30 years and its remaining economic life is 40 years. What is the building's economic life?

    a.   70 years.

    b.   90 years.

    c.   20 years.

    d.   80 years.

5.8   The economic life of the building is 65 years and its remaining economic life is 42 years. What is the effective age of the building?

    a.   23 years.

    b.   42 years.

    c.   65 years.

    d.   107 years.

5.9   A brand new house has just been built. It would be considered an over improvement if the value it adds to the property:

    a.   is more than the cost of its construction.

    b.   is less than the cost of its construction.

    c.   is the same as the cost of its construction.

    d.   reduces the value of the land.

5.10   The subject building was constructed in 1890. The economic life of a building in the area has always been 60 years. How can this building still have a remaining economic life since it is older than 60 years?

    a.   A building can be renovated resulting in an extension to its remaining economic life.

    b.   This happens where the effective age is greater than its economic life.

    c.   This happens where the remaining life is greater than its economic life.

    d.   It can happen if the building is of a solid brick or stone construction.

CHAPTER 6

Direct Comparison Approach

Introduction

The most common method of valuing single-family homes is of course the Direct Comparison Approach. Comparing the subject property to similar homes that have sold recently in the same neighbourhood provides the best indication of value. It is a good indication of value, providing there are a sufficient number of good comparable sales, because it reflects the actions of typical buyers and sellers.

In the normal course of events, a salesperson takes a prospective buyer through a number of listed properties, many of which later sell. When the buyer is about to make an offer on a property, the salesperson reminds him/her of all the properties they have seen and indicates what they have since sold or are still listed for. Of course, the sales-person will also show the buyer sales and listings of properties they might not have seen. The buyer then compares all these properties and prices to the property they are about to buy and then makes a decision as to what he or she is willing to pay. By doing this, the buyer is really substituting one property for another (principle of substitution) and this is the basis for the Direct Comparison Approach.

The key to an accurate valuation using the Direct Comparison Approach is selecting good comparables sales. The less adjustments required, the better the comparable.

Appraisers who spend extra time at the front end of the appraisal assignment and find good comparables end up with a more accurate valuation. They spend less overall time on the appraisal assignment than appraisers who chose poor comparables quickly and then end up having to estimate numerous adjustments and make difficult judgment calls at the back end of the appraisal assignment.

Learning Outcomes

At the conclusion of this chapter, students will be able to:

- List the steps in the Direct Comparison Approach.
- Describe the essential elements of a good comparable sale and listing.
- Explain what steps need to be undertaken if there is a lack of good comparable sales.
- Describe how the use of comparable listings can help in the valuation process.
- Describe the different types of adjustments and methods for quantifying those adjustments.
- Calculate the dollar amount for different adjustments.
- Explain what is involved in a reconciliation.
- Estimate the value of a property using the Direct Comparison Approach.

STEPS IN THE DIRECT COMPARISON APPROACH

In order to complete the valuation of a property in an accurate and efficient manner, you will need to follow the steps outlined below:

1. Select a sufficient number of good comparable properties that have recently sold in the area.

2. Gather all necessary data on these properties to make a proper comparison.

3. Compare each of the sales with the subject for differences that may exist.

4. Make the necessary adjustments to the sale price of each comparable based on those differences.

5. Reconcile the adjusted sale price of the comparables into an indication of value of the subject property.

ESSENTIALS OF GOOD COMPARABLE SALES

In selecting comparable sales, you need to ensure that they possess the four basic qualities as follows:

1. The sale should be on, or as close as possible, to the date of valuation. The older the sale, the less reliable it is likely to be, especially if significant economic, physical, location or political changes have taken place between the date of the comparable sale and the date of valuation. It is the difficulty of being able to accurately assess and quantify the dollar impact on value of any changes that makes a dated sale less reliable.

2. The comparable sales should be located within the subject neighbourhood, preferably on the subject street or as close as possible.

3. The comparable sale should be truly physically similar in nature. The test is: *"Would the buyer of the subject property look at purchasing the comparable sale as an alternative?"* In valuing a two-bedroom bungalow, comparables need to be two-bedroom bungalows. It would not make sense to select three-storey duplexes as comparables for a two-bedroom bungalow. It would be highly unlikely that a buyer who is looking for a two-bedroom bungalow would make an alternative decision to buy a three-storey duplex instead. In addition, it would be impossible to adjust for the differences in appeal and utility between the two kinds of homes.

4. The comparable sale should be an arms-length transaction under conditions that would meet the definition of market value.

Explaining Your Choice of Comparables		CAUTION	

If you are forced to use poor comparables because of a lack of market activity in the neighbourhood or because the subject property is not standard for the area, explain this to the client and detail why you are using the comparables that you eventually used.

EXAMPLE   *Avoiding Non Arm's Length Transactions*

You have been asked to value the subject property (Property A) for listing purposes as of today's date. The subject is a detached two-storey, 1,500 square foot brick home. Mary Smith owns a detached two-storey, 1,500 square foot brick home (Property B) located in the subject neighbourhood that was sold a week ago for $200,000 to her son Mike Smith. Detached two-storey homes in the subject neighbourhood have been selling over the past three months between $220,000 and 240,000. Prices have stayed stable during this time frame. It would not be a good idea to use Property B as a comparable sale, even though it is a similar property located in the subject neighbourhood and sold recently. This is not an arm's length transaction. It is clear that the mother/son relationship has resulted in a sale below market value and accordingly it will not provide you with any worthwhile assistance in valuing the subject. It is not possible to make an adjustment for motivation, such as love.

Choosing Comparables   FOCUS

During an economic boom, you are likely to find a number of highly comparable recent sales located close by the subject. During an economic recession, the chances are that very few comparable recent sales located close by will have occurred. You cannot manufacture good comparable sales. If there are none, widen the area of search in terms of sale date, physical comparability and/or location. In these circumstances the search for and choice of comparables should be guided by the following:

- Choose a comparable sale that would appeal to the same or a similar buyer as would buy the subject.

- Choose a comparable sale where you would be relatively confident as to the accuracy of adjustments needed to take account of any necessary time, location or physical differences.

EXAMPLE   *Making Choices When It Comes to Comparables*

You have been asked to estimate today's value of a property (Property A) for listing purposes. It is a 3-bedroom, 1,500 square foot bungalow.

You have already chosen two comparable sales, but need one more to complete the valuation. Unfortunately, the market has not been active and there is a lack of good comparable sales. However, you do have a choice of using either Sale C or D as the third comparable. Comparable C is a detached 4-bedroom 1,600 square foot bungalow that sold 12 months ago and is located in the subject neighbourhood three blocks from the subject. Prices have gone up significantly over the past year. Comparable D is a detached 3-bedroom 1,750 square foot bungalow that sold one week ago, but is located seven blocks away from the subject in a slightly superior neighbourhood.

You feel confident that you can make accurate adjustments for location, number of bedrooms and size, but feel uncertain as to what time adjustment is needed to account for the sale of 12 months ago. While neither C nor D can be considered ideal comparables, you have to make a choice in order to have a third sale for comparison. There is no reason to believe that the typical purchaser of the subject would not have considered sales C and D as an alternative purchase despite the differences. However, given the uncertainty as to the adjustment needed for the time difference for Comparable C, you should consider choosing sale D as the third comparable.

Of course, it would make sense to keep Comparable C as a back up comparable in your file in support of your primary sales. You may also be questioned by your client as to why it was not used in the Appraisal Form itself.

PRINCIPLES OF APPRAISAL

USING COMPARABLE LISTINGS
TO ESTIMATE VALUE

Current comparable listings can be helpful in estimating value especially in a fast moving market (i.e., prices changing on a week by week basis), or in a slow moving market (i.e., very few sales are occurring). In the first instance, even a 2-month-old sale may not be a good comparison because of the adjustment needed to take account of the time difference. In the second instance, there may be very few or no good comparable sales and you may be forced to make many adjustments. A current comparable listing can indicate what a property is not worth. The following examples may help explain this further.

EXAMPLE   *Comparable Listings*

Scenario 1

You have been asked to value the subject property (Property A) for listing purposes. It is a detached two-storey, 2,000 square foot home. Property prices have risen 10–15% over the past six months. You have selected three comparable sales that sold as follows:

- Comparable Sale #1 sold for $200,000 two months ago
- Comparable Sale #2 sold for $210,000 three months ago
- Comparable Sale #3 sold for $220,000 1 month ago

Each comparable sale required four or five adjustments including time adjustments. It has not been easy to estimate and quantify the adjustments. However, you have done the best you can based on the available market information. Accordingly, you arrive at the following adjusted selling prices:

- Comparable Sale #1 Adjusted Price: $210,000
- Comparable Sale #2 Adjusted Price: $212,000
- Comparable Sale #3 Adjusted Price: $214,000

After careful consideration, you feel the subject's value should be estimated at $212,000. Subsequent to the estimate of $212,000, you discover a current listing that has been on the market for 50 days and is priced at $209,000. There have been no offers on that property in a market where well-priced properties usually sell in 30–60 days. This listing is a detached two-storey 2,000 square foot home located one block from the subject. This property is very similar to the subject and might even be in slightly superior condition.

Clearly, this current listing is telling you that the subject property is not worth $212,000. Despite your best efforts, one or all of your adjustments have not been as accurate as you would have hoped. The listing has told you that the subject is worth less than $212,000 and allows you to go back and check your calculations and adjustments in order to arrive at a revised and more accurate estimate of value. In reality, your revised estimate should probably be somewhere below $209,000.

Scenario 2

You are valuing the subject property (Property A) which is a detached 3-bedroom 1,400 square foot bungalow. There have been very few comparable sales over the past 12 months in the subject neighbourhood. This means that you will have to look for comparable sales that are somewhat dated and located further from the subject. In addition, the comparables eventually chosen will need a number of significant adjustments for physical differences. As a result, you are not sure as to what price range of comparable sales you should start looking in.

continued...

Scenario 2 *(continued)*

Fortunately, there is a very comparable current listing (Property B). This is a highly similar detached 3-bedroom 1,475 square foot bungalow. It has one extra bathroom than the subject and has been listed for 45 days at $189,000. Given the similarity between the subject and Property B, the above tells us that the subject's value probably lies somewhere between $175,000 and $189,000. Accordingly, you should be looking for comparable sales as close to this price range as possible.

Underpriced Listings	CAUTION

What if a very comparable listing has been under priced? If any of the circumstances of either a comparable sale or listing do not meet the conditions of market value (e.g., unusual financing, motivation or marketing techniques) or do not assist you in your valuation, you would not use that property as a comparable listing.

Of course, comparable listings cannot be used as, or substituted for, comparable sales.

ADJUSTMENTS

Even in a neighbourhood of new homes, it is difficult to find three comparables that require no adjustments at all. The older the neighbourhood and the more varied the housing, the more adjustments will likely be needed. It is not uncommon to see several adjustments for each comparable used in estimating the value of a property. Adjustments are made to the selling prices of the comparables. This is done in order to eliminate any significant differences between them and the subject, so that the adjusted selling prices reflect the subject's value.

EXAMPLE   *Why Adjustments Are Needed*

You are trying to value the subject property that is a detached two-storey 2,000 square foot brick house. You find a great comparable sale that is identical to the subject, except that it has an extra bathroom and second fireplace. This comparable sold for $225,000. The extra bath is worth $3,000 and the second fireplace is valued at $2,000.

Once you deduct the $5,000 from the sale price of the comparable property, you arrive at an adjusted selling price of $220,000. Deducting the bath and second fireplace values effectively makes the comparable identical to the subject. This being so, the adjusted value of $220,000 should be an indication of the value of the subject.

Types Of Adjustments

The type of adjustment can fall under one of the following six main headings:

1. RIGHTS CONVEYED BY THE TRANSACTION

This involves the type of ownership that a person has in the property being appraised and the legal rights affecting it. You could value a property where the client's interest is either *Life Estate*, *Leasehold* or *Fee Simple*. Given the nature of the majority of transactions in residential real estate, you need only, for the purposes of this course, concern yourself with estimating the value of a home where the ownership is fee simple. Restrict choices of comparables to those where the sale involves a fee simple estate. Other adjustments under this heading could be where either the subject or comparable has an easement, encroachment or restrictive covenant.

2. FINANCING TERMS

Given that mortgages are arranged because of the personal finances of an owner or buyer, the subject property is, in most instances, valued as if it were free and clear and capable of attracting typical financing. However, there may be instances where the comparables used have been sold with non-typical financing. These instances might include:

- A comparable sold with a seller take back mortgage well below current market rates. In this case the buyer would have been given an advantage and the seller would have been disadvantaged. As a result, it would not be unreasonable to expect that the buyer may have been induced to pay, and the seller may have demanded, a higher sale price.
- A comparable sold with a buyer assuming a mortgage with below current market rates. Here the seller will not be able to transfer the mortgage to his/her new home. In this case the buyer would have been given an advantage and the seller a disadvantage. As a result, it would not be unreasonable to expect that the buyer may have been induced to pay, and the seller may have demanded, a higher sale price.

In both of the above situations, an adjustment may be warranted to take care of the difference between the subject's valuation as if free and clear (normal financing) and the comparable's appealing non-typical financing arrangement.

It is possible that you could be asked to value a subject property where it has a large mortgage on it at well below current market rates, but where the comparables sold free and clear and with the buyers having obtained typical financing. Providing the subject's mortgage is easily assumable and is sufficiently large enough to appeal to most buyers, then it is possible that an adjustment would be required to take account of this difference in financing.

3. MOTIVATION OF PARTIES

In valuing a property for sale or mortgage purposes, market value is used as the standard. Market value assumes that there has been no unusual motivation or undue pressure on either party to the sale of a property.

Clearly, all buyers and sellers must be motivated to a reasonable degree, otherwise there would not have been any reason for them to engage in a real estate transaction. However, you may discover that one of your comparable sales sold under what could be described as undue pressure or unusual motivation.

Undue pressure or unusual motivation can of course impact what a property has been bought or sold for. The following circumstances are examples of scenarios where undue pressure or motivation may be suspected.

- The sellers are under financial pressure with the bank threatening Power of Sale.
- The seller is moving within three weeks of the property being listed.
- The buyer is being relocated by his/her employer and only has time to spend three days looking for a home.
- The buyer is desperate to buy a home next to his/her elderly parents.
- The seller has already bought a house which is closing in four weeks.
- The buyer has already sold a house that is closing in three weeks.

Adjustments for undue pressure or unusual motivation are very difficult to quantify and support. Therefore, if you feel that the comparable selling price has been affected by pressure or motivation, then the best recommendation is that you discard it and look for an alternative sale.

4. MARKET CONDITIONS (TIME)

The majority of the comparable sales will have sold some time in the past. It is rare to find a good comparable sale that occurred on the date of valuation. Price levels can change over any given period of time, whether it is a month or six months. The question you should always be asking yourself is—*If the comparable were to be sold as at the date of valuation, what would its selling price have been?*

Changing Price Levels	MARKET MEMO

Traditionally, price changes are shown as a percentage per month and calculated in terms of whole months. It is not easy to find reliable market data that will accurately indicate price changes on a week-by-week or bi-weekly basis during a given time frame. Nevertheless, practitioners should be sensitive to the fact that market prices can change on a weekly basis and can change at different rates from one week to another.

> **EXAMPLE**   *Calculating Realistic Price Level Changes*
> In valuing the subject property, you find a comparable sale that sold five months and four days ago for $200,000. You estimate that prices have increased by about ½% per month over the past several months. It has not been easy to identify and extract this information with a great deal of certainty from the market data available. The estimated price change is not considered that significant and the market can be described as steady but improving.
>
> Based on the above, you would probably make a 2½% time adjustment (5 months x ½% per month) to the selling price of the comparable. Given the slow changing nature of the market, together with relatively low degree of certainty of the time adjustment, it is not unreasonable to assume that no price changes occurred over the extra four days. In addition, the impact of being out four days would not be that significant in terms of value.

5. LOCATION

There are two locational differences that can occur. 1) The comparable may actually be located within a different neighbourhood to the subject; or 2) the comparable may be situated within the same neighbourhood, but affected by different influences such as:

- the subject may back onto a park, whereas the comparable is located backing onto a railway; and/or
- the subject may be on a busy main road, whereas the comparable is on a quiet side street.

The question to be asked by you is: *How much more or less would the comparable have sold for if it had the same location as the subject?*

6. PHYSICAL CHARACTERISTICS

Chances are there will be physical differences between the comparable sale and the subject. Each physical adjustment must be broken down and shown separately, and not lumped together with other adjustments under one general heading such as *Physical Differences*. Physical differences may range from size, layout and condition to garage, fireplace, style and central air conditioning.

CALCULATING ADJUSTMENTS

Time, locational and physical adjustments probably represent 99% of the adjustments ever made. Occasionally, adjustments are made for special financing or for an encroachment or easement. Accordingly, this course will concentrate on calculating time, locational and physical adjustments, while also addressing how to estimate an adjustment for special financing.

Calculating Time Adjustments (Market Conditions)

There are two basic ways to estimate the changes in prices over a given period of time:

1. from the local real estate board's published statistics; and/or

2. the Time Resale Method.

PUBLISHED STATISTICS METHOD

Real estate boards track changing market conditions by publishing, on a monthly basis, a set of statistics showing such information as the number of sales, number of listings, and the average and median prices for each month. These figures are usually shown for the combined board area, and also broken down for each of the districts within that area. Of course, with the advent of the internet, salespeople can now actually access the changing statistics on a daily or weekly basis (depending on the real estate board they belong to).

    The average or median prices published can be used to calculate the price change as illustrated below.

EXAMPLE   *Calculating a Time Adjustment—Published Statistics Method*

You are valuing the subject property with a valuation date of August 30, 20xx. One of the comparable sales you have chosen sold for $200,000 three months prior on May 28, 20xx.

    You know that prices have increased over the past three months and the local real estate board's published figures show that the average house price as at August 30, 20xx was $225,000, but was $215,000 on May 28, 20xx. These prices are for the whole real estate board area.

    Given that the time frames of the average prices from the published statistics mirror the time frames indicated by the valuation date and comparable sale date, you can make the following analysis and application to the comparable for a time adjustment.

Analysis	
Average House Price—August 30, 20xx	$225,000
Average House Price—May 28, 20xx	−215,000
Price Increase Over the 3 Month Period	$ 10,000
Percentage Increase *(10,000 ÷ 215,000 x 100)*	**4.65%**
Application To Comparable	
Comparable Selling Price—May 28, 20xx	$200,000
Time Adjustment (4.65%)	+ 9,300
Time Adjusted Selling Price—August 30, 20xx	**$209,300**

NOTE: Given the inherent weaknesses of this adjustment method/process (i.e., availability of sufficient information and reliability of information collected), the convention in this course will be as follows: Comparable sales that sold within 3 weeks of the effective date will not require time adjustments—they will be considered current sales.

Calculating Adjustments is a Combination of Science, Art and Judgement   MARKET MEMO

It is important to understand that valuation, and more specifically calculating adjustments, is not an exact science. First of all, it is not easy to obtain a set of perfect information from the market because you are dealing with the results of the actions of many people who all have a different range of motivation, objectives, needs, desires and abilities to negotiate. Secondly, you still have to interpret all the information and that means using your own judgement that may differ from other people.

In short, you will be presented with scientific methods in order to calculate adjustments, but the use of judgement and resulting answers may not be perfect. The good news is that you will only ever be asked to be logical in your choice of answers and be able to support viewpoints.

The Problem with the Published Statistics Method   CAUTION

While the *published statistics method* is often quoted and used by salespeople/appraisers and the public, there are some inherent problems with it.

Price changes can occur in each neighbourhood at different times and at different rates. Within a neighbourhood, different types of homes might also experience price changes at varying times and rates. By using the average or median prices for the whole real estate board area, you may not be obtaining the specific price changes for the subject neighbourhood. In addition, the average or median prices may include all types of housing; i.e., condos, freehold, two-storeys, bungalows and split-level.

You could use the average and median sale price statistics for a particular district of the real estate board that most closely mirrors the borders of the subject neighbourhood. The problem here is that a relatively small number of trans-actions may have taken place resulting in possible significant distortions, depending on which properties sold within the given months.

EXAMPLE   *The Distortions of the Published Statistics Method of Time Adjustments*

You are valuing a subject property with a valuation date as at August 10, 20xx. You have found a comparable sale that sold for $190,000 on June 8, 20xx.

Prices have increased over this 2-month period and you are going to use the average prices from the local real estate board's Published Price Statistics.

However, instead of employing the average prices of the whole area, you decide to use the numbers from one of the 15 districts in the board (District A) that closely mirrors the borders of the subject neighbourhood.

You find that in June 20xx, the average price for District A is $198,000 (15 homes having sold that month). The average price for August 20xx turns out to be $194,000 (13 homes having sold that month).

The average prices make no sense to you, as you are absolutely certain that prices have improved over the time period in question. However, you find out that in District A the major-ity of the 15 homes that sold in June were the larger, more expensive two-storey homes, while the majority of the 13 properties that sold in August were the much smaller, less expensive bungalows.

Clearly, the resulting distortion in the published statistics reflects the monthly difference in types of homes sold, rather than the difference in market prices.

THE TIME RESALE METHOD

The idea behind this method is that, where a property sells and resells, within a given time frame, any difference in the price should be a reflection of a change in the market due to time. Ensure that the price change is a result of the passage of time, and not due to any physical changes or motivational factors. The best resales would be located in the same neighbourhood and be of a similar type to the subject. The illustration below describes the mechanics of how to calculate a monthly time adjustment using the Time Resale Method.

EXAMPLE   *Calculating a Monthly Time Adjustment—The Time Resale Method*

You are valuing the subject property (Property A) with a valuation date of December 30, 20xx. You find a comparable property (Property B) which sold for $145,000 and is very similar to the subject, except that it sold eight months prior (April 30, 20xx).

Prices have been increasing over the past year. Three properties (C, D and E) in the neighbourhood sold and resold during the year 20xx, and you are able to confirm that no legal, financial, physical, motivational or locational changes occurred to these properties between the time of their sale and resale. Details of the properties follows.

Analysis

PROPERTY	C	D	E
Sale Price	150,000 (Apr)	153,500 (May)	148,000 (Jan)
Resale Price	162,000 (Dec)	164,200 (Dec)	162,800 (Dec)
Price Increase	12,000	10,700	14,800
% Increase	8% (12,000 ÷ 150,000 x 100)	6.97% (10,700 ÷ 153,500 x 100)	10% (14,800 ÷ 148,000 x 100)
Time Difference	8 months	7 months	11 months
% Increase/ Month	1% (8% ÷ 8)	1% (6.97% ÷ 7)	0.91% (10% ÷ 11)

Based on the above analysis, a price increase per month of 1% is estimated.

Application To Comparable

Comparable Selling Price *(April 30, 20xx)*		$145,000
Time Difference *(December—April)*	8 months	
% Increase in 8 months *(1% x 8)*	8%	
Time Adjustment *($145,000 x 8%)*		+11,600
Time Adjusted Selling Price For Comparable		**$156,600**

Clearly, the closer the time frame of the resale property being used matches the time frame of the comparable sale date and the valuation date, the more accurate the adjustment is going to be. The accuracy of the adjustment is also going to depend on the time resales being as similar in type and appeal as possible to the subject property. If you cannot find similar types of properties in the subject neighbourhood that sold and resold within an acceptable time frame, then you may need to:

- expand the search within the subject neighbourhood in terms of the types of residential properties used as time resales (obviously, you wouldn't use a time resale of a triplex, if the subject were a single-family bungalow);
- use time resales from similar neighbourhoods that are nearby and would appeal to the same type of buyers as in the subject area; and/or

- use two properties within the subject neighbourhood that were very similar to each other, where one sold close to the sale date of the comparable and the other sold close to the valuation date.

EXAMPLE   *Calculating a Monthly Time Adjustment Using the Paired Sales Method of Two Different Properties*

You are valuing the subject property (Property A) with the valuation date of April 10, 20xx. You find a comparable sale (Property B) which is very similar to the subject which sold on January 7, 20xx. You are unable to find any similar properties in the subject neighbourhood that sold and resold in the current or prior years, however, you find properties C and D which are almost identical to each other. Property C sold for $192,000 on the 4th of January, 20xx and Property D sold for $198,000 on April 2, 20xx. With no significant differences between Properties C and D, you can use the sale price variances to estimate the time adjustment required.

Of course, had there been physical differences between Properties C and D, then you would have to adjust out those differences (see calculation of locational and physical adjustments), and then use the adjusted selling prices to calculate the time adjustment.

CALCULATING LOCATION ADJUSTMENTS

The calculation of dollar adjustments for differences between the comparable and subject for location is done by using the Paired Sales Method. The basis for this method is that you select two sales that are identical to each other except for a difference in location, the same locational difference as between the comparable and the subject. The sales should have occurred roughly at the same time. Accordingly, any variance in the selling price between the two sales would represent the adjustment in value between the locations. Ensure that the paired sales are identical or very similar to each other, except for the same difference in location that you have observed between the comparable and the subject. They should also be of a similar type and in the same price range as the subject; i.e., if the subject is a detached single-family home worth $200,000–225,000, the paired sales should not be attached duplexes in the $350,000–400,000 range. As a rule of thumb, try to select three sets of paired sales in order to be more certain of the results.

Preferably, paired sales will have come from the same neighbourhood as the subject. If not, they should come from a neighbourhood that is nearby and would appeal to the same buyer as in the subject neighbourhood.

EXAMPLE   *Calculating the Adjustment for Location*

You are estimating the value of the subject property (Property A) as of March 10, 20xx. It is a detached two-storey single-family home backing onto a park. You are able to find a comparable sale (Property B) which is very similar to the subject, except that it backs onto a busy main road. It sold for $180,000 on March 3, 20xx. In analyzing the location adjustment, you are able to find two sets of paired sales. All of the properties within the pairings are detached single-family homes located within the subject neighbourhood.

Paired Sales #1 are Properties C and D which are very similar to each other, except that C backs onto a busy main road and D backs onto a park. C sold for $195,000 on February 7, 20xx and D sold for $205,000 on February 19, 20xx.

Paired Sales #2 are Properties E and F also very similar to each other, except that E backs onto a busy main road and F backs onto a park. E sold for $205,000 on January 10, 20xx and F sold for $215,000 on January 16, 20xx.

continued...

EXAMPLE　　*Calculating the Adjustment for Location* (continued)

How much more would the comparable have sold for had it backed onto the park?

Analysis

	PAIR #1	PAIR #2
Sale Price C & E	$195,000	$205,000
Sale Price D & F	$205,000	$215,000
Locational Difference	$10,000	$10,000
% Superiority of Park Home Over Main Road	5.13% *(10,000 ÷ 195,000 x 100)*	4.88% *(10,000 ÷ 205,000 x 100)*

It is therefore estimated that backing onto a park is 5% better than backing onto a main road.

Application To Comparable

Comparable Selling Price	$180,000
Location Adjustment *(180,000 x 5%)*	+9,000
Location Adjusted Selling Price	**$189,000**

CALCULATING PHYSICAL ADJUSTMENTS

The calculation of dollar adjustments for physical differences between the comparable and subject is done by using the Paired Sales Method. The basis for this method is to select two sales that are identical to each other, except for a specific physical difference (the same specific physical difference as between the comparable and the subject). The sales should have occurred roughly at the same time. Accordingly, any variance in the selling price between the two sales would represent the adjustment in value for the physical difference.

Ensure that the paired sales are identical or very similar to each other, except for the same physical difference that you have observed between the comparable and the subject. They should also be of a similar type and in the same price range as the subject (i.e., if the subject is a detached single-family home worth $200,000–225,000, the paired sales should not be attached duplexes in the $350,000–400,000 range). As a rule of thumb, try to select three sets of paired sales in order to be more certain of the results.

Preferably, your paired sales will have come from the same neighbourhood as the subject. If not, they should come from a neighbourhood that is close by and would appeal to the same buyer as in the subject neighbourhood.

EXAMPLE　　*Calculating the Adjustment for Physical Differences*

You are estimating the value of the subject property (Property A) as of February 25, 20xx. It is a detached two-storey single-family home that enjoys the use of two bathrooms.

You are able to find a comparable sale (Property B) which is very similar to the subject, except that it only has the use of one bathroom. It sold for $205,000 on January 13, 20xx.

In analyzing the physical adjustment, you are able to find two sets of paired sales. All of the properties within the pairings are detached single-family homes located within the subject neighbourhood.

Paired Sales #1 are Properties C and D which are very similar to each other, except that C has one bathroom and D has two bathrooms. Property C sold for $195,000 on January 7, 20xx and property D sold for $198,000 on January 19, 20xx.

continued...

EXAMPLE *Calculating the Adjustment for Physical Differences (continued)*

Paired Sales #2 are Properties E and F which are very similar to each other, except that E has the use of one bathroom and F has the use of two bathrooms. Property E sold for $209,000 on January 10, 20xx and Property F sold for $212,000 on January 16, 20xx.

How much more would the comparable have sold for if it had two bathrooms instead of one?

Analysis

	PAIR #1	PAIR #2
Sale Price C & E	$195,000	$209,000
Sale Price D & F	$198,000	$212,000
Physical Difference	**$3,000**	**$3,000**

Given the above information, it is estimated that an extra bathroom adds $3,000 to value.

Application To Comparable

Comparable Selling Price	$205,000
Physical Adjustment	+3,000
Physical Adjusted Selling Price	**$208,000**

OTHER METHODS OF CALCULATING PHYSICAL AND LOCATIONAL ADJUSTMENTS

If you are concerned with the reliability of the Paired Sales Method or just are unable to find any acceptable paired sales, you could turn to the Survey Method.

This method of calculating an adjustment follows the premise that the dollar adjustment used should reflect the actions of the buyer. What better way of gauging the actions of buyers than surveying the buyers that have recently bought properties with the very items/components that you need to calculate an adjustment for. In other words, simply ask the buyers what value they attributed to specific items or parts of the house they just bought.

You could do this on a formal basis; i.e., send out a survey which you ask recent buyers to complete and return.

EXAMPLE *The Formal Survey Method*

You are estimating the value of the subject property (Property A) as of today's date.

You are going to use Property B as a comparable. It is a similar detached two-storey home that sold for $198,000. Property B has a 3-year-old gas fireplace in good condition in the living room. The subject property does not have a fireplace. In attempting to quantify the adjustment for a gas fireplace, you look for paired sales. Unfortunately, you cannot find any where the only difference between the properties in the paired sales would be the gas fireplace.

However, you do know that over the past six months 25 properties in the area have sold with a gas fireplace. All of these sales have been detached homes in the $180,000–230,000 price range. Accordingly, you send out the following letter to all 25 owner/buyers:

continued...

EXAMPLE   *The Formal Survey Method (continued)*

Dear _____,

I am studying the effect of gas fireplaces on real estate values. I understand that you recently purchased a home with a fireplace in the living room and would be interested in your opinion. I would very much appreciate it if you would provide me with the following information:

Make and Type of Fireplace: _____

Approximate Age of Fireplace: _____

Condition of Fireplace:

     Excellent: ☐   Good: ☐   Average: ☐   Fair: ☐   Poor: ☐

How much do you think the presence of a fireplace adds to the value of the property?
$_____

Did you have a fireplace in any of your previous homes? _____

Additional Remarks: _____

Would you like the results of my study sent to you at no charge:

     Yes: ☐   No: ☐

I am enclosing a self-addressed stamped envelope for your convenience and would ask you to respond as soon as possible. Should you have any questions about this study, please feel free to call me at my office at (555) 777 4444. Thanking you in advance for your assistance.

Sincerely,
Mary Thomas

Out of the 25 letters you send out, 10 responses are received.

PROPERTY	SALE PRICE	AGE OF FIREPLACE	CONDITION	PRICE PAID
C	189,000	10 years	FAIR	2,000
D	181,000	1 years	GOOD	4,000
E	210,000	4 years	EXCELLENT	4,000
F	220,000	6 years	GOOD	3,000
G	207,000	3 years	AVERAGE	3,000
H	211,000	7 years	AVERAGE	3,000
I	186,000	6 years	GOOD	4,000
J	193,000	10 years	AVERAGE	2,000
K	198,000	8 years	AVERAGE	3,000
L	229,000	4 years	AVERAGE	4,000

Based on the above survey, it looks like purchasers will pay between $2,000 and $4,000 for a fireplace. Given the age and condition of the fireplace in the comparable, you may want to estimate a gas fireplace adjustment as being $4,000.

FINANCING TERMS ADJUSTMENT

If the comparable sold with a significant mortgage having a rate noticeably higher/lower than the market rate as at the date of valuation, then an adjustment may be required. The adjustment is based on the difference between the face amount of the mortgage and the amount the mortgage would actually sell for on the open market.

In order to make this calculation, you will need the use of a *Discounted Mortgage Evaluation Table.* Please note that the *Annual Rate* is the rate of interest actually charged on the mortgage and the *Yield Rate* is the market rate of interest as at the date of valuation (i.e., the current rate).

EXAMPLE   *Calculating the Adjustment for Financing Terms*

In estimating the market value of the subject as of today's date, you find a comparable sale where the seller has taken back a mortgage of $100,000, with an interest rate of 8% per annum, calculated semi-annually not in advance. The mortgage is to run for a 3-year term and the blended monthly payments are amortized over 25 years.

The current rate of interest on this type of mortgage is 10%. The comparable sold for $150,000. *How much less would the comparable have sold for if only financing at market rates had been available?*

	DISCOUNTED MORTGAGE EVALUATION TABLE									
	Per $1,000 Outstanding Principal									
	Annual Rate 8 %					Amortization **25 YRS**				
YIELD RATE	REMAINING TERM IN YEARS									
	1	2	**3**	4	5	6	7	8	9	10
8.00	1000	1000	1000	1000	1000	1000	1000	1000	1000	1000
8.50	995	991	987	984	980	978	975	973	971	969
9.00	990	982	975	968	962	956	952	947	943	940
9.50	986	974	962	953	944	936	929	923	917	912
10.00	981	965	**951**	938	926	916	907	899	892	885
10.25	979	961	945	930	917	906	896	887	879	872
10.50	977	957	939	923	909	896	885	876	867	860
10.75	975	953	933	916	900	887	875	864	855	847
11.00	972	948	927	908	892	877	865	853	844	835
11.25	970	944	921	901	884	868	854	842	832	823

Analysis

The seller on sale of mortgage would receive $951 per $1,000 of mortgage. Therefore, the sale of this mortgage would net the seller $95,100 (100 x 951).

Seller's Loss	$100,000 – 95,100 =	$4,900
Financing Adjustment		**$4,900**

Application To Comparable	
Selling Price of Comparable	$150,000
Less Financing Adjustment	– 4,900
Finance Adjusted Selling Price of Comparable	**$145,100**

Clearly, the seller is losing $4,900 and the buyer is getting an advantage by having payments at an interest rate 2% below current market levels. Accordingly, the seller will want and the buyer should be willing to pay more for the property. Both the listing and selling agent would more than likely be sharing all this information with the seller and buyer of the comparable, and that is why this method of adjustment for financing makes sense. Of course, the only way to really substantiate the adjustment, if any, is to interview the participants to the sale, including the agent. It is ultimately up to the appraiser to decide whether to adjust for the full amount of the discount for the mortgage.

Salespeople use the paired sales or survey method to calculate adjustments everyday without realizing it. Jim and Mary are salespeople, both working for ABC Realty Ltd. Listen to their conversation:

Jim: *Hi Mary. I saw your two bedroom bungalow sold for $10,000 more than mine did at 123 Main Street.*

Mary: *Yes, my bungalow had that finished basement—yours didn't.*

You have just witnessed the paired sales method in action. A finished basement ads $10,000 to value. Take a look at another conversation between Jim and Mary:

Jim: *Hi Mary. What are your buyers paying for a finished basement?*

Mary: *I had a couple who just paid $10,000 more for a bungalow with a finished basement.*

You have just witnessed the survey method. Mary told you what buyers were willing to pay for a finished basement.

RECONCILIATION

After analyzing, comparing and adjusting the selling prices of the comparables used in order to come up with a value for the subject, a number of different but closely aligned adjusted selling prices should emerge. These close but different adjusted selling prices need to be reconciled into one single point estimate of value. In the reconciliation of the Direct Comparison Approach, you need to:

- consider the range in value shown by the adjusted sale prices. This range in value must make sense when compared to the listings that the subject will compete with. It will also be useful in your final conclusions.
- consider which sale is the most recent, as this is one of the best indicators of market conditions at the time of appraisal.
- consider which sale has the fewest adjustments. This means it is the most comparable to the subject property.
- select the sale or sales that best represent(s) the estimated sale price of the subject property, and give that sale (or sales) most weight in selecting the final estimate of value.

Under no circumstance should you average the three adjusted sale prices together and use the average as your estimate. There is no judgement implied in averaging, and it is a discredited practice for the appraisal process.

KNOWLEDGE INTEGRATION

Notables

- There are five steps in the *Direct Comparison Approach*.

- There are 4 essential elements that need to be considered when selecting good comparable sales and listings.

- Good comparable listings assist in telling the appraiser what a property is not worth; i.e., it sets the upper limit of value.

- There are 6 possible, but 3 main types of adjustments that might be required to be applied to comparable sales.

- There are several methods used in order to quantify the percentages or dollar adjustments required to take account of differences between properties.

- Inferior comparables require plus adjustments, superior comparables will require minus adjustments.

- Adjustments are made to the comparables and not to the subject.

- Reconciling the fully adjusted values of a set of comparable sales requires judgment and involves the selection of the best comparable based on the adjustments made.

Chapter Mini-Review

Solutions are located in the Appendix.

1. Adjustments are made to the subject property in order to estimate a value for it.

   ○ True   ○ False

2. One of the essential elements of a good comparable sale is that it should be located within the subject neighbourhood.

   ○ True   ○ False

3. The asking price of a comparable listing would set the lower limit of value.

   ○ True   ○ False

4. One of the methods for calculating time adjustments would be the Time Resale Method, which looks at the difference in selling price of a property that sells and resells over a given period of time.

   ○ True   ○ False

5. Properties used in the Paired Sales Method for calculating adjustments should be as similar as possible to the subject.

   ○ True   ○ False

6. If prices have increased over the past 6 months, a minus adjustment would need to be applied to a comparable that sold 6 months ago.

   ○ True   ○ False

7. When calculating a dollar adjustment for locational differences, the properties being used in the Paired Sales Method should be very similar to each other, except for the locational difference being assessed.

   ○ True   ○ False

8. The more comparable a property is to the subject, the more adjustments you will have to make to that comparable to bring it into line with the subject.

   ○ True   ○ False

9. You will want to avoid using comparables that sold with undue motivation.

   ○ True   ○ False

10. If the comparable is inferior to the subject, then a minus adjustment will need to be applied to that comparable's selling price.

    ○ True   ○ False

Active Learning Exercises

Solutions are located in the Appendix.

■ Exercise 1   Estimates of Value

Based on the following time resales, what is the indicated percentage increase in value per month for the neighbourhood?

- Property A sold on February 4, 20xx for $120,000 and resold on June 6, 20xx for $127,000.
- Property B sold on November 9, 20xx for $126,000 and resold on April 8, the following year for $135,690.
- Property C sold on July 30, 20xx for $120,000 and resold on June 1, the following year for $137,640.

PROPERTY	A	B	C
Sale Price			
Resale Price			
$ Change			
% Change			
Time Difference			
% Change/Month			

■ Exercise 2

You are valuing the subject property as at July 1, 20xx. You have been able to select three comparable sales as follows:

- Sale #1 sold on February 19, 20xx for $72,300
- Sale #2 sold on April 13, 20xx for $73,500
- Sale #3 sold on May 20, 20xx for $76,400

Research of the local real estate board's MLS® monthly average sale price reveals the following:

January 19, 20xx	$71,400	February 19, 20xx	$72,064
March 13, 20xx	$73,002	April 13, 20xx	$73,220
May 20, 20xx	$76,376	June, 20xx	$77,101
July 1, 20xx	$77,161		

Based on the above, what would the time adjustment be in percentages for each comparable sale and what would the time adjusted sale price be for each comparable?

PROPERTY	1	2	3
Average Price (as of sale date)			
Average Price (current)			
$ Change			
% Change			
Comparable Sale Price			
Time Adjusted Sale Price			

Exercise 3

You are being asked to estimate the value of 18 Flutie St. as at April 2, 20xx by analyzing the following information and completing the Direct Comparison Approach sections of the appraisal form provided on the following page.

- The local real estate board's average prices for January 15, February 28 and April 2, 20xx are $198,600, $195,750 and $193,250 respectively.
- An inner lot is worth $5,000 more than a corner lot.
- Each additional 1 foot frontage is worth an extra $1,000.
- A double garage is worth $5,000 more than a single garage.
- Buyers will pay $5,000 more for a property that has a general exterior condition that is rated good as opposed to average.
- People will pay $2,500 more for each extra 50 square feet of above grade living space.
- A third 4-piece bathroom is worth an extra $5,000.
- A 90% finished basement is worth $5,000 more than a 50% finished basement.
- A second fireplace is worth $3,000.

Exercise 3   Standard Appraisal Report—Sales Analysis, Page 1 of 1

Sales Analysis

Item	Subject	Comparable 1		Comparable 2		Comparable 3	
Address	18 Flutie Street	46 Riverside Drive		27 Mainside Rd.		15 Clover Blvd.	
Distance To Subject		2 blocks		1 block		3 blocks	
Date Sold		Feb. 28, 20xx		March 23, 20xx		Jan. 15, 20xx	
Sale Price		$194,000		$210,000		$222,000	
Days On Market		40 days		30 days		45 days	
Time Adjustment							
Time Adjusted Price							
Location	Inner lot	Inner lot		Inner lot		Corner lot	
Lot Size	50' x 120'	45' x 120'		50' x 120'		55' x 120'	
House Style	Detached 2-Storey	Det. 2-Storey		Det. 2-Storey		Det. 2-Storey	
Age of House	9 Years	7 Years		8 Years		10 Years	
Total Sq. Footage	2,500 Sq. Ft.	2,350 Sq. Ft.		2,600 Sq. Ft.		2,650 Sq. Ft.	
Family Room	Yes	Yes		Yes		Yes	
Bedrooms	4	4		4		4	
Bathrooms	3-4pcs., 1-2pc.	2-4pcs., 1-2pc.		3-4pcs., 1-2pc.		3-4pcs., 1-2pc.	
Basement/% Finished	Full/50%	Full/50%		Full/50%		Full/90%	
Rec Room	Yes	Yes		Yes		Yes	
Garage/Parking	Double/Private	Single/Private		Double/Private		Double/Private	
Interior Condition	Average	Average		Average		Average	
Exterior Condition	Average	Good		Average		Average	
Fireplaces	One	One		One		Two	
Total Adjustments							
Totally Adj. Sale Price							

Comments, Reconciliation And Estimate Of Value By The Direct Comparison Approach

Based on the above information and analysis, a value by the Direct Comparison Approach is estimated to be: ($..)

Form 700   2008   **Page 5 of 6**

■ **Exercise 4**

Briefly describe the Direct Comparison Approach and list the basic steps in applying this.

■ **Exercise 5**

Name the four qualities required of a good comparable.

Exercise 6

For each of the following scenarios, indicate whether the required adjustment will be a minus or plus adjustment:

SCENARIO	TYPE OF ADJUSTMENT *PLUS OR MINUS*
The comparable has two fireplaces, whereas the subject has only one fireplace.	
The comparable building has 1,500 square feet in living area, whereas the subject has 1,300 square feet.	
The comparable lacks a garage whereas the subject has a single garage.	
The comparable's lot frontage is 40 feet, whereas the subject's lot frontage is 35 feet.	
The subject has two bathrooms, whereas the comparable only has one bathroom.	
The subject is located backing to a park, whereas the comparable is located backing onto a railway line and paint factory.	

Exercise 7

The subject property is developed with a 9-year-old detached single-family two-storey brick dwelling in good condition. The dwelling has 2,500 square feet in living space with 4 bedrooms and 3 bathrooms, and the lot measures 50' x 120'. This property has a private drive and a double garage.

The MLS® system reveals six sales as follows:

Sale #1	Developed with a 50-year-old detached two-storey fully rented triplex in good condition. The dwelling has 2,700 square feet in living space and the lot measures 30 x 110 feet. This property has a mutual drive and no garage. It sold two months ago and is located 1 block away from the subject.
Sale #2	Developed with an 11-year-old detached two-storey single-family brick dwelling in good condition. The dwelling has 2,650 square feet in living space with 4 bedrooms and 4 bathrooms, and the lot measures 52 x 130 feet. This property has a private drive and a double garage. It sold two months ago and is located three blocks away from the subject.
Sale #3	Developed with a 5-year-old detached two-storey single-family brick dwelling in excellent condition. The dwelling has 2,750 square feet in living space with 4 bedrooms and 3 bathrooms, and the lot measures 55 x 120 feet. This property has a private drive and a triple garage. It sold three months ago and is located one block away from the subject.

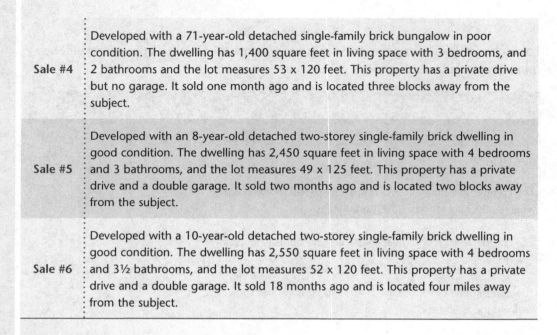

Sale #4   Developed with a 71-year-old detached single-family brick bungalow in poor condition. The dwelling has 1,400 square feet in living space with 3 bedrooms, and 2 bathrooms and the lot measures 53 x 120 feet. This property has a private drive but no garage. It sold one month ago and is located three blocks away from the subject.

Sale #5   Developed with an 8-year-old detached two-storey single-family brick dwelling in good condition. The dwelling has 2,450 square feet in living space with 4 bedrooms and 3 bathrooms, and the lot measures 49 x 125 feet. This property has a private drive and a double garage. It sold two months ago and is located two blocks away from the subject.

Sale #6   Developed with a 10-year-old detached two-storey single-family brick dwelling in good condition. The dwelling has 2,550 square feet in living space with 4 bedrooms and 3½ bathrooms, and the lot measures 52 x 120 feet. This property has a private drive and a double garage. It sold 18 months ago and is located four miles away from the subject.

Which of the above sales would you not want to use as a comparable? Clearly indicate the key reasons for your choices.

■ Exercise 8   Multiple Choice

In this case study, you are being asked to answer seven multiple choice questions based on the information provided.

CASE STUDY FOR QUESTIONS 8.1 TO 8.7

Jim Sandler has been asked to estimate the value of 24 Evans Avenue as at October 8th, 20xx. He has collected the following information and partially completed the Sales Analysis Chart on the next page.

- The local real estate board's average prices for July 10, August 27 and October 8, 20xx are $240,525, $243,725 and $244,900 respectively.

- Buyers will pay $2,000 more for a property that has landscaping that is rated average as opposed to fair.

- Each additional 1 foot frontage of lot is worth an extra $2,000.

- A single garage is worth $5,000.

- Buyers will pay $3,000 more for a property that has a general exterior condition that is rated good as opposed to average.

- Buyers will pay $5,000 more for a property that has a general interior condition that is rated good as opposed to average.

- Buyers will pay $5,000 more for a property that has a general interior condition that is rated average as opposed to fair.

- Buyers will pay $5,000 more for a property with a private driveway as opposed to a mutual driveway.

- Central air is worth $3,000.

- A second four piece bathroom is worth an extra $5,000.

- A 90% finished basement is worth $5,000 more than a 30% finished basement.

- A 30% finished basement is worth $3,000 more than a completely unfinished basement.

- A fireplace is worth $3,000.

You may want to use the Sales Analysis Chart and space below to complete the calculation needed to answer the multiple choice questions that follow.

Sales Analysis

Item	Subject	Comparable 1	Comparable 2	Comparable 3
Address	24 Evans Avenue	200 Evans Avenue	40 Fleming Street	321 Maple Street
Distance To Subject		1/2 block	2 blocks	3 blocks
Date Sold		October 1, 20xx	August 27, 20xx	July 10, 20xx
Sale Price		$235,000	$216,000	$258,000
Days On Market		25 days	30 days	29 days
Time Adjustment				
Time Adjusted Price				
Location	Inner lot	Inner lot	Inner lot	Inner lot
Lot Size	30' x 125'	30' x 125'	29' x 130'	31' x 125'
House Style	Det. Bungalow	Det Bungalow	Det Bungalow	Det Bungalow
Age of House	55 Years	52 Years	56 Years	57 Years
Total Sq. Footage	1,200 Sq. Ft.	1,200 Sq. Ft.	1,200 Sq. Ft.	1,200 Sq. Ft.
Family Room	No	No	No	No
Bedrooms	3	3	3	3
Bathrooms	1 — 4 pc.	1 — 4 pc.	1 — 4 pc.	2 — 4 pc.
Basement/% Finished	Full/30%	Full/30%	Full/0%	Full/90%
Rec Room	Yes	Yes	No	Yes
Garage/Parking	No/Private	No/Private	No/Mutual	Single/Private
Interior Condition	Average	Average	Fair	Good
Exterior Condition	Average	Average	Average	Good
Landscaping	Fair	Average	Average	Average
Central Air	No	No	Yes	No
Fireplaces	One	One	None	One
Total Adjustments				
Totally Adj. Sale Price				

Comments, Reconciliation And Estimate Of Value By The Direct Comparison Approach

Based on the above information and analysis, a value by the Direct Comparison Approach is estimated to be: ($...)

8.1   Calculate the time adjusted price for Comparable #1.

    a.   244,900

    b.   235,000

    c.   240,525

    d.   243,725

8.2   Calculate the time adjusted price for Comparable #2.

    a.   243,725

    b.   219,931

    c.   217,037

    d.   216,000

8.3   Calculate the time adjusted price for Comparable #3.

    a.   258,000

    b.   262,695

    c.   240,525

    d.   259,238

8.4   What would the totally adjusted selling price be for Comparable #1?

    a.   233,000

    b.   237,000

    c.   235,000

    d.   230,000

8.5   What would the totally adjusted selling price be for Comparable #2?

    a.   230,037

    b.   229,000

    c.   204,037

    d.   232,931

8.6   What would the totally adjusted selling price be for Comparable #3?

    a.   231,000

    b.   235,695

    c.   232,238

    d.   262,695

8.7   The final estimate of value for the subject property would be:

    a.   232,000

    b.   230,000

    c.   233,000

    d.   236,000

8.8 In valuing the subject property, you have decided to use a very comparable property that sold last week for $125,000. You discover that the seller took back a second mortgage of $22,000 at an interest rate of 10 per cent per annum, calculated semi-annually not in advance and repayable in blended monthly payments of interest and principal, amortized over 25 years. The mortgage is for a term of 3 years. Current interest rates for this type of mortgage is 8%.

Based on the above information and using the Discounted Mortgage Evaluation Table below, calculate the amount of the dollar adjustment to reflect this STB financing.

a. +1,100

b. −1,100

c. +1,694

d. −1,694

DISCOUNTED MORTGAGE EVALUATION TABLE
Per $1,000 Outstanding Principal

Annual Rate **10%**   Amortization **25 YRS**

YIELD RATE	REMAINING TERM IN YEARS									
	1	2	3	4	5	6	7	8	9	10
8.00	1018	1035	1050	1064	1077	1089	1099	1109	1117	1125
8.50	1013	1026	1037	1048	1057	1065	1073	1080	1086	1092
9.00	1009	1017	1024	1031	1037	1043	1048	1052	1056	1060
9.50	1004	1008	1012	1015	1018	1021	1023	1025	1027	1029
10.00	1000	1000	1000	1000	1000	1000	1000	1000	1000	1000
10.25	997	995	993	992	990	989	988	987	986	985
10.50	995	991	987	984	981	979	976	974	973	971
10.75	993	987	981	977	972	969	965	962	960	957
11.00	990	982	975	969	963	959	954	950	947	944
11.25	988	978	969	962	955	949	943	939	934	931
11.50	986	974	964	954	946	939	933	927	922	918
11.75	984	970	958	947	938	929	922	916	910	905
12.00	982	966	952	940	929	920	912	904	898	893
12.25	979	962	946	933	921	910	901	893	887	881
12.50	977	958	941	926	913	901	891	883	875	869
12.75	975	954	935	919	904	892	881	872	864	857
13.00	973	950	929	912	896	883	872	862	853	846
13.25	971	946	924	905	888	874	862	851	842	834
13.50	969	942	918	898	881	865	852	841	832	823
13.75	966	938	913	891	873	857	843	831	821	813
14.00	964	934	907	885	865	848	834	822	811	802

8.9 The subject property (123 Main Street) is being valued as at 1st July, 20xx. You have found a very good comparable property at 164 Main Street. It sold for $265,000 on April 15th, 20xx. The Anycity Real Estate Board Published Average Selling Prices show as follows:

April 15	$245,730
May 15	$243,840
July 1	$239,750

Based on this information, what time adjustment needs to be applied to 164 Main Street?

a. +6,440
b. −6,599
c. +6,599
d. −6,440

8.10 If the comparable sale is superior to the subject, then:
a. a negative adjustment is applied to the comparable selling price.
b. a positive adjustment is applied to the comparable selling price.
c. a negative adjustment is applied to the subject's value.
d. a positive adjustment is applied to the subject's value.

CHAPTER 7

The Cost Approach

Introduction

The Cost Approach is based on the principle of substitution, which maintains that no prudent purchaser will pay more for a property than the cost of producing or creating an equally desirable substitute, provided there is no delay in making the substitution. In other words, at any point in time, building values cannot rise above their reproduction or replacement cost. This approach is best used when dealing with new or proposed construction when it represents the highest and best use of the site. It is also applicable in estimating the market value of unique or special purpose properties, when sales information is unavailable or scarce.

This approach is rarely used by appraisers as a primary approach to value. *So why is it included in this course?* One of the main reasons is that the banks insist on it being included because they like to see what the ratio of the value of the building to land is. Banks do not like to place residential mortgages on properties that would primarily sell for land value or where the remaining economic life of the building is less than the remaining amortization of the mortgage.

Another reason to include the cost approach is that it teaches you how to value a site. It is not uncommon for an appraiser/salesperson to have a client who is a builder looking to purchase a vacant site or a property purely for its land value. In addition, clients are often asking what houses cost to build or renovate and the cost approach deals with costing a building and its components. It is also important to understand how a building depreciates and how that impacts its value.

Learning Outcomes

At the conclusion of this chapter, students will be able to:

- List the steps in the Cost Approach.
- Explain units of comparison used in site valuation.
- Outline the elements of adjustments to be used in site valuation.
- Describe the different methods of valuing land and estimate land value using the Comparative Sales Method and the Abstraction Method.
- Explain the difference between Reproduction Cost New and Replacement Cost New.
- Describe the different methods used in arriving at a building cost new and estimate the cost new of a building using the Cost Services Method and the Comparative Square Metre Method.
- Describe and explain the different types of depreciation and methods of estimating depreciation.
- Estimate the depreciation of a building and other improvements using the Economic Age-Life Method and the Comparable Sales—Abstraction Method.

THE STEPS IN THE COST APPROACH

In order to value a single-family home by the Cost Approach, follow these steps:

STEP 1   Estimate the land/site value.

STEP 2   Estimate the cost new of the building (including any attached or built-in garage).

STEP 3   Estimate the depreciation of the building (i.e., how much value the building has lost due to its age, functionality and location).

STEP 4   Estimate the current value of the building; i.e., **Current Value = Cost New – Depreciation** (step 2–step 3).

STEP 5   Estimate the Current Value of Other Improvements (Includes detached garage and landscaping); i.e., **Current Value = Cost New – Depreciation**.

STEP 6   Add the current value of the site to the current value (cost new–depreciation) of all the improvements (buildings, garages, landscaping etc.). Ensure the *Indicated Value By Cost Approach* is appropriately rounded.

EXAMPLE   *Summary of Cost Approach*

Your investigation into the value of 27 Anywhere Street by the Cost Approach reveals:

- The subject's land value is estimated at $250,000.

- The subject building is a 60-year-old, 150 square metre, 2-storey home. The cost new of this building is estimated at $1,100 per square metre ($165,000).

- The depreciation of the subject building is estimated at $41,250.

- There is a detached garage where the cost new is estimated at $8,000 with the depreciation at $2,000.

- The cost new of the landscaping is estimated at $25,000, with the depreciation at $10,000.

Given this information, the *Cost Approach To Value Section* of the *Standard Appraisal Report—Single Family* (OREA Form 700) can be completed as follows:

COST APPROACH TO VALUE

Land Value .... $ 250,000

Improvements	Cost New	Depreciation	Current Value	
Building	$ 165,000	$ 41,250	$ 123,750	
Garage	$ 8,000	$ 2,000	$ 6,000	
Landscaping	$ 25,000	$ 10,000	$ 15,000	
	$	$	$	
	$	$	$	
	Total Current Value of All Improvements	$ 144,750		$ 144,750
	Indicated Value by the Cost Approach			$ 394,750
	Value Rounded to			$ 395,000

SITE (LAND) VALUE

Units of Comparison

The selling prices of lots (vacant land/sites) are usually reduced to an appropriate unit of comparison. The unit of comparison to be used is usually determined by the physical attributes of the comparable sites and the subject site, so that standardized comparisons of lots can be made. The appropriate units of comparison can then be applied to individual lots to formulate estimates of value. Ideally, they should represent units in terms of which lots are in fact sold.

The three *Units of Comparison* that can be used in site/land valuation are:

1.	Bulk Sales Price
2.	Price Per Front Foot
3.	Price per Square Foot

BULK SALES PRICE

A Bulk Sales Price means a price per lot. It can be used when all the lots in the particular neighbourhood are approximately the same size and where minor changes in size may not affect market value. Caution is advised in bulk price comparisons as these lack the precision of other units of comparison such as price per front foot/metre or price per square foot/metre. Bulk basis is often viewed as a rule of thumb method, as opposed to a precise method of site valuation.

> **EXAMPLE**   *Bulk Basis—Site Valuation*
>
> Developer Reed is attempting to value a potential development site. According to the preliminary plan, 15 more or less equal lots can be created and no significant differences in value can be attributed. All lots are relatively level with no distinguishing characteristics, views or special value attributed to abutting lands; e.g., parkland. Based on research in the immediate area, lots are being sold for $34,000 each. Therefore, based on a bulk basis valuation, Reed estimates that the potential lots are worth approximately:
>
> $$15 \times \$34,000 = \$510,000$$

PRICE PER FRONT FOOT/METRE

This is a method of comparison that is regularly used with residential lots. The price per front foot/metre conveys no information about the depth or the width of the lot, but is presumed that the rate takes into consideration these other factors. Care must be exercised in using this unit of comparison, since the value of a site may not continue to increase beyond useful frontage. Extra frontage may, in fact, be an indication of excess land leading to a proportionate reduction in unit value.

> **EXAMPLE**   *Price Per Front Foot/Metre*
>
> 123 Main Street is a 10 metre by 70 metre vacant lot that sold for $200,000. The selling price per front metre would be $20,000 (200,000 ÷ 10). The subject site (220 Main Street) is a very similar vacant lot appealing to the same type of buyer except that it is 11 by 70 metres in size. Using the price per front metre of $20,000, the subject would be worth $220,000 (11 x 20,000). Of course, if there were physical or locational differences between the lots, the price per front metre of 123 Main Street would have to be adjusted accordingly.

In the above example it is assumed that the additional 1 metre frontage of the subject offers a proportional increase in value to the lot. If the subject had a frontage of 16 metres, then it may be that you would not be able to use the price per front metre from 123 Main Street as it might not be in that case a truly comparable lot appealing to the same type of buyer.

PRICE PER SQUARE FOOT/METRE

A price per square foot/metre is often used in the valuation of apartment, commercial and industrial sites. This measure has validity when used on lots with shapes and depths that are standard for a specific neighbourhood, but can cause difficulties when lots have excessive depths or unusual shapes, since proportional utility must be considered.

> **EXAMPLE**   *Price Per Square Foot/Metre—Industrial*
>
> Industrial land (unserviced) is selling for approximately $2.00 per sq. ft. The property being appraised is a normal rectangular tract measuring 300' by 300' or a total of 90,000 square feet. The value is estimated to be ($2.00 x 90,000) or $180,000 as the lot was judged typical for the area.

METHODS OF VALUING LAND/SITES

There are two main methods of valuing land/site where the highest and best use of the site would be for a single-family residential home:

1.	The Comparative Sales Method
2.	The Abstraction Method

During each method, we will be using price per front metre/foot as the unit of comparison.

Comparative Sales Method

The comparative sales method estimates value based on a comparison of the site being appraised with the most recent sales of similar sites, preferably in the same neighbourhood. The assumption is made that, if the subject site had been vacant and offered for sale, it would have competed with the comparable site sales and appealed to the same type of buyer.

The Site As If Vacant   CAUTION

Remember that you may be using the Comparative Sales Method to value a site that is vacant or a site that is improved with buildings. If there are improvements on the site, these will have to be ignored for the moment (i.e., until you come to estimating the current value of the improvements later on) and you will need to value the site as if vacant and ready to be put to its highest and best use. If you end up valuing a site that has not been improved to its highest and best use, then those improvements will be depreciated down to zero during the depreciation stage of the cost approach.

STEPS IN THE COMPARATIVE SALES METHOD

1.	Select a sufficient number of good comparable sites that have recently sold in the area.
2.	Gather all necessary data on these sites to make a proper comparison.
3.	Compare each of the sales with the subject for differences that may exist.
4.	Make the necessary adjustments to the sale price of each comparable based on those differences.
5.	Reconcile the adjusted sale price of the comparables into an indication of value of the subject site.

Comparative Sales Method = Direct Comparison Approach   CAUTION

While usually called the Comparative Sales Method when valuing a site, it is basically the same method/approach as the Direct Comparison Approach which was used in the previous chapter for improved properties.

ELEMENTS OF ADJUSTMENTS

It is unlikely that two sites will be identical. There are always going to be some differences. If the differences are significant enough, adjustments will need to be made. Six elements of adjustments are considered when comparing sites to the subject property:

1.	Rights conveyed by the transaction
2.	Financing terms
3.	Motivation of the parties
4.	Market conditions (time)
5.	Location
6.	Physical characteristics

We will only be dealing with the most common adjustments that relate to the final three adjustments—market conditions (time); location; and physical characteristics. The two main methods of showing adjustments are percentages (most common for site valuation) and dollar adjustments. The process of making adjustments under the comparative sales method is essentially the same as used in the direct comparison approach.

The example below shows a completed tabular analysis of adjustments for three site sales. The headings show you the process in arriving at an adjusted value for each comparable site. The reconciliation outlines how the adjusted values lead to an estimate of value. The information of course is made up—please do not spend time trying to figure out where the information came from. In the course exercises, information will be provided to you—in real life you will need to collect and analyze the information yourself.

EXAMPLE   *Site Value Tabular Analysis*

SALE	1	2	3
Front Metre	10.4	10.9	10.3
Sale Price	177,500	181,500	192,000
Sale Price Per F.M.	17,067	16,651	18,641
Time Adjustment	0%	– 4%	–3%
T.A. Sale Price/F.M.	17,067	15,985	18,082
Physical Adjustment	+2%	+3%	+2%
Location Adjustment	0%	+4%	–5%
Total Net Adjustment	+2%	+7%	–3%
Fully Adjusted Sale Price/F.M.	17,408	17,104	17,540

Reconciliation

An adjusted value range of between $17,104 and $17,540 per front metre has emerged from the above analysis. Within this range, most attention has been paid to comparable sale #1, as it is the most recent sale and required only one relatively minor physical adjustment. Its price per front metre is well supported by the other two comparables. Therefore the value of the subject site is calculated as:

10 x 17,408 = $174,080
Rounded To $174,000

Clearly, this is the best method of valuing a vacant site. However, it is dependent on finding at least three recent comparable site sales. This may not be easy, although even in older neighbourhoods, it is very often not uncommon to find old homes being knocked down to make way for modern infill. A comparable site sale can include a property with a house on it, providing the building adds no value to the site and the property is sold with the clear intention that the home is going to be knocked down to make way for a new building. The presence of the old building of course requires a physical adjustment related to the cost of having to tear down the building.

Calculating Adjustments in the Comparative Sales Method

The calculation of adjustments is the same as outlined in the Direct Comparison Approach. There is one exception and that is in the calculation of physical adjustments. For the Comparative Sales Method, it can be the actual cost of the difference that is used in the adjustment; e.g., the subject site has poor drainage, whereas the comparable sale has excellent drainage. A contractor would charge $10,000 to bring the subject site's drainage into line with the comparable. Therefore, the adjustment for physical differences is a minus $10,000, the comparable being superior.

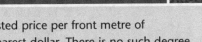
Abstraction Method

This method is used when there is an insufficient number or no comparable site sales in the subject area. The idea for this is simple. First of all, you need to find the sale of properties where the site is similar or the same as the subject site. Then, knowing the sale price of the property, all you need to do is deduct the current value of the improvements. The remaining number or abstracted number should represent the value of the site, providing no adjustments are now needed for differences between the sites, such as location, etc. If there are difference between the sites, you would apply adjustments to the abstracted land value. All of this is easier said than done. The problems occur in estimating the current value of the improvements and the adjustments needed to the abstracted comparable site values. However, if there are no land/site sales, this may be the only method left available to you.

EXAMPLE   *Abstraction Method—Site Valuation*

A developer is marketing new homes as a package that includes the lot and improvements. The buyer wants to establish how much the site is worth at the time of acquiring the property. The site value could be determined as follows:

Total Purchase Price	$187,500
Value of Improvements *(includes house, landscaping, services, etc.)*	−125,000
Value of Site	**$62,500**

The illustration of the Tabular Analysis of the Abstraction Method below shows the steps and adjustments required to use this method. The information of course is made up—please do not spend time trying to figure out where the information came from. In the course exercises information will be provided to you—in real life you will need to collect the information yourself.

EXAMPLE   *Tabular Analysis of the Abstraction Method*

The subject site has a lot size of 10 metres by 35 metres. Given the following sales of properties with similar lots, what is the value of the subject site?

	COMPARABLE #1	COMPARABLE #2	COMPARABLE #3
Address	20 Fleet Street	35 Bread Street	98 Shoe Road
Sale Date	2 Months Ago	1 Month Ago	4 Days Ago
Sale Price	$356,000	$351,000	$360,000
Time Adjustment	+2%	+1%	0
Time Adjusted Sale Price	363,120	354,510	360,000
Building Value	180,000	176,000	182,000
Value of Other Improvements	18,000	16,000	18,200
Land Value	165,120	162,510	159,800
Location Adjustment	0	–5%	0
Physical Adjustment	+2%	+4%	0
Total Net Adjustment	+2%	–1%	0
Fully Adjusted Land Value	168,422	160,885	159,800
Front Metre	10.5	10	9.9
Adjusted Value Per Metre	16,040	16,089	16,141

Reconciliation

An adjusted value range of between $16,040 and $16,141 per front metre has emerged from the above analysis. Within this range, most attention has been paid to comparable sale #3, as it is the most recent sale and required no physical or location adjustments. Its price per front metre is well supported by the other two comparables. Therefore the value of the subject site is calculated as:

10 x 16,141 = $161,410
Rounded To $161,000

ESTIMATING BUILDING COST NEW

While you should always try to estimate the Reproduction Cost New of the building you are valuing, the reality is that you will invariably end up arriving at a Replacement Cost New for the building. However, whatever you do and whatever method of calculating Building Cost New you use, remember that you are still trying to arrive at the Cost New (value) of constructing the exact same subject building. Let's now take a look at the actual difference between Reproduction Cost New versus Replacement Cost New.

REPRODUCTION COST NEW

Reproduction Cost New is the cost of construction, at current prices, of an exact duplicate or replica, using the same materials, construction standards, design, layout and quality of workmanship, while embodying all the deficiencies, superadequacies and obsolescence of the subject building.

REPLACEMENT COST NEW

Replacement Cost New is the cost of construction, at current prices, of a building having utility equivalent to the building being appraised, but built with modern materials and according to current standards, design and layout.

Building Cost New Considerations   MARKET MEMO

Appraisers would theoretically prefer in most instances to use reproduction cost new since it involves a costing of the actual building to be appraised. However, replacement cost new may end up being used, for example, in an older building where the materials used are no longer available and/or when the building suffers from severe forms of obsolescence, such as excessive foundation walls or ceiling heights. In these instances, replacement cost would more easily handle the difficulty of estimating the current costs of materials no longer available and would eliminate the need for estimating the obsolescence due to the super-adequacy. In reality, the decision to use reproduction or replacement cost is the appraiser's responsibility—it will of course depend on the information available. The appraiser just has to keep in mind that:

- The older the building, the more likely the replacement cost new estimate will be used.

- The newer the building, the more likely that the reproduction cost new estimate will be used.

METHODS FOR ARRIVING AT THE BUILDING COST NEW

The two methods we will be using in this course to estimate the RCN (Reproduction/ Replacement Cost New) are:

1.	The Cost Services Method (manuals)
2.	The Comparative Square Metre Method

NOTE: Detached garages and landscaping are valued separately from the main building. Attached or built-in garages will be valued as part of the main building.

Cost Services Method

This is a method of estimating *Replacement Cost* using dollar costs provided by cost service manuals.

Costing manuals provide basic unit costs for a range of building structures of differing qualities. Also included are costs of physical considerations; e.g., fireplace, finished basement and cost differences based on the size and the shape of building. This information is provided in the form of photographs, charts and tables, with supplements provided on a periodic basis. These supplements furnish the necessary time and geographic location adjustments, by way of multipliers, which are then applied to the basic costing manual.

The appraiser's job is to select a structure within the chosen manual that is most similar to the subject property. Physical differences between the subject and the manual's bench-mark structure must be adjusted based on amounts obtained from the manual.

Then, geographic and time differences must be taken care of with the appropriate adjustments supplied by the manual supplements. The cost services method can be an effective method of estimating building costs, provided that the appraiser selects the most comparable building and appropriate adjustments are made. No two buildings are identical, therefore adjustments are likely required and the accuracy of the cost services method depends on the appraiser's choices.

EXAMPLE   *Cost Services Method*

The purpose of this example is to illustrate the steps and headings required in order to arrive at a *cost new* of the subject building.

Base Building Cost	
160 Sq. Meters x $700	$112,000
Area/Shape Multiplier *(the subject shape is less costly than in manual)*	x .98
Adjusted Base Cost	**$109,760**
Add 3rd bathroom *(subject has but not included in the $700)*	+10,000
Add single attached garage *(subject has but not included in the $700)*	+12,000
Deduct central vacuum *(subject does not have but is included in $700)*	–2,000
Fully Adjusted Base Cost	**$129,760**
Location Multiplier *(subject area more expensive than base area)*	x 1.04
Location Adjusted Cost	**$134,950**
Cost Multiplier *(prices have gone up since date of manual)*	x 1.06
Total Reproduction Cost New	**$143,047**

Rounded To $143,000

Types of Manuals   MARKET MEMO

There are a number of published manuals that provide for the costing of buildings and other improvements. Your job is to chose a manual that is recognized, and then select the information (numbers) from that manual that best represents the subject property. What is a recognized manual? Find out what manuals or publications are being used by professional appraisers, contractors, or other experienced salespeople in your area. Your local real estate board may be helpful here.

Comparative Square Metre Method

A method that involves calculating the known cost per square metre (or its imperial equivalent) of a newly-constructed building similar to the subject, and then multiplying this unit cost by the number of square metres in the subject structure. The accuracy of this method depends on the refinements/adjustments made by the appraiser to cover the differences between the properties from which the unit cost is derived and the property being appraised.

It would be incorrect to ascertain the square metre cost of a two-storey house and apply this unit cost as a basis for estimating the cost of a bungalow. It would also be incorrect to apply the square metre cost of an odd shaped one-storey house to estimate the cost of a more conventional structure. To prevent this kind of inaccuracy, the appraiser ensures that the buildings from which a cost estimate is derived are truly comparable to the subject building being appraised, and that all cost estimates are current and apply as of the effective date of the appraisal.

The basic steps in this method are:

1.	Find sales of new homes or properties on which new buildings have recently been constructed and that are as similar as possible to the subject.
2.	Deduct the site value and any other improvements other than the main building from the property selling price; e.g., landscaping, detached garage, etc. This will give you the building cost.
3.	Make any necessary adjustments to the building cost including those for time and physical differences.
4.	Reconcile the adjusted building costs per square metre into an estimated RCN for the subject building.

All of this is illustrated in the tabular analysis below. The table shows the steps to arrive at a value.

EXAMPLE   *Tabular Analysis—Comparative Square Metre*

SALE	SALE #1	SALE #2	SALE #3
Sale Price of Property	$200,000	$218,000	$208,000
Site Value	–90,000	–96,000	–90,000
Value of Outside Improvements	–4,000	–6,000	–3,000
Building Cost	106,000	116,000	115,000
Building Time Adjustment	+4,000	0	0
Time Adjusted Building Cost	110,000	116,000	115,000
Bathroom Adjustment	–3,000	–3,000	–3,000
Quality of Materials Adjustment	–3,000	0	0
Recreation Room Adjustment	0	–5,000	0
Total Net Adjustment	–6,000	–8,000	–3,000
Fully Adjusted Building Cost	104,000	108,000	112,000
Size (m²)	208 m²	215 m²	225 m²
Indicated Cost per Square Metre	**$500.00**	**$502.23**	**$497.78**

Reconciliation

A value range of between $497.78/m² and $502.33/m² has emerged from this analysis. Within this range, most weight has been given to Sale #3, since it requires the fewest adjustments and is a recent sale with no time adjustment. Accordingly, the estimated reproduction cost new of the subject building (with an area of 210 m²), as of the effective date of the appraisal, is calculated as follows:

$$\$497.78 \times 210 = \$104,533 \text{ (rounded to } \$104,500)$$

ADVANTAGES OF THE COMPARATIVE SQUARE METRE METHOD

This method is practical, particularly with new construction, provided that site values (that must be deducted from the sale price of the property) can be accurately estimated.

If you have neighbourhoods in your town where properties are being sold for their land value and new homes are being constructed on them for sale by contractors/builders, then this method can be used. The beauty of this method is that building costs are valid for a town or city and so you do not have to stay in the subject neighbourhood in order to calculate the building cost new using this method. Clearly, the new homes being built have to be similar to your property. The chances are you will still have to make adjustments for differences between the new building being constructed and your property.

Local Contractors	MARKET MEMO

Clearly, if you know or have dealings with local reputable and active contractors in the subject area, then there is no reason why this would not be a valid way to estimate building cost new. When using this method, you would need to get a quote from three contractors, and, as in any other method, you would need the quotes to end up being reasonably close to each other in order to make sense of them.

Reproduction/Replacement Cost New	CURIOSITY

Use the method that you believe gives the most accurate number. That, of course, will be based on your ability to obtain information and the confidence you have in the information. By the way, you would use contractors or a published manual/booklet in estimating individual item costs or the costs of detached garages or landscaping. A contractor or published manual/booklet could extend to a national building supply retailer or an established home inspection company.

CALCULATING THE DEPRECIATION OF A BUILDING

Accrued Depreciation

Accrued depreciation is a loss of value, measured as of the date of appraisal, indicating the difference between reproduction cost new (RCN) or replacement cost new (RCN) of improvements, and the present worth/value of those improvements. Accrued depreciation is sometimes referred to as diminished utility. This loss of value or *diminished utility* of the improvements to real property can be caused by the following types of depreciation:

1.	Physical Deterioration
2.	Functional Obsolescence
3.	Locational Obsolescence

PHYSICAL DETERIORATION

Physical deterioration is a reduction in utility and consequently a loss in value resulting from an impairment of physical condition. Physical deterioration occurs as a result of wear and tear, decay and structural defects. Examples would be worn carpet, flaking of paint, broken window, curling shingles on a roof, kitchen cupboard door off its hinges, etc.

FUNCTIONAL OBSOLESCENCE

Functional obsolescence is a loss in utility and consequently a loss in value, due to the inability of the building, any component part of the structure or any item of equipment to perform in terms of today's standards and requirements. Standards and requirements could refer to the building or any component within it that is outdated, inadequate, unattractive, unappealing, over improved, etc. Examples would be poor floor plan, 60 amp electrical service, new but unattractive carpeting, installation of a $80,000 swimming pool in a home worth only $200,000, etc.

LOCATIONAL OBSOLESCENCE

Locational obsolescence is a loss in utility and consequently a loss in value that a structure incurs as a result of negative environmental forces beyond the boundaries of the property. Examples could be connected to the building being located next to a gas station, car park, nightclub, major highway, etc.

Understanding Specific Terminology

Before proceeding to calculate the depreciation of a building, it is important to understand the terminology surrounding depreciation. Some of the terminology has been addressed in Chapter 5. Nevertheless, some of the information is worth repeating again.

ECONOMIC LIFE OF A BUILDING

The period over which the improvements to a site contribute to the value of the property as a whole. The economic life of a structure refers to the amount of time that a structure (from the day it is built) would be useful or habitable given no renovation, updating or modernization over that time period. Most appraisers would use 50 to 60 years as a rule of thumb for physical economic life. In reality, economic life is estimated by looking at/ researching how long buildings similar to the subject in the same neighbourhood have remained liveable/useful/valuable before they have had to be renovated/modernized or demolished.

REMAINING ECONOMIC LIFE

The estimated number of years remaining in the economic life of a building as from the effective date of the appraisal. You can extend the remaining life of a building (without changing the economic life) by renovating/modernizing it.

ACTUAL AGE

The actual number of years that have passed since a structure was built; also referred to as the chronological age. The actual age of a structure must be differentiated from its effective age for appraisal purposes.

EFFECTIVE AGE

The estimated age in years based on the amount of care and attention a building has received. Care and attention could include renovation and modernization.

If a building has had better than average maintenance, its effective age may be less than its actual age. If there has been inadequate maintenance, it may be greater. A 40-year-old building may have an effective age of 20 years due to rehabilitation or modernization.

Recap of Formulas for Economic Life From Chapter 5   MARKET MEMO

> Economic Life = Effective Age + Remaining Economic Life
>
> Effective Age = Economic Life − Remaining Economic Life
>
> Remaining Economic Life = Economic Life − Effective Age

While in real life the economic life of a building can change, it is usually the one constant in the equation at any given time.

CURABLE AND INCURABLE ITEMS

During the inspection of a building, the component parts of that building (e.g., floors, furnace, roof, etc.) need to be classified into curable and incurable items (components) simply in order to measure the loss in value suffered by that item. The classification of each item (component) will of course depend on the age, condition and general appeal of that component. Curable and incurable can refer to an item that is suffering from either physical or functional obsolescence.

Curable Items

Curable items refer to those components in a building that are economically feasible to cure and therefore customarily repaired or replaced by a prudent property owner or buyer.

The term *curable* is used as it would be economically sound for an owner to correct the physical situation based on repair costs. Curable depreciation can arise either through physical deterioration or functional obsolescence.

> **EXAMPLE**   *Curable Item*
>
> The roof at 123 Main Street has a life expectancy of 20 years and has an effective age of 20 years. In short, the roof is in such bad condition that it requires replacing immediately (i.e., holes in roof, many shingles missing). The roof is clearly going to be a curable item because the typical owner/buyer would replace the roof straight away. The cost of doing so will be offset by the value increase to the property.

Incurable Items

This refers to a component/item that has suffered a loss in value resulting from physical deterioration or functional obsolescence that either cannot be corrected, or can only be corrected at a cost greater than its contribution to the value of the property.

Incurable depreciation applies to items in a structure that are not yet ready to be cured, that cannot be cured, or for which it is not economically sound to cure at this time since the cost of correcting the condition or effecting a cure is greater than the anticipated increase in value. While the correction of a condition may well be physically or technically possible, the criterion is whether or not it is economically sound to cure.

INCURABLE PHYSICAL DETERIORATION (SHORT-LIVED VERSUS LONG-LIVED)
For purposes of appraisal analysis, incurable physical deterioration may be divided into short-lived and long-lived elements.

Short-Lived Items

These are components that are not yet ready to be replaced, but that will require replacement sometime before the end of the remaining economic life of the structure. In other words, their life expectancy is less than the remaining economic life of the building.

EXAMPLE   *Short-Lived Items*

The subject building has an actual age of 30 years, but an effective age of 10 years and an economic life of 60 years. Based on this information, the building has a remaining life of 50 years.

   The carpet in this building has an effective age of 2 years and a remaining life of 6 years (life expectancy of 8 years). Clearly, the carpet will require replacing before the end of the life of the building. As a result, the carpet is considered a short-lived item because its remaining life is less than the remaining life of the building as a whole. Typically, items such as furnaces, roofs, kitchen cabinetry, stoves, fridges, etc., end up as being short-lived items.

Long-Lived Items

These are components that have suffered some physical deterioration but will not require replacement any time during the economic life of the structure.

EXAMPLE   *Long-Lived Items*

The subject building has an actual age of 30 years, but an effective age of 10 years and an economic life of 60 years. Based on this information, the building has a remaining life of 50 years.

   The copper plumbing in this building has an effective age of 30 years and a remaining life of 50 years (life expectancy of 80 years). Clearly, the plumbing will not require replacing before the end of the life of the building. As a result, the plumbing is considered a long-lived item because its remaining life is at least the same as the remaining life of the building as a whole. Typically, items such as foundations, framing, etc., are long-lived items.

METHODS OF ESTIMATING ACCRUED DEPRECIATION

There are a number of methods that can be used for measuring depreciation in a building. They include:

1.	Economic Age-Life Method
2.	Comparable Sales—Abstraction
3.	Economic Age-Life Method Modified
4.	Observed Condition (Breakdown) Method

   You may be asked to measure depreciation using the Comparable Sales—Abstraction Method and/or the Economic Age-Life Method. You will not be asked to measure depreciation using either the Economic Age-Life Method Modified or the Observed Condition (Breakdown) Method. However, it is important for you to understand how the last two methods work so as to give you a good insight into all the forms of depreciation and its impact on the minds of buyers and sellers.

The Economic Age-Life Method

In the Economic Age-Life Method (traditionally referred to as the Age-Life Method), an estimate is made of both the effective age of a building and its remaining economic life. The effective age and remaining economic life together comprise the economic life of the building. The ratio of the effective age to the economic life multiplied by the reproduction/replacement cost of the structure is a measure of the accrued depreciation. The economic age-life method takes physical deterioration into account, but does not measure loss in value due to functional and/or external causes. Accordingly, this approach is often viewed solely as a rule of thumb or cross check for more complex methods.

The formula is **Effective Age ÷ Economic Life x Cost New = Depreciation** (please note that the formula does not say *Remaining Economic Life*. It says *Economic Life* which in essence means *Total Economic Life*).

EXAMPLE   *Economic Age-Life Depreciation Method*

Assume that a building has an actual age of 15 years, an estimated effective age of ten years, a remaining economic life of 40 years and a reproduction cost on the date of the appraisal of $71,150. The accrued depreciation estimated by the age-life method would be as follows:

Effective Age ÷ Economic Life	= 10 ÷ 50
	= 20% or .20
Accrued Depreciation	= .20 x $71,150
	= $14,230

The Comparable Sales—Abstraction Method

The key steps in this method of measuring depreciation is as follows:

1.	Find property sale where the building is comparable and has the same age and condition/appeal as the subject building.
2.	Estimate the RCN of that building and the value of the site and any other improvements.
3.	Deduct the value of the site and any other improvements from the sale price to find the current value of the building.
4.	Deduct the current value of the building from the RCN to provide the depreciation of that building.
5.	Divide the depreciation by the RCN of that building to give a percentage depreciation rate.
6.	Apply that depreciation rate to the RCN of the subject building.

EXAMPLE   *Comparable Sales—Abstraction Method*

You are trying to estimate the depreciation of a 40-year-old, detached 2-storey, 2,000 square foot house in very good condition. Its RCN would be $200,000.

Two weeks ago, a property sold for $375,000. What is interesting about this property is that the house is also a 40-year-old, detached 2-storey home in very good condition. This house is however 2,500 square feet. The property's lot is 35 feet by 140 feet and your analysis shows that the value of the site and the landscaping is $200,000. You know that the RCN of this comparable building would be $100 per square foot, resulting in a total RCN of $250,000. Given this information, you can make the following calculations:

RCN Comparable Building		$250,000
Sale Price of Property	375,000	
Site Value (including landscaping)	200,000	
Current Value of Structure		175,000
Accrued Depreciation		**$75,000**

Accrued depreciation as a percentage = Accrued Depreciation ÷ RCN
Therefore: 75,000 ÷ 250,000 = 30%

Now apply this 30% depreciation rate to the subject building and you will get a depreciation of $60,000 and a current value (cost) of $140,000 as follows:

$$200,000 \times 30\% = \$60,000$$
$$200,000 - 60,000 = \$140,000$$

NOTE: Find 3 or 4 comparables in order to ensure that the depreciation rate you calculate is valid.

The Modified Age-Life Method

A modified measure of depreciation of a property based on the anticipated life of a structure using the economic age-life method.

This modified approach breaks down and measures the depreciation of the physical components of the building structure based on three categories:

1.	Curable Physical Deterioration
2.	Incurable Physical Deterioration—Short-Lived
3.	Incurable Physical Deterioration—Long-Lived

However, as with economic age-life depreciation, the modified method does not take into account either functional and/or external obsolescence. Consequently, appraisers normally use this approach only when it is apparent that the property being appraised is not affected by such factors; or when this method is combined with other techniques that do account for functional and/or external obsolescence.

CURABLE PHYSICAL DETERIORATION
This type of depreciation is measured by the cost to cure.

> **EXAMPLE**   *Measuring Curable Physical Deterioration*
>
> The roof on 123 Main Street is at the end of its life—shingles are missing/broken and there are holes everywhere. The owner would have to pay $15,000 to have the roof replaced—as a result the $15,000 is the measurement of depreciation that has taken place. So, if the RCN of the house was $200,000, you would deduct the $15,000 from that amount.

INCURABLE PHYSICAL DETERIORATION

For purposes of the measurement of depreciation, incurable physical deterioration is divided into short-lived and long-lived elements.

Incurable Physical Deterioration—Short-Lived Items

These items are components that are not yet ready to be replaced but that will require replacement sometime before the end of the remaining economic life of the structure. In other words, their remaining life expectancy is less than the remaining economic life of the building. The depreciation is measured by taking the ratio of the effective age (by observation) of the component to its life expectancy, and applying it to the reproduction cost of the item. Actual age in lieu of effective age could be used for certain components whose ages are more readily discernible than effective age.

> **EXAMPLE**   *Measuring Incurable Physical Deterioration*
>
> The carpet at 123 Main Street has an effective age of 2 years and a life expectancy of 8 years. It is a short-lived item because the carpet would need to be replaced before the end of the life of the building, which has a remaining economic life of 40 years. The RCN of the carpet is $10,000. Therefore, the calculation is as follows:
>
> RCN $10,000 x 2(effective age) ÷ 8 (life expectancy) = **$2,500 depreciation**
>
> Current value of carpet is $10,000 – 2,500 = **$7,500**

Long-Lived Items

These items are components that have suffered some physical deterioration, but will not require replacement during the economic life of the structure. Depreciation is measured by taking the ratio of the effective age of the structure as a whole to its economic life, and applying it to the balance of the reproduction cost; i.e., the total reproduction cost less the reproduction cost of the items considered under curable physical deterioration and incurable physical deterioration short-lived. (The reproduction cost of the curable physical and the incurable short-lived are deducted because these items have already been depreciated).

EXAMPLE   *Incurable Physical Deterioration—Long-Lived Items*

123 Main Street is a 20-year-old house with a remaining economic life of 45 years. It has an effective age of 15 years. If the house had been new, its RCN would have been $300,000.

You have already depreciated parts of the house under Curable Physical Deterioration and Incurable Physical Deterioration—Short-Lived Items. The RCN of the items considered under Curable Physical Deterioration and Incurable Physical Deterioration—Short-Lived Items was $100,000 of the $300,000. In other words, the depreciation of ⅓ of the house has now been looked at with the depreciation actually coming out of the $100,000 being $40,000.

If the RCN of the house is $300,000 and $100,000 of that has been looked at already, it means that $200,000 of the RCN must now be looked at under Incurable Physical Deterioration —Long-Lived Items (remember, you must look at the whole house for depreciation and the whole house is represented by the $300,000 RCN).

Given that the formula for depreciation under Incurable Physical Deterioration—Long-Lived Items is Remaining RCN x Effective Age ÷ Economic Life, the calculation for depreciation here would be:

$$200,000 \times 15 \div 60 = \textbf{\$50,000}$$

The RCN of the whole house was $300,000 and we found $40,000 worth of depreciation under Curable Physical Deterioration and Incurable Physical Deterioration—Short-Lived Items and we found $50,000 worth of depreciation under Incurable Physical Deterioration—Long-Lived Items. Therefore, the current value (cost) of the house would be:

$$\$300,000 - 40,000 - 50,000 = \textbf{\$210,000}$$

The Observed Condition (Breakdown) Method

This is a method of estimating accrued depreciation that separately considers and estimates the deductions for physical deterioration, functional obsolescence and economic obsolescence. These estimates are then added to provide a lump sum deduction from reproduction/replacement cost new. Under this method, accrued depreciation is broken down and measured under the following classifications:

1.	Physical Deterioration—Curable
2.	Physical Deterioration (Short-Lived And Long-Lived)—Incurable
3.	Functional Obsolescence—Curable
4.	Functional Obsolescence—Incurable
5.	External (Economic Or Locational) Obsolescence

We have already looked at how to measure both Physical Deterioration—Curable and Physical Deterioration (short-lived and long-lived)—Incurable. We will now look at how to measure the depreciation of items 3, 4 and 5 above.

FUNCTIONAL OBSOLESCENCE—CURABLE

There are 3 main types of depreciation/deterioration here and they include Deficiency, Modernization and Superadequacy (over improvement). Since the problem of superadequacy can be taken care of by using the Replacement Cost New rather than the Reproduction Cost New, we will only concern ourselves with measuring depreciation due to deficiency and lack of modernization.

Deficiency

This depreciation is measured by deducting the cost new of installing the missing component during construction from the cost new of installing the missing component once the house has been fully finished. It is obviously cheaper to install a second bathroom at the time of construction than it would be to install after the construction is complete. This differential in cost is the measure of depreciation.

Modernization

Depreciation is measured by the cost to cure. It is the cost of the new item to be installed less the current value of the obsolete item.

EXAMPLE *Modernization*

The kitchen cabinets at 123 Main Street have an actual physical age of 20 years. They have been so well maintained that they have an effective physical age of 15 years, with a remaining physical life of 5 years. The RCN of the cabinets are $5,000 and the RCN of the building is $250,000. Physically, the cabinets have been depreciated as an incurable physical short-lived item as follows:

$$5,000 \times 15 \div 20 = 3,750 \ (depreciation)$$

The current value of the cabinets would of course be 5,000 – 3,750 = $1,250.

The problem is that even though the cabinets are physically worth $1,250, a typical purchaser of 123 Main Street would look at the cabinets as being old-fashioned and would want to put in new cabinets anyway. The style of new cabinets being put into houses, such as 123 Main Street would cost $6,000.

The depreciation for the functional obsolescence would therefore be:

$$6,000 – 1,250 = \$4,750$$

FUNCTIONAL OBSOLESCENCE—INCURABLE

There are two types of obsolescence here—deficiency and superadequacy. The problem of superadequacy (over improvement) can be taken care of if you are using the Replacement Cost rather than the Reproduction Cost. Therefore, we will concentrate only on measuring a deficiency. Deficiency under Functional Obsolescence—Incurable items can measured by taking the estimated or actual rental loss arising from the deficiency and multiplying it by the gross income multiplier. (The gross income multiplier is the relationship between the annual rent and the sale price; e.g., sale price $425,000 Annual rent $28,000; GIM is 425,000 ÷ 28,000 = 15.18)

EXAMPLE *Functional Obsolescence—Incurable*

123 Main Street is a 700 square foot bungalow. It has been renovated and is very attractive. However, the only bathroom is in the basement. This is not functionally very appealing and would result in a loss in value to the subject building. The property rents for $1,000 per month.

An investigation of other rentals in the area reveals that if the subject had a bathroom on the main floor, the bungalow would have rented for $50 a month more ($600 a year more). The gross income multiplier is estimated as being 15. Accordingly the accrued depreciation for this deficiency (loss in value) can be estimated as follows:

$$\$600 \times 15 = \$9,000$$

LOCATIONAL (EXTERNAL) OBSOLESCENCE

This type of depreciation is measured by taking the estimated or actual rental loss arising from the locational obsolescence and multiplying it by the gross income multiplier. It is important to remember that the loss actually applies to both the land and to the building. Since the locational obsolescence of the site is already reflected in its estimated market value, only the loss to the building (improvements) must now be charged as depreciation.

EXAMPLE   *Locational (External) Obsolescence*

The subject property is a 40-year-old, 1,200 square foot, 3-bedroom bungalow located next to a gas station. Its location is having a negative impact on value on the property (land and buildings). This property rents for $1,500 per month. Research tells you that had the property been located next to other houses it would have rented for $115 per month more ($1,380 per annum more). The gross income multiplier for the area is estimated at 15 and a market analysis shows that buildings represent about 25% of the value of the property. Given this information, the loss in value (depreciation) can be calculated as follows:

$$\$1,380 \times 15 = 20,700$$

$$\$20,700 \times 25\% = \textbf{\$5,175} \text{ (loss of value to the building)}$$

Other Ways to Estimate Depreciation   PERSPECTIVE

Take a look at the following conversation between Alice (the appraiser) and Janet (the homeowner) regarding measuring depreciation.

JANET   I can see that using the Observed Condition (Breakdown) Method would be the most accurate way of measuring the depreciation in a building when using the Cost Approach to Value. I can also see that the Age-Life Method is much faster, but the problem is being able to accurately measure the effective age of the building. The Comparable Sales—Abstraction Method seems relatively straightforward, although actually finding and isolating the information may not be that easy. Is there some other recognized way of measuring depreciation?

ALICE   You could use published depreciation rates that require you to answer questions on the age and condition of the building and based on your answers provide you with a depreciation rate.

DEPRECIATING OTHER IMPROVEMENTS

In this course you will depreciate a detached garage and the landscaping individually. The formula for depreciating other improvements is:

Reproduction/Replacement Cost New x Effective Age ÷ Life Expectancy = Depreciation

EXAMPLE   *Calculating Depreciation and Current Value of Other Improvements*

ITEM	COST NEW	EFFECTIVE AGE	LIFE EXPECTANCY	DEPRECIATION	CURRENT COST
Concrete Drive	$1,000	15	20	$750	$250
Fencing	$2,000	10	25	$800	$1,200
Wood Deck	$2,000	5	15	$667	$1,333
Sod/Trees	$3,000	N/A	N/A	$0	$3,000
	$8,000			$2,217	$5,783

SUMMARY OF THE COST APPROACH

Once you have completed each of the six steps of the Cost Approach (land value, repro-duction cost new, depreciation, etc.), the estimates of value from each step need to be put together into a summary. We will use the following example to show how the estimates from each step are entered into this summary (taken from page four of the *Standard Appraisal Report—Single Family* (OREA Form 700)).

EXAMPLE   *Summary of Cost Approach*

Your investigation into the value of 57 Anywhere Street by the Cost Approach reveals the following information:

- The subject's land value is estimated at $175,000.

- The subject building is a 50-year-old, 200 square metre, 2-storey home. The cost new of this building is estimated at $1,200 per square metre ($240,000).

- The depreciation of the subject building is estimated at $48,000.

- There is a detached garage where the cost new is estimated at $10,000, with the depreciation at $2,500.

- The cost new of the landscaping is estimated at $35,000 with the depreciation at $12,000.

Given the above information, the Cost Approach To Value Section of the *Standard Appraisal Report—Single Family* (OREA Form 700) can be completed as follows:

COST APPROACH TO VALUE

Land Value .... $ 175,000

Improvements	Cost New	Depreciation	Current Value
Building	$ 240,000	$ 48,000	$ 192,000
Garage	$ 10,000	$ 2,500	$ 7,500
Landscaping	$ 35,000	$ 12,000	$ 23,000
	$	$	$
	$	$	$

Total Current Value of All Improvements $ 222,500 $ 222,500

Indicated Value by the Cost Approach $ 397,500

Value Rounded to $ 398,000

KNOWLEDGE INTEGRATION

Notables

- There are six steps in the cost approach to value.

- Units of comparison are often used when estimating the value of a site.

- There are six possible, but three main types of adjustments that may be required to be applied in a site valuation.

- There are two methods commonly used in valuing land where the highest and best use is a single-family home.

- There is a difference between Reproduction Cost New and Replacement Cost New. Which cost new of a building is actually arrived at will depend on the type of property and information available.

- There are two methods commonly used in estimating the cost new of a single-family home.

- There are many different ways in which a building can depreciate physically and functionally.

- There are several methods of estimating depreciation in a building—however only two methods are commonly used by appraisers of single-family homes; i.e., the Economic Age-Life Method and the Comparable Sales—Abstraction Method.

- The economic life and effective age of a building is used in estimating depreciation using the Economic Age-Life Method.

Solution Strategies

Economic Life = Effective Age + Remaining Economic Life

Effective Age = Economic Life – Remaining Economic Life

Remaining Economic Life = Economic Life – Effective Age

Chapter Mini-Review

Solutions are located in the Appendix.

1. In the Cost Approach to Value, the current value of a building is estimated by deducting the land value from the Reproduction/Replacement Cost New.

    ⭘ True   ⭘ False

2. In the Comparative Sales Method, the selling prices of comparable residential sites are normally reduced to a price per front foot/metres.

    ⭘ True   ⭘ False

3. The Comparative Square Metre Method is an alternative to the Comparative Sales Method in valuing vacant sites.

    ⭘ True   ⭘ False

4. The Comparative Sales Method is the best method for valuing a single-family vacant site providing you have sufficient comparable land sales.

    ⭘ True   ⭘ False

5. One of the steps in the Abstraction Method involves deducting the value of the site and other improvements from the selling price of the comparable in order to arrive at a cost of the building for that comparable.

    ⭘ True   ⭘ False

6. Replacement cost is the cost of construction, at current prices, of an exact duplicate or replica building, using the same materials, construction standards, design, layout and quality of workmanship, while embodying all the deficiencies, superadequacies and obsolescence of the subject building.

    ⭘ True   ⭘ False

7. In the Cost Approach to Value, the Comparative Square Metre Method uses location and cost multipliers to arrive at the RCN of the subject building.

    ⭘ True   ⭘ False

8. If the cost of replacing a roof is offset by the value increase to the property and a typical buyer or owner would in fact make the change, then the roof would be considered a curable item for the purpose of depreciation.

    ⭘ True   ⭘ False

9. For depreciation purposes, a long-lived item is a component of a house that has suffered some functional obsolescence, but would not require replacement before the end of the economic life of the building.

    ⭘ True   ⭘ False

10. Curable physical deterioration is measured by the cost to cure.

    ⭘ True   ⭘ False

Active Learning Exercises

Solutions are located in the Appendix.

Estimating Value Exercises

▣ Exercise 1   Site Valuation

In estimating the value of 46 Huron Street, a site 18m x 36.5m that is situated on a quiet residential street on the east side of the neighbourhood, you locate four reasonably good comparable vacant lots, all sold within the last year.

Two of these lots front on Main Street, a heavily travelled road on the east side of the neighbourhood. A survey of sales indicates that residential lots on Main Street are 5% inferior to similar lots on the quiet residential street nearby, and that lots on the west side of the neighbourhood are 5% superior to those on the east side.

In order to develop a percentage monthly time adjustment, you have located three time resales which occurred within the subject neighbourhood:

Property Resales

Site A sold 10 months ago for $78,000 and resold this month for $85,800.

Site B sold 8 months ago for $92,000 and resold this month for $99,360.

Site C sold 9 months ago for $77,000 and resold last month for $83,160.

The following is the data on the comparable lot sales:

Sale #1: 37 Main Street
18m x 36.5m; sold 5 months ago for $96,000. It was a treed lot, making it 5% superior to the subject. Its location was inferior, being on Main Street.

Sale #2: 26 Lindsay Street
15.25m x 36.5m; sold 4 months ago for $83,000. Located on the west side in a more expensive residential area of the neighbourhood. It was low-lying, making it inferior to the subject by 4% of its sale price.

Sale #3: 47 Main Street
Sold this month for $88,000. Size 16.5m x 36.5m. Its location was inferior to subject.

Sale #4: 87 Jane Street
Sold 4 months ago for $102,000. Size 18m x 36.5m. Located on the west side of the neighbourhood. Had very much the same physical features as the subject.

What is the value of the subject site? Show your adjustments in tabular form. Additional answer space is provided on the following page.

■ **Exercise 1   Site Valuation** (continued)

Monthly Time Adjustment Calculations

Site Value Tabular Analysis

	SALE #1	SALE #2	SALE #3	SALE #4
Front Metre				
Sale Price				
Sale Price Per F.M.				
Time Adjustment				
T.A. Sale Price/F.M.				
Physical Adjustment				
Location Adjustment				
Total Net Adjustment				
Fully Adjusted Sale Price/F.M.				

Reconciliation

■ Exercise 2   Site Valuation

Based on the following comparables located in the same subdivision as the subject, estimate the market value of the subject site as of today. It has a frontage and depth of 17m x 34m and zoned to permit a single-family dwelling. Land values have been increasing by 1% per month over the past 6 months. Show all calculations in the space provided.

Sale #1:
15m x 34m single-family lot sold 5 months ago for $30,000. This comparable is superior to the subject by 5% for location and by 6% for physical features.

Sale #2:
17m x 34m single-family lot sold 3 months ago for $28,600. This comparable is inferior to the subject by 8% for location.

Sale #3:
17m x 34m single-family lot sold 6 months ago for $29,975. Similar to subject in all respects.

	SALE #1	SALE #2	SALE #3
Front Metre			
Sale Price			
Sale Price Per F.M.			
Time Adjustment			
T.A. Sale Price/F.M.			
Physical Adjustment			
Location Adjustment			
Total Net Adjustment			
Fully Adjusted Sale Price/F.M.			

■ Exercise 3   Site Valuation, The Abstraction Method

The subject site has a lot size of 12.25 metres by 44 metres. Given the following information, calculate the value of the subject site.

In order to calculate any price increases, you find the following properties that have sold and resold over the past several months.

Property Resales

Property A sold 8 months ago for $453,000 and resold a few days ago for $547,500.

Property B sold 9 months ago for $465,000 and resold a few days ago for $565,000.

Property C sold 5 months ago for $482,000 and resold a few days ago for $542,000.

Comparable #1

41 Given Way is a property which sold 2 months ago for $518,500. Property prices have clearly risen over the past 2 months. It has a 12 metre by 44 metre lot. The current value of the 6-year-old house on the lot is $325,000 and the current value of the landscaping is estimated to be $18,000. The lot has an inferior location for which a 2% adjustment is required and it is physically superior to the subject for which a 5% adjustment is warranted. The lot appears to be very similar to the subject lot in all other respects.

Comparable #2

31 Cumberland Street is a property which sold 4 days ago for $545,000. It has a 12.2 metre by 44 metre lot. The current value of the 5-year-old house on the lot is $330,000 and the current value of the landscaping is estimated to be $20,000. The lot is physically inferior to the subject for which a 3% adjustment is warranted. The lot appears to be very similar to the subject lot in all other respects.

Comparable #3

4 Ashland Grove is a property which sold 3 months ago for $480,000. Property prices have clearly risen over the past 3 months. It has a 12.5 metre by 44 metre lot. The current value of the 9-year-old house on the lot is $292,000 and the current value of the landscaping is estimated to be $15,000. The lot has a superior location for which a 3% adjustment is required and it is physically inferior to the subject for which a 2% adjustment is warranted. The lot appears to be very similar to the subject lot in all other respects.

Monthly Time Adjustment Calculations

Site Value Tabular Analysis (Abstraction Method)

	COMPARABLE #1	COMPARABLE #2	COMPARABLE #3
Address			
Sale Date			
Sale Price			
Time Adjustment			
Time Adjusted Sale Price			
Building Value			
Value Other Improvements			
Land Value			
Location Adjustment			
Physical Adjustment			
Total Net Adjustment			
Fully Adjusted Land Value			
Front Metre			
Adjusted Value Per Metre			

Reconciliation

◼ Exercise 4   Reproduction (or Replacement) Cost Estimate

You have been asked to appraise a 12-year-old brick bungalow containing 120 square metres, with 6 rooms, 1 bath, unfinished basement and attached garage. The quality of materials and workmanship are typical of the new buildings being built in the neighbourhood. Estimate the reproduction/replacement cost new of this building, based on the following three recently built homes which sold last week.

Sale #1: 37 Applewood Place
A 128 square metre bungalow, sold for $161,000. It had the same features as the subject, except that it had a partly finished basement currently costing $6,000. It was built on a lot having an appraised value of $70,000 at the time this new property sold.

Sale #2: 24 Winding Trail
A 140.93 square metre bungalow, sold for $165,000. It had all the same features as the subject, except that it had an attached carport instead of an attached garage. The savings in building a carport instead of a garage is $2,000. The builder purchased the lot three months ago at the going market price of $68,500. Sale prices of similar lot sales in this area indicate a market price increase of $1,500 per month for each of the last three months.

Sale #3: 16 Chestnut Crescent
Builder Anderson completed construction of this new bungalow and sold the property for $163,000. Other than having air-conditioning which the subject did not have, it had very much the same features as the subject. The air-conditioning involved an additional construction cost of $3,500. This building was the exact same size as the subject. The market value of the site on the date this new property sold was appraised at $76,300. Other (site) improvements were estimated at $2,800, based on replacement cost on the date of sale of the property.

Estimate reproduction/replacement cost new of the subject building in the space provided.

	SALE #1	SALE #2	SALE #3
Sale Price			
Site Value			
Outside Improvements			
Building Cost			
Building Time Adjustment			
Time Adjusted Building Cost			
Basement Finish			
Carport			
Air Conditioning			
Total Net Adjustment			
Fully Adjusted Building Cost			
Size of Building			
Indicated Cost Per Sq. M.			

Reconciliation

■ Exercise 5   Reproduction (or Replacement) Cost Estimate

Based on the use of a cost service manual, estimate the reproduction (or replacement) cost new of a 20 year-old building, given the following information:

The subject is a detached two-storey rectangular shaped brick building of average quality. The ground floor outside measurements are 10 metres x 12 metres and it includes a finished basement of 30 square metres; an attached garage containing 20 square metres; central air conditioning; and a fireplace. The building does, however, lack a second bathroom. The property is located in Uptown, Ontario. The cost services manual you are using has details of a benchmark structure which indicates a $425 cost* per square metre and an area-shape multiplier of 1.078. The manual also indicates that a finished basement adds $150 per square metre; central air conditioning adds $3,000; a fireplace adds $4,000; and an attached garage adds $200 per square metre. The cost of a 2nd bathroom shows as $5,000. A current update of the manual indicates a location multiplier of 1.27 for Uptown Ontario and a cost multiplier for time of 1.13.

* This cost includes the use of a 2nd bathroom, but not the use of a finished basement, garage, central air or a fireplace.

Estimate reproduction or replacement cost new of the subject building in the space provided below:

▣ Exercise 6   Chapter Consolidation

Given the following information, you are to estimate the value of the subject property by completing the Cost Approach To Value section of the *Standard Appraisal Report— Single Family* (OREA Form 700) located at the end of the exercise.

Subject Information

The subject property is a 10-year-old bungalow with outside measurements of 7 metres by 13.11 metres at ground level. It has a lot size measuring 8.5 metres by 30 metres. There is no garage and the basement is unfinished.

Estimating Cost New

Sale #1: 1602 Kingsbank Court

This bungalow sold about one week ago for $190,000. The value of the site on the date that this new property sold, was estimated at $69,000. It had a recreation room which accounts for $4,000 of the current building cost. It had no garage. It had an area of 102.19 m². The outside improvements were estimated at $7,000.

Sale #2: 1301 Princeton Road

A newly built 85.79 m² bungalow sold 6 months ago for $176,000. It had a finished recreation room which accounts for $4,000 of the current building cost. Other site improvements had a value of $8,000 on the date of the sale. Since the date of sale, construction costs have increased by about 1% per month. The site was purchased 10 months ago for $71,000. A market survey of residential vacant site sales in this area indicates that site values have been increasing at approximately $1,000 per month for the last year.

Sale #3: 18 Durie Street

A new bungalow sold last week for $183,000. The estimated value of the site at the time this new property sold was $74,500, and the other (site) improvements were estimated at $9,000. Like the subject property, it did not have a garage. It had an area of 91.31 m².

Estimate the reproduction (or replacement) cost new of the subject building in the space provided below.

	SALE #1	SALE #2	SALE #3
Sale Price			
Site Value			
Outside Improvements			
Building Cost			
Building Time Adjustment			
Time Adjusted Building Cost			
Recreation Room			
Total Net Adjustment			
Fully Adjusted Building Cost			
Size of Building			
Indicated Cost Per Sq. M.			

Reconciliation

Estimate Current Value of Subject Building

The subject building is very well maintained and has enjoyed some renovation and updating. As a result, its effective age has been estimated as being 8 years, with a remaining economic life of 42 years.

Estimate Current Value of Other Improvements (Landscaping)

Information with respect to the subject's other improvements (landscaping) is as follows: The asphalt driveway is effectively 10 years old with a remaining life expectancy of 5 years; the wood deck is effectively 4 years old with a life expectancy of 25 years; the fence is effectively 10 years old with a remaining life expectancy of 40 years.

ITEM	COST NEW	EFFECTIVE AGE	LIFE EXPECTANCY	DEPRECIATION	CURRENT VALUE
Asphalt Driveway	$2,200				
Fencing	$2,800				
Wood Deck	$3,000				
Sod and Trees	$1,500				
Totals					

Estimating Land Value
The subject site has a lot size of 8.5 metres by 30 metres. Given the following sales of properties with similar lots, calculate the value of the subject site.

Comparable #1
19 Hamilton Way is a property which sold 3 months ago for $171,000. Property prices have risen 1% per month over the past 3 months. It has a 8.5 by 30 metre lot. The current value of the house on the lot is $97,000 and the current value of the landscaping is estimated to be $6,000. The lot has an inferior location for which a 1% adjustment is required and it is physically superior to the subject for which a 3% adjustment is warranted. The lot appears to be very similar to the subject lot in all other respects.

Comparable #2
27 Trafalgar Road is a property which sold 1 month ago for $185,000. Property prices have risen 1% per month over the past 3 months. It has a 8.9 by 30 metre lot. The current value of the house on the lot is $108,000 and the current value of the landscaping is estimated to be $5,000. The lot is physically inferior to the subject for which a 2% adjustment is warranted. The lot appears to be very similar to the subject lot in all other respects.

Comparable #3
48 Nelson Boulevard is a property which sold 4 days ago for $180,000. It has a 8.6 by 30 metre lot. The current value of the house on the lot is $99,000 and the current value of the landscaping is estimated to be $9,000. The lot appears to be very similar to the subject lot in all other respects.

	COMPARABLE #1	COMPARABLE #2	COMPARABLE #3
Address			
Sale Date			
Sale Price			
Time Adjustment			
Time Adjusted Sale Price			
Building Value			
Value Other Improvements			
Land Value			
Location Adjustment			
Physical Adjustment			
Total Net Adjustment			
Fully Adjusted Land Value			
Front Metre			
Adjusted Value Per Metre			

Reconciliation

Completion of Cost Approach to Value Section of Appraisal Form Report
Using the information you have already calculated, complete a summary of the Cost Approach on the form provided below.

COST APPROACH TO VALUE

Land Value .... $....................................

Improvements	Cost New	Depreciation	Current Value
Building	$...........................	$...........................	$...........................
Garage	$...........................	$...........................	$...........................
....	$...........................	$...........................	$...........................
....	$...........................	$...........................	$...........................
....	$...........................	$...........................	$...........................

Total Current Value of All Improvements $........................... $....................................

Indicated Value by the Cost Approach $....................................

Value Rounded to $....................................

■ Exercise 7   Case Study—Land Value

There are a number of multiple choice questions at the end of this case study. The questions are based on the information provided below and involve estimating the value of the subject site as of today's date.

The subject site is 10 metres by 38 metres in size.

Site Resales
Site A sold 7 months ago for $195,000 and resold a few days ago for $210,000.
Site B sold 5 months ago for $179,000 and resold a few days ago for $188,000.
Site C sold 4 months ago for $192,000 and resold a few days ago for $199,500.

Land Sale #1
25 Goorien Way sold 5 months ago for $174,000. It had a 9.7 metre frontage by 38 metre depth, with an inferior location on a busy street for which a 3% adjustment is warranted.

Land Sale #2
56 Barrack Road sold for $209,000 3 months ago. This site had a 10.1 metre frontage by 38 metre depth on a superior location backing to a park for which a 3% adjustment was felt warranted. In addition, 56 Barrack Road had a superior appeal in terms of its drainage and soil quality worth about 5% in adjustments.

Land Sale # 3
89 Dayanne Avenue sold for $195,000 about 1 week ago. This site had a 10.2 metre frontage by 38 metre depth. This site was physically inferior due to its more steeply sloping topography for which a 2% adjustment was warranted.

Monthly Time Adjustment Calculations

	LAND SALE #1	LAND SALE #2	LAND SALE #3
Front Metre			
Sale Price			
Sale Price Per F.M.			
Time Adjustment			
T.A. Sale Price/F.M.			
Physical Adjustment			
Location Adjustment			
Total Net Adjustment			
Fully Adjusted Sale Price/F.M.			

Reconciliation

7.1   Calculate the monthly percentage time adjustment indicated by the Site Resale A.
   a.   +1.1%
   b.   −1.1%
   c.   +1.02%
   d.   −1.02%

7.2   What is the fully adjusted sale price per front metre for Sale #1?
   a. $19,400
   b. $18,300
   c. $18,700
   d. $18,800

7.3 What is the fully adjusted sale price per front metre for Sale #2?

    a. $19,609

    b. $21,314

    c. $23,019

    d. $19,228

7.4 What is the fully adjusted sale price per front metre for Sale #3?

    a. $18,600

    b. $19,100

    c. $19,500

    d. $19,700

7.5 What is the estimate of value for the subject site?

    a. $186,000

    b. $195,000

    c. $191,000

    d. $197,000

7.6 Jim Smith is an appraiser who has been asked to value a vacant site at 123 Main Street using the Comparative Sales Method (i.e., comparable land sales). Jim's investigation reveals that 140 Main Street, which sold for $220,000, has a very comparable site, however it is improved with a 1,200 square foot bungalow. Jim can use 140 Main Street as a land sale in the Comparative Sales Method providing:

    a. the home is in poor to average condition and the buyer would consider living in it only for a short until it needs tearing down to make way for a new home.

    b. the intention of the buyer is to tear it down the bungalow in order to construct a new home even though he/she paid extra for the bungalow.

    c. he deducts the estimated depreciation of the improvements from the selling price of the property.

    d. the house does not add value to the site and the intention of the buyer is to tear it down in order to construct a new home.

7.7   In the Abstraction Method of estimating site values, the appraiser needs to know the current value of all the improvements to the comparable site. Why is this information important in this method?

    a. The current value of all the improvements is deducted from the time adjusted sale price of the comparable property in order to arrive at the land value of that comparable.

    b. The current value of all the improvements is added to the time adjusted sale price of the comparable property in order to arrive at the land value of that comparable.

    c. The current value of all the improvements is deducted from the time adjusted sale price of the comparable property in order to arrive at the RCN of that comparable.

    d. The current value of all the improvements is deducted from the time adjusted sale price of the comparable property in order to arrive at the depreciated value of that comparable.

7.8   Which of the following would be a good example of functional obsolescence in a house?

    a. The roof is in very poor shape and needs replacing.

    b. The paint in the bedrooms is flaking and looks in poor condition.

    c. The bungalow's only bathroom is in the basement.

    d. The bungalow is located next to a gas station.

7.9   The subject building is 90 years old. It has an effective age of 25 years and a remaining economic life of 35 years. The RCN of the building is $151,500. What is the amount of the building's depreciation using the Economic Age-Life Method?

    a. $108,214

    b. $63,125

    c. $42,083

    d. $58,917

7.10   The subject building is 20 years old. It has an effective age of 25 years and an economic life of 60 years. The RCN of the building is $225,000. What is the current value of the building using the Economic Age-Life Method?

    a. $150,000

    b. $75,000

    c. $93,750

    d. $131,250

7.11   Under which of the following scenarios would a furnace be depreciated as an incurable physical short-lived item?

   a.   At the date of the appraisal, the subject building has a remaining life of 35 years and the furnace has an effective age of 15 years with a life expectancy of 15 years.

   b.   At the date of the appraisal, the subject building has a remaining life of 35 years and the furnace has an effective age of 5 years with a life expectancy of 15 years.

   c.   At the date of the appraisal, the subject building has a remaining life of 10 years and the furnace has an effective age of 3 years with a life expectancy of 15 years.

   d.   At the date of the appraisal, the subject building has a remaining life of 10 years and the furnace has an effective age of 5 years with a life expectancy of 15 years.

7.12   The subject building at 123 Main Street is a 70-year-old house with an RCN of $180,000. 270 Main Street is a property which sold recently for $550,000. The site value (including landscaping) of 270 Main Street is estimated at $400,000 and the RCN of the building is $200,000. The building on 270 Main Street is very similar to the subject in terms of its age, condition and appeal. Based on this information, the current value of the subject building could be estimated as being:

   a. $135,000

   b. $50,000

   c. $130,000

   d. $150,000

7.13   The subject building at 45 High Street is a 20-year-old house with an RCN of $295,000. 100 High Street sold recently for $800,000. The site value (including landscaping) of 100 High Street is estimated at $560,000 and the RCN of the building is $330,000. The building on 100 High Street is very similar to the subject in terms of its age, condition and appeal. Based on this information, the current value of the subject building could be estimated as being:

   a. $205,000 exactly.

   b. $80,447 rounded to $80,000.

   c. $214,550 rounded to $215,000.

   d. $205,615 rounded to $206,000.

7.14 Based on the following information, what would be the estimated current value of the improvements to the site (i.e., landscaping)?

> The asphalt driveway (cost new $3,000) is effectively 7 years old, with a remaining life expectancy of 11 years; the wood deck (cost new $3,500) is effectively 8 years old, with a remaining life expectancy of 12 years; the wood fence (cost new $4,000) is effectively 5 years old, with a life expectancy of 20 years; the interlocking brick patio (cost new $1,000) is effectively 25 years old, with a life expectancy of 30 years. The cost new of the sod and trees was estimated at $2,500.

   a. $10,178

   b. $9,600

   c.   4,400

   d.   7,924

CHAPTER 8

Concluding the Appraisal Report

Introduction

In many instances, an appraiser will be asked to value a property by both the *Direct Comparison* and *Cost Approach To Value*. However, the client will still expect that a single point estimate of value be given.

The values arrived at by the two different approaches to value should end up being close but will almost never be identical. As a result, the appraiser must now make a choice as to which approach to value yields the more accurate and best supported conclusions. This choice is called Final Reconciliation.

In order to successfully complete a valuation and appraisal report, it is essential to understand and be able to convey to clients all the circumstances, conditions and limitations involved in the valuation process. The general *Assumptions and Limiting Conditions* within an appraisal report on the final page satisfy this requirement. The Certification Statement on the same page provides the client with a level of comfort that the appraisal assignment has been carried out ethically and professionally.

It is also important to enhance your report with documents that are relevant to the appraisal assignment. In addition, because many of your clients will ask you to value their property for sale purposes, it is essential that you understand the significance and relevance of a market driven listing price.

Learning Outcomes

At the conclusion of this chapter, students will be able to:

- Explain the Certification Statement on the final page of the *Standard Appraisal Report—Single Family* (OREA Form 700).
- Outline the attachments necessary to enhance an appraisal report.
- Describe and explain the general Assumptions and Limiting Conditions found on the final page of the *Standard Appraisal Report—Single Family* (OREA Form 700).
- Develop assumptions and limiting conditions to meet specific circumstances.
- Outline the strengths and weaknesses of each of the approaches to value.
- Describe how a final reconciliation is developed to arrive at a final estimate of value.
- Explain the relationship between market value and a suggested list price for the subject property.

THE CERTIFICATION STATEMENT

The Certification Statement on the last page of the appraisal report (illustrated below) sets up the parameters for both the appraiser and the reader of the report as to how, and under what circumstances, the valuation assignment was carried out. The statements are designed to give the reader of the appraisal report confidence that the appraiser completed a thorough, competent and objective valuation, with no undue pressure or influences either toward the property or the people involved in or affected by the appraisal. Here "people" could refer to the client, current owner or prospective owner (a buyer). Take the time to read the certification statement below.

FINAL RECONCILIATION, CERTIFICATION AND FINAL ESTIMATE OF VALUE

Given the nature of the subject property, the level and quality of information, the reliability of the necessary adjustments, and the actions of typical buyers in the subject neighbourhood, most weight has been given to the value arrived at by the .... Approach.

• This valuation and report is subject to the attached assumptions and limiting conditions.

• This valuation and report has been completed in accordance with the Canadian Real Estate Association's Code of Ethics and Standard of Business Practice, as well as the Code of Ethics of the Real Estate and Business Brokers Act.

• I confirm that I personally inspected the subject property and that I have no current or contemplated interest or bias (positive or negative) towards the subject property.

• Unless otherwise detailed in writing within this report, I can confirm that I have no personal relationship or bias (positive or negative) towards any of the parties using or affected by this valuation and report.

• I can confirm that my being employed and paid to complete this valuation is not conditional on the amount of the valuation or on any specific information being included or excluded in this appraisal report.

Therefore, based on a .... day marketing period, a reasonable market value for the subject property as at

................................., 20............. is estimated to be:

.... Dollars ($...)

Appraiser's Signature: ....   Date of Signature: ....

Appraiser's Name: ....   Company: ....
Appraiser's Address: ....   Phone No: ....
....   Fax No: ....
....   E-mail: ....

EXAMPLE   *The Certification Statement As A Guide*

1. Mary Smith, an appraiser, just sold her home at 37 Main Street, Bigtown to a buyer who is seeking a mortgage from Bigtown Bank. Bigtown Bank has asked Mary to appraise the property for the mortgage. Clearly Mary has a vested interest in the subject property and this issue is dealt with by the third statement in the certification.

2. Mary Smith is an appraiser whose sister has just sold 46 Dunn Ave, Bigtown for $250,000. The purchaser is seeking a mortgage from Bigtown Bank who has asked Mary to do the appraisal. Obviously Mary has a personal relationship with her sister who will be affected by the end result of the appraisal and this issue is dealt with by the fourth statement in the certification.

3. Mr Bloggs, the owner of 76 Peterson Blvd, Bigtown, needs an appraiser to value his property at $225,000 in order to get a mortgage. Mr Bloggs approaches Mary Smith and tells her that he will pay $500 for her to do an appraisal if she is prepared to value his property for at least $225,000. This dishonest issue is covered by the fifth statement in the certification.

ATTACHMENTS

Clearly the collection of information, analysis and conclusions in estimating a value are essential to an appraisal valuation. However, you still need to communicate and support your findings and results in writing by way of an appraisal report. A report that paints a clear and concise picture will not only help you make your case but will win the client's confidence.

The following is a list of supporting attachments that should be included in an appraisal report in order to support the value estimate:

NEIGHBOURHOOD MAP
Preferably include a map that shows features such as schools, shopping, parks, railway lines, landmarks etc. Include on this map the location of the subject and comparables used. Highlight negative and positive features shown on the map.

COPIES OF MLS® LISTINGS OF PROPERTIES USED AS COMPARABLES
Attach copies of the *MLS®* listings for each comparable you have used. It is preferable to include those listings that have pictures. By doing this, you are giving the client a more comprehensive background of the comparables used and are allowing him/her to see more easily why they have been included as comparisons to the subject.

PHOTOS
As a minimum, include a photo of the front and rear of the exterior of the home and the interior rooms. Given that a picture is worth a thousand words (and maybe a couple of hours of typing) you should include photos of anything that you think is going to have a significant negative or positive impact on value; e.g., water damage in the basement; a railway line at the rear of the lot; a factory a few doors away from the subject. Photos can save you a lot of time and ensure that the client has a clear understanding of what it is you are taking account of in the valuation.

SURVEY
This is a very important document that not only shows the shape and size of the lot and the location of buildings, but will also show easements and encroachments. Obviously the more recent the survey, the better chance that it will show all the current buildings and improvements.

SITE/BUILDING SKETCH
If there is no survey, you may want to show the client a sketch of the site indicating its shape and size and where the buildings are located. Clearly, this is going to be a *rough*, *approximate* sketch that is for visualization purposes only. The client needs to understand that the sketch should not be relied on for anything else other than a visualization guide. Your sketch of the building should show the exterior shape and dimensions. As with the site sketch, it does not need to be to scale. Obviously the closer to scale it is, the better.

ADDITIONAL INFORMATION/ANALYSIS
Don't feel that your comments have to be restricted or limited by the appraisal form used. If you need to describe something important in detail and it will not fit into the form as is, then attach a separate page at the back of the report while indicating its presence in the appropriate section of the form.

ADDITIONAL ASSUMPTIONS/LIMITING CONDITIONS

You should, at minimum, include the Assumptions and Limiting Conditions as shown below. Of course you should add limiting conditions and assumptions as necessary and determined by the facts of the appraisal.

OTHER

Very often it is a good idea to include other documents that have a bearing on the information you have briefly described in the main part of the appraisal form report. These documents might include one of the following: Zoning By-laws, Lease Agreements, Water Tests, Certificate of Approval for Septic System, UFFI Tests and Architectural Drawings.

Assumptions and Limiting Conditions

ASSUMPTIONS AND LIMITING CONDITIONS

1. This report may not be read or used by anyone other than the client without the written authorization of the appraiser. This report should only be used for the property and purpose identified within it. The appraiser accepts no responsibility or liability should the information contained within this report be used by anyone other than the client (or other authorized user) or for any other purpose or property other than that specified within this report.

2. Values are subject to varying and continual changes in market conditions and neighbourhood factors. Accordingly, the value presented in this report can only be relied on as the value estimated as of the effective date of appraisal specified in this report. Should the user of this report wish to know the value of the subject property as of another date, the appraiser will need to complete an update or a new appraisal report.

3. A search on title and ownership has not been performed. A good title with respect to the subject property has been assumed. Therefore, other than what is noted in this report, the appraiser assumes no responsibility for matters legal in nature that may affect the subject property's title, ownership, marketing or value.

4. Any sketches in this report are included solely for the purpose of assisting the reader in visualizing the property.

5. The appraiser has carried out a visual cosmetic inspection of the subject property only. This inspection and the ensuing appraisal report is not and should not be considered a structural, environmental or mechanical inspection and report. Accordingly, unless stated otherwise in this appraisal report, the appraiser is unaware of any hidden or not apparent structural, environmental or mechanical defects or problems and assumes for the purposes of this report and valuation that there are none. Therefore, should it subsequently become known that there is a structural, mechanical or environmental problem or defect, then the appraiser reserves the right to alter the value given in this appraisal report.

6. This appraisal has been based on the assumption that the subject property is in compliance with the applicable zoning, building codes, by-laws, and environmental regulations. Should this in fact turn out not to be so, the appraiser reserves the right to make any necessary changes to the final estimate of value.

7. This valuation has been based on the assumption that the information collected from industry recognized sources and professionals is in fact correct and can be relied upon for the purpose of this appraisal.

The Assumptions and Limiting Conditions illustrated above are a series of statements that outline for the reader:

- What can or cannot be done with the appraisal report.
- Who can and cannot use the report.
- What is or is not included in the appraisal report.
- How the appraisal report was or was not completed.
- What restrictions were imposed on the appraiser in completing the appraisal report.
- What the reader can and cannot rely on.
- What the appraiser did or did not do to complete the appraisal report.

In other words, Assumptions and Limiting Conditions provide the framework and circumstances under which the appraiser completed the valuation and appraisal report.

The Assumptions and Limiting Conditions illustrated are the minimum statements that should be included in any appraisal report and valuation. Obviously, there may be times some of the statements will need to be altered to reflect the specifics to a particular property. Seek advice before altering any of the statements provided as they may have legal ramifications.

EXAMPLE   *Assumptions and Limiting Conditions—Changing Market Conditions*

You completed an appraisal on the subject (Property A) as at February 3, 20xx. This date is clearly shown in the appraisal report. The valuation was for mortgage purposes and you arrived at an estimate of $275,000. The client, BigBank, gave a mortgage of $200,000 based on your appraisal.

One year later, the owner wanted to refinance her home and needed a $250,000 mortgage. The owner did not want to pay for another appraisal and BigBank decided to use the value estimated in your original appraisal as the current value. Based on that original value, BigBank gives the owner a mortgage of $250,000.

Unfortunately the market has declined by 20% in the intervening 12 months. The mortgage given is actually greater than the value of the property. If the owner of the subject defaults on the mortgage, BigBank may lose considerably as a result of relying on your original estimated value. However, the reader/user of your appraisal report is forewarned by Statement #2. The reality of this situation is that you should not be held responsible for BigBank using an outdated value estimate. You clearly warned the bank of how values are constantly changing and that an updated/new appraisal is required if they wanted a value estimate as of a date other than February 3rd, 20xx.

EXAMPLE   *Assumptions and Limiting Conditions—Relying on Information*

You are valuing the subject (Property A) as at March 24, 20xx. It is a detached two-storey home and the appraisal was requested for mortgage purposes.

You find an identical detached two-storey home (Property B) which according to the MLS® sold for $265,000 on March 20, 20xx. It is a great comparable to use. Of the three sales used, Property B is by far the best comparable. Accordingly, you arrive at a value of $265,000.

A month later you find out that the MLS® had made a mistake and Property B in fact sold for $260,000. Clearly you have over-appraised the subject property. However, the reader/user of your appraisal report is forewarned by Statement #7 which covers and outlines this very point. The reality of the situation in this case is that you used and relied on information from a recognized source (MLS®). As a result you should not be penalized for the mistake made by the MLS®.

EXAMPLE   *Adding a Needed Assumption and Limiting Condition*

You have been asked to appraise the subject property (Property A) for the purpose of mortgage financing for Bigbank (the mortgagee).

Property A is a detached two-storey home with a basement apartment which is tenanted. You have inspected the house except for the basement—the tenant is not being co-operative. The above grade part of the property appears to be in good condition with no observed structural, cosmetic or mechanical problems noted or repairs required. After talking to the owner and Bigbank, you are instructed to value the property without inspecting the basement. You get a description of the basement and foundation from the owner and from a copy of an old listing of the subject.

Clearly, not inspecting the basement limits your ability to complete a full and thorough appraisal. As a result, it is important to convey in the appraisal report what the limitations were and what assumptions you had to make in order to complete a valuation and report. The following is an example which should be included in the appraisal report:

> *I have been unable to gain access and inspect any part of the basement. After outlining the circumstances and implications to BigBank, they have requested that I complete a valuation and report on the assumption that the basement and foundation is as described by the owner and a listing dated 22nd February, 20xx and is in a condition similar to the above grade part of the home, there being no structural, mechanical or cosmetic problems requiring repair. Should the assumptions turn out to be incorrect, then I retain the right to alter this appraisal report and estimated value accordingly.*

Final Estimate of Value

The final estimate of value is an estimate of value made in the appraisal process following the selection of the most appropriate approach to value for the property being appraised and the completion of the final reconciliation.

The final estimate can be given as a single point estimate or range of value. Usually, clients will ask for a single point estimate. However, if a range is requested, it should be realistic as a wide range will not be of practical use. The final estimate of value should be given in rounded, as opposed to exact terms, since the appraisal process uses judgement and experience, and the value given is an estimate only.

Final Reconciliation

A final estimate of value is based on the conclusions of a final reconciliation. Single-family residential homes can use two approaches to value in the valuation process; i.e., the Direct Comparison Approach and the Cost Approach. Commercial properties could also use the Income Approach.

Using two approaches to value will likely result in two different value estimates for the subject. In the final reconciliation, the appraiser will evaluate the strengths and weaknesses of each approach and give more weight to the approach that provides the best indication of value.

The illustration below briefly summarizes the advantages and disadvantages of the three approaches to value. The basic concept of the final reconciliation is to discuss the advantages of the approach you are selecting as your primary approach and the disadvantages of the approach that you are selecting as your secondary but supporting approach.

	ADVANTAGES	DISADVANTAGES
THE COST APPROACH	• People understand it. • Often the only method to use in the appraisal of special-purpose properties. • Relatively easy to make a cost calculation.	• Difficult to estimate depreciation, particularly in older buildings. • While the cost of construction appears relatively easy to estimate, no exact cost figure can be given as several methods yield varying costs. • Construction costs are constantly changing.
THE INCOME APPROACH	• Applicable in estimating the value of investment properties by means of cash flow analysis.	• Difficulty in selecting an appropriate capitalization for direct capitalization (or a discount rate in the case of yield capitalization). • Estimating income and operating expenses can sometimes prove difficult, and a slight error in either estimate is magnified on capitalization. • Of limited use in the appraisal of owner-occupied and/or special-purpose properties.
THE DIRECT COMPARISON APPROACH	• Consumers generally understand and use it. • Avoids various problems associated with estimating and forecasting; e.g., building costs, depreciation, revenues, expenses and cash flows. • Generally accepted by courts and the general public.	• Sometimes difficult to obtain good comparable sales. • Making adjustments for differences in properties requires careful judgement and experience. In some instances, such adjustments are often difficult to support and explain satisfactorily. • Difficult to obtain relevant information relating to each sale, particularly with reference to seller or buyer motivation. • The data is historical in nature.

EXAMPLE   *Final Reconciliation*

The following is a hypothetical final reconciliation and final estimate of value for a single-family residential property:

Two value estimates have emerged as follows:

> Value indicated by Cost Approach $185,000.00
>
> Value indicated by Direct Comparison Approach $180,000.00

The Cost Approach required three separate value estimates (i.e., site value, current building and site improvement costs, and depreciation), and as a result required a significant number of calculations and adjustments. In addition, estimating the current reproduction (or replacement) cost and accrued depreciation of a 25-year-old building, such as the subject, was found difficult to measure and support. Apart from these difficulties, a typical purchaser would likely find it hard to think of a 25-year-old building in terms of reproduction cost new less accrued depreciation. As a result, less weight has been given to this approach, although its use tends to support the value indicated by the Direct Comparison Approach.

The Direct Comparison Approach was found to reflect market behavior, and is most widely used and understood by a typical purchaser for the subject property. Furthermore, this approach required far fewer adjustments with the comparables being relatively recent sales. In addition, the quality of the data left no doubts as to its reliability. Accordingly, bearing in mind the purpose of this appraisal and the type of value required, most weight was given to this approach.

Final Estimate of Value:

Therefore, the market value of the subject property as of [the effective date of appraisal], is estimated to be:

ONE HUNDRED AND EIGHTY THOUSAND DOLLARS ($180,000.00)

Market Value and the Listing Price

The listing price is a key component of the valuation and sale of a property in the marketplace. The closer the list price to market value, the more likely that a higher sale price will be realized within a reasonable period of time. A list price at or close to market value will attract the most number of serious buyers. A heightened demand will usually translate into a higher selling price.

Simply put, a buyer, upon seeing a well priced property, will become anxious to make a good offer before anyone else realizes the property's excellent value. As a result, it will be the seller and not the buyer who will be able to negotiate from a position of strength. Therefore, under normal circumstances, it is very likely that the buyer will pay top price to get the property before anyone else does.

While there are no absolutes concerning listing prices, it is generally recommended that the list price be no more than 2–3% above the estimated value or value range. If the estimated value is $205,000, then perhaps a list price of $209,900 should be recommended. Of course you should also look at your competition in determining the proper listing price.

Often, sellers misunderstand the process of determining a listing price. You can often hear them say *Let's list the property 10% higher just in case we get lucky* or *We need to list the property 10% higher to leave room for negotiations*. In both cases, a listing price 10% higher than the market value could very well be overpricing the seller's property. If the list price is indeed too high, then the seller's property will probably be eliminated by the serious buyers who otherwise would have considered buying it. In fact, serious buyers may either not look at the property at all or will use it to justify buying another property that is much better priced in comparison.

Of course a buyer may still make an offer on an overpriced property. However, in these situations, it is the buyer that will be in a position of strength in the negotiations as he/she will be aware that they will not be in competition for the property. Indeed they may be the only offer that comes along. As a result, they will often be able to negotiate a price at the low end of or below market value (depending on how long the property has been on the market and how frustrated and desperate the seller has become).

Some sellers will counter the argument that the listing price is too high by saying *You can always lower the listing price later.* The problem here is that a property will after a time suffer from the problem of Market Staleness. As the weeks drag on, fewer and fewer buyers will look at the property. Buyers will often ask how long a property has been on the market for and be very suspicious of a property that has been listed for a while. Even where a property is finally realistically listed after nine months of marketing, buyers will make remarks such as *There must be something wrong with the home, its been on the market so long* or *The property has been on the market so long it must be overpriced* or *The property has been on the market so long, the sellers must be desperate.* The end result is often that an overpriced property is on the market longer than necessary and the price received is generally lower than it would have been if it had been listed realistically in the first place.

EXAMPLE   *The Importance of Connecting the Listing Price to the Value*

On March 4, 20xx, you appraised three identical detached two-storey homes (Properties A, B, C) located on the same street with a value range of $220,000–$227,000 and a final estimate of $225,000. The estimates were done for the purpose of listing and selling each home. The homes were all owned by different sellers.

Well priced homes in the neighbourhood are selling within 45 days. All three properties were listed on March 10, 20xx. Property A–$229,900; Property B–$249,900; and Property C–$275,900. Jim Smith is looking to buy a house and is willing to pay up to $250,000 for the right property. Based on his criteria, Jim agrees to look at Properties A and B. Property C does not even come up on the MLS® search as it is above the price that Jim is willing to pay.

After inspecting Properties A and B, Jim realizes that A is a great buy compared to B. As a result he is anxious to make an offer on Property A before other prospective buyers put him into a competitive bid situation. On March 18th, Jim agrees to buy Property A for $227,000 (the top end of your estimated value range) with a 60 day closing. On April 19th, Property B is reduced to an asking price of $229,900 and sells on April 28, 20xx for $222,000 (the low end of your estimated range). On August 30, 20xx Property C is finally reduced to $231,900 and sells on September 20th for $216,000 (below your estimated range of values). Many of the prospective buyers looking at Property C after August 30th were wondering what was wrong for it to be listed so long or were commenting that it must be overpriced to be on the market for such a length of time. The owner of Property C was also becoming frustrated at the lack of showings and offers.

By being well priced from the beginning, Property A sells within a few days for top price. In being overpriced, Property B was *used* to sell Property A. Property B sold fairly quickly once it had been well priced but did not obtain as good a price due to some level of over-exposure. Property C's eventual sale after six months of listing shows the classic signs of being *stale* and was only able to sell below market value given its long listing reputation and the owners frustration.

KNOWLEDGE INTEGRATION

Notables

- The Certification Statement provides the client with confirmation that the appraisal assignment has been carried out ethically and professionally.

- Attachments such as photos, maps and copies of listings support and enhance appraisal reports.

- Assumptions and Limiting Conditions provide the client with the framework and conditions under which the appraisal assignment was carried out.

- It is important to understand the strengths and weaknesses of each approach to value. This assists the appraiser in completing a final reconciliation leading to a final estimate of value.

- A final reconciliation explains to the client which approach to value was given most weight and why.

- Listing prices should be closely aligned to the final estimate of value.

Chapter Mini-Review

Solutions are located in the Appendix.

1. One of the disadvantages of the cost approach is that it is difficult to estimate depreciation particularly in older buildings.

   ○ True   ○ False

2. One of the advantages of the Direct Comparison Approach is that the data is historical in nature.

   ○ True   ○ False

3. The list price should be at least 10% above the estimated value of the subject property.

   ○ True   ○ False

4. One of the advantages of the Direct Comparison Approach is that buyers tend to understand the method and use it.

   ○ True   ○ False

5. In final reconciliation, the appraiser averages the estimates of value from the Cost Approach and the Direct Comparison Approach in order to arrive at a final estimate of value for the subject.

   ○ True   ○ False

6. One of the disadvantages of the Direct Comparison Approach is that it is sometimes difficult to obtain good comparable sales.

   ○ True   ○ False

7. The final estimate of value is shown in an appraisal report in words and figures.

   ○ True   ○ False

8. A typical certificate statement used in an appraisal report would be *"This valuation has been based on the assumption that the information collected from industry recognized sources and professionals is in fact correct and can be relied upon for the purpose of this appraisal"*.

   ○ True   ○ False

9. A typical Assumption and Limiting Condition used in an appraisal report would be *"Values are subject to varying and continual changes in market conditions and neighbourhood factors. Accordingly, the value presented in this report can only be relied on as the value estimated as of the effective date of appraisal specified in this report. Should the user of this report wish to know the value of the subject property as of another date, the appraiser will need to complete an update or a new appraisal report"*.

   ○ True   ○ False

10. A typical certificate statement used in an appraisal report would be *"I confirm that I did not inspect the subject property and that I have a contemplated interest towards the subject property"*.

    ○ True   ○ False

Active Learning Exercises

Solutions are located in the Appendix.

▣ Exercise 1   Multiple Choice

Select the specific certification statement(s) that may conflict with the scenario presented.

1.1   You have been asked to appraise 67 Waterloo Street for the owner who wants to put the property up for sale using your valuation as the basis for the listing price. You are thinking about putting in an offer to buy the property.

   a.   This valuation and report is subject to the attached assumptions and limiting conditions.

   b.   I confirm that I personally inspected the subject property and that I have no current or contemplated interest or bias (positive or negative) towards the subject property.

   c.   Unless otherwise detailed in writing within this report, I can confirm that I have no personal relationship or bias (positive or negative) towards any of the parties using or affected by this valuation and report.

   d.   I can confirm that my being employed and paid to complete this valuation is not conditional on the amount of the valuation or on any specific information being included or excluded in this appraisal report.

1.2   Jim Smith appraised 67 Waterloo Street without actually inspecting the property. He did the valuation quickly by looking at old MLS® listings of the home.

   a.   This valuation and report is subject to the attached assumptions and limiting conditions.

   b.   I confirm that I personally inspected the subject property and that I have no current or contemplated interest or bias (positive or negative) towards the subject property.

   c.   Unless otherwise detailed in writing within this report, I can confirm that I have no personal relationship or bias (positive or negative) towards any of the parties using or affected by this valuation and report.

   d.   I can confirm that my being employed and paid to complete this valuation is not conditional on the amount of the valuation or on any specific information being included or excluded in this appraisal report.

1.3   Jim Smith has been asked to value 67 Waterloo Street for a bank that will put a mortgage on the property based on his appraisal. Jim's sister owns the property.

   a.   This valuation and report is subject to the attached assumptions and limiting conditions.

   b.   I confirm that I personally inspected the subject property and that I have no current or contemplated interest or bias (positive or negative) towards the subject property.

   c.   Unless otherwise detailed in writing within this report, I can confirm that I have no personal relationship or bias (positive or negative) towards any of the parties using or affected by this valuation and report.

   d.   I can confirm that my being employed and paid to complete this valuation is not conditional on the amount of the valuation or on any specific information being included or excluded in this appraisal report.

1.4   Jim Smith is being asked to appraise 67 Waterloo Street. The owner needs a mortgage based on a valuation of $400,000. The owner will only hire and pay Jim a fee of $1,000 if he values the property for $400,000 and doesn't mention the water damage in the basement.

     a.   This valuation and report is subject to the attached assumptions and limiting conditions.

     b.   I confirm that I personally inspected the subject property and that I have no current or contemplated interest or bias (positive or negative) towards the subject property.

     c.   Unless otherwise detailed in writing within this report, I can confirm that I have no personal relationship or bias (positive or negative) towards any of the parties using or affected by this valuation and report.

     d.   I can confirm that my being employed and paid to complete this valuation is not conditional on the amount of the valuation or on any specific information being included or excluded in this appraisal report.

1.5   You are being asked to value a three-acre single-family rural home with a well and septic tank. You have only had experience valuing inner city homes with municipal water and sewage.

     a.   This valuation and report has been completed in accordance with the Canadian Real Estate Association's Code of Ethics and Standard of Business Practice, as well as the Code of Ethics of the *Real Estate and Business Brokers Act, 2002.*

     b.   I confirm that I personally inspected the subject property and that I have no current or contemplated interest or bias (positive or negative) towards the subject property.

     c.   Unless otherwise detailed in writing within this report, I can confirm that I have no personal relationship or bias (positive or negative) towards any of the parties using or affected by this valuation and report.

     d.   I can confirm that my being employed and paid to complete this valuation is not conditional on the amount of the valuation or on any specific information being included or excluded in this appraisal report.

For the following questions, select the specific Assumption and Limiting Condition that covers the scenario being presented.

ASSUMPTIONS AND LIMITING CONDITIONS

1. This report may not be read or used by anyone other than the client without the written authorization of the appraiser. This report should only be used for the property and purpose identified within it. The appraiser accepts no responsibility or liability should the information contained within this report be used by anyone other than the client (or other authorized user) or for any other purpose or property other than that specified within this report.

2. Values are subject to varying and continual changes in market conditions and neighbourhood factors. Accordingly, the value presented in this report can only be relied on as the value estimated as of the effective date of appraisal specified in this report. Should the user of this report wish to know the value of the subject property as of another date, the appraiser will need to complete an update or a new appraisal report.

3. A search on title and ownership has not been performed. A good title with respect to the subject property has been assumed. Therefore, other than what is noted in this report, the appraiser assumes no responsibility for matters legal in nature that may affect the subject property's title, ownership, marketing or value.

4. Any sketches in this report are included solely for the purpose of assisting the reader in visualizing the property.

5. The appraiser has carried out a visual cosmetic inspection of the subject property only. This inspection and the ensuing appraisal report is not and should not be considered a structural, environmental or mechanical inspection and report. Accordingly, unless stated otherwise in this appraisal report, the appraiser is unaware of any hidden or not apparent structural, environmental or mechanical defects or problems and assumes for the purposes of this report and valuation that there are none. Therefore, should it subsequently become known that there is a structural, mechanical or environmental problem or defect, then the appraiser reserves the right to alter the value given in this appraisal report.

6. This appraisal has been based on the assumption that the subject property is in compliance with the applicable zoning, building codes, by-laws, and environmental regulations. Should this in fact turn out not to be so, the appraiser reserves the right to make any necessary changes to the final estimate of value.

7. This valuation has been based on the assumption that the information collected from industry recognized sources and professionals is in fact correct and can be relied upon for the purpose of this appraisal.

1.6   Eliza Smith valued the subject property a year ago for $210,000. The appraisal was done for a bank. The bank now wants to use the same report and value to approve a new first mortgage on the property.

    a.   Assumption and Limiting Condition #1 covers this situation.

    b.   Assumption and Limiting Condition #2 covers this situation.

    c.   Assumption and Limiting Condition #6 covers this situation.

    d.   Assumption and Limiting Condition #7 covers this situation.

1.7   Jim Smith has valued the subject property for the owner who will use the report to obtain a second mortgage. In addition to giving the appraisal report to the bank, the owner also gives the report to a friend. The friend wants to use it to figure out what he should pay for a property similar to the subject located three blocks away.

    a.   Assumption and Limiting Condition #1 covers this situation.

    b.   Assumption and Limiting Condition #2 covers this situation.

    c.   Assumption and Limiting Condition #5 covers this situation.

    d.   Assumption and Limiting Condition #7 covers this situation.

1.8   Six months ago, Eliza Smith completed an appraisal on the subject property. Her report indicated that there were no problems with the property. A month ago, a hidden underground storage tank was discovered. This tank has leaked and contaminated the property's soil and drinking water. The clean up cost will be $40,000.

    a.   Assumption and Limiting Condition #2 covers this situation.

    b.   Assumption and Limiting Condition #5 covers this situation.

    c.   Assumption and Limiting Condition #6 covers this situation.

    d.   Assumption and Limiting Condition #7 covers this situation.

1.9   Jim Smith has based his appraisal on a comparable sale which was reported by the MLS® as being sold for $208,000. It turns out that the comparable actually sold for $212,000.

    a.   Assumption and Limiting Condition #1 covers this situation.

    b.   Assumption and Limiting Condition #5 covers this situation.

    c.   Assumption and Limiting Condition #6 covers this situation.

    d.   Assumption and Limiting Condition #7 covers this situation.

1.10   Eliza Smith has appraised the subject property for $210,000. She has given full value to a large wood deck built at the rear of the building. It turns out that there is no permit for the wood deck and it violates the local zoning by-laws.

    a.   Assumption and Limiting Condition #1 covers this situation.

    b.   Assumption and Limiting Condition #2 covers this situation.

    c.   Assumption and Limiting Condition #5 covers this situation.

    d.   Assumption and Limiting Condition #6 covers this situation.

■ Exercise 2

The subject property has been listed at $249,900 for 90 days. There have been 12 showings, but no offers. Over the past few months, a well-priced property in the subject neighbourhood had sold within 20–30 days, with between 40–50 showings having taken place. Based on the above information, what are you able to say about the subject's listing price?

■ Exercise 3

Name three disadvantages of the Cost Approach and three advantages of the Direct Comparison Approach.

■ Exercise 4   Appraisal Form Completion

TASK 1

Using the information provided below, complete the first three pages of the *Standard Appraisal Report—Single Family* (OREA Form 700) provided on the following pages. For information that should be entered into the comments sections in the form, you may put "*See Attached*" rather than write out the comments.

Janet Fields is the owner and occupant of 25 Landsend Drive, Anycity, ON, M1X 9Z0, phone number: 453-888-9708, fax number: 453-888-9709, and e-mail jfields@orea.com. Janet is thinking of selling her home and would like to know what it is currently worth before she lists the property for sale. Janet calls and engages Mike Leung, an MVA with ABC Realty Inc., to complete the appraisal using the *Standard Appraisal Report—Single Family* (OREA Form 700). The Appraisal reference is 112/xx.

Mike inspects the property on the July 15th, 20xx (also being the effective date of appraisal). His investigation reveals that the legal description of the subject property is Part Lot 534 Plan 212, City of Anycity, Regional Municipality of Anyregion. The tax assessment is $305,000 and the taxes for the year 20xx (this year) are calculated as being $3,702. The zoning is R1 Single-Family Residential with the existing use being the highest and best use. The property last sold four years ago for $290,000 after being on the market for 78 days. The current typical exposure time to sell a property on the subject street and in the neighbourhood in general is between 30 to 60 days. As of the date of appraisal the supply and demand is in balance and as a result property values are currently stable. The subject property is not listed for sale.

Mike has collected the following information and data on the neighbourhood in which Janet Field's property is located. You are to take the information and complete the Neighbourhood Information section of the form provided. The subject property is located within a 100% developed residential neighbourhood that can be described as prestigious. The area trend is considered stable with homes selling from around $250,000–650,000 in the neighbourhood and between $300,000–600,000 for homes on the subject street itself. The age range for the typical property in the area and on the street is 50 to 60 years. The subject is typical for the area and the adjoining homes are comparable. The distance to the elementary school, secondary school, public transit, shopping, downtown and recreational facilities are 2 blocks, 3 blocks, 1 block, 2 blocks, 2 miles and 1 block respectively.

General comments on the neighbourhood are as follows: The subject is located in an older well-established neighbourhood that appeals to the middle to upper middle income segment of the population. Its popularity lies in a well-maintained quality housing stock, quiet-tree lined streets and proximity to downtown Anycity. A rail track and light industry are located a short distance to the south, but do not appear to have any significant negative impact on the subject area's desirability. 95% of the properties are owner occupied with a 5% tenancy rate. In terms of new construction activity, some of the older frame bungalows have been replaced by modern quality 2-storey infills. In essence the overall appeal/rating of the neighbourhood can be regarded as good to excellent.

Mike has collected the following information and data on the subject site. You are to take the information and complete the Site Information section of the form provided. The subject site has an inner lot location and is 11 x 45 metres deep, with a total area of 495 square metres. It has a rectangular shape with a topography that is even. The site appeal is considered as average. The subject street is municipal, paved and has sidewalks and curbs. There are storm and sanitary sewers, with the water being municipal. Utilities also include hydro, gas, telephone and cable. Street lighting and over-ground wiring is present. There are no registered easements or encroachments. There is a private paved driveway with an attached single car garage. Landscaping includes sod, trees, flower beds and a small interlocking brick patio. Comments on the subject site are as follows: The subject site is located on the south side of a quiet residential street giving the backyard good exposure to sunlight. The lot is standard in terms of its size, shape, topography and condition.

Mike has collected the following information and data on the improvements. The subject property is a detached 55-year-old, 105 square metre bungalow with a 21 year effective age. The economic life of a building such as the subject would be 60 years. It has a brick veneer exterior finish with an asphalt shingle roof and concrete block foundation. The windows are a combination of single and thermal pane with wood frame and vinyl material. The construction quality and exterior condition and appeal were seen to be average with no evidence of UFFI. The floor plan consists of a recreation room, laundry room and a 2-piece washroom in the basement with three bedrooms, 4-piece bathroom, a living room, dining room and kitchen on the main level. The room sizes are medium. The kitchen and bathrooms are considered outdated, although the closets are adequate. There is a full basement that is 50% finished. The flooring is a combination of hardwood and vinyl tile, and the walls/ceilings being a mixture of drywall, plaster and tile. The heating is forced air gas and the plumbing has copper and plastic piping. There is a 100 amp circuit breaker electrical system. The floor plan and interior condition are average. There is one fireplace. The chattels staying with the property are a hot water tank, fridge, stove, washer, dryer, central air conditioning, humidifier and dishwasher. No equipment or chattels are leased and there are no special features to mention.

For general comments on improvements, the following could be said: The subject is a solidly built home that has been well maintained and has enjoyed a moderate amount of updating and modernization over the years, including the installation of a new air conditioning unit one year ago, a new hot water tank two years ago, a new electrical service three years ago and five new double glazed windows four years ago. The kitchen and bathroom/washroom are somewhat outdated and this will be reflected in the Direct Comparison Approach adjustments when compared to other properties. Although the insulation is inadequate, this is quite common in the area for homes of the subject's age and accordingly no adjustments will be made for this. The subject is considered to be average for the neighbourhood in both condition and overall appeal.

Exercise 4   Task 1: Standard Appraisal Report—Single Family, Page 1 of 6

Standard Appraisal Report
Single Family

OREA Ontario Real Estate Association

Form **700**
for use in the Province of Ontario

CLIENT: .... Client Ref No: ....

Client: Phone No: (............)................................... Fax No: (............)................................... E-mail: ....

Client's Customer: .... Appraiser: .... Appraiser's Ref No: ....

GENERAL APPRAISAL AND PROPERTY INFORMATION

Property Address: ....

Municipality: ....

Full Legal Description: ....

Owner: .... Assessment: Total .... Taxes $ .... Year ....

This Appraisal is to estimate **MARKET VALUE** for a: ☐ Sale   ☐ Financing   ☐ Other ....

Effective Date of Appraisal: .... Date of Inspection: ....

Highest and Best Use is: ☐ Current   ☐ Other (*) ....

Zoning: .... Occupancy: ☐ Homeowner   ☐ Tenant   ☐ Vacant

SUBJECT & MARKET HISTORY

Subject Last Sold	**Subject Currently Listed**	**Property Values**	**Demand/Supply**
Date:	☐ Yes ☐ No	☐ Stable	☐ In Balance
Sale Price: $	Current List Price $	☐ Increasing	☐ Under Supply
Days on Market:	Days On Market	☐ Decreasing	☐ Over Supply

Typical Exposure Time Required for Properties to Sell in Subject Neighborhood is: ....

Typical Exposure Time Required for Properties to Sell on Subject Street is: ....

NEIGHBOURHOOD INFORMATION

Type		**Trend**	**Subject For Area is**	**Adjoining Homes**
☐ Rural	☐ Prestige	☐ Improving	☐ Comparable	☐ Comparable
☐ Residential	☐ Average	☐ Stable	☐ Superior *	☐ Superior
☐ Commercial	☐ Starter	☐ Declining	☐ Inferior	☐ Inferior
☐ Industrial				

Neighbourhood is: ....% Developed

Distance to

Elementary School	....	Age Range of Typical Property in Neighbourhood: .... to .... Years
Secondary School	....	Age Range of Typical Property on Subject Street: .... to .... Years
Public Transit	....	
Shopping	....	Price Range of Properties on Subject Street: $.................................. to $..............................
Downtown	....	
Recreational Facilities	....	Price Range of Properties in Neighbourhood: $.................................. to $..............................

Comments: (include any positive or negative factors that will have a measurable impact on the subject's marketability and value - items with an * should be discussed) ....

....

....

....

Form 700   Revised 2008   **Page 1 of 6**

SITE INFORMATION
Utilities & Services

Street
- [ ] Paved
- [ ] Municipal
- [ ] Sidewalks
- [ ] Street Lighting
- [ ] Underground Wiring
- [ ] Aboveground Wiring

- [ ] Gravel
- [ ] Private
- [ ] Curbs

Drainage
- [ ] Open Ditch
- [ ] Sanitary Sewer
- [ ] Other ....

- [ ] Storm Sewer
- [ ] Septic Tank

Water
- [ ] Municipal
- [ ] Cistern
- [ ] Other ....

- [ ] Private Well
- [ ] Shared Well

Utilities
- [ ] Hydro
- [ ] Gas
- [ ] Telephone
- [ ] Cable

Site Dimensions: ....   Encroachments: [ ] Yes*   [ ] No

Total Site Area: ....   Easements: [ ] Yes*   [ ] No

Site Shape: ....

Topography: Lot in relation to street grade: [ ] Even   [ ] Above   [ ] Below

Parking
Driveway
- [ ] Laneway
- [ ] Private
- [ ] Mutual
- [ ] Other ....

- [ ] None
- [ ] Paved
- [ ] Gravel

Garage (Indicate # of cars):
- [ ] Attached # ....
- [ ] Detached # ....
- [ ] Built In # ....
- [ ] Carport # ....

Site Appeal
- [ ] Excellent
- [ ] Good
- [ ] Average

- [ ] Fair*
- [ ] Poor*

Landscaping Includes: ....
....
....

Comments: (include any positive or negative factors that will have a measurable impact on the subject's marketability and value - items with an * should be discussed) ....
....
....

INFORMATION ON IMPROVEMENTS (BUILDINGS)
Building Type:
- [ ] Detached
- [ ] Semi-detached
- [ ] Attached Row
- [ ] Other ....

- [ ] High Ranch
- [ ] Apartment
- [ ] Split

- [ ] 1 Storey
- [ ] 1 1/2 Storey
- [ ] 2 Storey
- [ ] 3 Storey

Sq. Ft. (Above Grade)
Level 1 ....   Level 4 ....
Level 2 ....   Level 5 ....
Level 3 ....
Total ....

Actual Age ....Years   Effective Age ....Years   Total Economic Life ....Years

Exterior Finish
- [ ] Brick Veneer
- [ ] Solid Brick
- [ ] Stucco
- [ ] Alum. Siding
- [ ] Other ....

- [ ] Vinyl Siding
- [ ] Wood Siding
- [ ] Solid Stone
- [ ] Artificial Stone

Roof Material
- [ ] Asphalt Shingle
- [ ] Cedar Shake
- [ ] Metal
- [ ] Other ....

- [ ] Wood Shingle
- [ ] Slate
- [ ] Tar & Gravel

Foundation
- [ ] Poured Concrete
- [ ] Concrete Block
- [ ] Brick
- [ ] Stone
- [ ] Preserved Wood
- [ ] Other ....

Window Type
- [ ] Single
- [ ] Other: ....

- [ ] Thermal

- [ ] Wood Frame   [ ] Aluminum   [ ] Vinyl

Evidence of UFFI   [ ] Yes *   [ ] No

Construction Quality   [ ] Excellent   [ ] Good   [ ] Average   [ ] Fair   [ ] Poor*

Exterior Condition/Appeal   [ ] Excellent   [ ] Good   [ ] Average   [ ] Fair   [ ] Poor*

Exercise 4   Task 1: Standard Appraisal Report—Single Family, Page 3 of 6

INFORMATION ON IMPROVEMENTS (INTERIOR)

Rooms	Living	Dining	Kitchen	Family	Beds	Bath	Wash	Rec	Other
Basement									
Main									
Second									
Third									

Room Sizes   ☐ Large   ☐ Medium   ☐ Small

Additional Information on Room Sizes (Optional): ....
....
....

Kitchen
☐ Modern
☐ Average
☐ Outdated

Bathrooms
☐ Modern
☐ Average
☐ Outdated

Closets/Storage
☐ Excellent
☐ Adequate
☐ Inadequate

Basement
☐ None
☐ Full
☐ Partial

☐ Crawl Space
% Finished ....

Floors
☐ Carpet
☐ Hardwood
☐ Vinyl Tile
☐ Ceramic
☐ Other ....

Walls/Ceilings
☐ Drywall
☐ Plaster
☐ Panelling
☐ Tile
☐ Other ....

Heating
☐ Forced Air
☐ Hot Water
☐ Baseboard
☐ Other ....
....

Fuel
☐ Gas
☐ Oil
☐ Electricity
☐ Other ....
....

Plumbing
☐ Copper
☐ Plastic
☐ Lead
☐ Galvanized
☐ Other ....

Electrical
☐ Fuses
☐ Circuit Breakers
Amps ....

Floor Plan
☐ Excellent   ☐ Good   ☐ Average   ☐ Fair   ☐ Poor*

Interior Condition
☐ Excellent   ☐ Good   ☐ Average   ☐ Fair   ☐ Poor*

Equipment/Built-Ins/Chattels Remaining With Property:
☐ HWT   ☐ Fridge   ☐ Central Vac   ☐ Wood Stove   ☐ Elect Air Cleaner
☐ Central Air   ☐ Washer   ☐ Humidifier   ☐ Hood   ☐ Garburator
☐ Heat Pump   ☐ Dryer   ☐ Security System   ☐ Oven   ☐ Water Purifier/Filter
☐ Stove   ☐ Dishwasher   ☐ Dehumidifier   ☐ Range   ☐ Central Intercom
☐ Fireplace(s) ....
☐ Other: ....

Equipment/Chattels Leased or Rented
....
....

Special Features
....
....

Comments: (include any positive or negative factors that will have a measurable impact on the subject's marketability and value - items with an * should be discussed) ....
....
....
....

PRINCIPLES OF APPRAISAL

TASK 2

Using the information provided in *Task 1* and below, complete both the required calculations and the Cost Approach section on page 4 of the *Standard Appraisal Report—Single Family* (OREA Form 700) found at the end of this chapter.

Building Cost New And Depreciation

You use a well known Cost Services Manual which supplies the following information:

A detached brick bungalow with 3 bedrooms costs $750 per square metre. This cost includes central vacuum, but does not include the use of a single attached garage, central air conditioning, a fireplace or a recreation room and 2 piece washroom in the basement.

- A basement recreation room adds $350 per square metre. The basement rec room is 22.04 sq. metres.
- The area/shape/size of the subject requires a multiplier of 1.02.
- A fireplace adds $5,500.
- A basement 2-piece washroom adds $4,000.
- Central air adds $3,800.
- Central vacuum adds $1,090.
- Single garage adds $7,000.
- There is a cost multiplier of 1.05 for Anytown.
- There is a location multiplier of .98 for Anytown.
- The manual suggests a depreciation for the building of 35%.

Calculate the RCN of the building in the space provided.

Current Value of Building

From information calculated from the Building Cost New and Depreciation exercise, you are able to calculate the building value.

Calculate the current value of the building.

Current Value of Other Improvements

From information provided by three local landscaping contractors, you estimate the:

Cost New of the subject's landscaping to be as follows.

- Concrete Driveway $3,000
- Interlocking Brick Patio $1,200
- Sod and Trees $2,500

The concrete driveway is effectively 15 years old with a life expectancy of 40 years and the interlocking brick patio is effectively 10 years old with a 40 year life expectancy.

Calculate the current value of the other improvements.

ITEM	COST NEW	EFFECTIVE AGE	LIFE EXPECTANCY	DEPRECIATION	CURRENT COST
Totals					

Land Value

You are able to find 3 good comparable site sales and three good site time resales as follows.

Site Resales:

- Site A sold 5 months ago for $260,000 and resold 3 days ago for $285,000.
- Site B sold 8 months ago for $225,000 and resold 5 days ago for $260,000.
- Site C sold 3 months ago for $240,000 and resold 8 days ago for $255,000.

Land Sale #1   25 Marton Way sold 2 months ago for $216,000. It had a 10.75 metre frontage by 45 metre depth, but had an inferior shape and steeply sloping topography for which a 5% adjustment warranted.

Land Sale #2   56 Warton Road sold for $242,000 3 months ago. This site had an 11.25 metre frontage by 45 metre depth on a corner location for which a 2% adjustment was felt warranted. However, 56 Warton Road had a superior appeal in terms of its drainage and soil quality worth about 4% in adjustments.

Land Sale #3   89 Parton Avenue sold for $245,000 about 1 week ago. This site had an 11 metre frontage by 45 metre depth. This site was more appealingly located, backing onto a park for which a 2% adjustment was warranted.

Calculate the estimated value of the subject site.

TASK 3

Using the following information, complete the Direct Comparison Approach section on the *Standard Appraisal Report—Single Family* (OREA Form 700) found on the following page and finalize the appraisal of 25 Landsend Drive. To facilitate the exercise, the information on competitive listings has already been included on the form.

Comparable #1

Address: 250 Landsend Drive; distance to subject – *1/2 block*; days on market – *45*; date sold – *20th April, 20xx*; sale price *$305,000*; location – *inner lot*; lot size – *11 metres by 46 metres*; house style – *detached bungalow*; age of house – *50 years*; total square footage – *115 square metres*; family room – *no*; bedrooms – *3*; bathrooms – *1-4pce*; basement – *full*; % basement finished – *50%*; recreation room – *yes*; driveway – *private*; garage – *none*; interior condition – *good*; exterior condition – *average*; central air conditioning – *yes*; fireplace – *none*; flooring – *carpet and vinyl tile.*

Comparable #2

Address: 18 North End Road; distance to subject – *1 block*; days on market – *35*; date sold – *4th July, 20xx*; sale price *$320,000*; location – *inner lot*; lot size – *11 metres by 45 metres*; house style – *detached bungalow*; age of house – *55 years*; total square footage – *106 square metres*; family room – *no*; bedrooms – *3*; bathrooms – *1-4pce*; basement – *full*; % basement finished – *50%*; recreation room – *yes*; driveway – *private*; garage – *single attached*; interior condition – *average*; exterior condition – *average*; central air conditioning – *no*; fireplace – *one*; flooring – *hardwood and vinyl tile.*

Comparable #3

Address – 114 Evans Road; distance to subject – *2 blocks*; days on market – *50*; date sold – *13th May, 20xx*; sale price *$345,000*; location – *corner lot*; lot size – *12 metres by 47 metres*; house style – *detached bungalow*; age of house – *53 years*; total square footage – *115 square metres*; family room – *no*; bedrooms – *3*; bathrooms – *2-4pce & 1-2piece*; basement – *full*; % basement finished – *50%*; recreation room – *yes*; driveway – *private*; garage – *single attached*; interior condition – *very good*; exterior condition – *average*; central air conditioning – *yes*; fireplace – *one*; flooring – *hardwood and vinyl tile*.

Comparable Sales Analysis

Based on the paired sales and time resale method together with the survey method, the following adjustment amounts are required;

- From April, 20xx to July, 20xx, prices have gone up 2.8%.

- From May, 20xx to July, 20xx, prices have gone up 1.38%.

- Corner lots are worth $5,000 less than inner lot locations.

- Properties with 12 metre frontages are worth $5,000 more than homes with 11 metre frontages.

- Single attached garages add $5,000 to the value of a home.

- Each additional 5 square metres of living space is worth an extra $1,500.

- An additional 2-piece washroom is worth $3,000, while an additional 4-piece bathroom is worth $2,000 more than an additional 2-piece washroom.

- Central air is worth $2,000.

- A fireplace is worth $4,000.

- A home where the interior is in good condition is worth $7,000 more than a home where the interior is in average condition.

- A home where the interior is in very good condition is worth $15,000 more than a home where the interior is in average condition.

- The presence of hardwood floors will add $3,000 to a home.

TASK 4

Complete the Final Reconciliation and Certification (page 6) of the *Standard Appraisal Report—Single Family* (OREA Form 700). Create any information necessary to fully complete this page of the appraisal report including the attachments.

COST APPROACH TO VALUE

Land Value .... $..............................

Improvements	Cost New	Depreciation	Current Value
Building	$............................	$............................	$............................
Garage	$............................	$............................	$............................
	$............................	$............................	$............................
	$............................	$............................	$............................
	$............................	$............................	$............................

Total Current Value of All Improvements $............................ $............................

Indicated Value by the Cost Approach $............................

Value Rounded to $............................

DIRECT COMPARISON APPROACH
Competitive Listings

Item	Subject	Listing #1	Listing #2	Listing #3
Address	25 Landsend Dr.	90 Landsend Dr.	40 North End Rd.	150 Landsend Dr.
Distance To Subject		1 block	1 block	1/2 block
Original List Price		$369,000	$365,000	$379,000
Current List Price		$339,000	$349,000	$355,000
Original List Date		05/06/xx	10/06/xx	19/05/xx
Date Price Last Revised		30/06/xx	13/07/xx	01/07/xx
House Style	Detached Bungalow	Detached Bungalow	Detached Bungalow	Detached Bungalow
Lot Size	11m x 45m	11m x 47m	11m x 46m	12m x 48m
Building Size	105 sq. m.	107 sq. m.	115 sq. m.	115 sq. m.
Age	55 years	51 years	55 years	55 years
Condition	Average	Average	Average	Average
Beds	3	3	3	3
Baths	1	1	1	2
Basement	Finished	Finished	Finished	Finished
Listing is: Inferior/Similar/Superior		Similar	Superior	Superior

Comments:

Exercise 4   Task 3: Standard Appraisal Report—Single Family, Page 5 of 6

Sales Analysis

Item	Subject	Comparable 1	Comparable 2	Comparable 3
Address				
Distance To Subject				
Date Sold				
Sale Price				
Days On Market				
Time Adjustment				
Time Adjusted Price				
Location				
Lot Size				
House Style				
Age of House				
Total Sq. Footage				
Family Room				
Bedrooms				
Bathrooms				
Basement/% Finished				
Rec Room				
Garage/Parking				
Interior Condition				
Exterior Condition				
Total Adjustments				
Totally Adj. Sale Price				

Comments, Reconciliation And Estimate Of Value By The Direct Comparison Approach

....
....
....
....
....
....
....

Based on the above information and analysis, a value by the Direct Comparison Approach is estimated to be: ($..)

Form 700   Revised 2008   **Page 5 of 6**

FINAL RECONCILIATION, CERTIFICATION AND FINAL ESTIMATE OF VALUE

Given the nature of the subject property, the level and quality of information, the reliability of the necessary adjustments, and the actions of typical buyers

in the subject neighbourhood, most weight has been given to the value arrived at by the .... Approach.

- This valuation and report is subject to the attached assumptions and limiting conditions.
- This valuation and report has been completed in accordance with the Canadian Real Estate Association's Code of Ethics and Standard of Business Practice, as well as the Code of Ethics of the Real Estate and Business Brokers Act.
- I confirm that I personally inspected the subject property and that I have no current or contemplated interest or bias (positive or negative) towards the subject property.
- Unless otherwise detailed in writing within this report, I can confirm that I have no personal relationship or bias (positive or negative) towards any of the parties using or affected by this valuation and report.
- I can confirm that my being employed and paid to complete this valuation is not conditional on the amount of the valuation or on any specific information being included or excluded in this appraisal report.

Therefore, based on a .... day marketing period, a reasonable market value for the subject property as at

................................., 20............. is estimated to be:

.... Dollars ($...)

Appraiser's Signature: ....   Date of Signature: ....

Appraiser's Name: ....   Company: ....

Appraiser's Address: ....   Phone No: ....

....   Fax No: ....

....   E-mail: ....

ATTACHMENTS

☐ Neighbourhood Map   ☐ Additional Information/Analysis: ....
☐ Copies of MLS Listing/Sales   ☐ Additional Assumptions/Limiting Conditions: ....
☐ Site/Building Sketch   ....
☐ Photos   ☐ Other: ....
☐ Survey   ....

ASSUMPTIONS AND LIMITING CONDITIONS

1. This report may not be read or used by anyone other than the client without the written authorization of the appraiser. This report should only be used for the property and purpose identified within it. The appraiser accepts no responsibility or liability should the information contained within this report be used by anyone other than the client (or other authorized user) or for any other purpose or property other than that specified within this report.

2. Values are subject to varying and continual changes in market conditions and neighbourhood factors. Accordingly, the value presented in this report can only be relied on as the value estimated as of the effective date of appraisal specified in this report. Should the user of this report wish to know the value of the subject property as of another date, the appraiser will need to complete an update or a new appraisal report.

3. A search on title and ownership has not been performed. A good title with respect to the subject property has been assumed. Therefore, other than what is noted in this report, the appraiser assumes no responsibility for matters legal in nature that may affect the subject property's title, ownership, marketing or value.

4. Any sketches in this report are included solely for the purpose of assisting the reader in visualizing the property.

5. The appraiser has carried out a visual cosmetic inspection of the subject property only. This inspection and the ensuing appraisal report is not and should not be considered a structural, environmental or mechanical inspection and report. Accordingly, unless stated otherwise in this appraisal report, the appraiser is unaware of any hidden or not apparent structural, environmental or mechanical defects or problems and assumes for the purposes of this report and valuation that there are none. Therefore, should it subsequently become known that there is a structural, mechanical or environmental problem or defect, then the appraiser reserves the right to alter the value given in this appraisal report.

6. This appraisal has been based on the assumption that the subject property is in compliance with the applicable zoning, building codes, by-laws, and environmental regulations. Should this in fact turn out not to be so, the appraiser reserves the right to make any necessary changes to the final estimate of value.

7. This valuation has been based on the assumption that the information collected from industry recognized sources and professionals is in fact correct and can be relied upon for the purpose of this appraisal.

CHAPTER 9

Other Property Types—
Standard Condominiums

Introduction

Condominiums have, over the past ten years, become an important part of the housing stock, especially in the larger urban areas. This trend is expected to continue, especially as the baby boomer bulge continues to age. There are some important differences between condominiums and single-family homes and they impact the legal, physical and locational information that is required to complete the valuation on this type of property.

While the buyer of a unit within a condominium building/complex takes ownership of the fee simple (freehold) of that unit itself, the buyer becomes a tenant in common with all the other owners of units in the condominium with respect to the common elements; e.g., hallways, gardens, underground garage, recreational facilities etc. As a result, the Cost Approach has no place in valuing an individual condominium unit. The appraiser looks purely to the Direct Comparison Approach. While some aspects of appraising a condominium unit are easier and quicker than appraising a single-family home, there are other aspects that can make it more difficult. Inspecting a 900 square foot unit and obtaining sales within the condominium unit does not usually take a lot of time, however floor level and exposure differences between the subject and comparables can sometimes be a serious challenge for the appraiser in terms of finding out and proving what is more desirable or valuable as a location.

Learning Outcomes

At the conclusion of this chapter, students will be able to:

- Describe what specific information is required for condominiums as opposed to single-family homes.
- Describe the specific sources of information for collecting information on condominiums.
- Estimate the value of a condominium unit.
- Explain how to value a condominium unit when there are no comparable sales within the condominium complex.

VALUING A CONDOMINIUM AS OPPOSED TO A SINGLE-FAMILY FREEHOLD

All the rules, discussions, comments, advice on collecting information, analyzing it, reaching conclusions and supporting those conclusions from the market place are just as valid for condominiums as they are for single-family freehold properties. However, it should be noted that some information needed for single-family freehold properties are not needed or do not hold the same relevance or importance for condominiums, and vice versa. To see the type of information needed to be collected on a condominium unit, take a look at the *Standard Appraisal Report—Condominium* (OREA Form 701) reproduced at the end of this chapter.

Collecting Information

As mentioned before, much of the information required for a single-family freehold property is very similar or identical to that required for a condominium. However there is some information which is particular to and commonly required for condominiums and that includes:

- the name and background of the property management company;
- the condition and appearance of the common elements;
- the monthly maintenance fees and what they include;
- details of any lawsuits against or on behalf of the condominium;
- details of any proposed or approved Special Assessments;
- the amount of money held in the Reserve Fund;
- whether parking and locker spaces are owned, rented, assigned or common element exclusive use; and
- what amenities or facilities are available to the unit holders.
- number of units in the building, exposure/view and floor number (level).

PROPERTY MANAGEMENT

Given that a condominium is generally managed and looked after by an external property management company, it is important to assess the quality and effectiveness of that management. That assessment can be undertaken by a physical inspection of the complex, the minutes of owner's meetings, the financial statements and by talking to unit owners. Clearly if a complex is not being well run, this may very well impact on value. Conversely, if the condominium is being well looked after, this will more than likely impact positively on value.

MAINTENANCE FEES

It is important to find out what monthly maintenance fees are being paid and what is included. The amount of maintenance fees is going to depend on the number of amenities included, what utilities and services are paid for by the condominium corporation, the size of the unit, the number of units in the complex and how well the condominium is being cared for.

If the subject condominium corporation has high maintenance fees relative to other similar complexes with comparable amenities, then the value of units within that subject condominium may be negatively impacted. The converse will be true if the maintenance fees are comparatively low.

SPECIAL ASSESSMENTS

Part of the monthly maintenance fee is put into the reserve fund. The reserve fund is meant to take care of replacing the depreciated items of a condominium's common elements; e.g., roof, replacing hallway carpets, resurfacing the driveway etc. However, a number of things can happen that may require a special assessment. These could include:

- the building is poorly managed and the reserve fund is not adequate to take care of items that would normally be expected to be repaired over the course of several years;
- an unexpected major structural problem may occur which is expensive to correct; and/or
- the residents may decide to significantly upgrade the building in terms of facilities or decorations/renovations.

Depending on the size of the special assessment and the reason for its requirement, buyers may be put off purchasing a condominium with a special assessment or may require a deep discount of the selling price. Clearly a special assessment can have an impact on value.

EXAMPLE 1   *The Impact of Special Assessments*

Six months ago, selling prices in the subject condominium ranged from $200,000–300,000. Five months ago, significant water damage to the building structure and envelope was discovered. A structural engineers report revealed that $1.5 million worth of repairs would be required to rectify the problem.

Two weeks ago, an owner's meeting was called and a special assessment of $30,000–50,000 for each unit was proposed. This assessment would probably have to be paid for within the next six months.

Listing prices in the subject condominium now range between $165,000–235,000. General prices of condominiums in the area have been stable over the past several months. Clearly this special assessment is having a significant negative impact on value. After all, a purchaser buying today might be responsible for paying the special assessment amount just to put the building back into the condition it should have been in the first place. In addition, the purchasers might still be at risk for further assessments if the repairs do not work. Of course there will always be the nuisance factor during the repair period.

Once the assessment is actually paid and the work is done, prices may return to their previous levels providing the complex does not earn a poor reputation or retain a stigma.

EXAMPLE 2   *The Impact of Special Assessment*

Six months ago, prices in the subject condominium ranged from $175,000–275,000. Four months ago, it was decided to upgrade the hallways with higher quality new carpeting and wallpaper. The cost of these renovations will be $300,000. At a special meeting three weeks ago, it was proposed and approved that a special assessment of $900 to $1,200 be levied against each unit to pay for these upgrades. The assessment will become due to be paid within the next six months and if required can be paid in monthly installments over a six-month period.

A quick analysis of selling prices over the past three weeks indicate that the price range of $175,000–275,000 for units within the subject complex has not changed despite the approved special assessment. Prices within the general condominium market have remained stable over the past several months.

It appears that buyers treated the special assessment as an improvement to the appeal of the complex and therefore its value. Accordingly, the buyers see this as a benefit. Once the renovations have been completed and all the assessments paid, the price range in the subject condominium complex may increase as a result.

ADDITIONAL SOURCES OF INFORMATION

Sources of information detailed in the *Site*, *Building* and *Neighbourhood* units also apply to condominiums. However, given the particular physical nature of condominiums with its different legal and financial obligations, you will need to collect information by using the following additional resources.

- Property Manager; e.g., the monthly maintenance fee and what is included.
- Condominium Declaration and Rules; e.g., whether owners can have pets and how many.
- Condominium Declaration; e.g., whether the parking and locker space is owned/assigned/rented/exclusive use.
- Reserve Fund Study; e.g., the condition of building and what repairs will be needed in the near future. Need for a special assessment or significant increase in maintenance fees.
- Financial Statements; e.g., the state of the finances and whether a special assessment may be needed.
- Annual General Meetings; e.g., how the residents feel the building is being managed.
- House Rules; e.g., what residents are or are not allowed to do.
- Status Certificate; e.g., amount of maintenance fees, special assessments, number of leased units.

METHODS OF VALUING A CONDOMINIUM UNIT

Given that a condominium unit is only a portion of the improvements of the condominium complex/building and that ownership of the common elements; e.g., hallways, gardens, recreational areas etc. is owned jointly with many other people, the cost approach is not a viable method of valuation. As a result, the Direct Comparison Approach is the only method of valuation for a single unit within a condominium complex/building.

The process/principles and steps in using the Direct Comparison Approach apply equally the same to single-family homes as well as condominium units.

| *Lack of Sales in the Subject Condominium Complex* | PERSPECTIVE |

Alice and Nathan are both salespeople working for ABC Realty Ltd. Nathan is a fairly new salesperson who is about to go on a listing presentation of a building where there have been no sales in the past 11 months. Listen to the advice that Alice, an experienced salesperson, gives to Nathan with respect to estimating a value under these circumstances.

NATHAN   What would you do if you were valuing a condominium unit with comparable listings, but no sales in the past 11 months.

ALICE   There are three steps that I would take:

- Investigate the listings in terms of activity or offers.
- Use a comparable sale in the subject condominium, making any time or other adjustments necessary to bring the sale to today's date in terms of selling price.
- Look for recent sales of comparable units in other similar condominium complexes within the area.

Based on all three steps, I should be able to accurately estimate a value for the subject unit.

EXAMPLE

You are valuing the subject condominium unit (Property A) as of today's date. It is a 1,350 square foot, 2-bedroom, 2-bathroom apartment on the 12th floor of a 20-storey, 190-unit building (Building 1). The last sale in Building 1 was 14 months ago when an identical 2 bedroom unit (Property B) on the 13th floor sold for $224,000. Your analysis of the condominium market indicates that prices have increased by 10% over the 14 months. There is a listing of a very similar 2-bedroom unit (Property C) in the subject building that has been priced at $269,900 for the past 60 days. Well-priced condominium units would sell within 30 to 60 days. There have been no offers on this listing.

You are able to find another high rise condominium building (Building 2) located in the general area that has had a number of recent sales. Building 2 is similar to Building 1 but is considered to be in a slightly superior condition with a marginally more appealing location. Your research (pairing sales between the two buildings on a per square foot basis) suggests a $10,000 adjustment for location and condition between the two buildings. Within Building 2 there have been three very recent sales (Properties D, E and F) of 2-bedroom, 2-bathroom, 1,400 square feet units. These units are almost identical to the subject except that they are slightly larger units. Properties D, E and F sold for $260,000, $265,000 and $275,000 respectively. An $8,000 adjustment is felt to be adequate to take care of the size difference.

Clearly, with no recent sales in the subject condominium building (Building 1), you will as a last resort need to use the sales of Properties D, E and F in Building 2 as comparables. It will of course be essential to compare not only the comparable units to the subject unit, but also the comparable building to the subject building. Comparing the buildings will not be easy and will require very careful research and a lot of judgement. Based on the above and after necessary adjustments ($18,000), Properties D, E and F will have adjusted values of $242,000, $247,000 and $257,000 respectively. In support of this value range for the subject, you can look at the listing (Property C) and the old sale in the subject building (Property B). Property C clearly tells you that the subject unit is worth somewhat less than $269,900. Using a 10% increase in condominium prices as a guide, Property B would suggest a current value of $246,000 that is in line with the adjusted values of the comparable sales used. Using all the information gathered, a value for the subject property of between $242,000 to $252,000 would not seem unreasonable or indefensible.

A blank *Standard Appraisal Report—Condominium* (OREA Form 701) is provided in *Chapter 1*.

KNOWLEDGE INTEGRATION

Notables

- Appraising a condominium requires the collection and analysis of information that in a number of instances is different to that required for single-family homes.

- A number of the sources of information will be different for a condominium, as opposed to a single-family home.

- The cost approach is not applicable in the valuation of a condominium unit.

- An appraiser needs to be able to identify comparable buildings when there are no or not sufficient relevant sales and listings in the subject building/complex.

Chapter Mini-Review

Solutions are located in the Appendix.

1. Information concerning the financial health of a condominium can be found in the Condominium Declaration.

   ◯ True   ◯ False

2. If there are no comparable sales to be found in the subject building, it is acceptable to find comparable sales in a similar building located within the subject neighbourhood.

   ◯ True   ◯ False

3. A special assessment needed to make necessary building repairs would normally have a negative impact on value.

   ◯ True   ◯ False

4. One of the questions that an appraiser needs to ask with respect to a condominium's parking space is whether it is owned in joint tenancy or tenancy in common.

   ◯ True   ◯ False

5. One of the questions that needs to be asked by an appraiser with respect to the reserve fund is the date as to when a reserve fund study was last completed.

   ◯ True   ◯ False

6. The lot size of the standard condominium unit is an important piece of information that needs to be considered by an appraiser when estimating the value of that unit.

   ◯ True   ◯ False

7. It is important to know the economic life of a condominium unit in coming up with an estimate of value of the property.

   ◯ True   ◯ False

8. In valuing a condominium unit, it is important to know the exposure and floor level of the subject, as well as the comparable sales being used, as this can affect values.

   ◯ True   ◯ False

9. In valuing a condominium, it is not important to know what the maintenance fees are and what expenses are included in those fees.

   ◯ True   ◯ False

10. A status certificate can confirm the number of units that are leased in a condominium complex.

    ◯ True   ◯ False

Active Learning Exercises

Solutions are located in the Appendix.

▣ Exercise 1

What concerns and questions would you have given the following circumstances?

1.1 A special assessment for each condominium unit has been approved by a special meeting of the condominium complex.

1.2 The subject condominium unit has the use of one underground parking space.

1.3 The condominium's contingency fund has $900,000 in it.

1.4 Condominiums in the subject building are taking 90 days to sell.

1.5   The subject condominium unit is currently listed.

■ Exercise 2   Appraisal Form Completion

TASK 1

Rita Lichman (an MVA-Residential) is an appraiser who has been asked to value Nathan Rekab's high rise condominium apartment for resale purposes. She has collected the following information and data on the subject property. You are to take the information and complete pages 1, 2, 3 and the top part of page 4 of the *Standard Appraisal Report–Condominium* (OREA Form 701) located at the end of Task 1.

To facilitate the exercise, some information on page 4 of the form has been completed.

General Information

The municipal address of the subject property is 6 Clair Ave, Suite 1505, Anycity, ON. The homeowner's office phone number is 411-699-3344. The appraiser's file # is 72-20xx and the appraiser works with ABC Realty Inc., 48 Clair Avenue, Anycity, Ontario. The appraiser's office telephone number is 411-699-1234; fax number is 411-699-4321; and e-mail address is rita@abcrealty.ca. The date of inspection and the effective date of appraisal is June 30, 20xx.

The legal description of the subject is *MBCP 421 Unit 5 Level 15, Parking Unit 12 Level "C"*, in the Municipality of Anyregion and it is occupied by the homeowner. The zoning is Residential Multi-Family and the current use of the property is its highest and best use. The assessed value for 20xx is $235,000, with the taxes being $2,750.

Subject & Market History

The subject unit is not currently listed, but did sell in November (nine years earlier) for $190,000 after 60 days on the market. Property values are stable, with supply and demand currently in balance. The typical exposure time for a property to sell is between 30 to 45 days for both the neighbourhood and the subject condominium complex/street.

Neighbourhood Information

The value range of condominiums in the neighbourhood is $200,000–850,000 and the age range of a typical condominium complex in the area is from brand new up to 20 years. The neighbourhood is 100% developed and is stable. The subject is typical for the area.

The subject is in a prestigious neighbourhood developed with single-family freehold homes, high rise rental buildings, high rise condominium buildings and commercial/retail space.

Distance to elementary schools, secondary schools, public transit, shopping, downtown and recreational facilities is 3 blocks, 1 block, immediate, 1 block, 2 miles and 1 block respectively.

Neighbourhood Comments

The subject unit is located in midtown Anycity within a short walk of the subway, which allows for quick and easy access to uptown and downtown Anycity with its entertainment and commercial sections. Despite its midtown location, parks and ravines are located within the neighbourhood.

General Information–Condominium Complex

The subject building was fully constructed and registered 20 years ago as a high rise condominium with 19 floors and 160 units. The building is currently 80% owner occupied and 20% rented. The units range in size from 700 square feet to 3,400 square feet and in value from $210,000 to $850,000 respectively. The subject unit has one underground parking space that is owned. There is the exclusive use of one locker space (4 feet by 6 feet). The condition/appeal of the interior/exterior common elements were seen to be average for the area.

Condominium Financial And Legal information

The subject's maintenance fees are $360 per month and include maintenance of common elements, security, insurance, water, heat, snow removal, garbage collection and lawn care. These fees are in line with other local condominium complexes. There are no lawsuits or special assessments levied or pending. The reserve fund contains $1,500,000 and is considered by the property management company to be adequate. There are no major repairs or improvements currently underway, but some are envisioned over the next two years. An independent reserve fund study was done on the October 23rd (two years previously).

Comments Regarding Condominium Complex

Common facilities include an indoor pool, sauna, whirlpool, change rooms, exercise room, party room and concierge. This building appears to be well maintained and has an attractive appearance. All the hallways will have new carpet and wallpaper within the next 6 months.

Subject Unit Information

The subject unit is a one-storey condominium apartment enjoying 850 square feet of living space. The exterior walls are concrete and the roof of the building is the original metal one. There is a poured concrete foundation. The windows are vinyl double-glazed. There is no evidence that UFFI was used.

   The floor plan, interior and exterior condition/appeal were seen to be average. The floor plan includes a combined living/dining room, kitchen, foyer, 1- bedroom and a 4-piece bathroom. The room sizes, kitchen and bathroom were seen to be average, with the closets/storage being adequate. Room measurements were not taken.

   The flooring is a combination of hardwood and ceramic tile. The walls are drywall and the ceilings are drywall with stucco. The subject unit itself has no basement and the heating is hot water gas fired. The plumbing is a combination of copper and plastic, with the 200 amp electrical service being circuit breakers.

   The chattels and equipment to be included in any sale would be the stove, fridge, washer, dryer and dishwasher. No equipment/chattels were leased or rented and there were no special features.

Comments on Subject Unit

Within the past three years, the owner has repainted the walls, replaced the carpeting with hardwood floors and re-stuccoed the ceilings. The subject unit has an unobstructed northeast view. Units two floors below with the same exposure face into a commercial office building. Conversely, units with a southwest exposure enjoy unobstructed downtown and lake views.

OREA Ontario Real Estate Association

Standard Appraisal Report
Condominium

Form 701
for use in the Province of Ontario

CLIENT: .... Client Ref No: ....

Client: Phone No: (.............).. Fax No: (.............)................................. E-mail: ....

Client's Customer: .... Appraiser: .... Appraiser's Ref No: ....

GENERAL APPRAISAL AND PROPERTY INFORMATION

Property Address: ....

Municipality: ....

Full Legal Description: ....

Owner: .... Assessment: Total .... Taxes $ .... Year ....

This Appraisal is to estimate **MARKET VALUE** for a: ☐ Sale   ☐ Financing   ☐ Other ....

Effective Date of Appraisal: .... Date of Inspection: ....

Highest and Best Use is: ☐ Current   ☐ Other (*) ....

Zoning: .... Occupancy: ☐ Homeowner ☐ Tenant ☐ Vacant

SUBJECT & MARKET HISTORY

Subject Last Sold	Subject Currently Listed	Property Values	Demand/Supply
Date:	☐ Yes ☐ No	☐ Stable	☐ In Balance
Sale Price: $	Current List Price $	☐ Increasing	☐ Under Supply
Days on Market:	Days On Market	☐ Decreasing	☐ Over Supply

Typical Exposure Time Required for Properties to Sell in Subject Neighborhood is: ....
Typical Exposure Time Required for Properties to Sell in Subject Complex: ....

NEIGHBOURHOOD INFORMATION

Type

		Trend	**For Area, Condo Building is**
☐ Single Family Homes	☐ Mixed Residential/Commercial	☐ Improving	☐ Comparable
☐ Low Rise Rental Buildings	☐ Mixed Residential/Industrial	☐ Stable	☐ Superior*
☐ High Rise Rental Buildings	☐ Prestige	☐ Declining*	☐ Inferior
☐ Town House Condos	☐ Average		
☐ Low Rise Condo Buildings	☐ Starter		
☐ High Rise Condo Buildings			

Distance to

Elementary School   ....
Secondary School   ....
Public Transit   ....
Shopping   ....
Downtown   ....
Recreational Facilities   ....

Neighbourhood is: ....% Developed

Price Range of Properties in Neighbourhood: $................................. to $...................................

Age Range of Typical Property in Neighbourhood: .... to .... Years

Comments: (include any positive or negative factors that will have a measurable impact on the subject's marketability and value - items with an * should be discussed) ....
....
....

Exercise 2   Task 1: Standard Appraisal Report—Condominium, Page 2 of 6

GENERAL INFORMATION - SUBJECT CONDOMINIUM COMPLEX

Type of Condominium Complex

☐ Townhouse   ☐ Garden Home   ☐ Apartment Building

☐ Other ....   # Storeys ....   # Units in Complex ....

Age of Condominium Complex ....Years   Size of Units in Complex From .... to ....

Price Range of Units in Complex from $............................... to $................................

Complex Occupancy	Owner Occupied ....%	Rented ....%	Vacant ....%

Type of Parking	**Parking Space is**	**Storage/Locker Space**	**Storage/Locker Space is**
☐ Not Applicable	☐ Not Applicable	☐ Yes	☐ Exclusive Use/Common Element
☐ Underground Garage	☐ Exclusive Use/Common Element	☐ No	☐ Owned
☐ Aboveground w/Garage	☐ Owned	☐ # Lockers	☐ Assigned
☐ Aboveground w/o Garage	☐ Assigned	☐ Locker Size .... x	☐ Rented @ $ .... per Mth.
☐ Other	☐ Other		
Subject has .... Spaces	☐ Rented @ $ .... per Mth.		

Condition/Appeal of Interior Common Elements   ☐ Excellent   ☐ Good   ☐ Average   ☐ Fair   ☐ Poor*

Condition/Appeal of Exterior Common Elements   ☐ Excellent   ☐ Good   ☐ Average   ☐ Fair   ☐ Poor*

CONDOMINIUM FINANCIAL AND LEGAL INFORMATION

Subject Unit's Maintenance Fees Are: $ .... Per Month

Are Fees in Line with Other Similar Condominium Complexes?   ☐ Yes   ☐ No*

Maintenance Fees Include

☐ Maintenance of Common Elements   ☐ Insurance   ☐ Water   ☐ Heat   ☐ Hydro

☐ Garbage Collection   ☐ Snow Removal   ☐ Cable   ☐ Lawn Care

☐ Other ....

Is a Special Assessment Currently being levied?   ☐ Yes*   ☐ No

Are any Special Assessments Pending or Contemplated?   ☐ Yes*   ☐ No

As at the Date of Appraisal, the Reserve Fund contains: $ ....

Does the Property Management Company believe the Reserve Fund to be adequate?   ☐ Yes   ☐ No*

Are any Major Repairs/Improvements currently underway?   ☐ Yes*   ☐ No

Are any Major Repairs/Improvements Pending or Contemplated over the next two years?   ☐ Yes*   ☐ No

Are there any outstanding or anticipated legal actions?   ☐ Yes*   ☐ No

Has an independent reserve fund study been completed?   ☐ Yes   ☐ No

Date of last reserve fund study ....

Comments Regarding Condominium Complex: (include any positive or negative factors that will have a measurable impact on the subject's marketability and value - items with an * should be discussed)

....

....

....

....

SUBJECT UNIT INFORMATION

Type Of Unit
- ☐ Detached Townhouse
- ☐ Semi-detached Townhouse
- ☐ Attached Townhouse
- ☐ Apartment
- ☐ Other ....

Style Of Unit
- ☐ 1 Story
- ☐ 2 Storey
- ☐ 3 Storey
- ☐ Other ....

Sq. Ft. (Above Grade)
Level 1 ....   Level 4 ....
Level 2 ....   Level 5 ....
Level 3 ....
Total ....

Exterior Finish
- ☐ Brick Veneer
- ☐ Solid Brick
- ☐ Stucco
- ☐ Aluminum Siding
- ☐ Other ....
- ☐ Vinyl Siding
- ☐ Wood Siding
- ☐ Solid Stone
- ☐ Artificial Stone

Roof Material
- ☐ Asphalt Shingle
- ☐ Cedar Shake
- ☐ Metal
- ☐ Other ....
- ☐ Wood Shingle
- ☐ Slate
- ☐ Tar & Gravel

Foundation
- ☐ Poured Concrete
- ☐ Concrete Block
- ☐ Brick
- ☐ Stone
- ☐ Preserved Wood
- ☐ Other ....

Window Type
- ☐ Single   ☐ Thermal   ☐ Wood Frame   ☐ Aluminum   ☐ Vinyl
- ☐ Other ....

Evidence of UFFI
- ☐ Yes*   ☐ No

Exterior Condition
- ☐ Excellent   ☐ Good   ☐ Average   ☐ Fair   ☐ Poor*

Exterior Appeal
- ☐ Excellent   ☐ Good   ☐ Average   ☐ Fair   ☐ Poor*

Rooms	Living	Dining	Kitchen	Family	Beds	Bath	Wash	Rec	Other
Basement									
Main									
Second									
Third									

Room Sizes
- ☐ Large   ☐ Medium   ☐ Small

Additional Information on Room Sizes (Optional):
....
....
....

Kitchen
- ☐ Modern
- ☐ Average
- ☐ Outdated

Bathrooms
- ☐ Modern
- ☐ Average
- ☐ Outdated

Closets/Storage
- ☐ Excellent
- ☐ Adequate
- ☐ Inadequate

Basement
- ☐ None
- ☐ Full
- ☐ Partial

- ☐ Crawl Space
- % Finished ....

Floors
- ☐ Carpet
- ☐ Hardwood
- ☐ Vinyl Tile
- ☐ Ceramic
- ☐ Other ....

Walls/Ceilings
- ☐ Drywall
- ☐ Plaster
- ☐ Panelling
- ☐ Tile
- ☐ Other ....

Heating
- ☐ Forced Air
- ☐ Hot Water
- ☐ Baseboard
- ☐ Other ....
- ....

Fuel
- ☐ Gas
- ☐ Oil
- ☐ Electricity
- ☐ Other ....
- ....

Plumbing
- ☐ Copper
- ☐ Plastic
- ☐ Lead
- ☐ Galvanized
- ☐ Other ....

Electrical
- ☐ Fuses
- ☐ Circuit Breakers
- Amps ....

Floor Plan
- ☐ Excellent   ☐ Good   ☐ Average   ☐ Fair   ☐ Poor*

Interior Condition
- ☐ Excellent   ☐ Good   ☐ Average   ☐ Fair   ☐ Poor*

Equipment/Built-Ins/Chattels Remaining With Property:

Exercise 2   Task 1: Standard Appraisal Report—Condominium, Page 4 of 6

Equipment/Built-Ins/Chattels Remaining With Property:

☐ HWT   ☐ Fridge   ☐ Central Vac   ☐ Wood Stove   ☐ Elect Air Cleaner
☐ Central Air ☐ Washer   ☐ Humidifier   ☐ Hood   ☐ Garburator
☐ Heat Pump   ☐ Dryer   ☐ Security System ☐ Oven   ☐ Water Purifier/Filter
☐ Stove   ☐ Dishwasher   ☐ Dehumidifier   ☐ Range   ☐ Central Intercom
☐ Fireplace(s) ....
Other: ....
....

Equipment/Chattels Leased or Rented

Special Features

Comments: (include any positive or negative factors that will have a measurable impact on the subject's marketability and value - items with an * should be discussed)

DIRECT COMPARISON APPROACH
Competitive Listings

Item	Subject	Listing #1	Listing #2	Listing #3
Address	6 Clair Ave. #1505	6 Clair Ave. #1306	6 Clair Ave. #1605	6 Clair Ave. #1207
Distance To Subject		Same complex	Same complex	Same complex
Original List Price		$259,000	$279,000	$289,900
Current List Price		$249,900	$259,000	$279,000
Original List Date		01/06/20xx	19/05/20xx	14/05/20xx
Date Price Last Revised		15/06/20xx	19/06/20xx	06/06/20xx
Unit Type/Style	Apartment	Apartment	Apartment	Apartment
Size	850 sq. ft.	900 sq. ft.	850 sq. ft.	900 sq. ft.
Age	20 years	20 years	20 years	20 years
Location				
Exposure	North east	North east	North east	South west
Condition	Average	Average	Superior	Average
Beds	1	1	1	1
Baths	1	1	1	1
Floor Level	15	13	16	12
Listing is: Inferior/Similar/Superior		Similar	Superior	Superior

Comments: All 3 comparable listings are one-bedroom units located within the subject complex and as such were felt to be good comparables. Listing #1 is slightly larger, but is located on a less appealing floor level looking directly into a commercial office building. Listing #2 enjoys the use of an updated kitchen and bathroom making it superior to the subject. Listing #3 is larger and has a spectacular southwest view making it superior to the subject. There is nothing unusual about the number of days on the market for each listing.

TASK 2

Using information provided in Task 1, as well as the information below and on the following page, answer 10 multiple choice questions. Use the forms provided to assist in making the calculations.

Time Adjustments

There are no time resales of one-bedroom units in the subject condominium complex that have occurred in 20xx. However, you do obtain the following information:

- Unit 1803 is a larger one-bedroom and a den (1,050 square feet) apartment that sold on February 20th, 20xx for $336,000. Unit 1903 is identical to 1803 and it sold on June 20th, 20xx for $352,000. There are no differences between the units except that unit 1903's higher floor level is worth $2,000 more.

- Unit 601 is a larger one-bedroom and a den (950 square feet) apartment that sold on March 18th, 20xx for $300,000. Unit 701 is identical to 601 except that it is on a higher floor worth $2,000 extra and has a superior condition worth $5,000 more. Unit 701 sold on June 18th, 20xx for $315,800.

Explanation of Adjustment Amounts

- A condominium with a fair interior condition is worth $5,000 less than one with an average interior.

- A condominium with an excellent interior condition will sell for $15,000 more than one with an average interior condition.

- A value of $285 per square foot is applied when it comes to adjusting for size differences.

- A north-facing unit on the 15th floor is worth $10,000 more than one on the 7th floor.

- A unit facing north on the 15th floor will sell for $2,000 more than one on the 14th floor.

- A unit on the 17th floor facing north is worth $4,000 more than one on the 15th floor.

Exercise 2   Task 2: Standard Appraisal Report—Condominium, Page 5 of 6

Sales Analysis

Item	Subject	Comparable 1		Comparable 2		Comparable 3	
Address	6 Clair Ave. #1505	6 Clair Ave. #705		6 Clair Ave. #1405		6 Clair Ave. #1706	
Distance To Subject		Same complex		Same complex		Same complex	
Date Sold		21/05/20xx		19/06/20xx		26/04/20xx	
Sale Price		$220,000		$238,000		$271,000	
Days On Market		38 days		30 days		45 days	
Time Adjustment	30/06/20xx						
Time Adjusted Price							
Exposure	North east	North east		North east		North east	
Unit Type/Style	Apartment	Apartment		Apartment		Apartment	
Age of Unit	20 years	20 years		20 years		20 years	
Total Sq. Footage	850 sq. ft.	850 sq. ft.		850 sq. ft.		900 sq. ft.	
Family Room	No	No		No		No	
Bedrooms	One	One		One		One	
Bathrooms	1-4 pc.	1-4 pc.		1-4 pc.		1-4 pc.	
Basement/% Finished	N/A	N/A		N/A		N/A	
Rec Room	N/A	N/A		N/A		N/A	
Garage/Parking	Basement/One	Bsmt./One		Bsmt./One		Bsmt./One	
Unit Condition	Average	Fair		Average		Excellent	
Exterior Condition	Average	Average		Average		Average	
Floor plan	Average	Average		Average		Average	
Floor level	15th	7th		14th		17th	
Total Adjustments							
Totally Adj. Sale Price							

Comments, Reconciliation And Estimate Of Value By The Direct Comparison Approach

Based on the above information and analysis, a value by the Direct Comparison Approach is estimated to be: ($...)

2.1   Calculate the percentage monthly time adjustment arrived at by using the information from Units 1803 and 1903.

a.   1.19%

b.   1.04%

c.   4.16%

d.   4.76%

2.2   Calculate the percentage monthly time adjustment arrived at by using the information from Units 601 and 701.

a.   .97%

b.   1.76%

c.   2.93%

d.   5.27%

2.3   Calculate the time adjusted price for Comparable Sale #1 (remember the effective date of the appraisal is June 30th, 20xx).

a. $217,772

b. $217,800

c. $222,800

d. $222,200

2.4   Calculate the time adjusted price for Comparable Sale #2.

a. $240,380

b. $235,620

c. $238,000

d. $237,000

2.5   Calculate the time adjusted price for Comparable Sale #3.

a. $265,580

b. $276,420

c. $273,710

d. $268,290

2.6   Calculate the totally adjusted sale price for Comparable Sale #1.

a. $207,200

b. $235,000

c. $205,000

d. $237,200

2.7 Calculate the totally adjusted sale price for Comparable Sale #2.

   a. $240,000
   b. $236,000
   c. $242,380
   d. $233,620

2.8 Calculate the totally adjusted sale price for Comparable Sale #3.

   a. $243,170
   b. $309,670
   c. $237,750
   d. $232,330

2.9 The estimate of value for the subject property would be based on:

   a. the totally adjusted sale price of Comparable #3 as it had the greatest amount and number of adjustments and was a dated sale.
   b. the totally adjusted sale price of Comparable #2 as it had the least amount and number of adjustments and was the most recent sale.
   c. the totally adjusted sale price of Comparable #1 as it had the least amount and number of adjustments and was the most recent sale.
   d. the average of the totally adjusted selling prices of Comparables 1, 2 and 3.

2.10 The final estimate of value for the subject property would be based on:

   a. a 28 day marketing period.
   b. a 45 day marketing period.
   c. a 20 day marketing period.
   d. a 10 day marketing period.

TASK 3

Complete page 6 of the *Standard Appraisal Report—Condominium* (OREA Form 701) using information from Tasks 1 and 2. Where necessary create information to fully complete that page. The form can be found on the following page.

CERTIFICATION AND FINAL ESTIMATE OF VALUE

- This valuation and report is subject to the attached assumptions and limiting conditions.

- This valuation and report has been completed in accordance with the Canadian Real Estate Association's Code of Ethics and Standard of Business Practice, as well as the Code of Ethics of the Real Estate and Business Brokers Act.

- I confirm that I personally inspected the subject property and that I have no current or contemplated interest or bias (positive or negative) towards the subject property.

- Unless otherwise detailed in writing within this report, I can confirm that I have no personal relationship or bias (positive or negative) towards any of the parties using or affected by this valuation and report.

- I can confirm that my being employed and paid to complete this valuation is not conditional on the amount of the valuation or on any specific information being included or excluded in this appraisal report.

Therefore, based on a .... day marketing period, a reasonable market value for the subject property as at

................................, 20.............. is estimated to be:

.... Dollars ($..)

Appraiser's Signature: ....   Date of Signature: ....

Appraiser's Name: ....   Company: ....
Appraiser's Address: ....   Phone No: ....
....   Fax No: ....
....   E-mail: ....

ATTACHMENTS

- ☐ Neighbourhood Map
- ☐ Copies of MLS Listing/Sales
- ☐ Site/Building Sketch
- ☐ Photos
- ☐ Survey

- ☐ Additional Information/Analysis: ....
- ☐ Additional Assumptions/Limiting Conditions: ....
  ....
- ☐ Other: ....
  ....

ASSUMPTIONS AND LIMITING CONDITIONS

1. This report may not be read or used by anyone other than the client without the written authorization of the appraiser. This report should only be used for the property and purpose identified within it. The appraiser accepts no responsibility or liability should the information contained within this report be used by anyone other than the client (or other authorized user) or for any other purpose or property other than that specified within this report.

2. Values are subject to varying and continual changes in market conditions and neighbourhood factors. Accordingly, the value presented in this report can only be relied on as the value estimated as of the effective date of appraisal specified in this report. Should the user of this report wish to know the value of the subject property as of another date, the appraiser will need to complete an update or a new appraisal report.

3. A search on title and ownership has not been performed. A good title with respect to the subject property has been assumed. Therefore, other than what is noted in this report, the appraiser assumes no responsibility for matters legal in nature that may affect the subject property's title, ownership, marketing or value.

4. Any sketches in this report are included solely for the purpose of assisting the reader in visualizing the property.

5. The appraiser has carried out a visual cosmetic inspection of the subject property only. This inspection and the ensuing appraisal report is not and should not be considered a structural, environmental or mechanical inspection and report. Accordingly, unless stated otherwise in this appraisal report, the appraiser is unaware of any hidden or not apparent structural, environmental or mechanical defects or problems and assumes for the purposes of this report and valuation that there are none. Therefore, should it subsequently become known that there is a structural, mechanical or environmental problem or defect, then the appraiser reserves the right to alter the value given in this appraisal report.

6. This appraisal has been based on the assumption that the subject property is in compliance with the applicable zoning, building codes, by-laws, environmental regulations and condominium by-laws and regulations. Should this in fact turn out not to be so, the appraiser reserves the right to make any necessary changes to the final estimate of value.

7. This valuation has been based on the assumption that the information collected from industry recognized sources and professionals is in fact correct and can be relied upon for the purpose of this appraisal.

Form 701   Revised 2008   **Page 6 of 6**

CHAPTER 10

Other Property Types—Commercial Properties

Introduction

Commercial properties can include apartment buildings, industrial buildings, office buildings, retail buildings including plazas and shopping centres or buildings that mix office with retail with residential components.

One of the challenges in valuing commercial properties relates to the amount and type of information that is required to be collected and analyzed as a result of their size and complexity as compared to single-family homes or condominium units.

In addition to being able to use the Direct Comparison Approach and the Cost Approach, the Income Approach can also be used. Which approach or approaches ends up being used will, of course, depend on the type of commercial property being appraised. There are some type of special purpose or single purpose industrial properties which can only be valued by the cost approach given that there are unlikely to be any comparable sales of similar buildings (Direct Comparison Approach) or sufficient lease/rental information (Income Approach).

The challenge with the Income Approach is that the appraiser needs to reconstruct the income and expenses of both the subject property and the comparables used to evaluate a capitalization rate. This reconstruction ensures that income and expenses between the properties are being compared the same way and that they reflect the basis upon which buyers would make an offer.

Learning Outcomes

At the conclusion of this chapter, students will be able to:

- Describe some of the specific type of information that needs to be collected for the different categories of commercial real estate.
- Outline the approaches to value that are available to be used in valuing commercial properties.
- Explain the units of comparison that are used in valuing commercial properties during the Direct Comparison Approach.
- Estimate the value of an apartment building using units of comparison.
- List the steps used in the Income Approach.
- Complete a reconstructed income and expense statement of a commercial property.
- Estimate the value of a commercial property using the Direct Method of Capitalization and both a gross income multiplier and an overall capitalization rate.

COLLECTING AND ANALYZING INFORMATION—COMMERCIAL PROPERTIES

The collection and analysis of information for commercial properties follows the same process as it does for single-family homes and condominium units; i.e., information is needed on the neighbourhood, site and improvements in order to be able to arrive at a value. The type of information that needs to be collected and analyzed will of course depend on the property being appraised.

Let's review some of the more specific information that an appraiser would want to look at when valuing an apartment, retail, office or industrial building.

APARTMENT BUILDINGS

Access to public transportation; proximity to educational facilities such as schools, colleges, universities; distance to shopping; proximity of recreational facilities such as parks, golf courses; theatres, skating rinks, stadiums, swimming pools, proximity to medical services; level of security in the neighbourhood and the building; parking above ground or underground; laundry facilities; amenities in the building such as a pool or exercise room.

OFFICE BUILDINGS

Proximity to shopping, restaurants, health clubs; distance to public transportation; frequency of public transportation services; availability of office services; availability of banks, lawyers and accountants; central telecommunication facilities; data processing facilities; condition/quality of entrance, lobby, elevators and common hallways; security; parking facilities for clients and employees.

RETAIL BUILDINGS

Identification of major traffic routes and patterns; pedestrian flow; access to public transportation; frequency of public transportation service; location of on and off street parking; population and income levels in the surrounding area; adequacy of parking; mix and presence of different retail stores (compatibility of the stores).

INDUSTRIAL PREMISES

Access routes for road transportation; distance to railway freight depots; availability of railway spurs; clear height to underside of trusses or beams; dock height loading bays; load bearing capacity of floors; adequate turning facilities for semi-trailers; local environmental standards; available labour pool in the area; industrial waste disposal; disposal of hazardous waste

OTHER INFORMATION REQUIRED

Other information that needs to be looked at for commercial properties also includes:

- Leasing Arrangements—this includes the remaining period on the lease and the rent being paid. Rents are quite straightforward for apartment buildings but can get complicated for shopping plazas. It is important to spend time and go through the lease to find out what the tenant is or is not paying for; e.g., retail store in a shopping centre—on top of a base rent, the tenant might be paying for a proportionate share of the common area maintenance expenses as well as a percentage of the tenants gross income.

- Operating and maintenance expenses for the subject building.
- Typical operating and maintenance expenses for similar buildings in the area.
- Vacancy rates for similar buildings in the area.
- Quality of the management.
- Rental rates for similar buildings in the area.

VALUING COMMERCIAL PROPERTIES

For the majority of commercial properties, three valuation methods can be used:

1.	Direct Comparison Approach
2.	Cost Approach
3.	Income Approach

Direct Comparison Approach

The process and steps involved in valuing a commercial/industrial property using this approach are basically the same as those followed in valuing single-family homes and condominium units.

The major difference would be in the complexity of a commercial/industrial property as opposed to a single-family home or condominium unit. This complexity results in some of the adjustments being very different than in residential homes.

When using the Direct Comparison Approach for commercial properties, the selling prices of the comparables would normally be broken down into one or two of the following units of comparison:

- Price Per Square Foot/Metre
- Price Per Front Foot/Metre
- Price Per Suite
- Price Per Unit

The decision as to which unit of comparison to use will depend on the type of property and the actions of typical buyers and sellers in the specific marketplace.

EXAMPLE   *Using Units of Comparison in the Direct Comparison Approach for Apartment Buildings*

The subject property is an apartment building with 20 3-bedroom units. It is approximately 2,000 square metres in size.

A comparable apartment building which sold for $1,200,000 has been located. It has 25 3-bedroom units, and is approximately 2,500 square metres in size. The property is otherwise very similar in condition and location to the subject. Based on this information, the price per suite and price per square metre of the comparable can be calculated as follows (remember a unit of comparison = selling price ÷ # of units):

Price per suite of comparable: $1,200,000 ÷ 25 = **$48,000 per suite**
Price per square metre of comparable: $1,200,000 ÷ 2,500 = **$480 sq. m.**

This information can now be applied to the subject property as follows:

Value of subject using price per suite $48,000 x 20 = **$960,000**
Value of subject using price per square metre $480 x 2,000 = **$960,000**

Clearly the value of the subject property is **$960,000**.

In order to use this method, the comparable properties (in real life the appraiser would use several to come up with a value) need to be comparable; i.e., you would not compare a 120 unit, 12,000 square metre building with the subject. In addition, adjustments would need to be made to the prices per suite or per square metre of the comparable properties if there were significant difference that warranted adjustments.

Adjustments for Commercial/Industrial Properties   FOCUS

With commercial/industrial properties, adjustments might need to be made for quality of offices and common area finishes, elevators, loading facilities, height clearance, floor loading capacity etc.

Unlike single-family homes or condominium units where adjustments are shown as lump sum dollars, adjustments for commercial/industrial properties may be shown in terms of a unit of comparison; e.g., price/dollars per square foot or as a percentage.

Cost Approach

The process and steps involved in valuing a commercial/industrial property using this approach are basically the same those followed in valuing single-family homes.

Commercial/industrial properties typically have more detailed calculations concerning reproduction/replacement cost new (RCN) and depreciation owing to the diversity of improvements; e.g., a number of main and accessory buildings, differing structure heights and grades of construction material, divergent uses within one large complex, and the range of adjustments required for other improvements involving parking areas, loading docks, mechanical systems and floor load requirements. Advanced, more detailed methods such as the Quantity Survey Method or Unit in Place Method may be needed for computing RCN.

Owner Occupied Properties	CAUTION

One of the significant challenges in valuing commercial properties arises when dealing with special purpose or single purpose industrial properties which are often owner occupied. Often the only approach that can be used with these type of properties is the Cost Approach. The Direct Comparison and Income Approaches are not usually viable because of a lack of sales of similar properties and the inability to estimate rental income as a result of a lack of market data.

Income Approach

For the remainder of this chapter, we shall focus on the one approach which has not been covered in this course so far and which is very relevant to income producing commercial properties—the Income Approach. Given that this is a brief introduction to commercial properties and there is a need to provide continuity, we shall focus the material on valuing an apartment building (one of the types of commercial properties) using the income approach. The overall process and steps remain the same for other types of commercial properties while the specific details might be slightly different depending on the property.

INTRODUCTION TO THE INCOME APPROACH

The income approach to value is based on the theory that the value of an investment (commercial) property is the present worth of the future income which this property is capable of producing. This involves capitalizing the net income of the property, by an appropriate rate, into an indication of value. The value of all types of income producing properties is related, to one degree or another, to the income producing potential of those properties. The higher the potential income, the higher will be the price that the property will command on the market.

The appraiser should, however, appreciate that each investor will have his or her own personal reasons for buying an investment (commercial) property. While the majority of investors will be interested in achieving the greatest income or capital gain within the confines of generally accepted risk levels, other considerations, for instance might be prestige, retirement, balancing an investment portfolio or tax savings.

However, whatever the reason is for buying an investment (commercial) property, the amount of money that a purchaser will end up paying will in one way or another be based on its income. In other words, there is a relationship between income and value.

STEPS IN THE INCOME APPROACH

There are five basic steps in the income approach and they are as follows:

1.	Estimate the potential annual gross income of the property.
2.	Deduct vacancy and bad debts from the potential annual gross income to arrive at the effective annual gross income.
3.	Estimate the total annual operating expenses.
4.	Deduct the total annual operating expenses from the effective annual gross income to arrive at the net operating income.
5.	Using the appropriate method of capitalization, convert the net operating income into value.

STEP 1   ESTIMATE THE POTENTIAL ANNUAL GROSS INCOME OF THE PROPERTY

The main idea behind estimating potential gross income is that the amount of money that a purchaser will probably pay for an investment property will be based on the rental income that it is capable of producing within the next year, or annually in the years following the effective date of appraisal.

This estimation of potential gross income is arrived at after considering a number of factors, the most important of which are as follows:

Market Rent	When estimating the market value of an income producing property, it is market rent and not contract rent that must be used. Market rent is the rental that each unit would most probably command, if it were vacant and available for rent on the open market as of the date of the appraisal. Contract rent is the rent that is actually being paid under contract by the tenant of each unit.
	NOTE: It is important to keep in mind that the appraiser may have to give consideration to the fact that long term leases on investment properties and rent control for residential buildings may make it unrealistic to rely on full market rent.
100% Occupancy	Calculation of the total potential annual gross income is based on the total revenue that could be received if all the apartments in the subject building were rented.
Typical Management	The potential annual gross income of an investment property is based on market rent, and on the assumption that there is, or will be, typically competent and prudent management. An appraiser will start the analysis of the potential income by comparing the owner's last 3 income statements to those of comparable properties in the area.

ANALYZING THE SUBJECT PROPERTY'S PAST AND PRESENT PERFORMANCE

The appraiser may start the analysis of the income potential of a property by reference to the owner's last 3 income statements. While these statements may be a useful guide, they may not necessarily be a reliable one for appraisal purposes. Some reasons for this could be:

- Perhaps the management of the property is unusually poor and the current rentals are well below what they should be, or rent collection is not efficient and there is an abnormally high ratio of uncollected rents.
- Perhaps some of the units have been vacant due to recent renovations/modernization and their potential income does not yet show up on the income statement.
- Perhaps the owner's statement shows income that is not being received. For example, it may include a one year lease for $12,000 where, in fact, the tenant is being given one month's free rent of $1,000. Therefore the actual rent being received is $11,000 and not $12,000 as shown in the statement.

ANALYZING MARKET COMPARABLES

Given that an estimate of the potential annual gross income of an investment property is based on market rather than contract rent, it is natural that the appraiser would go from looking at the subject's past and present performance to the next stage which is analyzing market comparables. It is from comparable properties that the appraiser will be able to estimate the market rent of the subject property.

Even though market rent is the objective in estimating the potential annual gross income of an investment property, consideration must still be given to the impact of rent control legislation on contract rent, in terms of the length of time it would take to achieve the respective market rent.

Of course, if the owners income statement is consistent with the appraisers analysis, then its number can be used in the appraisers work. If not, then the appraiser will give more attention to the figures arrived at through his/her own market research.

STEP 2   DEDUCT THE ESTIMATED VACANCY AND BAD DEBTS FROM THE ESTIMATED POTENTIAL ANNUAL GROSS INCOME TO ARRIVE AT THE EFFECTIVE ANNUAL GROSS INCOME

It should be remembered that an investor/purchaser, and, as a result, an appraiser, will be interested in the income that the subject is likely to produce, rather than what it could produce if it was always fully occupied with the tenants paying their rent in full and on time. It is only natural to expect that a property will suffer some income loss, and accordingly an allowance for vacancy an bad debts should be made. This allowance is calculated as a percentage of the estimated potential annual gross income, and will vary according to the location, condition, quality of tenants and level of the rents of the subject property as well as the competition and vacancies in comparable buildings. Once again the subject's past and present performance is compared to the vacancy and bad debts being suffered by comparable buildings in the area. If there is a discrepancy, then the appraiser uses his/her judgment with an eye to the market.

When the amount allowed for vacancies and bad debts is subtracted from the potential annual gross income, the resulting amount is known as the effective gross income.

STEP 3   ESTIMATE THE TOTAL ANNUAL OPERATING EXPENSES

Net income is used by appraisers in estimating the value of investment properties. Net income is arrived at by subtracting the total annual operating expenses from the effective gross income. In arriving at the estimated total annual operating expenses, the following guidelines should be used:

- Include only the expenses that are necessary to maintain the flow of rental income estimated as of the date of appraisal.
- The nature and level of expenses should be based on typical management and should be consistent with market expenses.
- Since some expenses are concentrated in one particular year and not in others, it is important to stabilize or smooth out the expenses on an annual basis.

In estimating the operating expenses, the appraiser would look at a minimum of three years operating experience through the owner's income and expense statements and compare them to the information taken from comparable properties in the area and published studies. If the subject's actual operating expenses are consistent with the figures taken from the comparable properties and/or the published studies, then the appraiser can use them in his/her estimate of operating expenses.

There are however, a number of reasons why the appraiser will usually end up with an estimated operating expense statement (i.e., a reconstructed statement) that has different numbers to those found in the owner's statement. Those reasons follows:

REASON A

The owner of an apartment building usually records expenses on a cash basis (when paid) whereas you need to look at expenses on the basis of when they were incurred. If the seller pays none of his bills that year, it doesn't mean that there are no expenses.

Cash Versus Accrued

Bill owns an apartment building which Mary is going to list for sale. Last year his hydro expenses were $28,000. Bill has not yet paid the bill and it therefore does not show in his expense statement.

Question—What would the impact be if Mary did not include the hydro in her reconstructed expense statement?

Answer—It would inflate the amount of income after expenses which would result in a higher valuation and listing price which the typical buyer could easily see through.

REASON B

The building may not have competent management and therefore the expenses may not be typical (e.g., higher) as a result.

On the other hand the building may be owned by someone who owns a number of buildings and as a result can purchase at a much lower cost than is typical. Remember the appraiser is valuing the building and not the owners abilities and management capabilities. All expenses should be in line with the market (i.e., other comparable buildings in the area).

REASON C

The owner's statements may include expenses that are not necessary to maintain the current income flow of the building.

Examples of this might be:

- Capital expenditures; e.g., new kitchens, bathrooms, flooring etc.
- Mortgage payments
- Depreciation
- Charitable donations
- Car allowances
- Business tax
- Reserves for Capital Expenditures

None of these expenses are necessary to keep the current flow of income going. A tenant will pay the same rent whether there is a mortgage on the property or whether the owner leases a car.

     Examples of whether an item is a Capital Expenditure or Maintenance (necessary expense) follow:

- Painting the walls—maintenance
- Replacing all the walls—capital expenditure
- Replacing a broken window—maintenance
- Installing all new windows—capital expenditure
- Cleaning the carpets—maintenance
- Replacing the carpets—capital expenditure
- Replacing a thermostat on a furnace—maintenance
- Replacing the furnace with a new one—capital expenditure.

Caution: *Reserves for Replacement of Short-Life Components*

The only time the appraiser may be justified in including a reserve for replacement of such short-life components in the operating expense statement is when the market indicates that this is normal practice adopted by property owners in the area and when the overall capitalization rate used by the appraiser in capitalizing the resulting net income has been extracted from comparable properties treated in the same way; i.e., provision was also made for reserves for replacement in arriving at their net operating income.

REASON D

Legitimate expenses can occur in some years and not in others. All legitimate expenses must be stabilized on an annual basis.

Stabilizing Expenses

Jim is a salesperson with ABC Realty Inc. He is valuing a 50-unit apartment building for listing purposes. The interior of the building is typically painted once every 5 years. It was last painted 2 years ago for $25,000.

Question—What amount should show in Jim's *Current Estimated Annual Total Expenses* with respect to the painting of the interior.

Answer—25,000 ÷ 5 = $5,000
If you don't do this, you will end up with an inflated net income during the years when the painting is not done and a deflated net income in the year that the painting is done.

REASON E

There may be expenses excluded from the sellers Income/ Expense Statement that should be included. Typical of this would be management fees. Even if the owners of an apartment building have been managing it themselves, a management fee should be included as "time is money".

If there is a superintendent that enjoys the use of a free apartment, the expected rental of that apartment should be included in the Gross Potential Annual Income and then shown as an expense.

A step-by-step example of an appraiser's reconstructed operating statement is illustrated on the following page, including:

- The owner's three-year operating statement;
- The appraiser's reconstructed statement; and
- An explanation of each adjustment in the reconstructed statement.

PRINCIPLES OF APPRAISAL

OWNER'S THREE-YEAR OPERATING STATEMENT

	3 yrs ago	2 yrs ago	1 yr ago	Ref.
REVENUE				
Rent Collections	$372,761	$379,964	$385,630	1
Parking/Laundry Income	33,975	35,375	35,450	2
Total Revenue	406,736	415,339	421,080	4
EXPENSES				
Realty Taxes	50,940	52,375	53,642	5
Superintendent—salary, etc.	9,500	10,500	11,500	6
Janitor—salary, etc.	4,800	5,280	5,808	7
Water	8,450	8,720	8,950	8
Electricity	974	1,135	1,217	9
Fuel	3,700	5,150	7,200	10
Insurance	2,000	2,000	2,000	11
Maintenance and repairs	5,800	6,800	4,000	12
Painting and decorating	16,400	10,500	18,400	13
Supplies	850	1,020	1,224	14
Legal and Audit	1,000	1,650	1,250	15
Elevator Maintenance	1,200	1,200	1,200	16
Depreciation	42,000	57,000	54,150	17
Mortgage Payments	206,750	206,750	206,750	18
Total Expenses	354,364	370,080	377,291	
NET INCOME	**$52,372**	**$45,259**	**$43,789**	

APPRAISER'S RECONSTRUCTED STATEMENT

		Ref.
POTENTIAL GROSS INCOME		
Rent Collections:		
18 1-bedroom units x $300/month x 12	$ 64,800	
78 2-bedroom units x $375/month x 12	351,000	
	415,800	1
ADDITIONAL INCOME		
Parking—96 spaces x $20 x 12	23,040	
Laundry—96 x $10 x 12	11,520	
	34,560	2
Total Gross Income Potential	450,360	
Less Vacancy and Credit Losses (5%)	–22,518	3
Effective Gross Income	427,842	4
OPERATING EXPENSES		
Realty taxes	$ 54,100	5
Superintendent	17,000	6
Janitor	9,989	7
Water	9,216	8
Electricity	1,320	9
Fuel	9,000	10
Insurance	2,700	11
Maintenance & repairs	4,000	12
Painting & decorating	18,000	13
Supplies	1,469	14
Legal and audit	1,300	15
Elevator maintenance	1,500	16
Management (3%)	12,835	19
Total Operating Expenses	142,429	
NET ANNUAL OPERATING INCOME	**$285,413**	

EXPLANATION

1. The potential annual gross income from rental collections is based on the market rent for each apartment with all suites fully rented. This amount would include the rental income collected for the suites presently occupied as well as those suites provided rent free for the superintendent and janitor.

2. In addition to normal rent, each tenant must pay $20 per month for parking and $10 per month for laundry facilities.

3. A vacancy and credit losses allowance of 5% of both rental and additional income is based on current competitive conditions as indicated by a survey of comparable properties in the area. Whether or not this factor applies to both gross income and additional income will depend on circumstances.

4. The effective gross income represents the total potential gross income less an allowance for vacancy and bad debts.

5. The current year's taxes as shown in the reconstructed operating statement were derived by multiplying the present assessment by this year's tax rate.

6. The superintendent's salary was adjusted upwards from last year's at the same rate of increase as previous years. Allowance of the free two-bedroom suite is also added.

7. The janitor's salary was adjusted upwards at the same rate as previous years. The allowance of a free one-bedroom suite occupied by the janitor was also added.

8. Water costs based on present consumption worked out to an average of $8.00 per suite per month. This checked out very closely to published figures for water consumption costs in this general area.

9. Electricity expenses pertain only to the public areas and to the equipment. The average current cost is estimated at $110 per month. Tenants are responsible for their own consumption, individually metered to each suite.

10. Fuel costs have been rising rapidly over the last three years. The estimate for the current year is based on the average consumption for the last three years at a rate quoted by the gas company for this year's heating season.

11. The annual insurance premium has now increased from $2,000 to a new rate for the current year of $2,700.

12. As a result of the property rehabilitation program undertaken almost two years ago, it is expected that expenses for maintenance and repairs will remain the same as last year's expense for at least the next two or three years.

13. The current year's painting and decorating expense is based on the cost of $500 per suite once every three years, and a total cost of $10,000 to paint the public areas and exterior trim once every five years.

14. Expenses for supplies have been increasing steadily by 20% per year. The current year's expenses are projected on this basis.

15. Legal and audit expenses for the current year are an average of the last three years.

16. Elevator maintenance expenses are based on a new three-year contract for $1,500 per year.

17. Depreciation is not a deductible expense for the purpose of deriving net operating income for appraisal purposes.

18. Mortgage payments of principal and/or interest are not a deductible expense in arriving at net operating income.

19. No management costs were reported in the owner's statements. The typical management cost for this type of property and operation in this area is 3% of the effective gross income.

STEP 4   DEDUCT THE TOTAL ANNUAL OPERATING EXPENSES FROM THE EFFECTIVE ANNUAL GROSS INCOME TO ARRIVE AT THE NET OPERATING INCOME

This is of course a purely mechanical/mathematical step.

STEP 5   USING THE APPROPRIATE METHOD OF CAPITALIZATION, CONVERT THE NET OPERATING INCOME INTO VALUE

Capitalization is the process of converting the income of a property into a capital value. A capitalization rate expresses the mathematical relationship between the income and capital value of an income producing property. Once the rate has been selected, a method has to be used in order to combine this rate with the defined income. The two basic methods of capitalization are the Direct Method and the Yield Method. The Direct method is most frequently associated with smaller income investment properties. The yield capitalization method applies more commonly to larger investment-grade commercial projects and properties. We shall focus on the Direct Method in our continuing look at an apartment building as our commercial property.

The two common rates used in the Direct Method of capitalization that we shall be looking at are the:

1.	Gross Income Multiplier
2.	Overall Capitalization Rate

GROSS INCOME MULTIPLIER

The gross income multiplier (GIM) simply expresses the relationship between the effective annual gross income (EGI) and the selling price of a property. It should be stressed that this rate is not expressed as a percentage but as a multiplier. The formula to calculate a GIM is as follows:

GIM = Sale Price ÷ Effective Gross Income (EGI)

The first step in calculating a GIM is to select a number of comparables from which sufficient information can be obtained. The comparable properties chosen must be just that—COMPARABLE. They should be similar in terms of size, utility, price, location, financing, and in expense ratios and rents. The appraiser should also look at the gross rents of the comparables, to ensure that they are being received on the same basis as the subject. In other words, if the subject's rents include heat and hydro, parking and appliances, so should the comparable rents. If this is not the case, then the relationship between the Effective Gross Income and sale price of the comparables cannot be used directly on the subject's Effective Gross Income without some sort of adjustment(s). The income figure ultimately used in the calculation for estimating the gross income multiplier from comparables is based on the appraiser's reconstructed statements of those comparables in much the same way as is done to estimate the subject's income:

EXAMPLE   *GIM*

The subject property has an effective gross income of $100,000. A comparable sale with an effective gross income of $112,000 is located. The comparable sold for $784,000. (In actual practice, several comparables should be located and analyzed). The GIM can be calculated as follows:

GIM = Sale Price ÷ Effective Gross Income (EGI)
Therefore: **784,000 ÷ 112,000 = 7 (GIM)**

This GIM can now be applied to the EGI of the subject property to arrive at a value as follows:

Value (V) = Gross Income Multiplier (GIM) x Effective Gross Income (EGI)
7 x 100,000 = $700,000 (Value of Subject)

In many instances, buyers of relatively small commercial properties will come up with a value by using the GIM, since it is easy to understand, calculate and apply. In addition, the relevant information is relatively easily obtained. However, this method does not take into account variations in expenses and mortgage financing, and is considered to be mainly a "rule of thumb" quick calculation.

OVERALL CAPITALIZATION RATE

The overall capitalization rate expresses the relationship between the current year's income and the value of the property. Once the overall capitalization rate is calculated, it is combined with the net operating income to arrive at a capital value for the whole subject property. The formula that is used to combine the net operating income with the overall capitalization rate is as follows:

Value of Property (V) = Net Operating Income (I) ÷ Overall Capitalization Rate (R)

In this course we shall look at calculating the overall capitalization rate through the use of comparable sales and the following formula:

Overall Capitalization Rate (R) = Net Operating Income (I) ÷ Sale Price (of comparable)

Once again, it must be stressed that the comparables should be just that—comparable in terms of income and expenses, financing, age, condition, type of property, size etc.

EXAMPLE   *Overall Capitalization Rate*

The subject property has a net operating income of $135,000. The appraiser finds a comparable property which has a net operating income of $150,000 and a selling price of $1,450,000. Given the above information, the overall capitalization rate (R) can be calculated as follows:

Overall Capitalization Rate (R) = Net Operating Income (I) ÷ Sale Price
Therefore: **150,000 ÷ 1,450,000 = 10.34% (Overall Capitalization Rate (R))**

(In actual practice, 4 or 5 comparable sales would be selected in order to estimate the overall capitalization rate.) This overall capitalization rate can now be combined with the net operating income of the subject property to arrive at a value as follows:

Value of Property (V) = Net Operating Income (I) ÷ Overall Capitalization Rate (R)

Therefore: **135,000 ÷ .1034 = $1,305,609 (Value)**
The $1,305,609 would be rounded to **$1,306,000**.

Calculating the value of the subject property, using comparable sales and the overall capitalization rate, is relatively easy. It is often used by investors and, accordingly, the rationale for the overall capitalization rate using the Direct Method of Capitalization is strongly supported by the actions of the marketplace. However, sufficient comparables are necessary in order to have enough information to successfully analyze and estimate the overall capitalization rate. Once again, the income figure ultimately used in the calculation for estimating the overall capitalization rate from comparables is based on the appraiser's reconstructed statements of those comparables in much the same way as is done to estimate the subject's income.

KNOWLEDGE INTEGRATION

Notables

- The collection and analysis of information for commercial buildings will likely be more complex and time consuming than it is for single-family homes or condominiums.
- In many instances, the Income Approach is a prime method for estimating the value of a commercial property.
- With special purpose or single purpose buildings, the Cost Approach may be the only method for estimating value.

- There are five steps in the Income Approach.
- The appraiser needs to reconstruct the income and expense statements of the owners of both the subject and comparable property sales used in the Direct Method of Capitalization.
- Gross income multipliers and overall capitalization rates are used in the Direct Method of Capitalization.

Chapter Mini-Review

Solutions are located in the Appendix.

1. Distance to railway freight depots and methods of disposal for hazardous waste are pieces of information that need to be collected when it comes to industrial properties.

    ○ True   ○ False

2. The net operating income of an investment property is arrived at by deducting the vacancy and bad debts from the effective annual gross income.

    ○ True   ○ False

3. One of the important factors that needs to be considered in arriving at an estimation of potential annual gross income is typical management.

    ○ True   ○ False

4. The estimate of market rent used in an appraiser's reconstructed income and expense statement is arrived at by analyzing the subject property's past performance.

    ○ True   ○ False

5. One of the reasons why some of the expenses shown in an appraiser's reconstructed expense statement may be different to the owner's expense statement is that the subject building may not have competent management and therefore the expenses may not be typical.

    ○ True   ○ False

6. A typical operating expense shown in an appraiser's reconstructed income and expense statement would be mortgage payments.

    ○ True   ○ False

7. In estimating the total annual operating expenses, an appraiser would compare the owner's expense statement to the operating expenses being experienced by comparable properties and/or operating expense ratios shown in published studies.

   ◯ True   ◯ False

8. In order to estimate the overall capitalization rate from comparable sales, the sale price of the comparable is divided by its annual net operating income (NOI).

   ◯ True   ◯ False

9. To capitalize the subject's annual net operating income (NOI) into value for the subject property, you would multiply it by the overall capitalization rate.

   ◯ True   ◯ False

10. The gross income multiplier (GIM) is a factor or a multiplier used to convert the potential annual effective gross income of the subject property into value.

    ◯ True   ◯ False

Active Learning Exercises

Solutions are located in the Appendix.

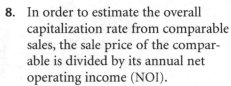 **Exercise 1**

Describe three factors that should be taken into account when estimating the potential annual gross income of a property.

■ Exercise 2

Why is it necessary to reconstruct the owner's annual income and expense statement in order to arrive at a net operating income for the property?

■ Exercise 3

Should the appraiser's reconstructed operating expense statement include reserves for the replacement of short-life components? Why?

■ Exercise 4

Using two different units of comparison, develop a comparable sales analysis chart and estimate the value of a 495 square metre, 7-suite apartment building, based on the following information:

Sale #1: An 8-suite, 565 square metre apartment building sold this month for $792,000.

Sale #2: A 435 square metre, 6-suite apartment building sold last week for $606,000.

Sale #3: An 8-suite, 550 square metre apartment building also sold last week for $784,000.

SALE #	SALE PRICE	SQ. M.	# UNITS	SALE PRICE/ SQ. M.	SALE PRICE/ UNIT

Value of Subject:

▣ Exercise 5

You are asked by Investor McKay to estimate the current market value of an apartment property containing eight two-bedroom suites. Investor McKay provides you with this 12-month income and expense statement prepared for income tax purposes by his accountant.

Gross Revenue For Last Year (12 Months)		**$71,000**
Operating Expenses for the same period:		
Water	1,680	
Heating and Air Conditioning	3,920	
Fire Insurance (1 year premium)	1,448	
Minor Repairs and Maintenance	3,180	
Electricity for Common Areas	600	
Landscaping Contract	1,000	
Realty Taxes	6,800	
Mortgage Interest	4,950	
Purchase of 2 Stoves And 3 Refrigerators	2,900	
Janitor's Salary	15,000	
Painting of Halls and Common Areas	1,500	
Painting and Decorating 3 Suites	2,100	
Carpeting Halls and Public Areas	2,500	
Depreciation	12,000	
Miscellaneous Sundry Expenses	300	
Total Operating Expenses		**$59,878**
NET OPERATING INCOME		**$11,122**

After inspecting the subject property and analyzing relevant market data, you conclude that:

a. Comparable suites in the area rent at $760 monthly.

b. Vacancy and bad debt rate applicable is 2%.

c. Market derived overall capitalization rate is 6¼%.

d. The owner manages the property. However, typical management fees are 3% of effective gross income.

e. Suites are painted once every four years.

f. Halls and common areas are painted every five years.

g. Janitor has a free suite in addition to his salary.

▣ Exercise 6

Given the following information, estimate the value of the subject property using:

1. A gross income multiplier.
2. An overall capitalization rate.

The effective gross income of the subject has been estimated at $80,750; and the net operating income estimated at $49,088. You have selected three comparable income properties with the following data: (the income data is based on the appraiser's reconstructed statements of these comparables):

Sale #1:
Sold for $535,000. The net operating income to be used is $50,022 and the effective gross income is $82,308.

Sale #2:
Sold for $561,000. The net operating income to be used is $52,510 and the effective gross income is $86,175.

Sale #3:
Sold for $495,000. The estimated effective gross income to be used is $76,154 and the net operating income is $46,282.

▣ Exercise 7

Given the following information, estimate the value of the subject property using:

1. A gross income multiplier.
2. An overall capitalization rate.

In reconstructing the owner's Income and Expense Statement, you estimate the:

Effective Gross Income of subject at: $150,000
Annual Operating Expenses of subject at: $90,000

An analysis of three comparable recent sales yielded the following data (based on the appraiser's reconstructed statements of these comparables):

SALE #	SALE PRICE	EFFECTIVE GROSS INCOME	NET INCOME
1	700,000	133,080	53,200
2	830,000	158,000	63,240
3	640,000	123,560	49,425

■ Exercise 8 Multiple Choice

You are to answer 10 multiple choice questions based on the following information. The questions will be found at the end of the case study.

You are asked by Investor McKay to estimate the current market value of a 10-suite apartment property. Investor McKay provides you with this 12 month income and expense statement prepared for income tax purposes by his accountant.

Gross Revenue (January 1 to December 31)		$144,000
Operating Expenses for the same period:		
Utilities (Electricity, Water And Gas)	3,420	
Heating And Air Conditioning	4,100	
Insurance	1,680	
Repairs And Maintenance	4,350	
Modernization Of 2 Bathrooms	5,000	
Realty Taxes	9,800	
Mortgage Interest	21,050	
Depreciation (Capital Cost Allowance)	9,618	
Superintendent Salary	18,500	
Carpeting Hallways	5,600	
Painting Exterior	6,000	
Painting Suites	1,500	
Painting Halls And Common Areas	2,500	
Cleaning Supplies	380	
Elevator Contract	1,000	
Landscaping And Snow Removal Contract	1,650	
Charitable Donations	500	
Owners Automobile Expenses	830	
Installation Of Water Softeners	2,400	
Reserves For Replacement Of Roof	850	
Roof Repairs	320	
Management (Annual Contract)	3,750	
Total Operating Expenses		**$104,798**
NET OPERATING INCOME		**$39,202**

After inspecting the subject property and analyzing relevant market data, you conclude that:

a. Market rent for comparable suites is $1,200 per month.

b. There are 20 extra parking spaces in the underground garage which rent for $30 each per month.

c. Applicable vacancy and bad debt rate on all income is 3%.

d. Suites are painted every 2 years. Owner painted 2 suites this year.

e. Halls and common areas were painted this year and are repainted every 5 years.

f. Exterior woodwork was painted this year and will be repainted every 6 years.

g. Superintendent has a free suite in addition to his salary. Furthermore, the owner paid $450.00 for Employment Insurance, Canada Pension and Workman's Compensation, as owner's contribution with respect to the superintendent's salary.

h. The assessment value is $625,000 and the applicable tax rate is 1.638%.

continued...

CASE STUDY FOR QUESTIONS 8.1— 8.10   *Continued*

You find the following comparable sales.

Comparable #1:
Sold for $575,000. It has an estimated EGI of $140,587 and estimated operating expenses of $67,467.

Comparable #2:
Sold for $614,000. It has an estimated EGI of $149,029 and estimated operating expenses of $67,779.

Comparable #3:
Sold for $664,000. It has an estimated EGI of $161,557 and estimated operating expenses of $74,417.

8.1 Calculate the effective gross income of the subject.

a. $151,200

b. $139,680

c. $146,664

d. $155,736

8.2 Calculate the net operating income of the subject.

a. $66,426

b. $72,176

c. $77,176

d. $77,626

8.3 Calculate Comparable #1's gross income multiplier.

a. 4.09

b. 8.52

c. 12.72

d. 7.86

8.4 Calculate Comparable #1's overall capitalization rate.

a. 11.73%

b. 12.72%

c. 7.86%

d. 4.13%

8.5 Calculate Comparable #2's gross income multiplier.

a. 9.06

b. 13.23

c. 4.12

d. 7.56

8.6   Calculate Comparable #2's overall capitalization rate.

    a. 11.04%

    b.   7.56%

    c. 4.17%

    d. 13.23%

8.7   Calculate Comparable #3's gross income multiplier.

    a. 8.92

    b. 13.12

    c. 7.62

    d. 4.11

8.8   Calculate Comparable #3's overall capitalization rate.

    a. 13.12%

    b. 11.21%

    c. 7.62%

    d. 4.23%

8.9   Calculate the value of the subject property using the gross income multiplier.

    a. $601,322 rounded to $601,000.

    b. $694,584 rounded to $695,000.

    c. $1,003,288 rounded to $1,003,000.

    d. $567,114 rounded to $567,000.

8.10   Calculate the value of the subject property using the overall capitalization rate.

    a. $671,095 rounded to $671,000.

    b. $735,010 rounded to $735,000.

    c. $981,679 rounded to $982,000.

    d. $593,662 rounded to $594,000.

APPENDIX

SOLUTIONS

CHAPTER 1
THE APPRAISAL PROFESSION

Chapter Mini-Review

1. An appraisal is an estimate of value which must be presented in written form.

    True   ✔ False

   An appraisal could be verbal.

2. In Ontario, there is no requirement for an appraiser to actually be licensed by either the government or any particular organization.

    ✔ True   False

   While there is no legislation that mandates that an appraiser must have a designation or license to carry out an appraisal assignment, it is more likely that a prudent bank, lawyer or accountant would hire a person with a recognized appraisal designation to carry out an appraisal where legal or financial considerations were involved.

3. It is not a problem for a salesperson to give advice about the value of a property that is listed in an area where the salesperson has no expertise or knowledge.

    True   ✔ False

   Section 6 of the REBBA 2002 Code of Ethics deals with this issue.

4. An appraiser with a CRA designation is qualified to appraise an office building.

    True   ✔ False

   CRAs are qualified in the appraisal and valuation of individual, undeveloped residential dwelling sites and housing containing not more than four self-contained units.

5. AVMs compete with professional appraisers for appraisal business especially when it comes to valuations for mortgage lending purposes.

    ✔ True   False

   AVMs are most effective when there are lots of sales in the neighbourhood, the properties are highly similar and the lending risk level is considered relatively low.

6. A form report would be used by an appraiser when estimating the market value of an office building.

    True   ✔ False

   Form reports are designed for residential properties with up to 4 self-contained units.

7. An appraisal completed by a letter of opinion does not require the same research, analysis and conclusions as does a valuation completed on a form report.

   True   ✔ False

   While the letter of opinion does not detail the research, analysis and all the conclusions, the file on the valuation must include this information in order to support the valuation.

8. Subjective value states that value exists in the minds of buyers and sellers.

    ✔ True   False

   In subjective value, the key is to look at what people are willing to pay for a property irrespective of what it costs to produce. People will base what they are willing to pay on what other people were willing to pay for similar properties.

9. The subjective concept of value dominates in real estate valuation.

 True   False

This concept is used in the Direct Comparison Approach which is used as the primary approach in valuing residential homes.

10. Market price and market value would always be the same.

 True   **False**

There are situations where a buyer might overpay for a property (sold their home and are desperate to find another home quickly) or underpay for a home (seller is in financial difficulties and needs to sell quickly at any cost).

11. John is thinking of paying $10,000 more for 123 Main Street than for 125 Main Street because it has a fireplace and central air conditioning not found in 125 Main Street. This is an example of the principle of anticipation.

 True   False

John is looking at the present value of something (the fireplace and central air conditioning unit) that he anticipates that he will enjoy in the future (i.e., when he moves into the property).

12. The definition of highest and best use is "that use which at the time of the appraisal is most likely to produce the greatest net return in money or amenities to the building over a given period of time."

○ True   ✓ **False**

Highest and best use applies to the use of the land.

Active Learning Exercises

■ Exercise 1

- The highest price in terms of money.
- An open market.
- A willing buyer and seller.
- No undue motivation or unusual circumstances.
- Equal and adequate knowledge.
- A reasonable time.

■ Exercise 2

2.1 Value In Use.

2.2 Market Value.

2.3 Objective Value.

2.4 Subjective Value.

CH1 EX3

■ Exercise 3

The market value of a property is an estimation based on the recent selling and listing prices of comparable properties located in the neighbourhood.

The market price is the actual selling price that a property achieved irrespective of its value. Market price can be the same, lower or higher than market value.

CH1 EX4

■ Exercise 4

- The objective concept of value bases value on the cost of creating or producing the item.
- The subjective concept of value looks at what people are prepared to pay for the item based on their opinion and preferences, irrespective of what it costs.

CH1 EX5

■ Exercise 5

Value in use is looked at from the point of view of a specific owner/seller or buyer, rather than from the point of view of the market place as a whole. The property may have features in it that have a specific appeal to the owner or buyer that is not important to the average buyer. Examples could be as follows:

- A swimming pool that the owner loves and uses, but which most buyers are indifferent to. The owner gives a significant value to the pool, but the average buyer would not.
- The property is located a block from the buyer's office. This may be important to a specific buyer, but would not be to the average buyer. That specific buyer may give added value to the location, but others would not.

Market value is looked at from the perspective of the average buyer with no special circumstances (value in use) included.

CH1 EX6

■ Exercise 6   Multiple Choice

6.1 Which of the following would assist in providing a necessary level of conformity within a neighbourhood?

a. Easements

Incorrect. An easement is a right enjoyed by one landowner over the land of another—there is no connection to this question.

b. Zoning

 CORRECT. Municipal zoning is used to ensure a certain level of compatibility of uses within a designated area; i.e., the zoning dictates what can and cannot be built.

c. Encroachments

Incorrect. An encroachment is the unauthorized intrusion onto the lands and property of another—there is no connection to this question.

d. Profits

Incorrect. Profit is a gain resulting from a business activity or investment—there is no connection to this question.

APPENDIX

6.2 Mike Smith is a salesperson who has been listing and selling single-family homes for several years in Anycity. He has been asked by one of his clients to value a condominium apartment unit in Anycity for capital gains tax purposes. Mike's training and experience is strictly limited to listing and selling single-family homes. What should he do?

a. Advise his client of his lack of training and experience, but proceed to complete the appraisal if the client still wishes.

Incorrect. This action would not be in keeping with a salesperson's obligations under Section 6 of the REBBA 2002 Code of Ethics.

b. Use his knowledge and experience of single-family homes to assist him in valuing the condominium.

Incorrect. This action would not be in keeping with a salesperson's obligations under Section 6 of the REBBA 2002 Code of Ethics.

c. **Turn down the client's request because of his lack of training and experience with respect to this type of property and assignment.**

✓ *CORRECT.* Section 6 of the REBBA 2002 Code of Ethics is quite specific about what a salesperson should do in these circumstances.

d. Complete the appraisal, but ensure that a limiting condition is put in the appraisal that outlines his lack of training and experience.

Incorrect. This action would not be in keeping with a salesperson's obligations under Section 6 of the REBBA 2002 Code of Ethics.

6.3 Which of the following statements accurately reflects the principle of regression?

a. The value of the better property will be affected positively by the presence of the property of lesser value.

Incorrect. This statement contradicts the principle of regression.

b. The property of lesser value will be negatively affected by the presence of the property of greater value.

Incorrect. This statement misinterprets the principle of progression as the property of lesser value would be positively affected by the presence of the property of greater value.

c. **The value of the better property will be affected adversely by the presence of the property of lesser value.**

✓ *CORRECT.* The value of a luxury 5,000 square foot house would be negatively affected by being surrounded by old run down 1,000 square foot bungalows.

d. The property of lesser value would not be positively or negatively affected by the presence of the property of greater value.

Incorrect. This statement misinterprets the principle of progression as the property of lesser value would be positively affected by the presence of the property of greater value.

6.4 An appraiser with a CRA designation is qualified to appraise a residential home containing up to a maximum of:

a. 6 self-contained units.

Incorrect. It would be unethical for a CRA to use their designation to appraise a building with this number of units.

b. 2 self-contained units.

Incorrect. A CRA can use their designation to appraise a duplex. However, the question requires you to identify the maximum number of units a CRA can appraise using their designation.

c. 10 self-contained units.

Incorrect. It would be unethical for a CRA to use their designation to appraise a building with this number of units.

d. **4 self-contained units.**

✔ *CORRECT.* The Appraisal Institute of Canada permits a CRA to use their designation in appraising properties developed with buildings containing up to 4 self-contained units.

6.5 For what type of appraisal would a form report not be used? The valuation of a:

a. **60-unit apartment building for mortgage financing purposes.**

✔ *CORRECT.* Remember that the question asks *"For what type of appraisal would a form report not be used?"* The form report does not accommodate the type and amount of information that would be required by an appraiser when valuing an apartment building; e.g., this type of property would require a valuation using the income approach—that approach is not traditionally contained in a form report.

b. Duplex for transfer or ownership purposes.

Incorrect. The form report was developed with single-family homes and duplexes in mind, and accommodates the information necessary to successfully complete this type of assignment.

c. Single-family home for estate purposes.

Incorrect. The form report was developed with single-family homes and duplexes in mind, and accommodates the information necessary to successfully complete this type of assignment.

d. Single-family home for capital gains taxes.

Incorrect. The form report was developed with single-family homes and duplexes in mind, and accommodates the information necessary to successfully complete this type of assignment.

6.6 Which of the following scenarios incorporates one of the main characteristics of market value?

a. **The property was marketed for a reasonable length of time before it sold.**

✔ *CORRECT.* A reasonable length of time is a characteristic contained in the definition of market value.

b. The property was located next to similar properties.

Incorrect. This answer is connected to the principle of conformity—it is not a characteristic contained in the definition of market value.

c. Supply and demand in the neighbourhood was balanced.

Incorrect. Supply and demand explains the state of the market (why prices are stable, increasing, decreasing), but is not a characteristic of market value.

d. Each additional bathroom cost $5,000, but increased value by $7,000.

Incorrect. This scenario is explained by the principle of contribution, but is not connected to any of the main characteristics within the definition of market value.

APPENDIX

6.7 Which of the following situations would be the most likely to cause the market value of a property to be different from its market price?

a. The property was being sold on MLS®.

Incorrect. The sale of a property on MLS® would indicate a sale on the open market, which would be one of the characteristics of market value. As a result, this example does not suggest a market value that would likely be different than the market price.

b. The property sold within a reasonable amount of time.

Incorrect. Selling within a reasonable time would be one of the characteristics of market value. As a result, this example does not suggest a market value that would likely be different than the market price.

c. **The seller needed to sell quickly because of financial difficulties.**

✓ *CORRECT.* Two characteristics of market value are that there are no unusual circumstances (e.g., undue pressure) and that a reasonable amount of time has been allowed to market a property. In this example, neither characteristic is present in the sale and the result could well be a selling price (market price) that is outside of the market value of the property.

d. The buyer and seller negotiated with both having equal and adequate knowledge.

Incorrect. Equal and adequate knowledge would be one of the characteristics of market value. As a result, this example does not suggest a market value that would likely be different than the market price.

6.8 Which principle would explain why an appraisal report would always include the effective date of the appraisal?

a. Highest and best use.

Incorrect. The principle of highest and best use alerts the appraiser to the fact that a property's value should be based on a legitimate use that would provide the owner with the highest value. That use could be the current use or an alternative use.

b. **Change.**

✓ *CORRECT.* The principle of change illustrates the fact that a value estimate provided by an appraiser is only valid as of a specific time—markets change. That specific time is identified by the effective date.

c. Anticipation.

Incorrect. The principle of anticipation relates to the price that a buyer will pay for a property based on the benefits that buyer anticipates he/she will enjoy from the ownership of that property.

d. Consistent use.

Incorrect. The principle of consistent use alerts the appraiser to the fact that the valuation of a property must be consistent with its highest and best use; e.g., if the land is being valued for its redevelopment potential, then you cannot add any value for the current improvements as they would be demolished in a redevelopment.

6.9 24 Main Street is a 25-year-old detached 1,900 square foot bungalow, surrounded by 3,200 square feet detached 2-storey 5-year-old homes. Describe what impact the above scenario would likely have on the value of 24 Main Street.

a.   There would be a negative impact on the value of 24 Main Street.

Incorrect. This interpretation of the impact would be a contradiction of the principle of progression.

b.   **There would be a positive impact on the value of 24 Main Street.**

✔ *CORRECT.* This impact is explained by the principle of progression.

c.   There would be no impact on the value of 24 Main Street.

Incorrect. This interpretation of the impact would be a contradiction of the principle of progression.

d.   There could be either a positive and negative impact on the value of 24 Main Street.

Incorrect. This interpretation of the impact would be a contradiction of the principle of progression.

6.10 In valuing properties, it is important to keep in mind that:

a.   **A prudent buyer will pay no more for a property than the cost of acquiring an equally desirable substitute in the market place.**

✔ *CORRECT.* This statement is explained by the principle of substitution. The principle provides the rationale for using comparables in valuing a property.

b.   An appraiser, in estimating market value, must only consider the current use of the property as being the highest and best use.

Incorrect. The highest and best use could be the current use or an alternative use. Market value assumes that the appraiser will take into account the highest and best use whether it is the current use or an alternative use.

c.   The value of a property will continue to increase as more and more amenities and features are added to it.

Incorrect. This would violate the principle of increasing and decreasing returns. Continuing to add features/amenities to a property will at some point add little or no value to a property, or may even decrease a property's value if needless amenities or features are added.

d.   Excessive profits will tend to decrease competition, which in turn will have a negative impact on value.

Incorrect. The opposite is actually true. Excessive profits will increase the value of a property/business and will increase competition.

APPENDIX

CHAPTER 2
ACCEPTING A REQUEST FOR AN APPRAISAL

CH2 MR

Chapter Mini-Review

1. The purpose of *Defining the Problem* is to understand what it is the appraiser is being asked to do in the appraisal assignment.

    True   False

   An appraiser, or salesperson for that matter, should not undertake an assignment until he/she fully understands what is involved in that assignment; e.g., what is the purpose of the appraisal, what is the effective date of the appraisal, etc.

2. One of the purposes for which an appraisal would be required would be to estimate market value.

    True   **False**

   Market value is not a purpose. The sale of a property or obtaining a mortgage would be a purpose. The value being used depends on the purpose.

3. Market value is the only type of value used by appraisers.

    True   **False**

   There are many types of value; e.g., insurance value.

4. One purpose for which an appraisal might be required is for a land use study.

    True   False

   A land use study is an appraisal assignment that looks at estimating the highest and best use of the land; i.e., the use that will provide the land with the greatest net return.

5. The effective date of an appraisal would be the date the appraisal report was completed.

    True   **False**

   The two dates are independent of each other. The effective date is dependent on the purpose of the appraisal and the requirements of the client.

6. The zoning of a property would not have an impact on the value of a property.

    True   **False**

   Zoning can change the highest and best use of a property, which as a result can have a significant impact on value.

7. The date of inspection and the effective date would not be the same when it comes to valuing a property for the purpose of a marriage separation.

    True   False

   The effective date would likely be some time in the past. It would not be up to you to determine or advise as to what the effective date should be. You would get your instruction from the client or their lawyer.

8. When completing the preliminary work in an appraisal assignment, the appraiser would want to establish if the subject property contained any functional obsolescence.

    True   **False**

   This would be done later during a physical inspection of the property.

APPENDIX

9. The highest and best use of a property does not change over a period of time.

   ○ True   ✔ False

   The principle of change tells us that change can occur at any time.

10. The accuracy of the Direct Comparison Approach will depend on being able to locate good comparable sales that require few, or relatively few, adjustments.

     ✔ True   ○ False

    The fewer the adjustments required, the more comparable the sale. A good comparable is one that requires few adjustments.

11. Assumptions and limiting conditions tell a client what an appraiser did or did not do, as well as what the appraiser is or is not responsible for in the valuation of their property.

     ✔ True   ○ False

    A client needs to understand the circumstances and conditions under which an appraisal assignment was carried out. If the client knows this up front, it is unlikely that they will have grounds for a complaint later on.

12. The property is developed with a detached two-storey building containing a store and apartment. If, after careful consideration, it is determined that this is not the highest and best use of the property, the highest and best use of the property would now be determined by looking at the property as if it were a vacant site, because the store and apartment would not add value to the land.

     ✔ True   ○ False

    If the current use of a property is not the highest and best use, then the improvements cannot in fact add any value to the site. The value of the land available for an alternative use would be worth more than the value of the property (including improvements) in its current use; e.g., as a store and apartment, the property might only be worth $400,000 to a buyer; as a piece of land that can have a 20-storey condominium built on it, the land (property) might be worth $2,000,000 to a buyer.

Active Learning Exercises

▣ Exercise 1

1.1 • Is the building legal or legal non-conforming?

• Is the building similar to the other homes in the area?

• Does the building add value to the site?

• Would a typical purchaser buying the property live in the building or knock it down and build something else?

• Is there a demand for this type of home or is another type of home in demand?

• If the house were to be knocked down and another home be constructed, would the increase in value equal the cost of doing so?

1.2 • What does the zoning allow you to build on the site?

• What types of homes are in demand in the area?

• What types of homes have already been built, recently built or are in the middle of construction?

• What type of house does the subject site physically allow for?

• Will the value of the house being proposed at least equal the cost of its construction?

▣ Exercise 2

Sometimes an appraiser is asked to inspect a property, but value it as at a specific date in the past. The past date required will depend on the circumstances, but could be as a result of a probate of will, fire insurance claim, legal dispute, separation/divorce, expropriation or capital gains. It is not the appraiser who decides on the value date, but the client.

▣ Exercise 3

Information sources include:

• Deed—Legal description;

• Lease—Tenant information;

• Tax Bill—Assessment;

• Client—Type of value, effective date of appraisal;

• Municipality—Zoning, building permits; and

• MLS®—Property values, sales, typical exposure time.

▣ Exercise 4

4.1 • Ask the owner if they have started the rezoning process.

• Check with the city to see how easy it will be to get rezoning, if at all.

• If rezoning is not possible or if it would be a long process with no certainty of success, then value as is based on the current zoning.

• If rezoning would be a simple, short process with a high certainty of success, discuss issue with Tarquin Trust and get their authorization as to how to proceed. If Tarquin wishes to proceed as if rezoned, make sure you develop an Assumption and Limiting Condition that will cover what you have been asked to do and what would happen if rezoning does not take place.

4.2   Yes. In this case, you could proceed with the valuation on the following basis:

- The buyers were going to use the appraisal for their own purposes only (i.e., how much to pay for the property).
- You were aware of and knew the buyers were aware of the realities of getting rezoning.
- You were assured that the valuation would not be used for or by a third party to justify a certain amount of financing.
- You made adequate cautions by way of Assumptions and Limiting Conditions that advised the reader of the possibility of rezoning, and that the report could only be used by the buyers and could not be used by a third party, either for financing or buying and reselling purposes.
- If you are not comfortable as to how the report will be used, do not do the appraisal.

◼ Exercise 5

The typical exposure time for properties to sell tells you the state of the neighbourhood market in terms of its activity. Knowing exposure times required for properties on the subject street is relevant as it shows the relative popularity and appeal, or lack of, as compared to the rest of the neighbourhood.

Most homes are valued based on their being marketed or exposed on the market for a reasonable length of time. That reasonable time is the typical exposure time required for properties to sell within the subject neighbourhood. As a result, this information is important to know. Choose comparables that sold within the typical exposure time.

◼ Exercise 6

The subject's previous listing time (days on market) and selling price will tell you how the property has been viewed previously in terms of the neighbourhood and other properties of comparable size and utility. This may or may not be relevant in today's market or valuation, but at least it will be a starting point and may warn you of potential difficulties or problems in the property itself, or in the valuation process.

Suppose the subject property took 253 days to sell in 1996 at a time when the typical sale occurred in 60 days. Suppose the subject had sold in 1996 for $350,000 when properties of comparable size and utility were selling for between $400,000 and $450,000. In both cases, you would want to know if the property had been overpriced and sold after becoming stale or whether there was some other factor relevant today, such as a location or physical/functional problem.

◼ Exercise 7

The current listing price of the subject property would in all likelihood set its upper limit of value. Suppose the subject property had been listed on the market at $490,000 for 120 days with no offers. It is unlikely you would want to value the property at $495,000. Treat the listing price as a starting guide.

APPENDIX

■ **Exercise 8   Multiple Choice**   CH2 EX8

8.1   The type of value required for an appraisal assignment will depend on the:

a.   zoning of the property.

Incorrect. The zoning may affect the estimated value, but it does not determine the type of value to be used in an assignment.

b.   effective date of the appraisal.

Incorrect. The effective date of the appraisal depends on the purpose of the appraisal, but does not determine the type of value to be used.

c.   highest and best use of the property.

Incorrect. The highest and best use may affect the estimated value, but it does not determine the type of value to be used in an assignment.

d.   **purpose of the appraisal.**

✔ *CORRECT.* There are many types of value; e.g., market value, insurance value, investment value, lending value. The type of value that will be used depends on the purpose of the appraisal, as requested by the client.

8.2   Jim has appraised 123 Main Street and estimated a value of $324,000 as of May 21st, 20xx. For what period of time would that value be valid?

a.   The value would be valid for 30 days after the effective date.

Incorrect. See Assumption and Limiting Condition #2.

b.   The value would be valid for a 45 to 60 day marketing period.

Incorrect. See Assumption and Limiting Condition #2.

c.   There is no specific time period for which a value would be valid.

Incorrect. See Assumption and Limiting Condition #2.

d.   **It would only be valid as of the effective date of the appraisal.**

✔ *CORRECT.* See Assumption and Limiting Condition #2.

8.3   Provide a circumstance in which the effective date and the date of inspection would not be the same.

a.   **A trustee needs an appraisal for probating a will.**

✔ *CORRECT.* The date will be some time in the past; i.e., usually the date of death.

b.   A buyer needs an appraisal for mortgage financing.

Incorrect. The bank would want a current valuation which would be the date that the appraiser inspected the property.

c.   A seller needs an appraisal for listing purposes.

Incorrect. The seller would want a current valuation which would be the date that the appraiser inspected the property.

d.   A buyer needs an appraisal for the purpose of making an offer.

Incorrect. The buyer would want a current valuation which would be the date that the appraiser inspected the property.

APPENDIX

8.4 What is the purpose of assumptions and limiting conditions?

a. They outline the circumstances and conditions under which an appraisal was completed.

✔ *CORRECT.* This makes sense if you read the Assumptions and Limiting Conditions as outlined on page six of the *Standard Appraisal Report—Single Family* (OREA Form 700).

b. They prevent a client from being able to sue the appraiser for negligent mistakes made during the valuation.

Incorrect. There is nothing in the Assumptions and Limiting Conditions that would suggest this to be true. It is unlikely that a court would allow an appraiser to escape from being responsible for negligence.

c. It is the certification of the appraiser's ability to appraise the client's property without limitations.

Incorrect. A quick read of the Assumptions and Limiting Conditions would suggest that this is not true.

d. They outline the problems in the client's property and what will be done to correct those problems.

Incorrect. A quick read of the Assumptions and Limiting Conditions would suggest that this is not true.

8.5 One of the factors that would be looked at in estimating the highest and best use of a vacant site would be the:

a. zoning of the property.

✔ *CORRECT.* If the proposed use is not legal, then it cannot be developed as such.

b. purpose of the appraisal.

Incorrect. This would not be one of the factors that would be looked at in estimating highest and best use.

c. tax value of the property.

Incorrect. This would not be one of the factors that would be looked at in estimating highest and best use.

d. type of value required.

Incorrect. This would not be one of the factors that would be looked at in estimating highest and best use.

8.6 Jim is appraising 123 Manin Road (a vacant site) for a bank for mortgage financing. He believes that the highest and best use of the site would be a six-storey 80-unit apartment building. There is demand for this use and it is physically possible. However, the current zoning only allows for a three-storey 40-unit apartment building. Under what circumstances would this property's highest and best use still be estimated as a 6-storey 80-unit apartment building?

CH2 EX8

a. If a change to the zoning were possible and an application had been made.

Incorrect. Possible is very different from probable. Anything is possible, but is it likely to happen. The six-storey building will make the land worth much more than a three-storey building. However, consider what would happen if the zoning change does not take place and the bank has lent a large sum of money in the belief that there would be a zoning change.

b. If the owner of the subject property had given Jim permission to do so.

Incorrect. Of course the owner is going to give permission as they undoubtedly would appreciate the extra funds. However, the bank is the client and the appraiser needs to protect the client.

c. Under no circumstances could Jim do that, unless permission was given by the zoning department.

Incorrect. The zoning department is not the institution relying on or requiring the appraisal.

d. **If a change in zoning for the subject property was probable and imminent.**

✓ *CORRECT.* The zoning change must be probable and imminent and it will be up to the bank to decide whether the appraisal can be based on a probable and imminent change to the zoning.

8.7 What would be one of the factors that an appraiser would look at in confirming that the current improvements of a site are its highest and best use?

a. The typical number of days it takes to sell a property in the neighbourhood.

Incorrect. While this is important information in valuing a property, it does not assist an appraiser in determining whether the current improvements are the highest and best use of the land.

b. **Whether the improvements conform to the other properties in the area.**

✓ *CORRECT.* If the current building is similar to the majority of other buildings in the area, then it may well be the highest and best use of the property. Of course, it is only one of the factors to be considered in estimating the highest and best use.

c. The change in prices experienced in the area over the past 12 months.

Incorrect. While this is important information in valuing a property, it does not assist an appraiser in determining whether the current improvements are the highest and best use of the land.

d. Value of the subject site as compared to the other sites in the area.

Incorrect. The value of the subject site will be based on the value (selling price) of other comparable sites. The value will, of course, depend on the subject's highest and best use.

APPENDIX

8.8 The property is developed with a single-family home on a main road. The zoning allows for a five-storey office building and the lot could easily physically accommodate that type of improvement. The cost of putting up the office building would be $2,000,000 and it would add $1,700,000 in value to the subject site. Would the five-storey office building in fact be the highest and best use of the land?

a. No, because the current use is always the best use of the property.

Incorrect. This answer does not attempt to address the facts of the case and it provides a blanket statement that cannot be true.

b. Yes, the zoning allows for it and it is physically possible.

Incorrect. This answer does not address the issue of the cost and expected return/value increase.

c. **No, because it would not be financially viable.**

✔ *CORRECT.* If the cost of development is greater than the expected return or value increase, then it clearly would not be the highest and best use of the property. What person would knowingly invest money in a project that they knew up front would lose them money?

d. Yes, because it would add much more value to the land than the single-family house.

Incorrect. Nobody is going to pay more money for the land just so they can make a loss of $300,000 ($2,000,000–$1,700,000).

8.9 You are appraising the market value of a property for sale purposes. You have estimated that a reasonable time to sell a property would be 60 days. How would you have come up with the 60 days?

a. The number of days it had taken to sell the subject property in previous years.

Incorrect. While this information will tell you something about the appeal of the subject property, it does not tell you what a reasonable time to sell is.

b. The average number of days that current listings had been on the market for.

Incorrect. Current listings will not tell you how long it will take to actually sell a property.

c. **The typical exposure time needed to sell similar properties in the neighbourhood.**

✔ *CORRECT.* A reasonable time is estimated by looking at the average number of days it takes to sell similar properties in the area.

d. The average number of days that expired listings had been on the market for.

Incorrect. An expired listing did not sell, so it cannot tell you how long it is taking to sell a property in the neighbourhood.

APPENDIX

8.10 What piece or pieces of information that you would note on an appraisal could help you identify if a specific property was going to be difficult to market and sell as compared to other similar properties?

CH2 EX8

a.	The previous listing and sale history of the property itself.	✓ *CORRECT.* The selling history of the subject property will give clues as to how it has been, and may in the future be, perceived in the marketplace.
b.	The assumptions and limiting conditions outlined in the appraisal report.	*Incorrect.* Assumptions and Limiting Conditions will tell you the conditions under which an appraisal was completed, it will not assist in identifying the appeal of the subject property.
c.	How many times the property had sold over the past several years.	*Incorrect.* While this is interesting information, it will not assist in identifying the appeal of the subject property.
d.	The supply and demand of comparable properties in the area.	*Incorrect.* While supply and demand will provide an insight into the state of the market in terms of prices, it will not assist in identifying the appeal of the subject property.

8.11 The subject property has been listed at $222,000 for 70 days. It is a very active market, but there have been no offers on the property. The typical exposure time for similar properties in the neighbourhood is 60 days. How does the listing price assist you in valuing the property?

a.	The current listing price sets the lower limit of value.	*Incorrect.* The opposite is true—in fact the subject cannot be worth more than $222,000. The property would have sold if it were really worth more than $222,000.
b.	The current listing price sets the upper limit of value.	✓ *CORRECT.* The subject cannot be worth more than $222,000. The property would have sold if it were really worth more than $222,000.
c.	It would tell you what the property is worth.	*Incorrect.* Only a sale can tell you what a property is worth. A listing can tell you what a property is not worth. The subject is not worth more than $222,000.
d.	It would not tell you anything as it is just a listing.	*Incorrect.* A listing can tell you what a property is not worth; the subject is not worth more than $222,000.

CHAPTER 3
NEIGHBOURHOOD ANALYSIS

Chapter Mini-Review

1. A typical example of a neighbourhood boundary would be a ravine or a major highway.

    True   False

   Neighbourhood boundaries are usually classified as man-made, natural or political.

2. A neighbourhood with easy access to transportation will be negatively affected.

    True   **False**

   Having access to public transportation would normally be appealing to buyers.

3. The four distinct features of a trend are: growth, stability, decline and renewal.

    True   **False**

   These are stages in the life cycle of a neighbourhood. The features are time, direction, cause and effect.

4. A trend in a neighbourhood can have an impact on the value of the subject property.

    True   False

   Lets look at an example—the subject property has an eat-in kitchen at the front of the house. The current trend for new homes or renovations is to have the kitchens combined with family rooms and have those rooms placed at the back of the home looking onto the backyard. As a result, the subject will not be as valuable as a property with a combined kitchen/family room at the back of the house.

5. A neighbourhood goes through 2 distinct phases of a life cycle.

    True   **False**

   There are 4 distinct phases—growth, stability, decline and renewal.

6. The subject's value is going to be determined by the prices being obtained by comparable properties in the neighbourhood.

    True   False

   Lets look at an example—if very comparable properties are selling in the $375,000 to $400,000 range, then that will dictate the value of the subject property; i.e., the subject property cannot be worth $500,000.

7. For a neighbourhood in decline you are more likely to see people of higher income levels moving into the area.

    True   **False**

   This would more likely be an indication of renewal and not decline.

8. The growth phase of a neighbourhood occurs when a neighbourhood is first being developed.

    True   False

   There are four phases that a neighbourhood can experience; i.e., growth, stability, decline and renewal.

APPENDIX

9. If the price range of properties on the subject street is at the high end of the price range for the neighbourhood, then the subject street will be considered as having one of the inferior locations in the neighbourhood.

 True   False

The opposite is in fact true. A high price range within a neighbourhood would suggest that the street represents one of the better locations.

10. The amount of time to sell a property in a neighbourhood that was in a renewal phase will likely be longer than if the neighbourhood were in decline.

 True   False

In fact, it should take a shorter period of time to sell a property in a period of renewal than if it were in a period of decline.

Active Learning Exercises

Exercise 1

1.1 The likelihood is that there will be a negative impact, which will actually lower the value of the subject.

1.2 The principle of conformity (regression).

1.3 By collecting information and data from the marketplace; i.e., sales, listings, expired listings that can show the expected value relationships and impact between the subject and surrounding homes. The relationship can be gleaned from the subject's prior sales or from the sale of similar homes in the past, or in other neighbourhoods. It would be ideal to contrast the sale of a home that is much superior than the surrounding properties, to the sale of a similar home surrounded by properties of the same size, quality and utility.

Exercise 2

- How well or poorly the homes are being maintained and what level of renovation or new construction is or is not taking place.
- The income levels of people moving in and out of the area.
- The changing level of owner or tenant occupation.
- Price levels and length of time needed for marketing—whether they are staying stable, improving or declining in terms of comparison with other similar neighbourhoods.

CH3 EX3   ■ Exercise 3 Multiple Choice

3.1 Ignoring neighbourhood trends in an appraisal assignment could result in an appraiser:

a. overvaluing or undervaluing the final value of the subject property.

✔ *CORRECT.* An example may help to explain further. The trend in the neighbourhood is to install hardwood floors, rather than carpet. As a result, a home with hardwood floors is worth more than a home with carpet. The subject property has carpet. If the appraiser was not aware of this trend, then he/she might not make an adjustment for the difference believing that the appeal/value of both types of flooring was similar.

b. arriving at a more accurate final value for the subject property.

Incorrect. The opposite is actually true. Understanding trends will assist the appraiser in identifying the best comparables and what adjustments are required.

c. being able to more easily establish the life cycle stage that a neighbourhood is going through.

Incorrect. The opposite is actually true. Knowing the individual and overall trends within a neighbourhood will help identify the life cycle stage that the subject neighbourhood is going through.

d. less easily able to identify the sources of the information that needs to be collected.

Incorrect. Ignoring trends may affect the information that the appraiser decides to collect, but it does not change the sources of that information.

3.2 What stage of the life cycle has Neighbourhood A been going through during the past five year period?

a. Stability

Incorrect. This conclusion is not supported by the information supplied in the case study.

b. Growth

Incorrect. This conclusion is not supported by the information supplied in the case study.

c. Decline

✔ *CORRECT.* Owner occupation has declined in favour of tenancy; average incomes have dropped; prices have risen much slower than in a comparable neighbourhood.

d. Renewal

Incorrect. This conclusion is not supported by the information supplied in the case study.

APPENDIX

3.3 What market data given in the case study would confirm the stage of the life cycle that Neighbourhood A had been going through over the past 5 years?

a. Prices in Neighbourhood A ranged from $200,000 to $225,000, while prices in Neighbourhood B ranged from $195,000 to $230,000 5 years ago.

Incorrect. These numbers are correct, but they are not sufficient to confirm the stage of the life cycle that Neighbourhood A had been going through over the past 5 years.

b. **Prices in Neighbourhood A have risen by less than 10% over the past 5 years while prices in Neighbourhood B have risen by between 25 and 30%.**

✓ *CORRECT.* Prices in Neighbourhood A went from $200,000–$225,000 to $215,000–$245,000, while in Neighbourhood B they went from $195,000–$230,000 to $250,000–$295,000. This information supports the analysis that Neighbourhood A has been in decline over the past 5 years.

c. Prices in Neighbourhood A have risen by between 25 and 30% over the past 5 years while prices in Neighbourhood B have gone up by less than 10%.

Incorrect. This analysis of the information provided is in fact incorrect.

d. Within the province, property prices have generally risen 15–30% over the past five years due to economic improvement and inflation.

Incorrect. While this information is in fact correct, it does not confirm the stage of the life cycle that Neighbourhood A had been going through over the past 5 years.

3.4 What is the impact on the value of the subject property as a result of it being surrounded by much larger homes?

a. **The subject's value has been positively impacted.**

✓ *CORRECT.* The bungalows in Neighbourhood A sell for $30,000 more than in Neighbourhood B. Clearly, the principal of progression is at work here.

b. There has been no impact on the subject's value.

Incorrect. This would contradict the evidence.

c. The subject's value has been negatively impacted.

Incorrect. This would contradict the evidence.

d. The impact will have been both positive and negative.

Incorrect. The bungalows in Neighbourhood A sell for $30,000 more than in Neighbourhood B. Clearly, the impact has been positive.

APPENDIX

CH3 EX3   **3.5** What market data would confirm the impact on the value of the subject?

a. 1,000 square foot bungalows in Neighbourhood A sell for $160,000, while they sell for $130,000 in Neighbourhood B.

✔ *CORRECT.* This market data clearly shows the positive impact.

b. The fact that Neighbourhood B is located next door to Neighbourhood A would confirm the impact.

Incorrect. While this information is correct, it is not the necessary market data; i.e., selling price differentials.

c. The only difference between Neighbourhood A and B is related to the size of the majority of homes in each area.

Incorrect. While this information is correct, it is not the necessary market data; i.e., selling price differentials.

d. 2,000–2,500 square foot homes in Neighbourhood A sell for between $190,000 and 210,000.

Incorrect. While this information is correct, it is not the necessary market data; i.e., selling price differentials.

3.6 What impact does the presence of two theatres and over a dozen restaurants have on Neighbourhood A?

a. It has a negative impact on value.

Incorrect. This contradicts the evidence from the market place. Prices in Neighbourhood A are higher than in Neighbourhood B, despite being very similar neighbourhoods.

b. It has no impact on value.

Incorrect. This contradicts the evidence from the market place. Prices in Neighbourhood A are higher than in Neighbourhood B despite being very similar neighbourhoods.

c. **It has a positive impact on value.**

✔ *CORRECT.* Prices in Neighbourhood A are higher than in Neighbourhood B, despite being very similar neighbourhoods.

d. It has both a positive and negative impact.

Incorrect. It cannot be both. Prices in Neighbourhood A are higher than in Neighbourhood B, despite being very similar neighbourhoods. This suggest a positive impact.

APPENDIX

3.7 What market data would confirm the impact on value within Neighbourhood A?

a. The fact that Neighbourhood A is located 3 miles away from Neighbourhood B.

Incorrect. While this information is correct, it does not in itself provide the market evidence as to what the impact is on Neighbourhood A.

b. Neighbourhood A is developed with older detached 2,000 to 2,500 square foot homes.

Incorrect. While this information is correct, it does not in itself provide the market evidence as to what the impact is on Neighbourhood A.

c. **House prices in Neighbourhood A are up to $10,000 more than in Neighbourhood B.**

✔ *CORRECT.* This is clear information from the market place that the presence of theatres and restaurants are having a positive impact.

d. Both neighbourhoods appeal to the middle income segment of the population.

Incorrect. While this information is correct, it does not in itself provide the market evidence as to what the impact is on Neighbourhood A.

3.8 A residential neighbourhood could be negatively affected by:

a. **declining family income levels.**

✔ *CORRECT.* Less income can mean less ability to maintain, renovate or purchase property, all of which has negative implications.

b. increasing job opportunities.

Incorrect. This should have a positive impact. Higher employment rates usually translates into more people being able to purchase homes or maintain/renovate their properties.

c. low interest rates.

Incorrect. This should have a positive impact. It will help make homes more affordable.

d. a wide range of amenities.

Incorrect. This should have a positive impact. It would make the neighbourhood more appealing.

3.9 A residential neighbourhood could be positively affected by:

a. a lack of schools in the area.

Incorrect. This could have a negative impact as it may prevent a number of people with children from wanting to move into the area.

b. **a growth in population.**

✔ *CORRECT.* Population growth can lead to more demand for housing.

c. a high crime rate.

Incorrect. This will likely have a negative impact.

d. a lack of tree-lined streets.

Incorrect. This will likely have a negative impact.

APPENDIX

CH3 **EX3**   **3.10** Describe what you would expect to see in a neighbourhood that is in a declining phase.

a. The neighbourhood would be increasing in popularity.

Incorrect. This would suggest growth or renewal.

b. Lots of new construction in the neighbourhood.

Incorrect. This would suggest growth or renewal.

c. Property prices would be rising faster than before.

Incorrect. This suggests that the neighbourhood has become quite popular and is in a renewal phase.

d. **Properties becoming less well maintained than before.**

✔ *CORRECT.* This could be as a result of families with lower incomes and less disposable incomes moving into the area. It could be as a result of property owners renting out their homes, rather than owner occupying them.

3.11 2% of the homes in the neighbourhood are 70-year-old 1,200 square foot bungalows sitting on 30 by 140 foot lots. 98% of the homes in the area are more expensive 70-year-old detached two-storey 2,500 square foot homes sitting on 50 by 150 foot lots. What impact would this scenario have on the bungalows?

a. It would tend to drive down the prices of the bungalows.

Incorrect. This would violate the principle of progression.

b. It would make the bungalows appear less appealing.

Incorrect. This would violate the principle of progression.

c. It would make the bungalows the same value as the detached two storey homes.

Incorrect. This would not make sense as the detached 2-storey home is clearly superior.

d. **It would tend to drive up the prices of the bungalows.**

✔ *CORRECT.* This statement is well supported by the principle of progression.

CHAPTER 4
SITE ANALYSIS

Chapter Mini-Review

1. Plottage occurs when assembled land creates a property with a highest and best use that is better than the highest and best use of the individual sites.

    True   False

   Plottage can only occur if there is a change in utility of the assembled land, as compared to the utility of the individual lots that go to make up the assembled land.

2. An easement can have either a positive or negative impact on the value of a property.

    True   False

   The owner of Property A has the right to access a beach by walking over Property B. Property A's value may be enhanced. Property B's value may be negatively affected.

3. If properties with and without a particular easement sell for roughly the same price, it is an indication that the easement is having a negative impact on value.

    True   **False**

   If properties with or without a particular easement are selling for the same price, then clearly the easement is having no impact.

4. In order to measure the impact of an environmental problem on a site, compare the selling prices of properties with the same environmental problem to the selling prices of properties without the environmental problem.

    True   False

   Dollar impacts can only be assessed by comparing the selling prices of properties with and without the specific problem.

5. There are only two types of factors that can have an impact on the value of a site; i.e., economic and locational.

    True   **False**

   There are in fact 4 types of factors; i.e., economic, locational, physical and legal-governmental.

6. Once the soil contamination present in a site has been cleaned up, the stigma associated with the contamination will disappear.

    True   **False**

   A stigma may result from the presence of soil contamination, but the stigma may remain after the soil is cleaned up. Stigma is related to the reputation of the site, not necessarily to its current physical condition.

7. A vacant site refers to a site that is improved with buildings.

    True   **False**

   A vacant site refers to a piece of land that is unimproved (not improved with any buildings).

APPENDIX

CH4 MR

8. A corner lot is generally associated as being a negative influence on value when it comes to a residential property, but a positive influence when it comes to a commercial property.

 True   ◯ False

Traditionally, residential properties on a corner lot are affected by factors such as a lack of privacy. Commercial properties are positively affected by factors such as exposure. Of course, only market data will determine whether there is an impact and what that impact actually is.

9. If an old landfill site is located next to or near the subject site, you would want to know whether the subject has been exposed to any contamination.

 True   ◯ False

Environmental issues can have significant impacts on a property's value especially if a clean up is required.

10. Inspecting a site to gather information on its functionality would involve looking at the condition of the site and its improvements.

◯ True   **False**

Functionality involves looking at a site in terms of its utility, appeal and popularity; e.g., a pie-shaped lot may be more appealing than a standard rectangular shape, irrespective of whether it's landscaping is in good condition or not.

Active Learning Exercises

CH4 EX1

▣ Exercise 1

1.1 Based on the information provided, it would appear that Elaine Smith is correct in thinking that the subject's extra 200 foot depth is in fact excess land. The key question to be asked here is whether the additional 200 feet provides a potential purchaser with any significant extra utility or enjoyment.

The three owners of the subject property have not developed the site any differently from the smaller properties. Indeed, the extra 200 feet is only landscaped with grass. The smaller sites could have much larger houses on them, but this has not been happening more than likely because there is no demand in the area for a greater development of the sites. While the subject property might provide more room for dogs and children to run around in, the time and cost of additional upkeep would also be greater. Accordingly, since there is nothing significantly more that a purchaser could do or enjoy with the subject's lot, there is little evidence that purchasers would want to pay any more or much more for the subject than they would for the smaller standard lots.

1.2 The above analysis would appear to be supported by the fact that Property B sold for only $5,000 to $7,000 more than Properties C and D, despite the fact that it's lot is twice the size. Had the extra 200 feet been equally valuable, then Property B would have sold for an additional $100,000. This clearly suggests that the subject property's extra size may only be worth marginally more than the standard 200 foot properties and certainly nowhere near the $400,000 suggested by the owner.

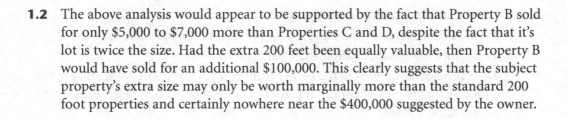

Exercise 2

2.1 There is clearly going to be a significant negative impact on value and marketing as a result of the subject property's location on Pleasant Blvd. This will be due to the restriction placed on the enjoyment and use of the property by the presence of noise and pollution, the lack of privacy, and the difficulty in getting the car out of the driveway.

2.2 This conclusion is supported by the fact that properties on Pleasant Blvd. seem to be selling for approximately $15,000 less than their identical counterparts on the quiet side streets located close by. In addition, the Pleasant Blvd properties seem to be taking up to 150 days longer to sell.

Exercise 3

- The Seller Property Information Statement—hidden defects, environmental issues, easements and encroachments.
- Surveys—shape and size of lot, easements, and encroachments.
- Inspection Reports—well flows and quality of well water, efficiency of septic systems, condition of trees.
- Neighbours—flooding, repairs of and additions to site improvements.
- Physical Inspection—topography, condition and quality of improvements; i.e., deck, grass, swimming pool, patio, fence.
- Environmental audits—contamination of soil or ground water, remedial action required, cost of remedial action.
- Invoices/receipts—details of work or repairs done to site and when.
- Municipality—services to the site.
- MLS®—selling and listing prices of sites.

Exercise 4

4.1
- Seek legal opinion as to the implications of the encroachment.
- What is the likelihood that the current or future owner of the subject property will have to remove or demolish the family room?
- If removal or demolition is required what will the cost be?
- Is there an encroachment agreement?
- Is title insurance an option?
- Is there a difference in selling price and marketing time between homes that have sold with this kind of encroachment and similar/identical homes that sold with no such encroachment?

4.2
- Is this easement common for the area?
- What percentage of the subject property does the easement take up?
- What does the easement allow the utility company to do?
- Does the easement prevent the owner from enjoying or doing something to the property that would be common place in the neighbourhood; e.g., landscaping or installing a pool?
- Is there a difference in selling price and marketing time between homes that have sold with this kind of easement and similar/identical homes that sold without this type of easement?

4.3
- Order an environmental audit and inspection.
- Has the subject property been contaminated by the landfill site?
- Has a previous environmental audit/inspection been done on the property?
- If the property is contaminated what would the cost of clean-up be?
- If the property has been contaminated, what impact will this have on value?
- If the property is contaminated and then cleaned up, will there still be a stigma resulting in a continuing negative impact on marketing and value?
- If the property is contaminated, look at the selling prices and marketing time of properties with similar contamination as compared to properties that sold without contamination.
- If the property was contaminated and is now cleaned up, look at the selling prices and marketing time of properties that had similarly been contaminated and cleaned up, as compared to properties that sold and had never been contaminated.

4.4
- Is this common for the neighbourhood?
- How steep is the slope?
- Is there a possibility of damage from flooding?
- Does the owner have to climb a lot of stairs to get to the front door of the house?
- Will the topography prevent further development and landscaping?
- What does the topography prevent in terms of use and enjoyment of the site?
- What do properties with a steeply sloping site sell for, as compared to sites with a more or less level topography?
- Does a property with a steeply sloping site take longer to sell?

■ **Exercise 5   Multiple Choice**

5.1   Based on the information provided above, is the encroachment likely to have a negative impact on value?

a.   Yes. The hydro company could request that the pool be removed once they find out about the encroachment. This will result in a cost as well as a loss in value due to the removal of the swimming pool.

Incorrect. The hydro company knows about the swimming pool encroachment and has not required that the pool be removed.

b.   **No. There is an encroachment agreement in place and over the past 5 years, there has been no request to remove the swimming pool. In addition, title insurance could cover any costs and consequences of this encroachment.**

✓ *CORRECT.* The reasoning is self-explanatory. The buyer of this property is highly unlikely to be involved in any costs or work.

c.   No. The pool sits within the subject lot and as a result the owner can ask the hydro company to remove its easement because it interferes with the enjoyment of the swimming pool. The cost of removing the easement would be borne by the hydro company.

Incorrect. It is the pool that encroaches on the easement and not the other way around.

d.   Yes. The presence of the encroachment agreement and the need for title insurance will alert a potential purchaser to the problem and will actually make the property difficult to sell.

Incorrect. It is the encroachment agreement and title insurance that in fact solves any potential problems for the buyer/owner of the property.

5.2   What market data would confirm the dollar impact on value of the encroachment on the subject property?

a.   The subject property has a 15' x 30' in-ground swimming where 2' x 30' of the pool encroaches onto a 20-foot hydro easement at the rear of the property.

Incorrect. While this information is correct, it does not support the contention that the encroachment will not have a negative dollar impact on value.

b.   **Property A had a similar encroachment and yet sold for the same price and within the same time frame as properties without the encroachment.**

✓ *CORRECT.* This is market data that shows that there is no negative dollar impact on value.

c.   Property A is a detached two-storey 1,500 square foot bungalow with a 60' x 200' lot. It has a similar encroachment.

Incorrect. While this information is correct, it does not make any reference to the value of Property A.

d.   The hydro company has an encroachment agreement which allows the company to ask for the removal of the pool from the easement at any time, should it so require.

Incorrect. While this information is correct, it does not support the contention that the encroachment will not have a negative dollar impact on value.

5.3 Do you think the easement will have any impact on the subject property's value and marketing?

a. Yes. The easement has resulted in only a detached 2,000 square foot house being placed on the property.

Incorrect. There is no evidence to support this explanation.

b. No. The easement has not prevented the owner from enjoying the use of the property; e.g., it has a deck.

Incorrect. This is not true. The easement has prevented the owner and any future buyer from installing a swimming pool.

c. **Yes. The easement is preventing the owner from installing a pool which is popular in the area.**

✔ *CORRECT.* The reasoning is self-explanatory. Anything that prevents a property from being developed to its full potential (as dictated by the local market) will have an impact on value.

d. No. The subject lot is fairly standard for the neighbourhood and therefore the easement will have no impact at all.

Incorrect. This explanation does not address the issue of why the easement will or will not impact the subject's marketing and value.

5.4 What market data can be used to confirm the dollar impact of the easement on the subject property's value?

a. Property B has an 11 foot easement similar to the subject and it has a deck, but no swimming pool.

Incorrect. While this information is correct, it does not support the contention that there will be a negative impact on value because of the easement.

b. Properties C and D are almost identical to Property B but are not subject to the municipal easement.

Incorrect. While this information is correct, it does not support the contention that there will be a negative impact on value because of the easement.

c. **Property B took much longer to sell and sold for $3,000 to $4,000 less than Properties C and D.**

✔ *CORRECT.* This market data clearly indicates that there will be a negative impact on value because of the easement.

d. Property A is a detached 2,000 square-foot, two-storey house on a 40' x 120' lot with a deck, but no swimming pool.

Incorrect. While this information is correct, it does not support the contention that there will be a negative impact on value because of the easement.

APPENDIX

5.5 You are appraising a property with a pie-shaped lot and would like to know what dollar impact this would have on the value of the subject. How would you be able to determine the dollar impact?

a. By looking at the marketing time needed to sell properties with a pie-shaped lot as compared to the marketing time of similar properties with standard shaped lots.

Incorrect. The market data required would come from looking at the selling prices of the properties with pie-shaped lots as compared to the selling prices of properties with standard shaped lots.

b. By looking at the listing prices of properties with a pie-shaped lot as compared to the listing prices of similar properties with standard shaped lots.

Incorrect. Only selling prices will assist in estimating the actual dollar impact.

c. **By looking at the selling prices of properties with a pie-shaped lot as compared to the selling prices of similar properties with standard shaped lots.**

✔ *CORRECT.* The actual dollar impact is assessed by looking at the market data.

d. By looking at the cost of constructing a home on pie-shaped lots as compared to the cost of constructing the same type of home on standard lots.

Incorrect. Construction costs will not provide the market data as to what impact the pie-shaped lot has on the value of the subject.

5.6 The subject property has a brand new swimming pool. Swimming pools are unpopular in the area, with very few houses having one. As a result, the pool can be seen to be:

a. in poor physical condition, but functionally good.

Incorrect. The opposite is in fact true.

b. both physically and functionally in good condition.

Incorrect. The fact that the pool is not popular makes it functionally poor.

c. both physically and functionally in poor condition.

Incorrect. The fact that the pool is brand new makes it physically in good condition.

d. **in good physical condition, but functionally poor.**

✔ *CORRECT.* The pool is new, but not popular.

APPENDIX

CH4 **EX5**

5.7   Which of the following is an example of plottage?

a. 123 Main Street is a vacant site worth $175,000 and 125 Main Street is a vacant site worth $200,000. If the two sites were assembled, the assembled site would be worth $475,000.

    ✅ **CORRECT.** The definition of plottage is "A value increment resulting from the assembly of two or more sites, when the combined utility is proportionately greater than the sum of the individual utilities". This example meets the criterion outlined in the definition of plottage.

b. 123 Main Street is a vacant site worth $175,000 and 125 Main Street is a vacant site worth $200,000. If the two sites were assembled, the assembled site would be worth $375,000.

    Incorrect. This example does not meet the criterion outlined in the definition of plottage.

c. 123 Main Street is a vacant site worth $175,000 and 125 Main Street is a vacant site worth $200,000. If the two sites were assembled, the assembled site would be worth less than $375,000.

    Incorrect. This example does not meet the criterion outlined in the definition of plottage.

d. 123 Main Street is a vacant site worth $175,000 and 125 Main Street is a vacant site worth $200,000. If the two sites were assembled, the assembled site would be worth between $175,000 and $200,000.

    Incorrect. This example does not meet the criterion outlined in the definition of plottage.

5.8   123 Main Street is a vacant site with a lot size of 40 by 150 feet. It sold for $250,000. 190 Main Street is an identical vacant site, except that it has a lot size of 40 feet by 300 feet. It sold for $258,000. 190 Main Street would be considered to:

a. be an example of plottage because it has a larger lot and is more valuable than 123 Main Street.

    Incorrect. The definition of plottage is *"A value increment resulting from the assembly of two or more sites, when the combined utility is proportionately greater than the sum of the individual utilities"*. The above scenario is clearly not an example of plottage.

b. have excess land because it is 200% larger in size, but worth only 3.2% more than 123 Main Street.

    ✅ **CORRECT.** Excess land refers to a site that is larger than standard, where the additional size does not provide proportional utility or a proportional increase in value.

c. have excess land because its value per front foot is greater than the front foot value of 123 Main Street.

    Incorrect. Having a greater value per front foot is not an explanation of why 190 Main Street would be considered to have excess land.

d. be an example of plottage because its value per front foot is greater than the front foot value of 123 Main Street.

    Incorrect. The definition of plottage is *"A value increment resulting from the assembly of two or more sites, when the combined utility is proportionately greater than the sum of the individual utilities"*. The above scenario is clearly not an example of plottage.

APPENDIX

5.9 Describe a physical factor that could have an influence on the value of a site.

a. **The topography of the site.**

✓ *CORRECT.* A steeply sloping lot might make the construction of a house and/or landscaping more expensive.

b. The site's tax assessment.

Incorrect. This is not a physical factor. It is an economic factor.

c. The site located on a corner.

Incorrect. This would be a locational factor.

d. The zoning of the site.

Incorrect. This would be a legal-governmental factor.

5.10 123 Main Street and 125 Main Street are sites with 30 foot frontages. They are both worth $60,000 per front foot. If these two lots were assembled, the price per front foot:

a. **might stay the same, increase or decrease depending on the utility of the assembled land.**

✓ *CORRECT.* Assembling land does not automatically result in an increase in value. It only results in an increase if there is a proportional increase in utility (i.e., a change in what can be done with the land).

b. would increase as assembled land provides greater utility than is present in the individual lots.

Incorrect. Assembled land may result in excess land if the utility of the assembled land does not increase.

c. would decrease as there is an inverse relationship between price and the site frontage.

Incorrect. The assembled land might be worth more than the sum of the two individual lots, resulting in an increase in the price per front foot. Perhaps, the individual lots can be developed with two 2,000 square foot houses, but the assembled land can be developed with a 3-storey 20 unit condominium.

d. might increase as a result of excess land being created by the assemblage of the sites.

Incorrect. If the assembled land resulted in excess land, then the price per front foot would decrease.

APPENDIX

CHAPTER 5
BUILDING ANALYSIS

Chapter Mini-Review

1. An example of functional data to be collected on a house would be the chronological age of the structure.

    True   **False**

   The chronological age would be general data.

2. Any component (e.g., a furnace) in a house can be in physically good condition but functionally poor.

    True   False

   The physical and functional condition of a house, or any component within it, has to be looked at separately. Something may be brand new, physically excellent, but it may be unpopular or may not perform as well as other products; i.e., it is functionally poor.

3. For appraisal purposes, any room that is partially above grade is included in the size of the house.

    True   **False**

   A room must be finished and 100% above grade to be included in the measurement of the area/size of a house.

4. If you suspect a house has a problem, then you need to find out what the problem is, what the cause of it is, what damage or further damage can be done, the solution to the problem and the cost of the solution.

    True   False

   A typical purchaser would want to fully understand the problem and its potential costs prior to making an unconditional offer.

5. The effective age of a building could be the same, greater or less than its actual age depending on the care and maintenance it has received.

    True   False

   A modernized building would have an effective age that is less than its actual age. A poorly maintained building would have an effective age greater than its actual age.

6. If you add the effective age of a building to its economic life you will arrive at the remaining life of a building.

    True   **False**

   If you deduct the effective age from the economic life of a building, you will arrive at the remaining life.

7. If a building no longer adds value to a property, it has come to the end of its economic life.

    True   False

   The economic life of a building refers to the period of time during which a building is useful/livable. If it is no longer livable or useful, it would no longer add value.

8. An over improvement can occur where a property is much larger, or of a much higher quality, than the other homes in the neighbourhood.

    ✔ **True**   ◯ False

    The principle of regression would come into play here—the value of the larger, higher quality home, is reduced by the value of the surrounding, smaller, inferior, homes. As a result, the value return of the larger, higher quality improvement, could end up being less than the cost of construction.

9. A seller take back mortgage at below current market mortgage rates might deflate the price paid for the building.

    ◯ True   ✔ **False**

    It might inflate the price paid by the buyer. The buyer is getting an advantage and the seller is getting a disadvantage. As a result, the buyer might be willing to pay more while the seller will want more for the house.

10. The rational for a building being an over improvement is explained by the principle of conformity.

     ✔ **True**   ◯ False

    In particular, it is the principle of regression that provides the rational for over improvement. An over improved property is larger and/or of higher quality than surrounding properties. The impact of the smaller lower quality properties act as a negative impact on the over improved property, ultimately resulting in a value that is less than the cost of its construction.

Active Learning Exercises

 Exercise 1

1.1 In terms of quality, John has built an over improved property. The result of doing this is that he will most likely sell the property for less than what he expects. John is charging $100 per square foot on construction in an area where most of the homes have been sold for $60–$75 per square foot. The majority of houses surrounding John's property are accordingly of much lower quality. Based on the principle of regression, it would be expected that the value of the higher quality home would be brought down closer to the value of the lower quality homes surrounding it.

1.2 The market data reveals the sale of a property in Neighbourhood A for $270,000. Clearly, this market data shows how the value of the property, although still higher than the general neighbourhood value range, has been brought down by the consistently lower values around it.

APPENDIX

■ Exercise 2

2.1 The inclusion of chattels will have a fairly significant positive impact on the value of the subject. A dishwasher, fridge, stove, dryer and microwave are all fairly standard chattels to be found in a fully functioning home today. People generally expect to see them as a part of the home. If they were not included, a prospective purchaser would have to pay up to $6,000 for new ones. Accordingly, a purchaser would likely reduce the price they would be willing to pay for the home, if they were not included.

2.2 The two sales in the subject neighbourhood support this conclusion. The sale with the chattels sold for $4,000 more than the home that sold without the chattels.

■ Exercise 3

The Seller Property Information Statement—hidden defects.

- A Survey—shape and size of building.
- Building or Zoning Department—permits, legal use of property.
- Neighbours—problems, additions, repairs.
- Home Inspection—condition, repairs recommended.
- Physical Inspection—condition, quality, problems, repairs required.
- Architects Drawings—floor plan, size, quality of construction.
- Previous MLS® Listings—problems, features.
- Owner's Receipts and Invoices—repairs, improvements, renovations, costs.

■ Exercise 4

4.1
- Is leasing a furnace common for the area?
- What are the lease terms?
- If it is common, what is the value impact and buyer reaction to a furnace being leased as opposed to owned?
- If it is not common, what is the value impact and buyer reaction to a furnace being leased as opposed to owned?

4.2
- Are crawl spaces common for the area?
- If crawl spaces are not common for the area, what will be the value impact and buyer reaction to the subject property's crawl space?
- If crawl spaces are not common, what will the impact be on the length of time required for marketing?

4.3
- How common are two bedroom floor plans for the neighbourhood?
- How easy would it be to convert the two bedroom floor plan to say a three bedroom?
- If two bedroom floor plans are not common, what will the value impact and buyer reaction be to this, as opposed to say a three bedroom floor plan?
- If two bedroom floor plans are not common, what will the impact be on the length of time required for marketing?

APPENDIX

▣ Exercise 5   Multiple Choice

5.1   How do you rate the physical condition and functional appeal of the subject flooring?

a.   The physical condition of the shag carpeting is poor, its functional appeal is excellent.

Incorrect. The opposite is actually true.

b.   The physical condition of the shag carpeting is poor, its functional appeal is poor.

Incorrect. The carpet is brand new, so physically it would be in excellent condition.

c.   The physical condition of the shag carpeting is excellent, its functional appeal is excellent.

Incorrect. Its functional appeal is actually poor given that it is not a popular type of flooring.

d.   **The physical condition of the shag carpeting is excellent, its functional appeal is poor.**

✔ *CORRECT.* While the carpeting is new, it is not very popular as can be seen by the fact very few homes have this type of flooring.

5.2   What value impact will the presence of earth-tone carpeting have on the subject property and what market data supports your conclusion?

a.   The presence of the earth-tone shag carpeting will have no value impact. Over 20 years ago, earth-tone shag carpeting was very popular in the subject neighbourhood.

Incorrect. The answer here goes against the evidence from the market place.

b.   **The presence of the earth-tone shag carpeting will have a negative value impact. The property with the shag carpeting sold for $5,000 less than the property with a standard beige pile carpeting.**

✔ *CORRECT.* Only market data can confirm the value impact of the carpeting.

c.   The presence of the earth-tone shag carpeting will have a positive value impact. The property with the shag carpeting sold for only $5,000 less than the property with a standard beige pile carpeting.

Incorrect. The evidence from the market place clearly shows that there is a negative impact.

d.   The presence of the earth-tone shag carpeting will have a positive value impact. Over 20 years ago earth-tone shag carpeting was very popular in the subject neighbourhood.

Incorrect. The answer here clearly goes against the evidence from the market place.

APPENDIX

CH5 EX5

5.3 The building is actually 30 years old, the effective age is 10 years. What could you possibly deduce from this information?

a. The building has probably been very poorly maintained and is most unlikely to have received any measure of modernization/renovation.

Incorrect. The answer here goes against the observations made about the building; i.e., its effective age is much less than its actual age.

b. The building has an economic life of 30 years and a remaining economic life of 10 years.

Incorrect. This answer cannot be deduced from the information provided.

c. **The building has been very well maintained and has most likely received a good deal of modernization/renovation.**

✔ *CORRECT.* The fact that the effective age of the building is much less than the actual age supports this answer.

d. The building has an economic life of 40 years and a remaining economic life of 30 years.

Incorrect. This answer cannot be deduced from the information provided.

5.4 The building is actually 30 years old, the effective age is 40 years. What could you possibly deduce from this information?

a. **The building has received less than average care and maintenance.**

✔ *CORRECT.* This answer is supported by the fact that the effective age is greater than the actual age.

b. The building has received well above average care and maintenance.

Incorrect. This answer here goes against the observations made about the building; i.e., its effective age is greater than its actual age.

c. The building has an economic life of 70 years and a remaining life of 30 years.

Incorrect. This answer cannot be deduced from the information provided.

d. The building has an economic life of 70 years and a remaining life of 40 years.

Incorrect. This answer cannot be deduced from the information provided.

5.5 A home inspection of 123 Main Street reveals the presence of UFFI. How would you go about measuring the dollar impact of the presence of UFFI in the home?

CH5 EX5

a. Compare the listing prices of homes with UFFI to the listing prices of similar homes without UFFI.

Incorrect. Selling prices, not listing prices, measure the dollar impact of the presence of UFFI in a home.

b. Compare the selling prices of homes with UFFI to the selling prices of similar homes without UFFI.

✔ *CORRECT.* The dollar impact is assessed by looking at the available market data.

c. Find out what the cost of removing all of the UFFI from 123 Main Street is going to be.

Incorrect. Cost may be a consideration, but it alone does not measure the dollar impact. This is related to the objective and subjective concepts of value. The principle of contribution comes into play.

d. Compare the listing prices of homes with UFFI to the selling prices of similar homes without UFFI.

Incorrect. Comparing listing prices to selling prices would not be consistent and, as a result, does not help in measuring dollar impacts.

5.6 The economic life of a building refers to:

a. the estimated total period of time remaining from the date of the appraisal that a building would be expected to continue to contribute to the value of a property given no renovations, updating or modernization.

Incorrect. This refers to the remaining economic life of a building.

b. the estimated total period of time during which a brand new building would be expected to contribute to the value of a property given no renovations, updating or modernization.

✔ *CORRECT.* Economic life refers to the period of time that a building would be usable/livable given no renovations/modernization.

c. the estimated total period of time during which a brand new building would be expected to contribute to the value of a property, given that appropriate renovations, updating and modernization takes place.

Incorrect. Estimating economic life requires the assumption that no renovations/modernization will take place during that period (life). Renovating/modernizing a building will extend the life of a building (increase the remaining life), but will not change the economic life of that building itself—at any point in time, economic life is a fixed number.

d. the estimated total period of time remaining from the date of the appraisal that a building would be expected to continue to contribute to the value of a property, given that appropriate renovations, updating and modernization takes place.

Incorrect. This refers to the remaining economic life of a building. The estimating of remaining economic life requires the assumption that no modernization/renovations will take place during that period (the remaining economic life). If renovations/modernization do take place, then that extends the remaining economic life, because it will decrease the effective age (remember that the economic life of a building remains fixed at any one point in time).

APPENDIX

5.7 The actual age of the building is 50 years, the effective age is 30 years and its remaining economic life is 40 years. What is the building's economic life?

a. 70 years.   ✓ *CORRECT.* 30 + 40 = 70.

b. 90 years.   *Incorrect.* You have incorrectly added actual age to the remaining economic life. The correct answer is obtained by using the formula "Effective Age + Remaining Economic Life = Economic Life".

c. 20 years.   *Incorrect.* You have incorrectly deducted effective age from actual age. The correct answer is obtained by using the formula "Effective Age + Remaining Economic Life = Economic Life".

d. 80 years.   *Incorrect.* You have incorrectly deducted effective age from actual age. The correct answer is obtained by using the formula "Effective Age + Remaining Economic Life = Economic Life".

5.8 The economic life of the building is 65 years and its remaining economic life is 42 years. What is the effective age of the building?

a. 23 years.   ✓ *CORRECT.* 65 – 42 = 23.

b. 42 years.   *Incorrect.* Reminder: Economic Life – Remaining Economic Life = Effective Age.

c. 65 years.   *Incorrect.* Reminder: Economic Life – Remaining Economic Life = Effective Age.

d. 107 years.   *Incorrect.* Reminder: Economic Life – Remaining Economic Life = Effective Age.

5.9 A brand new house has just been built. It would be considered an over improvement if the value it adds to the property:

a. is more than the cost of its construction.   *Incorrect.* This would not be an over improvement as the return is greater than the cost.

b. **is less than the cost of its construction.**   ✓ *CORRECT.* An owner has over improved their property where the return on value is less than the cost incurred.

c. is the same as the cost of its construction.   *Incorrect.* There is no over improvement, providing the return is at least equal to the cost.

d. reduces the value of the land.   *Incorrect.* The relationship presented here just does not exist. The value of the land is affected by its highest and best use.

APPENDIX

5.10 The subject building was constructed in 1890. The economic life of a building in the area has always been 60 years. How can this building still have a remaining economic life since it is older than 60 years?

a. **A building can be renovated resulting in an extension to its remaining economic life.**

    CORRECT. Economic life refers to the period of time that a building would be livable/usable (add value to the land) given that no renovation/modernization has taken place.

b. This happens where the effective age is greater than its economic life.

    Incorrect. If the effective age were greater than the economic life, then this building would have no remaining economic life and in fact would not be livable/usable.

c. This happens where the remaining life is greater than its economic life.

    Incorrect. This would not be possible.

d. It can happen if the building is of a solid brick or stone construction.

    Incorrect. Even a brick or stone building would require modernization for the remaining economic life to be extended.

CHAPTER 6
DIRECT COMPARISON APPROACH

Chapter Mini-Review

1. Adjustments are made to the subject property in order to estimate a value for it.

    ○ True   ✔ **False**

   Adjustments are made to the comparable selling prices in order to estimate a value for the subject.

2. One of the essential elements of a good comparable sale is that it should be located within the subject neighbourhood.

    ✔ **True**   ○ False

   The comparable should be subject to the same factors and forces as is the subject property.

3. The asking price of a comparable listing would set the lower limit of value.

   ○ True   ✔ **False**

   A truly comparable listing would set the upper limit of value.

4. One of the methods for calculating time adjustments would be the Time Resale Method which looks at the difference in selling price of a property that sells and resells over a given period of time.

     ✔ **True**   ○ False

   The other method for calculating time adjustments is the published statistics method which looks at the change in average prices over a given period of time.

5. Properties used in the Paired Sales Method for calculating adjustments should be as similar as possible to the subject.

     ✔ **True**   ○ False

   If the properties used in the Paired Sales Method for calculating adjustments do not appeal to the same kind of buyers as would purchase the subject property, then the adjustments estimated from this method might not be applicable.

6. If prices have increased over the past 6 months, a minus adjustment would need to be applied to a comparable that sold 6 months ago.

     ○ True   ✔ **False**

   Given that the comparable property would sell for more money today, a plus adjustment would need to be made.

7. When calculating a dollar adjustment for locational differences, the properties being used in the paired sales method should be very similar to each other, except for the locational difference being assessed.

     ✔ **True**   ○ False

   If there are other differences other than location, then those differences would have to be adjusted out in order to isolate the price differential for the location.

8. The more comparable a property is to the subject, the more adjustments you will have to make to that comparable to bring it into line with the subject.

    ( ) True   False

    The more comparable a property is to the subject, the fewer adjustments you will have to make to that comparable to bring it into line with the subject.

9. You will want to avoid using comparables that sold with undue motivation.

     True   ( ) False

    It is extremely difficult to quantify adjustments for motivation differences.

10. If the comparable is inferior to the subject, then a minus adjustment will need to be applied to that comparable's selling price.

    ( ) True   False

    If the comparable is inferior, a plus adjustment needs to be made in order to bring it into line with the subject property.

Active Learning Exercises

 Exercise 1

PROPERTY	A	B	C
Sale Price	120,000	126,000	120,000
Resale Price	127,000	135,690	137,640
$ Change	7,000	9,690	17,640
% Change	5.83% (7,000 ÷ 120,000 x 100)	7.69% (9,690 ÷ 126,000 x 100)	14.7% (17,640 ÷ 120,000 x 100)
Time Difference	4 months	5 months	10 months
% Increase/ Month	1.46% (5.83% ÷ 4)	1.54% (7.69% ÷ 5)	1.47% (14.7% ÷ 10)

The indicated increase per month is estimated at 1.5%

APPENDIX

CH6 EX2

■ Exercise 2

PROPERTY	1	2	3
Average Price (as of sale date)	$72,064 (Feb 19, 20xx)	$73,220 (Apr 13, 20xx)	$76,376 (May 20, 20xx)
Average Price (current)	$77,161 (July 1, 20xx)	$77,161 (July 1, 20xx)	$77,161 (July 1, 20xx)
Dollar Change	5,097	3,941	785
% Change	7.1% (5,097 ÷ 72,064 x 100)	5.4% (3,941 ÷ 73,220 x 100)	1% (785 ÷ 76,376 x 100)
Comparable Sale Price	72,300	73,500	76,400
Time Adjusted Sale Price	**$77,433** (72,300 + 7.1%)	**$77,469** (73,500 + 5.4%)	**$77,164** (76,400 + 1%)

CH6 EX3

■ Exercise 3

TIME ADJUSTMENT	SALE 1	SALE 2	SALE 3
Avg Price (as of sale date)	195,750 (Feb 28)		198,600 (Jan 15)
Avg Price (current)	193,250 (April 2)		193,250 (April 2)
Price Decrease	2,500		5,350
% Decrease	1.28% (2,500 ÷ 195,750 x 100)		2.69% (5,350 ÷ 198,600 x 100)
Time Adjustment	–$2,483 (194,000 x 1.28%)		–$5,971 (222,000 x 2.69%)

No time adjustment was necessary for Sale #2 as it sold within 2 weeks of the effective date.

Exercise 3 Standard Appraisal Report—Sales Analysis, Page 1 of 1 **CH6** **EX3**

Sales Analysis

Item	Subject	Comparable 1		Comparable 2		Comparable 3	
Address	18 Flutie Street	46 Riverside Drive		27 Mainside Rd.		15 Clover Blvd.	
Distance To Subject		2 blocks		1 block		3 blocks	
Date Sold		Feb. 28, 20xx		March 23, 20xx		Jan. 15, 20xx	
Sale Price		$194,000		$210,000		$222,000	
Days On Market		40 days		30 days		45 days	
Time Adjustment		February	−2,483	Current	0	January	−5,971
Time Adjusted Price		$191,517		$210,000		$216,029	
Location	Inner lot	Inner lot	0	Inner lot	0	Corner lot	+5,000
Lot Size	50' x 120'	45' x 120'	+5,000	50' x 120'	0	55' x 120'	−5,000
House Style	Detached 2-Storey	Det. 2-Storey	0	Det. 2-Storey	0	Det. 2-Storey	0
Age of House	9 Years	7 Years	0	8 Years	0	10 Years	0
Total Sq. Footage	2,500 Sq. Ft.	2,350 Sq. Ft.	+7,500	2,600 Sq. Ft.	−5,000	2,650 Sq. Ft.	−7,500
Family Room	Yes	Yes	0	Yes	0	Yes	0
Bedrooms	4	4	0	4	0	4	0
Bathrooms	3-4pcs., 1-2pc.	2-4pcs., 1-2pc.	+5,000	3-4pcs., 1-2pc.	0	3-4pcs., 1-2pc.	0
Basement/% Finished	Full/50%	Full/50%	0	Full/50%	0	Full/90%	−5,000
Rec Room	Yes	Yes	0	Yes	0	Yes	0
Garage/Parking	Double/Private	Single/Private	+5,000	Double/Private	0	Double/Private	0
Interior Condition	Average	Average	0	Average	0	Average	0
Exterior Condition	Average	Good	−5,000	Average	0	Average	0
Fireplaces	One	One	0	One	0	Two	−3,000
Total Adjustments		+ 17,500		− 5,000		− 15,500	
Totally Adj. Sale Price		$209, 017		$205,000		$200,529	

Comments, Reconciliation And Estimate Of Value By The Direct Comparison Approach

A narrow range of adjusted values has emerged from the comparable sales analysis of $200,529 to $209,017. Within this range, most attention has been paid to sale #2, as it was the most recent sale with only one relatively minor adjustment required.

Based on the above information and analysis, a value by the Direct Comparison Approach is estimated to be: ($ 205,000 ....)

APPENDIX

Exercise 4

This is an approach where the appraiser compares the subject property with similar properties that have sold recently in the same general area. Since very few properties are identical, adjustments usually have to be made for the differences that exist between the comparables and the subject property. This adjustment process provides for an indication of what the comparables would have sold for had they been identical or highly similar to the subject. As a result of this, the adjusted comparables are able to tell you what the subject would likely sell for (i.e., be worth).

The basic fundamental principle underlying the Direct Comparison Approach is the principle of substitution which says that where a property is replaceable, its value tends to be set by the cost of acquiring a similar and equally desirable property, provided there is no delay in making the acquisition.

The basic steps in applying the approach are:

- Select at least three comparable sales and three current listings.
- Collect relevant information on each of the comparables being used.
- Identify any significant differences between the comparables and the subject.
- With respect to the comparable sales, make the necessary dollar adjustments to them in order to take account of any significant differences. With respect to the comparable listings, assess whether they are inferior, similar or superior to the subject.
- Reconcile the adjusted comparable sales values into a final estimate of value. Use the current comparable listings to assist in your estimate.

Exercise 5

- The comparable sales should be located within the subject neighbourhood, preferably on the subject street or as close as possible.
- The sale should be on, or as close as possible to, the date of valuation.
- The comparable sale should be truly physically similar in nature.
- The comparable sale should have occurred as a result of an arms-length transaction under conditions that would meet the definition of market value.

Exercise 6

SCENARIO	TYPE OF ADJUSTMENT PLUS OR MINUS
The comparable has two fireplaces, whereas the subject has only one fireplace.	MINUS
The comparable building has 1,500 square feet in living area, whereas the subject has 1,300 square feet.	MINUS
The comparable lacks a garage whereas the subject has a single garage.	PLUS
The comparable's lot frontage is 40 feet, whereas the subject's lot frontage is 35 feet.	MINUS
The subject has two bathrooms, whereas the comparable only has one bathroom.	PLUS
The subject is located backing to a park, whereas the comparable is located backing onto a railway line and paint factory.	PLUS

▣ Exercise 7

You would not want to use:

- Sale #1 because it is a 50-year-old rental property (triplex) with a mutual driveway. The lot is only 30 x 110 feet.
- Sale #4 because it is a 71-year-old 1,400 square foot bungalow in poor condition.
- Sale #6 because it is located four miles away and sold 18 months ago.

▣ Exercise 8   Multiple Choice

TIME ADJUSTMENT	SALE 1	SALE 2	SALE 3
Avg Price (as of sale date)		243,725 (Aug 27)	240,525 (Jul 10)
Avg Price (current)		244,900 (Oct 8)	244,900 (Oct 8)
Price Increase		1,175	4,375
% Increase		0.48% (1,175 ÷ 243,725 x 100)	1.82% (4,375 ÷ 240,525 x 100)
Time Adjustment		+$1,037 (216,000 x 0.48%)	+$4,695 (258,000 x 1.82%)

There is no time adjustment for Sale #1 as this sale sold within two weeks of the effective date.

Sales Analysis

Item	Subject	Comparable 1		Comparable 2		Comparable 3	
Address	24 Evans Avenue	200 Evans Avenue		40 Fleming Street		321 Maple Street	
Distance To Subject		1/2 block		2 blocks		3 blocks	
Date Sold		October 1, 20xx		August 27, 20xx		July 10, 20xx	
Sale Price		$235,000		$216,000		$258,000	
Days On Market		25 days		30 days		29 days	
Time Adjustment		Current	0	August	+1,037	July	+4,695
Time Adjusted Price		$235,000		$217,037		$262,695	
Location	Inner lot	Inner lot	0	Inner lot	0	Inner lot	0
Lot Size	30' x 125'	30' x 125'	0	29' x 130'	+2,000	31' x 125'	−2,000
House Style	Det. Bungalow	Det Bungalow	0	Det Bungalow	0	Det Bungalow	0
Age of House	55 Years	52 Years	0	56 Years	0	57 Years	0
Total Sq. Footage	1,200 Sq. Ft.	1,200 Sq. Ft.	0	1,200 Sq. Ft.	0	1,200 Sq. Ft.	0
Family Room	No	No	0	No	0	No	0
Bedrooms	3	3	0	3	0	3	0
Bathrooms	1 — 4 pc.	1 — 4 pc.	0	1 — 4 pc.	0	2 — 4 pc.	−5,000
Basement/% Finished	Full/30%	Full/30%	0	Full/0%	+3,000	Full/90%	−5,000
Rec Room	Yes	Yes	0	No	0	Yes	0
Garage/Parking	No/Private	No/Private	0	No/Mutual	+5,000	Single/Private	−5,000
Interior Condition	Average	Average	0	Fair	+5,000	Good	−5,000
Exterior Condition	Average	Average	0	Average	0	Good	−3,000
Landscaping	Fair	Average	−2,000	Average	−2,000	Average	−2,000
Central Air	No	No	0	Yes	−3,000	No	0
Fireplaces	One	One	0	None	+3,000	One	0
Total Adjustments			−2,000		+13,000		−27,000
Totally Adj. Sale Price		$233,000		$230,037		$235,695	

Comments, Reconciliation And Estimate Of Value By The Direct Comparison Approach

A narrow range of adjusted values has emerged from the comparable sales analysis. Within this range of $230,037 to $235,695 most attention has been given to sale #1 as it is the most recent sale with only one relatively minor adjustment required.

Based on the above information and analysis, a value by the Direct Comparison Approach is estimated to be: ($ 233,000 ....)

APPENDIX

8.1   Calculate the time adjusted price for Comparable #1.

CH6 EX8

a.   244,900   *Incorrect.* This was a current sale—no time adjustment was required. See answer above.

b.   235,000   ✔ *CORRECT.* Please review answer shown above.

c.   240,525   *Incorrect.* This was a current sale—no time adjustment was required. See answer above.

d.   243,725   *Incorrect.* This was a current sale—no time adjustment was required. See answer above.

8.2   Calculate the time adjusted price for Comparable #2.

a.   243,725   *Incorrect.* Please review answer shown above. Reminder—you need to use the correct average prices from August and October.

b.   219,931   *Incorrect.* Please review answer shown above. Reminder—you need to divide the average dollar price increase by the original average price (earlier month) to arrive at the percentage price increase between August and October.

c.   217,037   ✔ *CORRECT.* Please review answer shown above.

d.   216,000   *Incorrect.* Please review answer shown above. Reminder—you need to apply the total percentage increase from August to October to the selling price of Comparable #2.

8.3   Calculate the time adjusted price for Comparable #3.

a.   258,000   *Incorrect.* Please review answer shown above. Reminder—you need to use the correct average prices from July and October.

b.   262,695   ✔ *CORRECT.* Please review answer shown above.

c.   240,525   *Incorrect.* Please review answer shown above. Reminder—you need to divide the average dollar price increase by the original average price (earlier month) to arrive at the percentage price increase between July and October.

d.   259,238   *Incorrect.* Please review answer shown above. Reminder—you need to apply the total percentage increase from July to October to the selling price of Comparable #3.

8.4   What would the totally adjusted selling price be for Comparable #1?

a.   233,000   ✔ *CORRECT.* Please review answer shown above.

b.   237,000   *Incorrect.* Please review answer shown above. Reminder—check to see if you had the correct Time Adjusted Price; the correct adjustments (+/–); correct total adjustments.

c.   235,000   *Incorrect.* Please review answer shown above. Reminder—check to see if you had the correct Time Adjusted Price; the correct adjustments (+/–); correct total adjustments.

d.   230,000   *Incorrect.* Please review answer shown above. Reminder—check to see if you had the correct Time Adjusted Price; the correct adjustments (+/–); correct total adjustments.

8.5 What would the totally adjusted selling price be for Comparable #2?

a. 230,037   ✔ *CORRECT.* Please review answer shown above.

b. 229,000   ***Incorrect.*** Please review answer shown above. Reminder—check to see if you had the correct Time Adjusted Price; the correct adjustments (+/–); correct total adjustments.

c. 204,037   ***Incorrect.*** Please review answer shown above. Reminder—check to see if you had the correct Time Adjusted Price; the correct adjustments (+/–); correct total adjustments.

d. 232,931   ***Incorrect.*** Please review answer shown above. Reminder—check to see if you had the correct Time Adjusted Price; the correct adjustments (+/–); correct total adjustments.

8.6 What would the totally adjusted selling price be for Comparable #3?

a. 231,000   ***Incorrect.*** Please review answer shown above. Reminder—check to see if you had the correct Time Adjusted Price; the correct adjustments (+/–); correct total adjustments.

b. 235,695   ✔ *CORRECT.* Please review answer shown above.

c. 232,238   ***Incorrect.*** Please review answer shown above. Reminder—check to see if you had the correct Time Adjusted Price; the correct adjustments (+/–); correct total adjustments.

d. 262,695   ***Incorrect.*** Please review answer shown above. Reminder—check to see if you had the correct Time Adjusted Price; the correct adjustments (+/–); correct total adjustments.

8.7 The final estimate of value for the subject property would be:

a. 232,000   ***Incorrect.*** Please review answer shown above. Reminder—check to see if you had the correct Total Adjustments for each of the comparables. You need to select the best comparable—you do not average the 3 Totally Adjusted Sale prices to arrive at a final value.

b. 230,000   ***Incorrect.*** Please review answer shown above. Reminder—check to see if you had the correct Total Adjustments for each of the comparables. You need to select the best comparable—you do not average the 3 Totally Adjusted Sale prices to arrive at a final value.

c. 233,000   ✔ *CORRECT.* Please review answer shown above.

d. 236,000   ***Incorrect.*** Please review answer shown above. Reminder—check to see if you had the correct Total Adjustments for each of the comparables. You need to select the best comparable—you do not average the 3 Totally Adjusted Sale prices to arrive at a final value.

APPENDIX

8.8 In valuing the subject property, you have decided to use a very comparable property that sold last week for $125,000. You discover that the seller took back a second mortgage of $22,000 at an interest rate of 10 per cent per annum, calculated semi-annually not in advance and repayable in blended monthly payments of interest and principal, amortized over 25 years. The mortgage is for a term of 3 years. Current interest rates for this type of mortgage is 8 %.

CH6 EX8

Based on the above information and using the Discounted Mortgage Evaluation Table provided, calculate the amount of the dollar adjustment to reflect this STB financing.

The seller would receive $1,050 per $1,000 of mortgage. Therefore, the present value of this mortgage to the seller is **$23,100 (22 x 1,050).**

Seller's Gain **$23,100 – 22,000 = $1,100**

Financing Adjustment + $1,100 (this suggests that the property would have sold for less (inferior) than market value, given that the seller is getting an advantage and the buyer a disadvantage.

a. +1,100   ✓ *CORRECT.* Please review answer shown above.

b. −1,100   *Incorrect.* Please review answer shown above. The minus sign is wrong as it suggests that the comparable property would have sold for more money because of the financing.

c. +1,694   *Incorrect.* Please review answer shown above. You have either used the wrong numbers from the Discounted Mortgage Evaluation Table or you have made a calculation error.

d. −1,694   *Incorrect.* Please review answer shown above. The minus sign is wrong as it suggests that the comparable property would have sold for more money because of the financing. In addition, you have either used the wrong numbers from the Discounted Mortgage Evaluation Table or you have made a calculation error.

APPENDIX

CH6 **EX8**   **8.9**   The subject property (123 Main Street) is being valued as at 1st July, 20xx. You have found a very good comparable property at 164 Main Street. It sold for $265,000 on April 15th, 20xx. The Anycity real estate board published average selling prices show as follows:

April 15	$245,730
May 15	$243,840
July 1	$239,750

Based on this information, what time adjustment needs to be applied to 164 Main Street?

$$245,730 - 239,750 = 5,980$$
$$5,980 \div 245,730 = 2.43\%$$
$$265,000 \times 2.43\% = 6,440$$

Prices are clearly declining, hence the minus adjustment.

a.   +6,440   *Incorrect.* Please review answer shown above. Reminder—plus sign indicates that prices have been increasing. In reality, prices have been declining.

b.   –6,599   *Incorrect.* Please review answer shown above. Check your math calculations. Reminder—you need to use the correct average prices from April and July ; you need to divide the average dollar price increase by the original average price (earlier month) to arrive at the percentage price increase between April and July. You need to apply the total percentage increase from April to July to the selling price of comparable 164 Main Street.

c.   +6,599   *Incorrect.* Please review answer shown above. Reminder—a plus sign indicates that prices have been increasing. In reality, prices have been declining. You need to use the correct average prices from April and July ; you need to divide the average dollar price increase by the original average price (earlier month) to arrive at the percentage price increase between April and July. You need to apply the total percentage increase from April to July to the selling price of comparable 164 Main Street.

d.   –6,440   ✅ *CORRECT.* Please review answer shown above.

8.10 If the comparable sale is superior to the subject, then:

a.   a negative adjustment is applied to the comparable selling price.   ✅ *CORRECT.* You need to bring the comparable sale into line with the subject.

b.   a positive adjustment is applied to the comparable selling price.   *Incorrect.* This will not bring the comparable sale into line with the subject.

c.   a negative adjustment is applied to the subject's value.   *Incorrect.* Adjustments are applied to the comparable sale—you are trying to estimate the value of the subject, not the comparable.

d.   a positive adjustment is applied to the subject's value.   *Incorrect.* Adjustments are applied to the comparable sale—you are trying to estimate the value of the subject, not the comparable.

APPENDIX

CHAPTER 7
THE COST APPROACH

CH7   MR

Chapter Mini-Review

1. In the Cost Approach to Value, the current value of a building is estimated by deducting the land value from the Reproduction/Replacement Cost New.

   ○ True   ✔ **False**

   You would deduct the accrued depreciation from the Reproduction/ Replacement Cost New to arrive at a current value for the building.

2. In the Comparative Sales Method, the selling prices of comparable residential sites are normally reduced to a price per front foot/metres.

   ✔ **True**   ○ False

   This makes it easier to compare sites with slightly differing frontages and avoids having to make adjustments for frontage differences.

3. The Comparative Square Metre Method is an alternative to the Comparative Sales Method in valuing vacant sites.

   ○ True   ✔ **False**

   The Comparative Square Metre Method is one of the methods used in estimating the RCN of a building.

4. The Comparative Sales Method is the best method for valuing a single-family vacant site providing you have sufficient comparable land sales.

   ✔ **True**   ○ False

   The other method is the Abstraction Method and it requires more steps and more adjustments/calculations. The more steps/adjustments required, the less ideal/appealing the method is.

5. One of the steps in the Abstraction Method involves deducting the value of the site and other improvements from the selling price of the comparable in order to arrive at a cost of the building for that comparable.

   ○ True   ✔ **False**

   In the abstraction method, you would deduct the value of all the improvements away from the selling price of the comparable property in order to arrive at a land value for that comparable.

6. Replacement Cost is the cost of construction, at current prices, of an exact duplicate or replica building, using the same materials, construction standards, design, layout and quality of workmanship, while embodying all the deficiencies, superadequacies and obsolescence of the subject building.

   ○ True   ✔ **False**

   Replacement Cost is the cost of construction, at current prices, of a building having utility equivalent to the building being appraised, but built with modern materials and according to current standards, design and layout.

7. In the Cost Approach to Value, the Comparative Square Metre Method uses location and cost multipliers to arrive at the RCN of the subject building.

   ○ True   ✔ **False**

   Cost and location multipliers are used in the Cost Services Method.

CH7 MR

8. If the cost of replacing a roof is offset by the value increase to the property and a typical buyer or owner would in fact make the change, then the roof would be considered a curable item for the purpose of depreciation.

 True   False

A curable item is an item in a home that a buyer or owner would replace immed-iately because it makes economic sense to do so; i.e., the return at least equals the cost.

9. For depreciation purposes, a long-lived item is a component of a house that has suffered some functional obsolescence but would not require replacement before the end of the economic life of the building.

 True   False

A long-lived item would have suffered physical depreciation and not functional obsolescence. Functional obsolescence is either curable or incurable—incurable functional obsolescence is not divided into short and long-lived items.

10. Curable Physical Deterioration is measured by the cost to cure.

 True   False

In the Cost Approach, it is assumed that any buyer would look at the cost of replacement as being the measure of depreciation; i.e., the amount of money that needs to be deducted from the RCN of that building.

Active Learning Exercises

CH7 EX1

■ Exercise 1   Site Valuation

Monthly Time Adjustment Calculation

Site A	85,800 – 78,000 = 7,800	(7,800 ÷ 78,000) ÷ 10 = .01 (or 1%)
Site B	99,360 – 92,000 = 7,360	(7,360 ÷ 92,000) ÷ 8 = .01 (or 1%)
Site C	83,160 – 77,000 = 6,160	(6,160 ÷ 77,000) ÷ 8 = .01 (or 1%)

1% is selected as percentage monthly increase.

APPENDIX

Site Value Tabular Analysis

	SALE #1	SALE #2	SALE #3	SALE #4
Front Metre	18M	15.25M	16.5M	18M
Sale Price	96,000	83,000	88,000	102,000
Sale Price Per F.M.	5,333.33	5,442.62	5,333.33	5,666.67
Time Adjustment	+5%	+4%	0%	+4%
T.A. Sale Price/F.M.	5,600	5,660.32	5,333.33	5,893.33
Physical Adjustment	–5%	+4%	0%	0%
Location Adjustment	+5%	–5%	+5%	–5%
Total Net Adjustment	0%	–1%	+5%	–5%
Fully Adjusted Sale Price/F.M.	5,600	5,603.72	5,600	5,598.67

Reconciliation

An adjusted value range of between $5,598.67 and $5,603.72 per front metre has emerged from the above analysis. Within this range, most attention has been paid to comparable sale # 3 as it is the most recent sale and required only one relatively minor location adjustment. Its price per front metre is well supported by the other three comparables. Therefore, the value of the subject site is estimated as:

$$18 \times 5,600 = \$100,800$$
$$\text{Rounded To } \$101,000$$

■ Exercise 2   Site Valuation

Site Value Tabular Analysis

	SALE #1	SALE #2	SALE #3
Front Metre	15M	17M	17M
Sale Price	30,000	28,600	29,975
Sale Price Per F.M	2,000	1,682.35	1,763.24
Time Adjustment	+5%	+3%	+6%
T.A. Sale Price/F.M.	2,100	1,732.82	1,869.03
Physical Adjustment	–6%	0%	0%
Location Adjustment	–5%	+8%	0%
Total Net Adjustment	–11%	+8%	0%
Fully Adjusted Sale Price/F.M.	1,869.00	1,871.44	1,869.03

Reconciliation

An adjusted value range of between $1,869 and $1,871.44 per front metre has emerged from the above analysis. Within this range, most attention has been paid to comparable Sale #3 as it required no location or physical adjustments. Its price per front metre is well supported by the other two comparables. Therefore, the value of the subject site is estimated as:

$$17 \times 1,869 = \$31,773$$
$$\text{Rounded To } \$32,000$$

APPENDIX

Exercise 3   Site Valuation, The Abstraction Method

Monthly Time Adjustment Calculation

PROPERTY A	547,500 − 453,000 = 94,500
	(94,500 ÷ 453,000) ÷ 8 = .02608 (or 2.61%)
PROPERTY B	565,000 − 465,000 = 100,000
	(100,000 ÷ 465,000) ÷ 9 = .02389 (or 2.39%)
PROPERTY C	542,000 − 482,000 = 60,000
	(60,000 ÷ 482,000) ÷ 5 = .02489 (or 2.49%)

2.5% is selected as percentage monthly increase.

Site Value Tabular Analysis (Abstraction Method)

	COMPARABLE #1	COMPARABLE #2	COMPARABLE#3
Address	41 Given Way	31 Cumberland St.	4 Ashland Grove
Sale Date	2 Months Ago	4 days ago	3 Months Ago
Sale Price	$518,500	$545,000	$480,000
Time Adjustment	+5%	0	+7.5%
Time Adjusted Sale Price	544,425	545,000	516,000
Building Value	325,000	330,000	292,000
Value Other Improvements	18,000	20,000	15,000
Land Value	201,425	195,000	209,000
Location Adjustment	+2%	0	−3%
Physical Adjustment	−5%	+3%	+2%
Total Net Adjustment	−3%	+3%	−1%
Fully Adjusted Land Value	195,382	200,850	206,910
Front Metre	12	12.2	12.5
Adjusted Value Per Metre	**16,281**	**16,463**	**16,553**

Reconciliation

For reconciliation, select Comparable #2 with acceptable rationale.

12.25M x 16,463 = $201,672
Rounded To $202,000

■ Exercise 4   Reproduction (or Replacement) Cost Estimate

	SALE #1	SALE #2	SALE #3
Sale Price	161,000	165,000	163,000
Site Value	70,000	68,500 +4,500 73,000	76,300
Outside Improvements	0	0	–2,800
Building Cost	91,000	92,000	83,900
Building Time Adjustment	0	0	0
Time Adjusted Building Cost	91,000	92,000	83,900
Basement Finish	–6,000	0	0
Carport	0	+2,000	0
Air Conditioning	0	0	–3,500
Total Net Adjustment	**–6,000**	**+2,000**	**–3,500**
Fully Adjusted Building Cost	85,000	94,000	80,400
Size of Building	128 Sq. M.	140.93 Sq. M.	120 Sq. M.
Indicated Cost Per Sq. M.	**664.06**	**667**	**670**

Reconciliation

An adjusted value range of between $664.06 and $670 per square metre has emerged from the above analysis. Within this range, most attention has been paid to comparable sale # 3 as it was the same size as the subject and only required one minor adjustment to the building cost. Its price per square metre is well supported by the other two comparables. Therefore, the RCN of the subject building is estimated as:

120 x 670 = $80,400

■ Exercise 5   Reproduction (or Replacement) Cost Estimate

Base Building Cost

10 x 12 x 2 = 240 Sq. Meters x $425/sq. m	$102,000
Area/Shape Multiplier	x 1.078
Adjusted Base Cost	109,956
Add Finished Basement Area (30 sq. m. x $150/sq. m.)	+4,500
Add Garage (20 sq. m. x $200/sq. m.)	+4,000
Add Central Air Conditioning	+3,000
Add Fireplace	+4,000
Deduct Lack of Second Bathroom	–5,000
Fully Adjusted Base Cost	120,456
Multiply the Location Multiplier	x 1.27
Location Adjusted Cost	$152,979
Multiply the Cost Multiplier	x 1.13
Total Reproduction Cost New	$172,866

Rounded To $172,900

APPENDIX

▣ Exercise 6   Chapter Consolidation

	SALE #1	SALE #2	SALE #3
Sale Price	190,000	176,000	183,000
Site Value	69,000	71,000 +4,000 ——— 75,000	74,500
Outside Improvements	7,000	8,000	9,000
Building Cost	114,000	93,000	99,500
Building Time Adjustment	0	+6%	0
Time Adjusted Building Cost	114,000	98,580	99,500
Recreation Room	–4,000	–4,000	0
Total Net Adjustment	**–4,000**	**–4,000**	**0**
Fully Adjusted Building Cost	110,000	94,580	99,500
Size of Building	102.19 Sq. M.	85.79 Sq. M.	91.31 Sq. M.
Indicated Cost Per Sq. M.	**1,076**	**1,102**	**1,090**

Reconciliation

An adjusted value range of between $1,076 and $1,102 per square metre has emerged from the above analysis. Within this range, most attention has been paid to comparable sale # 3 as it was the closest in size to the subject and required no adjustments to the building cost. Its price per square metre is well supported by the other two comparables. Therefore, the value of the subject building is estimated as:

$$91.77 \times 1,090 = \$100,029$$

Estimate Current Value of Building

$$\$100,029 \times 8 \div 50 = \$16,005$$
$$\$100,029 - 16,005 = \$84,024$$

Estimate Current Value of Other Improvements (Landscaping)

ITEM	COST NEW	EFFECTIVE AGE	LIFE EXPECTANCY	DEPRECIATION	CURRENT VALUE
Asphalt Driveway	$2,200	10	15	$1,467	$733
Fencing	$2,800	10	50	$560	$2,240
Wood Deck	$3,000	4	25	$480	$2,520
Sod and Trees	$1,500	N/A	N/A	$0	$1,500
Totals	$9,500			$2,507	$6,993

Estimating Land Value

	COMPARABLE #1	COMPARABLE #2	COMPARABLE #3
Address	19 Hamilton Way	27 Trafalgar Road	48 Nelson Blvd.
Sale Date	3 Months Ago	1 Month Ago	4 Days Ago
Sale Price	$171,000	$185,000	$180,000
Time Adjustment	+3%	+1%	0%
Time Adjusted Sale Price	176,130	186,850	180,000
Building Value	97,000	108,000	99,000
Value Other Improvements	6,000	5,000	9,000
Land Value	73,130	73,850	72,000
Location Adjustment	+1%	0%	0%
Physical Adjustment	–3%	+2%	0%
Total Net Adjustment	–2%	+2%	0%
Fully Adjusted Land Value	71,667	75,327	72,000
Front Metre	8.5	8.9	8.6
Adjusted Value Per Metre	8,431	8,464	8,372

Reconciliation

An adjusted value range of between $8,372 and $8,464 per front metre has emerged from the above analysis. Within this range, most attention has been paid to comparable sale # 3 as it is the most recent sale and required no physical or location adjustments. Its price per front metre is well supported by the other two comparables. Therefore, the value of the subject site is estimated as:

$$8.5 \times 8,372 = \$71,162$$
Rounded To $71,000

Completion of Cost Approach to Value Section of Appraisal Form Report

COST APPROACH TO VALUE

Land Value .... $ 71,000

Improvements	Cost New	Depreciation	Current Value
Building	$ 100,029	$ 16,005	$ 84,024
Garage	$	$	$
Other Improvements	$ 9,500.	$ 2,507	$ 6,993
	$	$	$
	$	$	$

Total Current Value of All Improvements $ 91,017 $ 91,017

Indicated Value by the Cost Approach $ 162,017

Value Rounded to $ 162,000

■ Exercise 7   Case Study—Land Value

Monthly Time Adjustment Calculation

SITE A	210,000 – 195,000 = 15,000	(15,000 ÷ 195,000) ÷ 7 = .01098 (or 1.1%)
SITE B	188,000 – 179,000 = 9,000	(9,000 ÷ 179,000) ÷ 5 = .01005 (or 1.01%)
SITE C	199,500 – 192,000 = 7,500	(7,500 ÷ 192,000) ÷ 4 = .00976 (or .98%)

1% selected as percentage monthly increase for the neighbourhood.

Site Value Tabular Analysis

	LAND SALE #1	LAND SALE #2	LAND SALE #3
Front Metre	9.7	10.1	10.2
Sale Price	174,000	209,000	195,000
Sale Price Per F.M.	17,938	20,693	19,118
Time Adjustment	+5%	+3%	0%
T.A. Sale Price/F.M.	18,835	21,314	19,118
Physical Adjustment	0%	–5%	+2%
Location Adjustment	+3%	–3%	0%
Total Net Adjustment	+3%	–8%	+2%
Fully Adjusted Sale Price/F.M.	**19,400**	**19,609**	**19,500**

Reconciliation

An adjusted value range of between $19,400 and $19,609 per front metre has emerged from the above analysis. Within this range, most attention has been paid to comparable sale # 3 as it is the most recent sale and required only one relatively minor physical adjustment. Its price per front metre is well supported by the other two comparables. Therefore, the value of the subject site is calculated as:

10 x 19,500 = $195,000
Rounded To $195,000

APPENDIX

7.1 Calculate the monthly percentage time adjustment indicated by the Site Resale A.

a. +1.1%   ✔ *CORRECT.* Please review answer shown above.

b. −1.1%   *Incorrect.* Please review answer shown above. Reminder—prices have been increasing and not decreasing.

c. +1.02%   *Incorrect.* Please review answer shown above. Reminder—you take the dollar difference in selling prices and divide it by the original selling price in order to arrive at a percentage. You then take that percentage and divide it by the number of months between selling prices to arrive at a percentage per month.

d. −1.02%   *Incorrect.* Please review answer shown above. Reminder—prices have been increasing and not decreasing. You take the dollar difference in selling prices and divide it by the original selling price in order to arrive at a percentage. You then take that percentage and divide it by the number of months between selling prices to arrive at a percentage per month.

7.2 What is the fully adjusted sale price per front metre for sale #1?

a. $19,400   ✔ *CORRECT.* Please review answer shown above.

b. $18,300   *Incorrect.* Please review answer shown above. Check your math, the time and other adjustments you made. Reminder—the percentage increase per month is 1%. This property sold 5 months ago.

c. $18,700   *Incorrect.* Please review answer shown above. Check your math, the time and other adjustments you made. Reminder—the percentage increase per month is 1%. This property sold 5 months ago.

d. $18,800   *Incorrect.* Please review answer shown above. Check your math, the time and other adjustments you made. Reminder—the percentage increase per month is 1%. This property sold 5 months ago.

7.3 What is the fully adjusted sale price per front metre for sale #2?

a. $19,609   ✔ *CORRECT.* Please review answer shown above.

b. $21,314   *Incorrect.* Please review answer shown above. Check your math, the time and other adjustments you made. Reminder—the percentage increase per month is 1%. This property sold 3 months ago.

c. $23,019   *Incorrect.* Please review answer shown above. Check your math, the time and other adjustments you made. Reminder—the percentage increase per month is 1%. This property sold 3 months ago.

d. $19,228   *Incorrect.* Please review answer shown above. Check your math, the time and other adjustments you made. Reminder—the percentage increase per month is 1%. This property sold 3 months ago.

APPENDIX

7.4 What is the fully adjusted sale price per front metre for Sale #3?

   a. $18,600   *Incorrect.* Please review answer shown above. Check your math, the time and other adjustments you made. Reminder—this is a current sale, there should be no time adjustment.

   b. $19,100   *Incorrect.* Please review answer shown above. Check your math, the time and other adjustments you made. Reminder—this is a current sale, there should be no time adjustment.

   c. $19,500   ✔ *CORRECT.* Please review answer shown above.

   d. $19,700   *Incorrect.* Please review answer shown above. Check your math, the time and other adjustments you made. Reminder—this is a current sale, there should be no time adjustment.

7.5 What is the estimate of value for the subject site?

   a. $186,000   *Incorrect.* Please review answer shown above. Reminder—check to see if you had the correct Fully Adjusted Sale price/F.M. for each of the comparables. You need to select the best comparable—you do not average the 3 Fully Adjusted Sale Prices /F.M. to arrive at a final value.

   b. $195,000   ✔ *CORRECT.* Please review answer shown above.

   c. $191,000   *Incorrect.* Please review answer shown above. Reminder—check to see if you had the correct Fully Adjusted Sale Price/F.M. for each of the comparables. You need to select the best comparable—you do not average the 3 Fully Adjusted Sale Prices /F.M. to arrive at a final value.

   d. $197,000   *Incorrect.* Please review answer shown above. Reminder—check to see if you had the correct Fully Adjusted Sale Price/F.M. for each of the comparables. You need to select the best comparable—you do not average the 3 Fully Adjusted Sale Prices /F.M. to arrive at a final value.

APPENDIX

7.6 Jim Smith is an appraiser who has been asked to value a vacant site at 123 Main Street using the Comparative Sales Method (i.e., comparable land sales). Jim's investigation reveals that 140 Main Street, which sold for $220,000, has a very comparable site, however it is improved with a 1,200 square foot bungalow. Jim can use 140 Main Street as a land sale in the Comparative Sales Method providing:

a. the home is in poor to average condition and the buyer would consider living in it only for a short until it needs tearing down to make way for a new home.

Incorrect. If the buyer is prepared to live in the current building, then this property did not sell for its land value.

b. the intention of the buyer is to tear it down the bungalow in order to construct a new home even though he/she paid extra for the bungalow.

Incorrect. If the buyer paid a price over and above the land value, then this property did not sell for its land value.

c. He deducts the estimated depreciation of the improvements from the selling price of the property.

Incorrect. If the selling price includes the value of anything above the land value, then this property did not sell for its land value.

d. **the house does not add value to the site and the intention of the buyer is to tear it down in order to construct a new home.**

✅ *CORRECT.* Clearly the property sold purely for its land value.

7.7 In the Abstraction Method of estimating site values, the appraiser needs to know the current value of all the improvements to the comparable site. Why is this information important in this method?

a. **The current value of all the improvements is deducted from the time adjusted sale price of the comparable property in order to arrive at the land value of that comparable.**

✅ *CORRECT.* Once the land value is isolated, its value can be used to estimate the subject's land value. Of course, adjustments for differences between the sites may need to be made.

b. The current value of all the improvements is added to the time adjusted sale price of the comparable property in order to arrive at the land value of that comparable.

Incorrect. The current value is deducted, not added.

c. The current value of all the improvements is deducted from the time adjusted sale price of the comparable property in order to arrive at the RCN of that comparable.

Incorrect. The deduction is made in order to isolate the land value of that comparable.

d. The current value of all the improvements is deducted from the time adjusted sale price of the comparable property in order to arrive at the depreciated value of that comparable.

Incorrect. The deduction is made in order to isolate the land value of that comparable.

APPENDIX

7.8 Which of the following would be a good example of functional obsolescence in a house?

a. The roof is in very poor shape and needs replacing.

Incorrect. This represents physical depreciation.

b. The paint in the bedrooms is flaking and looks in poor condition.

Incorrect. This represents physical depreciation.

c. **The bungalow's only bathroom is in the basement.**

✓ *CORRECT.* Clearly, this is a floor plan that would not have popular appeal. Therefore, the value of the building would be negatively affected (obsolescence).

d. The bungalow is located next to a gas station.

Incorrect. This would represent locational obsolescence.

7.9 The subject building is 90 years old. It has an effective age of 25 years and a remaining economic life of 35 years. The RCN of the building is $151,500. What is the amount of the building's depreciation using the Economic Age-Life Method?

a. $108,214

Incorrect. Check your math. Reminder—the formula for completing this calculation is RCN x Effective Age/Economic Life = Depreciation. The economic life is the effective age plus the remaining economic life. Actual age is immaterial.

b. $63,125

✓ *CORRECT.* 151,500 x 25 ÷ 60 = $63,125

c. $42,083

Incorrect. Check your math. Reminder—the formula for completing this calculation is RCN x Effective Age/Economic Life = Depreciation. The economic life is the effective age plus the remaining economic life. Actual age is immaterial.

d. $58,917

Incorrect. Check your math. Reminder—the formula for completing this calculation is RCN x Effective Age/Economic Life = Depreciation. The economic life is the effective age plus the remaining economic life. Actual age is immaterial.

7.10 The subject building is 20 years old. It has an effective age of 25 years and an economic life of 60 years. The RCN of the building is $225,000. What is the current value of the building using the Economic Age-Life Method?

$$\$225,000 \times 25 \div 60 = \$93,750$$
$$\$225,000 - 93,750 = \$131,250$$

a. $150,000

Incorrect. Please review answer shown above. Check your math. Reminder—the formula for calculating depreciation is RCN x Effective Age/Economic Life. Then you would deduct the depreciation from the RCN.

b. $75,000

Incorrect. Please review answer shown above. Check your math. Reminder—the formula for calculating depreciation is RCN x Effective Age/Economic Life. Then you would deduct the depreciation from the RCN.

c. $93,750

Incorrect. Please review answer shown above. Check your math. Reminder—the formula for calculating depreciation is RCN x Effective Age/Economic Life. Then you would deduct the depreciation from the RCN.

d. $131,250   ✔ *CORRECT.* Please review answer shown above.

7.11 Under which of the following scenarios would a furnace be depreciated as an incurable physical short-lived item?

a. At the date of the appraisal, the subject building has a remaining life of 35 years, and the furnace has an effective age of 15 years with a life expectancy of 15 years.

Incorrect. Based on the numbers, the furnace would be a curable item; i.e., it needs to be replaced immediately—it has no remaining life.

b. **At the date of the appraisal, the subject building has a remaining life of 35 years, and the furnace has an effective age of 5 years with a life expectancy of 15 years.**

✔ *CORRECT.* The remaining life of the furnace is less than the remaining life of the building. This makes the furnace a short-lived item.

c. At the date of the appraisal, the subject building has a remaining life of 10 years, and the furnace has an effective age of 3 years with a life expectancy of 15 years.

Incorrect. Given that the furnace has a remaining life that is longer than the remaining life of the whole building, the furnace would be considered an incurable physical long term item.

d. At the date of the appraisal, the subject building has a remaining life of 10 years, and the furnace has an effective age of 5 years with a life expectancy of 15 years.

Incorrect. Given that the furnace has a remaining life that is the same as the remaining life of the whole building, the furnace would be considered an incurable physical long term item.

APPENDIX

7.12 The subject building at 123 Main Street is a 70-year-old house with an RCN of $180,000. 270 Main Street is a property which sold recently for $550,000. The site value (including landscaping) of 270 Main Street is estimated at $400,000 and the RCN of the building is $200,000. The building on 270 Main Street is very similar to the subject in terms of its age, condition and appeal. Based on this information, the current value of the subject building could be estimated as being:

RCN Comparable Building		$200,000
Sale Price of Property	550,000	
Site Value (including landscaping)	400,000	
Current Value of Structure		150,000
Accrued Depreciation		**$50,000**

Accrued Depreciation as a percentage = Accrued Depreciation ÷ RCN
Therefore: 50,000 ÷ 200,000 = 25%

Now apply this 25% depreciation rate to the subject building and you will get a depreciation of $45,000 and a current value (cost) of $135,000 as follows:

180,000 x 25% = $45,000
180,000 – 45,000 = $135,000

The steps to follow are:

1. Deduct the value of the site and any other improvements from the sale price to arrive at a current value of the comparable building.

2. Deduct the current value of the comparable building from its RCN to arrive at the depreciation of the structure.

3. Divide the depreciation of the structure by the RCN of that structure to arrive at a depreciation rate.

4. Apply the depreciate rate to the RCN of the subject building to arrive at the subject building's depreciation.

5. Deduct the subject's depreciation from its RCN to arrive at the current value of the subject building.

a. $135,000   ✓ *CORRECT.* Please review answer shown above.

b. $50,000   *Incorrect.* Please review answer shown above. Check your math. Reminder—follow the steps outlined.

c. $130,000   *Incorrect.* Please review answer shown above. Check your math. Reminder—follow the steps outlined.

d. $150,000   *Incorrect.* Please review answer shown above. Check your math. Reminder—follow the steps outlined.

APPENDIX

7.13 The subject building at 45 High Street is a 20-year-old house with an RCN of $295,000. 100 High Street sold recently for $800,000. The site value (including landscaping) of 100 High Street is estimated at $560,000 and the RCN of the building is $330,000. The building on 100 High Street is very similar to the subject in terms of its age, condition and appeal. Based on this information, the current value of the subject building could be estimated as being:

RCN Comparable Building		$330,000
Sale Price of Property	800,000	
Site Value (including landscaping)	560,000	
Current Value of Structure		240,000
Accrued Depreciation		**$90,000**

Accrued Depreciation as a percentage = Accrued Depreciation ÷ RCN
Therefore: 90,000 ÷ 330,000 = 27.27%

Now apply this 27.27% depreciation rate to the subject building and you will get a depreciation of $80,447 and a current value (cost) of $214,553 as follows:

295,000 x 27.27% = $80,447

295,000 – 80,447 = $214,553

Rounded to $215,000

The steps to follow are:

1. Deduct the value of the site and any other improvements from the sale price to arrive at a current value of the comparable building.

2. Deduct the current value of the comparable building from its RCN to arrive at the depreciation of the structure.

3. Divide the depreciation of the structure by the RCN of that structure to arrive at a depreciation rate.

4. Apply the depreciate rate to the RCN of the subject building to arrive at the subject building's depreciation.

5. Deduct the subject's depreciation from its RCN to arrive at the current value of the subject building.

a. $205,000 exactly.   *Incorrect.* Please review answer shown above. Check your math. Reminder—follow the steps outlined.

b. $80,447 rounded to $80,000.   *Incorrect.* Please review answer shown above. Check your math. Reminder—follow the steps outlined.

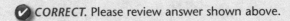

c. **$214,550 rounded to $215,000.**   ✓ *CORRECT.* Please review answer shown above.

d. $205,615 rounded to $206,000.   *Incorrect.* Please review answer shown above. Check your math. Reminder—follow the steps outlined.

7.14 Based on the following information, what would be the estimated current value of the improvements to the site (i.e., landscaping)?

The asphalt driveway (cost new $3,000) is effectively 7 years old, with a remaining life expectancy of 11 years; the wood deck (cost new $3,500) is effectively 8 years old, with a remaining life expectancy of 12 years; the wood fence (cost new $4,000) is effectively 5 years old, with a life expectancy of 20 years; the interlocking brick patio (cost new $1,000) is effectively 25 years old, with a life expectancy of 30 years. The cost new of the sod and trees was estimated at $2,500.

ITEM	COST NEW	EFFECTIVE AGE	LIFE EXPECTANCY	DEPRECIATION	CURRENT VALUE
Asphalt Driveway	$3,000	7	18	$1,167	$1,833
Wood Deck	$3,500	8	20	$1,400	$2,100
Wood Fencing	$4,000	5	20	$1,000	$3,000
Brick Patio	$1,000	25	30	$833	$167
Sod and Trees	$2,500	N/A	N/A	$0	$2,500
Totals	$14,000			$4,400	$9,600

a. $10,178   *Incorrect.* Please review answer shown above. Reminder—the formula for calculating the depreciation of improvements to the site is RCN x Effective Age-Life Expectancy. The sod and trees did not need to be depreciated. The depreciation needs to be deducted from the cost new of that improvement in order to arrive at its current value.

b. $9,600   ✓ *CORRECT.* Please review answer shown above.

c. 4,400   *Incorrect.* Please review answer shown above. Reminder—the formula for calculating the depreciation of improvements to the site is RCN x Effective Age-Life Expectancy. The sod and trees did not need to be depreciated. The depreciation needs to be deducted from the cost new of that improvement in order to arrive at its current value.

d. 7,924   *Incorrect.* Please review answer shown above. Reminder—the formula for calculating the depreciation of improvements to the site is RCN x Effective Age-Life Expectancy. The sod and trees did not need to be depreciated. The depreciation needs to be deducted from the cost new of that improvement in order to arrive at its current value.

CHAPTER 8
CONCLUDING THE APPRAISAL REPORT

Chapter Mini-Review

1. One of the disadvantages of the cost approach is that it is difficult to estimate depreciation particularly in older buildings.

     True   ◯ False

    The difficulty lies in estimating the effective age and economic life of a building when using the Economic Age-Life method or selecting a truly comparable building when using the Comparable Sales—Abstraction Method of Depreciation.

2. One of the advantages of the Direct Comparison Approach is that the data is historical in nature.

    ◯ True   **False**

    This would in fact be a disadvantage. We are trying to value the property today using information from the past. Markets may have changed in the meantime.

3. The list price should be at least 10% above the estimated value of the subject property.

    ◯ True   **False**

    This would likely result in the subject property being overlooked by motivated purchasers who would be looking for similar properties in a more realistic price range. The closer the listing price is to the properties market value, the more likely the property will sell more quickly and for a higher price.

4. One of the advantages of the Direct Comparison Approach is that buyers tend to understand the method and use it.

     True   ◯ False

    The reality of the market place is that buyers will compare properties that have sold or are listed to the property they are about to make an offer on.

5. In final reconciliation, the appraiser averages the estimates of value from the Cost Approach and the Direct Comparison Approach in order to arrive at a final estimate of value for the subject.

    ◯ True   **False**

    In final reconciliation, the appraiser uses his/her judgment by evaluating the strengths and weaknesses of each approach to value and then selecting the approach to value that gives the best indication of value for the subject.

6. One of the disadvantages of the Direct Comparison Approach is that it is sometimes difficult to obtain good comparable sales.

     True   ◯ False

    Good comparables are a key to an accurate valuation. Finding good comparables in a slow market or where the subject property is not typical for the area will be a challenge.

APPENDIX

7. The final estimate of value is shown in an appraisal report in words and figures.

 True   ◯ False

This is to ensure that there is no misunderstanding or mistake.

8. A typical certificate statement used in an appraisal report would be *"This valuation has been based on the assumption that the information collected from industry recognized sources and professionals is in fact correct and can be relied upon for the purpose of this appraisal".*

◯ True   **False**

This is in fact an Assumption and Limiting Condition.

9. A typical Assumption and Limiting Condition used in an appraisal report would be *"Values are subject to varying and continual changes in market conditions and neighbourhood factors. Accordingly, the value presented in this report can only be relied on as the value estimated as of the effective date of appraisal specified in this report. Should the user of this report wish to know the value of the subject property as of another date, the appraiser will need to complete an update or a new appraisal report".*

 True   False

This is Assumption and Limiting Condition #2 on page six of the *Standard Appraisal Report—Single Family* (OREA Form 700).

10. A typical certificate statement used in an appraisal report would be *"I confirm that I did not inspect the subject property and that I have a contemplated interest towards the subject property".*

◯ True   **False**

The certificate statement would normally read "I confirm that I personally inspected the subject property and that I have no current or contemplated interest or bias (positive or negative) towards the subject property".

APPENDIX

Active Learning Exercises

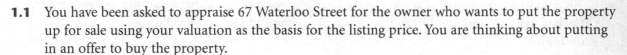

▣ Exercise 1   Multiple Choice

1.1 You have been asked to appraise 67 Waterloo Street for the owner who wants to put the property up for sale using your valuation as the basis for the listing price. You are thinking about putting in an offer to buy the property.

a. This valuation and report is subject to the attached assumptions and limiting conditions.

Incorrect. The scenario does not deal with assumptions and limiting conditions.

b. **I confirm that I personally inspected the subject property and that I have no current or contemplated interest or bias (positive or negative) towards the subject property.**

✔ *CORRECT.* You do have a contemplated interest—you are thinking about putting in an offer. Clearly a conflict of interest.

c. Unless otherwise detailed in writing within this report, I can confirm that I have no personal relationship or bias (positive or negative) towards any of the parties using or affected by this valuation and report.

Incorrect. In this scenario, there is no personal relationship or bias towards the owner.

d. I can confirm that my being employed and paid to complete this valuation is not conditional on the amount of the valuation or on any specific information being included or excluded in this appraisal report.

Incorrect. This scenario does not indicate that the appraisal is being carried out based on a specific value being reported or that specific information be included or excluded.

1.2 Jim Smith appraised 67 Waterloo Street without actually inspecting the property. He did the valuation quickly by looking at old MLS® listings of the home.

a. This valuation and report is subject to the attached assumptions and limiting conditions.

Incorrect. The scenario does not deal with assumptions and limiting conditions.

b. **I confirm that I personally inspected the subject property and that I have no current or contemplated interest or bias (positive or negative) towards the subject property.**

✔ *CORRECT.* This property is not being inspected. How accurate is Jim's valuation if he did not inspect the property.

c. Unless otherwise detailed in writing within this report, I can confirm that I have no personal relationship or bias (positive or negative) towards any of the parties using or affected by this valuation and report.

Incorrect. In this scenario, there is no personal relationship or bias towards the owner.

d. I can confirm that my being employed and paid to complete this valuation is not conditional on the amount of the valuation or on any specific information being included or excluded in this appraisal report.

Incorrect. This scenario does not indicate that the appraisal is being carried out based on a specific value being reported or that specific information be included or excluded.

APPENDIX

CH8 **EX1** **1.3** Jim Smith has been asked to value 67 Waterloo Street for a bank that will put a mortgage on the property based on his appraisal. Jim's sister owns the property.

a. This valuation and report is subject to the attached assumptions and limiting conditions.

Incorrect. The scenario does not deal with assumptions and limiting conditions.

b. I confirm that I personally inspected the subject property and that I have no current or contemplated interest or bias (positive or negative) towards the subject property.

Incorrect. This scenario does not deal with inspections or bias towards the subject property.

c. **Unless otherwise detailed in writing within this report, I can confirm that I have no personal relationship or bias (positive or negative) towards any of the parties using or affected by this valuation and report.**

✓ *CORRECT.* Clearly, there will be a perception, if not the reality, of Jim being biased in estimating the value of his sister's home.

d. I can confirm that my being employed and paid to complete this valuation is not conditional on the amount of the valuation or on any specific information being included or excluded in this appraisal report.

Incorrect. This scenario does not indicate that the appraisal is being carried out based on a specific value being reported or that specific information be included or excluded.

1.4 Jim Smith is being asked to appraise 67 Waterloo Street. The owner needs a mortgage based on a valuation of $400,000. The owner will only hire and pay Jim a fee of $1,000 if he values the property for $400,000 and doesn't mention the water damage in the basement.

a. This valuation and report is subject to the attached assumptions and limiting conditions.

Incorrect. The scenario does not deal with assumptions and limiting conditions.

b. I confirm that I personally inspected the subject property and that I have no current or contemplated interest or bias (positive or negative) towards the subject property.

Incorrect. This scenario does not deal with inspections or bias towards the subject property.

c. Unless otherwise detailed in writing within this report, I can confirm that I have no personal relationship or bias (positive or negative) towards any of the parties using or affected by this valuation and report.

Incorrect. In this scenario, there is no evidence of a personal relationship or bias towards the owner.

d. **I can confirm that my being employed and paid to complete this valuation is not conditional on the amount of the valuation or on any specific information being included or excluded in this appraisal report.**

✓ *CORRECT.* This appraisal is conditional on a particular valuation and on excluding certain information—clearly it would be unethical to accept an appraisal assignment based on fulfilling the owner's demands.

APPENDIX

1.5 You are being asked to value a three-acre single-family rural home with a well and septic tank. You have only had experience valuing inner city homes with municipal water and sewage.   CH8 EX1

a.	**This valuation and report has been completed in accordance with the Canadian Real Estate Association's Code of Ethics and Standard of Business Practice, as well as the Code of Ethics of the *Real Estate and Business Brokers Act, 2002.***	✔ *CORRECT.* You should not accept assignments for which you have little or no experience, unless you partner with someone who does—see section 6 of the Code of Ethics in REBBA 2002.
b.	I confirm that I personally inspected the subject property and that I have no current or contemplated interest or bias (positive or negative) towards the subject property.	*Incorrect.* This scenario does not deal with inspections or bias towards the subject property.
c.	Unless otherwise detailed in writing within this report, I can confirm that I have no personal relationship or bias (positive or negative) towards any of the parties using or affected by this valuation and report.	*Incorrect.* In this scenario, there is no evidence of a personal relationship or bias towards the owner.
d.	I can confirm that my being employed and paid to complete this valuation is not conditional on the amount of the valuation or on any specific information being included or excluded in this appraisal report.	*Incorrect.* This scenario does not indicate that the appraisal is being carried out based on a specific value being reported or that specific information be included or excluded.

1.6 Eliza Smith valued the subject property a year ago for $210,000. The appraisal was done for a bank. The bank now wants to use the same report and value to approve a new first mortgage on the property.

a.	Assumption and Limiting Condition #1 covers this situation.	*Incorrect.* This scenario is not about an appraisal being read and used by another person, other than the client.
b.	**Assumption and Limiting Condition #2 covers this situation.**	✔ *CORRECT.* The appraisal is a year old and values/market conditions change. A new appraisal report would be needed.
c.	Assumption and Limiting Condition #6 covers this situation.	*Incorrect.* This scenario is not about compliance with zoning, building codes, etc.
d.	Assumption and Limiting Condition #7 covers this situation.	*Incorrect.* This scenario is not about relying on recognized sources for information.

APPENDIX

1.7 Jim Smith has valued the subject property for the owner who will use the report to obtain a second mortgage. In addition to giving the appraisal report to the bank, the owner also gives the report to a friend. The friend wants to use it to figure out what he should pay for a property similar to the subject located three blocks away.

a. **Assumption and Limiting Condition #1 covers this situation.**

✔ *CORRECT.* The client has given the appraisal report to a friend for that friend to use.

b. Assumption and Limiting Condition #2 covers this situation.

Incorrect. This scenario is not about using the value in an old appraisal report.

c. Assumption and Limiting Condition #5 covers this situation.

Incorrect. This scenario is not about inspections and identifying hidden defects.

d. Assumption and Limiting Condition #7 covers this situation.

Incorrect. This scenario is not about relying on recognized sources for information.

1.8 Six months ago, Eliza Smith completed an appraisal on the subject property. Her report indicated that there were no problems with the property. A month ago, a hidden underground storage tank was discovered. This tank has leaked and contaminated the property's soil and drinking water. The clean up cost will be $40,000.

a. Assumption and Limiting Condition #2 covers this situation.

Incorrect. This scenario is not about using the value in an old appraisal report.

b. **Assumption and Limiting Condition #5 covers this situation.**

✔ *CORRECT.* There is a hidden underground storage tank. This situation is clearly covered by Assumption and Limiting Condition #5.

c. Assumption and Limiting Condition #6 covers this situation.

Incorrect. This scenario is not about compliance with zoning, building codes, etc.

d. Assumption and Limiting Condition #7 covers this situation.

Incorrect. This scenario is not about relying on recognized sources for information.

1.9 Jim Smith has based his appraisal on a comparable sale which was reported by the MLS® as being sold for $208,000. It turns out that the comparable actually sold for $212,000.

a. Assumption and Limiting Condition #1 covers this situation.

Incorrect. This scenario is not about an appraisal being read and used by another person other than the client.

b. Assumption and Limiting Condition #5 covers this situation.

Incorrect. This scenario is not about inspections and identifying hidden defects.

c. Assumption and Limiting Condition #6 covers this situation.

Incorrect. This scenario is not about compliance with zoning, building codes, etc.

d. **Assumption and Limiting Condition #7 covers this situation.**

✔ *CORRECT.* There is a mistake in the MLS®. The MLS® is a recognized source for information.

APPENDIX

1.10 Eliza Smith has appraised the subject property for $210,000. She has given full value to a large wood deck built at the rear of the building. It turns out that there is no permit for the wood deck and it violates the local zoning by-laws.

a. Assumption and Limiting Condition #1 covers this situation.

Incorrect. This scenario is not about an appraisal being read and used by another person other than the client.

b. Assumption and Limiting Condition #2 covers this situation.

Incorrect. This scenario is not about using the value in an old appraisal report.

c. Assumption and Limiting Condition #5 covers this situation.

Incorrect. This scenario is not about inspections and identifying hidden defects.

d. Assumption and Limiting Condition #6 covers this situation.

✓ *CORRECT.* This scenario is about compliance with zoning by-laws.

▣ Exercise 2

Clearly the subject is overpriced. It has been on the market about three times longer and with a quarter of the showings than would be expected if it were well priced.

▣ Exercise 3

Disadvantages of Cost Approach

- It is difficult to estimate reproduction cost new and depreciation, especially of older buildings.
- Numerous valuations and adjustments are required in order to complete this approach; i.e., cost new of buildings and landscaping, depreciation of buildings and landscaping and site valuation.
- Costs are constantly changing.

Advantages of Direct Comparison Approach

- People understand and use it.
- It requires only one valuation analysis and one set of adjustments.
- Information is generally readily and easily available through the MLS® system.

▣ Exercise 4   Appraisal Form Completion

TASK 1

See the first three pages of the completed form on the following pages.

APPENDIX

Standard Appraisal Report
Single Family

Form 700
for use in the Province of Ontario

CLIENT: Janet Fields   Client Ref No: N/A

Client: Phone No: 453-888-9708   Fax No: 453-888-9709   E-mail: jfields@orea.com

Client's Customer: N/A   Appraiser: Mike Leung   Appraiser's Ref No: 112/xx

GENERAL APPRAISAL AND PROPERTY INFORMATION

Property Address: 25 Landsend Drive, Anycity, Ontario M1X 9ZO

Municipality: Anycity, Anyregion

Full Legal Description: Part Lot 534, Plan 212, City of Anycity, Regional Municipality of Anyregion

Owner: Janet Fields   Assessment: Total $305,000.00   Taxes $ 3,702.00   Year 20xx

This Appraisal is to estimate **MARKET VALUE** for a: ☑ Sale ☐ Financing ☐ Other

Effective Date of Appraisal: 15th July 20xx   Date of Inspection: 15th July 20xx

Highest and Best Use is: ☑ Current ☐ Other (*)

Zoning: R1 Single Family Residential   Occupancy: ☑ Homeowner ☐ Tenant ☐ Vacant

SUBJECT & MARKET HISTORY

Subject Last Sold	Subject Currently Listed	Property Values	Demand/Supply
Date: 4 Years Ago	☐ Yes ☑ No	☑ Stable	☑ In Balance
Sale Price: $ 290,000	Current List Price $	☐ Increasing	☐ Under Supply
Days on Market: 78	Days On Market	☐ Decreasing	☐ Over Supply

Typical Exposure Time Required for Properties to Sell in Subject Neighborhood is: 30 to 60 Days
Typical Exposure Time Required for Properties to Sell on Subject Street is: 30 to 60 Days

NEIGHBOURHOOD INFORMATION

Type		Trend	Subject For Area is	Adjoining Homes
☐ Rural	☑ Prestige	☐ Improving	☑ Comparable	☑ Comparable
☑ Residential	☐ Average	☑ Stable	☐ Superior *	☐ Superior
☐ Commercial	☐ Starter	☐ Declining	☐ Inferior	☐ Inferior
☐ Industrial				

Neighbourhood is: 100 % Developed

Distance to

Elementary School	2 blocks
Secondary School	3 blocks
Public Transit	1 block
Shopping	2 blocks
Downtown	2 miles
Recreational Facilities	1 block

Age Range of Typical Property in Neighbourhood: 50 to 60 Years

Age Range of Typical Property on Subject Street: 50 to 60 Years

Price Range of Properties on Subject Street: $ 300,000 to $ 600,000

Price Range of Properties in Neighbourhood: $ 250,000 to $ 650,000

Comments: (include any positive or negative factors that will have a measurable impact on the subject's marketability and value - items with an * should be discussed)

See Attached

SITE INFORMATION
Utilities & Services

Street	Drainage	Water	Utilities
☑ Paved ☐ Gravel	☐ Open Ditch ☑ Storm Sewer	☑ Municipal ☐ Private Well	☑ Hydro
☑ Municipal ☐ Private	☑ Sanitary Sewer ☐ Septic Tank	☐ Cistern ☐ Shared Well	☑ Gas
☑ Sidewalks ☑ Curbs	☐ Other	☐ Other	☑ Telephone
☑ Street Lighting			☑ Cable
☐ Underground Wiring			
☑ Aboveground Wiring			

Site Dimensions: 11m x 45m   Encroachments: ☐ Yes* ☑ No

Total Site Area: 495 sq. m   Easements: ☐ Yes* ☑ No
Site Shape: Rectangular

Topography: Lot in relation to street grade: ☑ Even   ☐ Above   ☐ Below

Parking

Driveway	Garage (Indicate # of cars):
☐ Laneway ☐ None	☑ Attached # Single
☑ Private ☑ Paved	☐ Detached # ....
☐ Mutual ☐ Gravel	☐ Built In # ....
☐ Other	☐ Carport # ....

Site Appeal

☐ Excellent ☐ Fair*	Landscaping Includes:	Sod, trees, flower beds and interlocking brick patio
☐ Good ☐ Poor*		
☑ Average		

Comments: (include any positive or negative factors that will have a measurable impact on the subject's marketability and value - items with an * should be discussed)

See Attached

INFORMATION ON IMPROVEMENTS (BUILDINGS)

Building Type:		Sq. Ft. (Above Grade)
☑ Detached ☐ High Ranch	☑ 1 Storey	Level 1 105.00 Level 4 ....
☐ Semi-detached ☐ Apartment	☐ 1 1/2 Storey	Level 2 .... Level 5 ....
☐ Attached Row ☐ Split	☐ 2 Storey	Level 3 ....
☐ Other	☐ 3 Storey	Total 105.00

Actual Age 55 Years   Effective Age 21 Years   Total Economic Life 60 Years

Exterior Finish	Roof Material	Foundation
☑ Brick Veneer ☐ Vinyl Siding	☑ Asphalt Shingle ☐ Wood Shingle	☐ Poured Concrete
☐ Solid Brick ☐ Wood Siding	☐ Cedar Shake ☐ Slate	☑ Concrete Block
☐ Stucco ☐ Solid Stone	☐ Metal ☐ Tar & Gravel	☐ Brick
☐ Alum. Siding ☐ Artificial Stone	☐ Other	☐ Stone
☐ Other		☐ Preserved Wood
		☐ Other ....

Window Type

☑ Single   ☑ Thermal   ☑ Wood Frame   ☐ Aluminum   ☑ Vinyl
☐ Other: ....

Evidence of UFFI   ☐ Yes *   ☑ No

Construction Quality   ☐ Excellent   ☐ Good   ☑ Average   ☐ Fair   ☐ Poor*

Exterior Condition/Appeal   ☐ Excellent   ☐ Good   ☑ Average   ☐ Fair   ☐ Poor*

INFORMATION ON IMPROVEMENTS (INTERIOR)

Rooms	Living	Dining	Kitchen	Family	Beds	Bath	Wash	Rec	Other
Basement							1 - 2 pc.	Yes	Laundry
Main	Yes	Yes	Yes		Three	1 - 4 pc.			
Second									
Third									

Room Sizes   ☐ Large   ☑ Medium   ☐ Small

Additional Information on Room Sizes (Optional):

Kitchen
☐ Modern
☐ Average
☑ Outdated

Bathrooms
☐ Modern
☐ Average
☑ Outdated

Closets/Storage
☐ Excellent
☑ Adequate
☐ Inadequate

Basement
☐ None
☑ Full
☐ Partial

☐ Crawl Space
   % Finished 50%

Floors
☐ Carpet
☑ Hardwood
☑ Vinyl Tile
☐ Ceramic
☐ Other ....

Walls/Ceilings
☐ Drywall
☐ Plaster
☐ Panelling
☑ Tile
☐ Other ....

Heating
☑ Forced Air
☐ Hot Water
☐ Baseboard
☐ Other ....

Fuel
☑ Gas
☐ Oil
☐ Electricity
☐ Other ....

Plumbing
☑ Copper
☐ Plastic
☐ Lead
☐ Galvanized
☐ Other ....

Electrical
☐ Fuses
☑ Circuit Breakers
   Amps 100

Floor Plan
☐ Excellent   ☐ Good   ☑ Average   ☐ Fair   ☐ Poor*

Interior Condition
☐ Excellent   ☐ Good   ☑ Average   ☐ Fair   ☐ Poor*

Equipment/Built-Ins/Chattels Remaining With Property:

☑ HWT   ☑ Fridge   ☐ Central Vac   ☐ Wood Stove   ☐ Elect Air Cleaner
☑ Central Air   ☑ Washer   ☑ Humidifier   ☐ Hood   ☐ Garburator
☐ Heat Pump   ☑ Dryer   ☐ Security System   ☐ Oven   ☐ Water Purifier/Filter
☑ Stove   ☑ Dishwasher   ☐ Dehumidifier   ☐ Range   ☐ Central Intercom
☑ Fireplace(s) One
☐ Other: .... N/A
....

Equipment/Chattels Leased or Rented

N/A

Special Features

N/A

Comments: (include any positive or negative factors that will have a measurable impact on the subject's marketability and value - items with an * should be discussed)

See Attached

TASK 2

Building Cost New And Depreciation

Base Building Cost

105 Sq. Meters x $750	$78,750
Area/Shape Multiplier	x 1.02
Adjusted Base Cost	**80,325**
Add Single Garage	+7,000
Add Central Air	+3,800
Add Fireplace	+5,500
Add Rec Room (22.04 x $350)	+7,714
Add Basement 2 Piece Washroom	+4,000
Deduct Central Vacuum	–1,090
Fully Adjusted Base Cost	**107,249**
Multiply the Location Multiplier	x .98
Location Adjusted Cost	**$105,104**
Multiply the Cost Multiplier	x 1.05
Total Reproduction Cost New	**$110,359**

Current Value of Building

$$110,359 \times 35\% = \$38,625 \text{ (Depreciation)}$$

$$110,359 - 38,625 = \$71,734$$

Current Value of Other Improvements

ITEM	COST NEW	EFFECTIVE AGE	LIFE EXPECTANCY	DEPRECIATION	CURRENT VALUE
Concrete Drive	$3,000	15	40	$1,125	$1,875
Patio	$1,200	10	40	$300	$900
Sod/Trees	$2,500	N/A	N/A	$0	$2,500
Totals	**$6,700**			**$1,425**	**$5,275**

Monthly Time Adjustment Calculation

SITE A	285,000 – 260,000 = 25,000	(25,000 ÷ 260,000) ÷ 5 = .0192 (or 1.92%)
SITE B	260,000 – 225,000 = 35,000	(35,000 ÷ 225,000) ÷ 8 = .0194 (or 1.94%)
SITE C	255,000 – 240,000 = 15,000	(15,000 ÷ 240,000) ÷ 3 = .0208 (or 2.08%)

2% selected as percentage monthly increase for the neighbourhood.

Site Value Tabular Analysis

	SALE #1	SALE #2	SALE #3
Front Metre	10.75	11.25	11
Sale Price	216,000	242,000	245,000
Sale Price Per F.M	20,093	21,511	22,273
Time Adjustment	+4%	+6%	0%
T.A. Sale Price/F.M.	20,897	22,802	22,273
Physical Adjustment	+5%	–4%	0%
Location Adjustment	0%	+2%	–2%
Total Net Adjustment	+5%	–2%	–2%
Fully Adjusted Sale Price/F.M.	**21,942**	**22,346**	**21,828**

Reconciliation

An adjusted value range of between $21,828 and $22,346 per front metre has emerged from the above analysis. Within this range most attention has been paid to comparable sale # 3 as it is the most recent sale and required only one location adjustment. Its price per front metre is well supported by the other two comparables. Therefore, the value of the subject site is calculated as:

11 x 21,828 = $240,108
Rounded To 240,000

TASKS 3 AND 4

Pages four, five and six of the completed *Standard Appraisal Report—Single Family* (OREA Form 700) are provided on the following pages.

COST APPROACH TO VALUE

Land Value .... $ 240,000

Improvements	Cost New	Depreciation	Current Value
Building	$ 110,359	$ 38,625	$ 71,734
Garage	$	$	$
Driveway	$ 3,000	$ 1,125	$ 1,875
Patio	$ 1,200	$ 300	$ 900
Sod/Trees	$ 2,500	$ 0	$ 2,500

Total Current Value of All Improvements $ 77,009 $ 77,009

Indicated Value by the Cost Approach $ 317,009

Value Rounded to $ 317,000

DIRECT COMPARISON APPROACH
Competitive Listings

Item	Subject	Listing #1	Listing #2	Listing #3
Address	25 Landsend Dr.	90 Landsend Dr.	40 North End Rd.	150 Landsend Dr.
Distance To Subject		1 block	1 block	1/2 block
Original List Price		$369,000	$365,000	$379,000
Current List Price		$339,000	$349,000	$355,000
Original List Date		05/06/xx	10/06/xx	19/05/xx
Date Price Last Revised		30/06/xx	13/07/xx	01/07/xx
House Style	Detached Bungalow	Detached Bungalow	Detached Bungalow	Detached Bungalow
Lot Size	11m x 45m	11m x 47m	11m x 46m	12m x 48m
Building Size	105 sq. m.	107 sq. m.	115 sq. m.	115 sq. m.
Age	55 years	51 years	55 years	55 years
Condition	Average	Average	Average	Average
Beds	3	3	3	3
Baths	1	1	1	2
Basement	Finished	Finished	Finished	Finished
Listing is: Inferior/Similar/Superior		Similar	Superior	Superior

Comments:

Form 700   2008   **Page 4 of 6**

APPENDIX

Sales Analysis

Item	Subject	Comparable 1		Comparable 2		Comparable 3	
Address	25 Landsend Dr.	250 Landsend Dr.		18 North End Rd.		114 Evans Rd.	
Distance To Subject		1/2 block		1 block		2 blocks	
Date Sold		20/04/20xx		04/07/20xx		13/05/20xx	
Sale Price		$305,000		$320,000		$345,000	
Days On Market		45		35		50	
Time Adjustment	15/07/20xx	3 months	+8,540	Current	0	2 months	+4,761
Time Adjusted Price		313,540		320,000		349,761	
Location	Inner lot	Inner lot	0	Inner lot	0	Corner lot	+5,000
Lot Size	11m x 45m	11m x 46m	0	11m x 45m	0	12m x 47m	−5,000
House Style	Det. Bungalow	Det Bungalow	0	Det Bungalow	0	Det Bungalow	0
Age of House	55 Years	50	0	55	0	53	0
Total Sq. Footage	105 sq. m.	115 sq. m.	−3,000	106 sq. m.	0	115 sq. m.	−3,000
Family Room	No	No	0	No	0	No	0
Bedrooms	3	3	0	3	0	3	0
Bathrooms	1-2pc, 1-4pc	1-4pc	+3,000	1-4pc	+3,000	1-2pc, 2-4pc	−5,000
Basement/% Finished	Full/50%	Full/50%	0	Full/50%	0	Full/50%	0
Rec Room	Yes	Yes	0	Yes	0	Yes	0
Garage/Parking	Single/Private	No/Private	+5,000	Single/Private	0	Single/Private	0
Interior Condition	Average	Good	−7,000	Average	0	Very Good	−15,000
Exterior Condition	Average	Average	0	Average	0	Average	0
CAC	Yes	Yes	0	No	+2,000	Yes	0
Fireplaces	1	None	+4,000	1	0	1	0
Flooring	Vinyl & Hardwood	Vinyl & Carpet	+3,000	Vinyl & Hwd	0	Vinyl & Hwd	
Total Adjustments		+5,000		+5,000		−23,000	
Totally Adj. Sale Price		$318,540		$325,000		$326,761	

Comments, Reconciliation And Estimate Of Value By The Direct Comparison Approach

A narrow range of adjusted values has emerged from the sales analysis of $318,540 to $326,761. Within this range, most attention has been paid to Sale #2 as it was the most recent sale with only two relatively minor adjustments required.

Based on the above information and analysis, a value by the Direct Comparison Approach is estimated to be: ($ 325,000 ....)

FINAL RECONCILIATION, CERTIFICATION AND FINAL ESTIMATE OF VALUE

Given the nature of the subject property, the level and quality of information, the reliability of the necessary adjustments, and the actions of typical buyers in the subject neighbourhood, most weight has been given to the value arrived at by the .... **Direct Comparison** .... Approach.

- This valuation and report is subject to the attached assumptions and limiting conditions.
- This valuation and report has been completed in accordance with the Canadian Real Estate Association's Code of Ethics and Standard of Business Practice, as well as the Code of Ethics of the Real Estate and Business Brokers Act.
- I confirm that I personally inspected the subject property and that I have no current or contemplated interest or bias (positive or negative) towards the subject property.
- Unless otherwise detailed in writing within this report, I can confirm that I have no personal relationship or bias (positive or negative) towards any of the parties using or affected by this valuation and report.
- I can confirm that my being employed and paid to complete this valuation is not conditional on the amount of the valuation or on any specific information being included or excluded in this appraisal report.

Therefore, based on a ....**60**.......... day marketing period, a reasonable market value for the subject property as at

....**15th July**........., 20.**xx**...... is estimated to be:

Three Hundred and Twenty-Five Thousand .... Dollars ($ **325,000** ....)

Appraiser's Signature: ...... *Mike Leung* ......   Date of Signature: ...**Learner to make up**

Appraiser's Name: ......**Mike Leung (MVA-Residential)**......   Company: .....**To be made up by learner**
Appraiser's Address: ......**Learner to make up**......   Phone No: .....**To be made up by learner**
Fax No: .....**To be made up by learner**
E-mail: .....**To be made up by learner**

ATTACHMENTS

☑ Neighbourhood Map
☑ Copies of MLS Listing/Sales
☐ Site/Building Sketch
☑ Photos
☑ Survey

☐ Additional Information/Analysis: ....
☐ Additional Assumptions/Limiting Conditions: ....
....
☐ Other: .... **Suggested Attachments ✔**
....

ASSUMPTIONS AND LIMITING CONDITIONS

1. This report may not be read or used by anyone other than the client without the written authorization of the appraiser. This report should only be used for the property and purpose identified within it. The appraiser accepts no responsibility or liability should the information contained within this report be used by anyone other than the client (or other authorized user) or for any other purpose or property other than that specified within this report.

2. Values are subject to varying and continual changes in market conditions and neighbourhood factors. Accordingly, the value presented in this report can only be relied on as the value estimated as of the effective date of appraisal specified in this report. Should the user of this report wish to know the value of the subject property as of another date, the appraiser will need to complete an update or a new appraisal report.

3. A search on title and ownership has not been performed. A good title with respect to the subject property has been assumed. Therefore, other than what is noted in this report, the appraiser assumes no responsibility for matters legal in nature that may affect the subject property's title, ownership, marketing or value.

4. Any sketches in this report are included solely for the purpose of assisting the reader in visualizing the property.

5. The appraiser has carried out a visual cosmetic inspection of the subject property only. This inspection and the ensuing appraisal report is not and should not be considered a structural, environmental or mechanical inspection and report. Accordingly, unless stated otherwise in this appraisal report, the appraiser is unaware of any hidden or not apparent structural, environmental or mechanical defects or problems and assumes for the purposes of this report and valuation that there are none. Therefore, should it subsequently become known that there is a structural, mechanical or environmental problem or defect, then the appraiser reserves the right to alter the value given in this appraisal report.

6. This appraisal has been based on the assumption that the subject property is in compliance with the applicable zoning, building codes, by-laws, and environmental regulations. Should this in fact turn out not to be so, the appraiser reserves the right to make any necessary changes to the final estimate of value.

7. This valuation has been based on the assumption that the information collected from industry recognized sources and professionals is in fact correct and can be relied upon for the purpose of this appraisal.

CHAPTER 9
OTHER PROPERTY TYPES— STANDARD CONDOMINIUMS

Chapter Mini-Review

1. Information concerning the financial health of a condominium can be found in the Condominium Declaration.

   ○ True   **False**

   You would need to look at the financial statements, status certificate or reserve fund study to find out about a condominium's financial condition.

2. If there are no comparable sales to be found in the subject building, it is acceptable to find comparable sales in a similar building located within the subject neighbourhood.

    True   ○ False

   You may have to make an adjustment for any value differences between the two buildings.

3. A special assessment needed to make necessary building repairs would normally have a negative impact on value.

    True   ○ False

   A special assessment is an expense to the owner and possible to a buyer of that unit. Potential buyers might also be worried as to whether there is anything else wrong with the building or whether the special assessment will be sufficient to cover the necessary repairs.

4. One of the questions that an appraiser needs to ask with respect to a condominium's parking space is whether it is owned in joint tenancy or tenancy in common.

   ○ True   **False**

   A parking space is either owned, common element exclusive use, assigned or rented—the appraiser needs to know which of these applies to the parking.

5. One of the questions that needs to be asked by an appraiser with respect to the reserve fund is the date as to when a reserve fund study was last completed.

    True   ○ False

   Take a look at page two of the *Standard Appraisal Report—Condominium* (OREA Form 701) under the section "Condominium Financial and Legal Information". This is one of the questions asked in that section.

6. The lot size of the standard condominium unit is an important piece of information that needs to be considered by an appraiser when estimating the value of that unit.

   ○ True   **False**

   The land that the condominium unit sits on belongs to all the owners of the condominium and as a result cannot be apportioned to any particular unit.

7. It is important to know the economic life of a condominium unit in coming up with an estimate of value of the property.

 True   **False**

Economic life is needed in order to estimate the depreciation of a building during the cost approach. The cost approach is not used in valuing condominium units.

8. In valuing a condominium unit, it is important to know the exposure and floor level of the subject, as well as the comparable sales being used, as this can affect values.

 True   False

View (exposure) and floor level are pieces of information that are provided by an appraiser in an appraisal report.

9. In valuing a condominium, it is not important to know what the maintenance fees are and what expenses are included in those fees.

 True   **False**

A comparatively high maintenance fee can have a negative impact on value and should be considered. A comparatively low maintenance fee may be indicative of a well managed condominium and may have a positive impact on value.

10. A status certificate can confirm the number of units that are leased in a condominium complex.

 True   False

This piece of information is required by the *Condominium Act, 1998*. It is required in the Status Certificate.

Active Learning Exercises

 Exercise 1

1.1
- How much is the special assessment for?
- What is the special assessment for?
- Is the special assessment to pay for repairs or for improvements/upgrades?
- How and when is the special assessment payable?
- Will the special assessment negatively impact the value of the condominiums in the complex?
- Will the special assessment make it difficult to market and sell the subject unit?

APPENDIX

1.2 • Is the parking space exclusive use—common element, owned, assigned or rented?
• If owned, can one buy another parking space?
• If rented, can one rent a second space?
• If rented, what is the monthly rental?
• If owned, what would it cost to buy another parking space?

1.3 • Is the amount sufficient to pay for expected needed repairs?
• What major repairs are envisioned over the next two years?
• When was the last independent Reserve Fund Study done?
• If the contingency fund is not adequate, will a special assessment be required?
• What will the reaction of buyers be if the contingency fund is inadequate?
• If the contingency fund is inadequate, what will the impact be on the value of the condominiums in the subject complex?

1.4 • What is the average time to sell condominium units in the general area?
• If it is taking longer to sell condominiums in the subject complex than in other condominiums in the general area, why is that?

1.5 • What is the name of the broker and salesperson?
• What is the current list price?
• How long has the property been listed?
• What was the original list price?
• If the list price has been changed, what was the date of the change?
• Have there been any offers?
• What has the reaction of prospective buyers been to the subject unit?

■ **Exercise 2   Appraisal Form Completion**

TASK 1
The first four pages of the completed *Standard Appraisal Report—Condominium* (OREA Form 701) are provided on the following pages.

OREA Ontario Real Estate Association

Standard Appraisal Report
Condominium

Form **701**
for use in the Province of Ontario

CLIENT: Nathan Rekab   Client Ref No: ...... N/A

Client: Phone No: 411-699-3344   Fax No: ...... N/A   E-mail: ...... N/A

Client's Customer: ...... N/A   Appraiser: ...... Rita Lichman   Appraiser's Ref No: ...72-20xx

GENERAL APPRAISAL AND PROPERTY INFORMATION

Property Address: ...... 6 Clair Ave., Suite 1505, Anycity, Ontario

Municipality: ...... Anyregion

Full Legal Description: ...... MBCP 421, Unit 5 Level 15, Parking Unit 12 Level C

Owner: ...... Nathan Rekab   Assessment: Total $235,000   Taxes $ 2,750   Year 20xx

This Appraisal is to estimate **MARKET VALUE** for a: ☑ Sale   ☐ Financing   ☐ Other ....

Effective Date of Appraisal: ...... 30th June 20xx   Date of Inspection: ...... 30th June, 20xx

Highest and Best Use is: ☑ Current   ☐ Other (*) ......

Zoning: Multi Family Residential   Occupancy: ☑ Homeowner ☐ Tenant   ☐ Vacant

SUBJECT & MARKET HISTORY

Subject Last Sold	Subject Currently Listed	Property Values	Demand/Supply
Date: November, 9 years ago	☐ Yes ☑ No	☑ Stable	☑ In Balance
Sale Price: $ 190,000	Current List Price $	☐ Increasing	☐ Under Supply
Days on Market: 60	Days On Market	☐ Decreasing	☐ Over Supply

Typical Exposure Time Required for Properties to Sell in Subject Neighborhood is: ...... 30 to 45 Days
Typical Exposure Time Required for Properties to Sell in Subject Complex: ...... 30 to 45 Days

NEIGHBOURHOOD INFORMATION

Type

		Trend	**For Area, Condo Building is**
☑ Single Family Homes	☑ Mixed Residential/Commercial	☐ Improving	☑ Comparable
☐ Low Rise Rental Buildings	☐ Mixed Residential/Industrial	☑ Stable	☐ Superior*
☑ High Rise Rental Buildings	☐ Prestige	☐ Declining*	☐ Inferior
☐ Town House Condos	☐ Average		
☐ Low Rise Condo Buildings	☐ Starter		
☑ High Rise Condo Buildings			

Distance to

Elementary School	3 blocks
Secondary School	1 block
Public Transit	Immediate
Shopping	1 block
Downtown	2 miles
Recreational Facilities	1 block

Neighbourhood is: ...... 100 ......% Developed

Price Range of Properties in Neighbourhood: $ 200,000 ...... to $ 850,000

Age Range of Typical Property in Neighbourhood: ...... 0 to ...... 20 Years

Comments: (include any positive or negative factors that will have a measurable impact on the subject's marketability and value - items with an * should be discussed)

The subject unit is located in midtown Anycity within a short walk of the subway which allows for quick and easy access to uptown and downtown Anycity with its entertainment and commercial sections. Despite its midtown location, parks and ravines are located within the neighbourhood.

GENERAL INFORMATION - SUBJECT CONDOMINIUM COMPLEX
Type of Condominium Complex

☐ Townhouse   ☐ Garden Home   ☑ Apartment Building
☐ Other ....   # Storeys .... 19 ....   # Units in Complex .... 160 ....

Age of Condominium Complex .... 20 ....Years   Size of Units in Complex From ..... 700 sq. ft. .... to ..... 3,400 sq. ft. ....

Price Range of Units in Complex from $ .210,000 .... to $ .850,000 ....

Complex Occupancy   Owner Occupied .... 80 ....%   Rented .... 20 ....%   Vacant ....%

Type of Parking	**Parking Space is**	**Storage/Locker Space**	**Storage/Locker Space is**
☐ Not Applicable	☐ Not Applicable	☑ Yes	☑ Exclusive Use/Common Element
☑ Underground Garage	☐ Exclusive Use/Common Element	☐ No	☐ Owned
☐ Aboveground w/Garage	☑ Owned	☐ # Lockers	☐ Assigned
☐ Aboveground w/o Garage	☐ Assigned	☐ Locker Size ..4'.. x ..6'..	☐ Rented @ $ .... per Mth.
☐ Other	☐ Other		
Subject has ...One... Spaces	☐ Rented @ $ .... per Mth.		

Condition/Appeal of Interior Common Elements   ☐ Excellent   ☐ Good   ☑ Average   ☐ Fair   ☐ Poor*

Condition/Appeal of Exterior Common Elements   ☐ Excellent   ☐ Good   ☑ Average   ☐ Fair   ☐ Poor*

CONDOMINIUM FINANCIAL AND LEGAL INFORMATION

Subject Unit's Maintenance Fees Are: $ .360 .... Per Month

Are Fees in Line with Other Similar Condominium Complexes?   ☑ Yes   ☐ No*
Maintenance Fees Include
☑ Maintenance of Common Elements   ☑ Insurance   ☑ Water   ☑ Heat   ☐ Hydro
☑ Garbage Collection   ☑ Snow Removal   ☐ Cable   ☑ Lawn Care
☑ Other .... Security ....

Is a Special Assessment Currently being levied?   ☐ Yes*   ☑ No

Are any Special Assessments Pending or Contemplated?   ☐ Yes*   ☑ No

As at the Date of Appraisal, the Reserve Fund contains: $ .1,500,000 ....

Does the Property Management Company believe the Reserve Fund to be adequate?   ☑ Yes   ☐ No*

Are any Major Repairs/Improvements currently underway?   ☐ Yes*   ☑ No

Are any Major Repairs/Improvements Pending or Contemplated over the next two years?   ☑ Yes*   ☐ No

Are there any outstanding or anticipated legal actions?   ☐ Yes*   ☑ No

Has an independent reserve fund study been completed?   ☑ Yes   ☐ No

Date of last reserve fund study ..23rd October, 2 years ago ....

Comments Regarding Condominium Complex: (include any positive or negative factors that will have a measurable impact on the subject's marketability and value - items with an * should be discussed)
Common facilities include an indoor pool, sauna, whirlpool, change rooms, exercise room, party room and concierge. This building appears to be well maintained and has an attractive appearance. All the hallways will be re-carpeted and re-wallpapered within the next 6 months.

Exercise 2   Task 1: Standard Appraisal Report—Condominium, Page 3 of 6   CH9   EX2

SUBJECT UNIT INFORMATION

Type Of Unit
- [ ] Detached Townhouse
- [ ] Semi-detached Townhouse
- [ ] Attached Townhouse
- [x] Apartment
- [ ] Other ....

Style Of Unit
- [x] 1 Story
- [ ] 2 Storey
- [ ] 3 Storey
- [ ] Other ....

Sq. Ft. (Above Grade)
Level 1 **850**   Level 4 ....
Level 2 ....   Level 5 ....
Level 3 ....
Total **850**

Exterior Finish
- [ ] Brick Veneer
- [ ] Solid Brick
- [ ] Stucco
- [ ] Aluminum Siding
- [x] Other   **Concrete**
- [ ] Vinyl Siding
- [ ] Wood Siding
- [ ] Solid Stone
- [ ] Artificial Stone

Roof Material
- [ ] Asphalt Shingle
- [ ] Cedar Shake
- [x] Metal
- [ ] Other ....
- [ ] Wood Shingle
- [ ] Slate
- [ ] Tar & Gravel

Foundation
- [x] Poured Concrete
- [ ] Concrete Block
- [ ] Brick
- [ ] Stone
- [ ] Preserved Wood
- [ ] Other ....

Window Type
- [ ] Single
- [x] Thermal
- [ ] Wood Frame
- [ ] Aluminum
- [x] Vinyl
- [ ] Other ....

Evidence of UFFI
- [ ] Yes*
- [x] No

Exterior Condition
- [ ] Excellent
- [ ] Good
- [x] Average
- [ ] Fair
- [ ] Poor*

Exterior Appeal
- [ ] Excellent
- [ ] Good
- [x] Average
- [ ] Fair
- [ ] Poor*

Rooms	Living	Dining	Kitchen	Family	Beds	Bath	Wash	Rec	Other
Basement									
Main	Comb.	Comb.	Yes		One	4 pc.			Foyer
Second									
Third									

Room Sizes
- [ ] Large
- [x] Medium
- [ ] Small

Additional Information on Room Sizes (Optional):

Kitchen
- [ ] Modern
- [x] Average
- [ ] Outdated

Bathrooms
- [ ] Modern
- [x] Average
- [ ] Outdated

Closets/Storage
- [ ] Excellent
- [x] Adequate
- [ ] Inadequate

Basement
- [x] None
- [ ] Full
- [ ] Partial

- [ ] Crawl Space
% Finished ....

Floors
- [ ] Carpet
- [x] Hardwood
- [ ] Vinyl Tile
- [x] Ceramic
- [ ] Other ....

Walls/Ceilings
- [x] Drywall
- [ ] Plaster
- [ ] Panelling
- [ ] Tile
- [x] Other   **Stucco**

Heating
- [x] Forced Air
- [x] Hot Water
- [ ] Baseboard
- [ ] Other ....

Fuel
- [x] Gas
- [ ] Oil
- [ ] Electricity
- [ ] Other ....

Plumbing
- [x] Copper
- [x] Plastic
- [ ] Lead
- [ ] Galvanized
- [ ] Other ....

Electrical
- [ ] Fuses
- [x] Circuit Breakers
Amps **200**

Floor Plan
- [ ] Excellent
- [ ] Good
- [x] Average
- [ ] Fair
- [ ] Poor*

Interior Condition
- [ ] Excellent
- [ ] Good
- [x] Average
- [ ] Fair
- [ ] Poor*

Equipment/Built-Ins/Chattels Remaining With Property:

☐ HWT	☑ Fridge	☐ Central Vac	☐ Wood Stove	☐ Elect Air Cleaner
☐ Central Air	☑ Washer	☐ Humidifier	☐ Hood	☐ Garburator
☐ Heat Pump	☑ Dryer	☐ Security System	☐ Oven	☐ Water Purifier/Filter
☑ Stove	☑ Dishwasher	☐ Dehumidifier	☐ Range	☐ Central Intercom
☐ Fireplace(s)	....			
Other:	....			

Equipment/Chattels Leased or Rented

N/A

Special Features

N/A

Comments: (include any positive or negative factors that will have a measurable impact on the subject's marketability and value - items with an * should be discussed)

Within the past 3 years, the owner has repainted the walls, replaced the carpeting with hardwood floors and re-stuccoed the ceilings. The subject unit has an unobstructed north east view. Units 2 floors lower with the same exposure look directly into a commercial office building. Conversely, units with a southwest exposure enjoy an obstructed downtown and lake view.

DIRECT COMPARISON APPROACH
Competitive Listings

Item	Subject	Listing #1	Listing #2	Listing #3
Address	6 Clair Ave. #1505	6 Clair Ave. #1306	6 Clair Ave. #1605	6 Clair Ave. #1207
Distance To Subject		Same complex	Same complex	Same complex
Original List Price		$259,000	$279,000	$289,900
Current List Price		$249,900	$259,000	$279,000
Original List Date		01/06/20xx	19/05/20xx	14/05/20xx
Date Price Last Revised		15/06/20xx	19/06/20xx	06/06/20xx
Unit Type/Style	Apartment	Apartment	Apartment	Apartment
Size	850 sq. ft.	900 sq. ft.	850 sq. ft.	900 sq. ft.
Age	20 years	20 years	20 years	20 years
Location				
Exposure	North east	North east	North east	South west
Condition	Average	Average	Superior	Average
Beds	1	1	1	1
Baths	1	1	1	1
Floor Level	15	13	16	12
Listing is: Inferior/Similar/Superior		Similar	Superior	Superior

Comments: All 3 comparable listings are one-bedroom units located within the subject complex and as such were felt to be good comparables. Listing #1 is slightly larger, but is located on a less appealing floor level looking directly into a commercial office building. Listing #2 enjoys the use of an updated kitchen and bathroom making it superior to the subject. Listing #3 is larger and has a spectacular southwest view making it superior to the subject. There is nothing unusual about the number of days on the market for each listing.

TASK 2
Time Adjustment Calculation

CH9 EX2

Time Resales

Unit 1803 Sale Price	336,000	(Feb)
Unit 1903 Sale Price (adjusted)	350,000	(Jun) (352,000 – 2,000)
Price Increase	**14,000**	
% Increase	4.16%	(14,000 ÷ 336,000 x 100)
Time Difference	4 months	
% Increase/Month	1.04%	(4.16 ÷ 4)
Unit 601 Sale Price	300,000	(Mar)
Unit 701 Sale Price (adjusted)	308,800	(Jun) (315,800 – 7,000)
Price Increase	**8,800**	
% Increase	2.93%	(8,800 ÷ 300,000 x 100)
Time Difference	3 months	
% Increase/Month	0.97%	(2.93 ÷ 3)

Reconciliation

Based on the above, 1% is estimated as the percentage monthly increase. The completed page five of the *Standard Appraisal Report—Condominium* (OREA Form 701) is shown on the following page.

Sales Analysis

Item	Subject	Comparable 1		Comparable 2		Comparable 3	
Address	6 Clair Ave. #1505	6 Clair Ave. #705		6 Clair Ave. #1405		6 Clair Ave. #1706	
Distance To Subject		Same complex		Same complex		Same complex	
Date Sold		21/05/20xx		19/06/20xx		26/04/20xx	
Sale Price		$220,000		$238,000		$271,000	
Days On Market		38 days		30 days		45 days	
Time Adjustment	30/06/20xx	1 month	+2,200	Current	0	2 months	+5,420
Time Adjusted Price		$222,200		$238,000		$276,420	
Exposure	North east	North east	0	North east	0	North east	0
Unit Type/Style	Apartment	Apartment	0	Apartment	0	Apartment	0
Age of Unit	20 years	20 years	0	20 years	0	20 years	0
Total Sq. Footage	850 sq. ft.	850 sq. ft.	0	850 sq. ft.	0	900 sq. ft.	−14,250
Family Room	No	No	0	No	0	No	0
Bedrooms	One	One	0	One	0	One	0
Bathrooms	1-4 pc.	1-4 pc.	0	1-4 pc.	0	1-4 pc.	0
Basement/% Finished	N/A	N/A	0	N/A	0	N/A	0
Rec Room	N/A	N/A	0	N/A	0	N/A	0
Garage/Parking	Basement/One	Bsmt./One	0	Bsmt./One	0	Bsmt./One	0
Unit Condition	Average	Fair	+5,000	Average	0	Excellent	-15,000
Exterior Condition	Average	Average	0	Average	0	Average	0
Floor plan	Average	Average	0	Average	0	Average	0
Floor level	15th	7th	+10,000	14th	+2,000	17th	-4,000
Total Adjustments		+ 15,000		+ 2,000		− 33,250	
Totally Adj. Sale Price		$ 237,200		$240,000		$243,170	

Comments, Reconciliation And Estimate Of Value By The Direct Comparison Approach

Within the adjusted selling price range of $237,200 and $243,170, most attention has been paid to Sale #2 as it is a very recent sale only requiring one adjustment for floor level. The adjusted selling prices of both sales 1 and 3 fully support the conclusions from Sale # 2.

Based on the above information and analysis, a value by the Direct Comparison Approach is estimated to be: ($ 240,000 ....)

APPENDIX

2.1 Calculate the percentage monthly time adjustment arrived at by using the information from Units 1803 and 1903.

CH9 EX2

a. 1.19%   *Incorrect.* Please review time adjustment calculations above. Reminder—you need to adjust the sale price of unit 1903 to take care of the difference in floor levels.

b. 1.04%   ✔ *CORRECT.* Please review answer shown above.

c. 4.16%   *Incorrect.* Please review answer shown above. Reminder—you need to divide the % increase by 4 months (the time difference).

d. 4.76%   *Incorrect.* Please review answer shown above. Reminder—you need to adjust the sale price of unit 1903 to take care of the difference in floor levels. You also need to divide the % increase by 4 months (the time difference).

2.2 Calculate the percentage monthly time adjustment arrived at by using the information from Units 601 and 701.

a. .97%   ✔ *CORRECT.* Please review answer shown above.

b. 1.76%   *Incorrect.* Please review answer shown above. Reminder—you need to adjust the sale price of unit 701 to take care of the condition difference.

c. 2.93%   *Incorrect.* Please review answer shown above. Reminder—you need to divide the % increase by 3 months (the time difference).

d. 5.27%   *Incorrect.* Please review answer shown above. Reminder—you need to adjust the sale price of unit 701 to take care of the condition difference. You also need to divide the % increase by 3 months (the time difference).

2.3 Calculate the time adjusted price for Comparable Sale #1 (remember the effective date of the appraisal is June 30th, 20xx).

a. $217,772   *Incorrect.* Please review answer shown above. Check your math. Reminder—the time adjustment should be added, not deducted; the percentage increase per month is 1%. This property sold 1 month ago.

b. $217,800   *Incorrect.* Please review answer shown above. Check your math. Reminder—the time adjustment should be added, not deducted; the percentage increase per month is 1%. This property sold 1 month ago.

c. $222,800   *Incorrect.* Please review answer shown above. Check your math. Reminder—the percentage increase per month is 1%. This property sold 1 month ago.

d. $222,200   ✔ *CORRECT.* Please review answer shown above.

2.4 Calculate the time adjusted price for Comparable Sale #2.

    a. $240,380   *Incorrect.* Please review answer shown above. This is a current sale—no time adjustment required.

    b. $235,620   *Incorrect.* Please review answer shown above. This is a current sale—no time adjustment required.

    c. **$238,000**   ✔ *CORRECT.* Please review answer shown above.

    d. $237,000   *Incorrect.* Please review answer shown above. This is a current sale—no time adjustment required.

2.5 Calculate the time adjusted price for Comparable Sale #3.

    a. $265,580   *Incorrect.* Please review answer shown above. Check your math. Reminder—the time adjustment should be added, not deducted; the percentage increase per month is 1%. This property sold 2 months ago.

    b. **$276,420**   ✔ *CORRECT.* Please review answer shown above.

    c. $273,710   *Incorrect.* Please review answer shown above. Check your math. Reminder—the percentage increase per month is 1%. This property sold 2 months ago.

    d. $268,290   *Incorrect.* Please review answer shown above. Check your math. Reminder—the time adjustment should be added, not deducted; the percentage increase per month is 1%. This property sold 2 months ago.

2.6 Calculate the totally adjusted sale price for comparable sale #1.

    a. $207,200   *Incorrect.* Please review answer shown above. Reminder—check to see if you had the correct Time Adjusted Price; the correct adjustments (+/–); correct total adjustments. You should have applied the total adjustments to the Time Adjusted Price.

    b. $235,000   *Incorrect.* Please review answer shown above. Reminder—check to see if you had the correct Time Adjusted Price; the correct adjustments (+/–); correct total adjustments. You should have applied the total adjustments to the Time Adjusted Price.

    c. $205,000   *Incorrect.* Please review answer shown above. Reminder—check to see if you had the correct Time Adjusted Price; the correct adjustments (+/–); correct total adjustments. You should have applied the total adjustments to the Time Adjusted Price.

    d. **$237,200**   ✔ *CORRECT.* Please review answer shown above.

2.7   Calculate the totally adjusted sale price for comparable sale #2.

a. $240,000   ✔ *CORRECT.* Please review answer shown above.

b. $236,000   *Incorrect.* Please review answer shown above. Reminder—check to see if you had the correct Time Adjusted Price; the correct adjustments (+/–); correct total adjustments. You should have applied the total adjustments to the Time Adjusted Price.

c. $242,380   *Incorrect.* Please review answer shown above. Reminder—check to see if you had the correct Time Adjusted Price; the correct adjustments (+/–); correct total adjustments. You should have applied the total adjustments to the Time Adjusted Price.

d. $233,620   *Incorrect.* Please review answer shown above. Reminder—check to see if you had the correct Time Adjusted Price; the correct adjustments (+/–); correct total adjustments. You should have applied the total adjustments to the Time Adjusted Price.

2.8   Calculate the totally adjusted sale price for comparable sale #3.

a. $243,170   ✔ *CORRECT.* Please review answer shown above.

b. $309,670   *Incorrect.* Please review answer shown above. Reminder—check to see if you had the correct Time Adjusted Price; the correct adjustments (+/–); correct total adjustments. You should have applied the total adjustments to the Time Adjusted Price.

c. $237,750   *Incorrect.* Please review answer shown above. Reminder—check to see if you had the correct Time Adjusted Price; the correct adjustments (+/–); correct total adjustments. You should have applied the total adjustments to the Time Adjusted Price.

d. $232,330   *Incorrect.* Please review answer shown above. Reminder—check to see if you had the correct Time Adjusted Price; the correct adjustments (+/–); correct total adjustments. You should have applied the total adjustments to the Time Adjusted Price.

2.9   The estimate of value for the subject property would be based on:

a.   the totally adjusted sale price of Comparable #3 as it had the greatest amount and number of adjustments and was a dated sale.   *Incorrect.* A property which is a dated sale and has the greatest number of adjustments would not be the best comparable.

b.   **the totally adjusted sale price of Comparable #2 as it had the least amount and number of adjustments and was the most recent sale.**   ✔ *CORRECT.* A recent comparable with a minimal number of adjustments would be the best basis for an estimate of value for the subject.

c.   the totally adjusted sale price of Comparable #1 as it had the least amount and number of adjustments and was the most recent sale.   *Incorrect.* This is an untrue statement. Check the answer above.

d.   the average of the totally adjusted selling prices of Comparables 1, 2 and 3.   *Incorrect.* An estimate of value requires reasoned judgment based on the most comparable sale. Averaging is purely a mechanical exercise.

APPENDIX

CH9   EX2

2.10 The final estimate of value for the subject property would be based on:

a. a 28 day marketing period.

Incorrect. Market Value requires a reasonable time to sell. 28 days is not typical for the subject neighbourhood and therefore would not meet the definition of reasonable. The typical number of days to sell comes from Task 1.

b. a 45 day marketing period.

✓ *CORRECT.* This appraisal is for sale purposes. On average, it is taking up to 45 days to market and sell a property within the subject neighbourhood. This information comes from Task 1.

c. a 20 day marketing period.

Incorrect. Market Value requires a reasonable time to sell. 20 days is not typical for the subject neighbourhood and therefore would not meet the definition of reasonable. The typical number of days to sell comes from Task 1.

d. a 10 day marketing period.

Incorrect. Market Value requires a reasonable time to sell. 10 days is not typical for the subject neighbourhood and therefore would not meet the definition of reasonable. The typical number of days to sell comes from Task 1.

TASK 3

The completed page six of the *Standard Appraisal Report—Condominium* (OREA Form 701) is shown on the following page.

APPENDIX

CERTIFICATION AND FINAL ESTIMATE OF VALUE

- This valuation and report is subject to the attached assumptions and limiting conditions.
- This valuation and report has been completed in accordance with the Canadian Real Estate Association's Code of Ethics and Standard of Business Practice, as well as the Code of Ethics of the Real Estate and Business Brokers Act.
- I confirm that I personally inspected the subject property and that I have no current or contemplated interest or bias (positive or negative) towards the subject property.
- Unless otherwise detailed in writing within this report, I can confirm that I have no personal relationship or bias (positive or negative) towards any of the parties using or affected by this valuation and report.
- I can confirm that my being employed and paid to complete this valuation is not conditional on the amount of the valuation or on any specific information being included or excluded in this appraisal report.

Therefore, based on a ....**45**...... day marketing period, a reasonable market value for the subject property as at

..**30th June**...., 20 **xx**.... is estimated to be:

..**Two Hundred and Forty Thousand**.. Dollars ($.**240,000**.....................)

Appraiser's Signature: ....*Rita Lichman*........   Date of Signature: ....**02/07/20xx**....

Appraiser's Name: ....**Rita Lichman**....   Company: ....**ABC Realty**....

Appraiser's Address: ....**48 Clair Avenue**....   Phone No: ....**411 699-1234**....

....**Anycity, Ontario**....   Fax No: ....**411 699-4321**....

E-mail: ....**rita@abcrealty.ca**....

ATTACHMENTS

- ☑ Neighbourhood Map
- ☑ Copies of MLS Listing/Sales
- ☐ Site/Building Sketch
- ☑ Photos
- ☐ Survey

- ☐ Additional Information/Analysis: ....
- ☐ Additional Assumptions/Limiting Conditions: ....
- ☑ Other: ....**Builders Floor Plan**....

ASSUMPTIONS AND LIMITING CONDITIONS

1. This report may not be read or used by anyone other than the client without the written authorization of the appraiser. This report should only be used for the property and purpose identified within it. The appraiser accepts no responsibility or liability should the information contained within this report be used by anyone other than the client (or other authorized user) or for any other purpose or property other than that specified within this report.
2. Values are subject to varying and continual changes in market conditions and neighbourhood factors. Accordingly, the value presented in this report can only be relied on as the value estimated as of the effective date of appraisal specified in this report. Should the user of this report wish to know the value of the subject property as of another date, the appraiser will need to complete an update or a new appraisal report.
3. A search on title and ownership has not been performed. A good title with respect to the subject property has been assumed. Therefore, other than what is noted in this report, the appraiser assumes no responsibility for matters legal in nature that may affect the subject property's title, ownership, marketing or value.
4. Any sketches in this report are included solely for the purpose of assisting the reader in visualizing the property.
5. The appraiser has carried out a visual cosmetic inspection of the subject property only. This inspection and the ensuing appraisal report is not and should not be considered a structural, environmental or mechanical inspection and report. Accordingly, unless stated otherwise in this appraisal report, the appraiser is unaware of any hidden or not apparent structural, environmental or mechanical defects or problems and assumes for the purposes of this report and valuation that there are none. Therefore, should it subsequently become known that there is a structural, mechanical or environmental problem or defect, then the appraiser reserves the right to alter the value given in this appraisal report.
6. This appraisal has been based on the assumption that the subject property is in compliance with the applicable zoning, building codes, by-laws, environmental regulations and condominium by-laws and regulations. Should this in fact turn out not to be so, the appraiser reserves the right to make any necessary changes to the final estimate of value.
7. This valuation has been based on the assumption that the information collected from industry recognized sources and professionals is in fact correct and can be relied upon for the purpose of this appraisal.

CHAPTER 10
OTHER PROPERTY TYPES— COMMERCIAL PROPERTIES

Chapter Mini-Review

1. Distance to railway freight depots and methods of disposal for hazardous waste are pieces of information that need to be collected when it comes to industrial properties.

 True   ◯ False

The need for raw materials and waste derived from industrial processes make the collection of this information important.

2. The net operating income of an investment property is arrived at by deducting the vacancy and bad debts from the effective annual gross income.

◯ True   False

Vacancy and bad debts are deducted from the potential annual gross income to arrive at the effective annual gross income, and then operating expenses are deducted from the effective annual gross income to arrive at the net operating income.

3. One of the important factors that needs to be considered in arriving at an estimation of potential annual gross income is typical management.

 True   ◯ False

For a buyer, the income that a property can reasonably be expected to generate would be based on the property being run by average competent management.

4. The estimate of market rent used in an appraiser's reconstructed income and expense statement is arrived at by analyzing the subject property's past performance.

◯ True   False

The estimate of market rent is arrived at by looking at the rents being obtained by comparable properties.

5. One of the reasons why some of the expenses shown in an appraiser's reconstructed expense statement may be different to the owner's expense statement is that the subject building may not have competent management and therefore the expenses may not be typical.

 True   ◯ False

Other reasons for differences between the two statements might be that 1) the owner has included expenses that are paid, but not needed to maintain the income flow of that building; e.g., charitable donation, car allowance, etc. 2) some expenses are payable in one year and not in others; e.g., painting done every 5 years—appraiser would stabilize on an annual basis.

6. A typical operating expense shown in an appraiser's reconstructed income and expense statement would be mortgage payments.

 True   ✓ False

One of the guidelines in arriving at the estimated total annual operating expenses is that only expenses that are necessary to maintain the flow of current income should be included in the appraiser's reconstructed expense statement. Mortgage payments may be needed by the owner of the building for personal/business reasons, but they are not required to ensure the continued flow of the rental income; i.e., a tenant will pay the rental whether there is a mortgage or not on a property.

7. In estimating the total annual operating expenses, an appraiser would compare the owner's expense statement to the operating expenses being experienced by comparable properties and/or operating expense ratios shown in published studies.

✓ True   False

This is to ensure the validity of the owner's expenses in terms of the nature and level of those expenses. Expenses need to conform to typical average management.

8. In order to estimate the overall capitalization rate from comparable sales, the sale price of the comparable is divided by its annual net operating income (NOI).

 True   ✓ False

The annual net operating income would be divided by the sale price of the comparable.

9. To capitalize the subject's annual net operating income (NOI) into value for the subject property, you would multiply it by the overall capitalization rate.

 True   ✓ False

You would divide the subject's annual net operating income by the overall capitalization rate in order to arrive at a value for the subject property.

10. The gross income multiplier (GIM) is a factor or a multiplier used to convert the potential annual effective gross income of the subject property into value.

✓ True   False

The GIM is estimated by looking at the selling prices of comparable properties and dividing their selling prices by the estimated annual effective gross incomes of those properties.

APPENDIX

Active Learning Exercises

■ Exercise 1

Market Rent

When estimating the market value of an income producing property, it is market rent and not contract rent that must be used. Market rent is the rental that each unit would most probably command, if it were vacant and available for rent on the open market as of the date of the appraisal. Contract rent is the rent that is actually being paid under contract by the tenant of each unit.

100% Occupancy

Calculation of the total potential annual gross income is based on the total revenue that could be received if all the apartments in the subject building were rented.

Typical Management

The potential annual gross income of an investment property is based on market rent, and on the assumption that there is, or will be, typically competent and prudent management.

■ Exercise 2

In arriving at the estimated total annual operating expenses, the appraiser needs to follow these guidelines:

- Include only the expenses that are necessary to maintain the flow of rental income estimated as of the date of appraisal.
- The nature and level of expenses should be based on typical management and should be consistent with market expenses.
- Since some expenses are concentrated in one particular year and not in others, it is important to stabilize or smooth out the expenses on an annual basis.

As a result, the appraiser will need to reconstruct the owner's income and expense statement for one or all of the following reasons:

- The owner of an apartment building usually records expenses on a cash basis (when paid) whereas the appraiser needs to look at expenses on the basis of when they were incurred.
- The building may not have competent management and therefore the expenses may not be typical (higher) as a result.
- The owner's statements may include expenses that are not necessary to maintain the current income flow of the building; e.g., charitable donations
- Legitimate expenses can occur in some years and not in others. All legitimate expenses must be stabilized on an annual basis.
- There may be expenses excluded from the seller's income/expense statement that should be included. Typical of this would be management fees. Even if the owners of an apartment building have been managing it themselves, a management fee should be included as "time is money". If there is a superintendent that enjoys the use of a free apartment, the expected rental of that apartment should be included in the gross potential annual income and then shown as an expense.

■ Exercise 3

No. The replacement of short-lived component parts would be considered a capital expenditure. While it is prudent for the owner to contribute into a reserve fund, the condition of the building is effectively taken care of by the overall capitalization rate being selected from comparables in the same condition requiring the same repairs and replacement.

Of course, the only time the appraiser may be justified in including a reserve for replacement of such short-life components in the operating expense statement is when the market indicates that this is normal practice adopted by property owners in the area, and when the overall capitalization rate used by the appraiser in capitalizing the resulting net income has been extracted from comparable properties treated in the same way; i.e., provision was also made for reserves for replacement in arriving at their net operating income.

■ Exercise 4

SALE #	SALE PRICE	SQ. M.	# UNITS	SALE PRICE/ SQ. M.	SALE PRICE/ UNIT
1	792,000	565	8	1,402 (792,000 ÷ 565)	99,000 (792,000 ÷ 8)
2	606,000	435	6	1,393 (606,000 ÷ 435)	101,000 (606,000 ÷ 6)
3	784,000	550	8	1,425 (784,000 ÷ 550)	98,000 (784,000 ÷ 8)

Value of Subject

1) Sale Price Per Sq. M.   495 x 1,400 = $693,000
2) Sale Price Per Unit   7 x 100,000 = $700,000

Exercise 5

Estimated Potential Annual Gross Income (760 x 12 x 8)	$72,960	
Vacancy & Bad Debt (72,960 x 2%)	$1,459	
Estimated Effective Gross Annual Income (EGI)		**$71,501**

Expenses:

Water	1,680
Heating and Air Conditioning	3,920
Fire Insurance (1 Year Premium)	1,448
Minor Repairs and Maintenance	3,180
Electricity for Common Areas	600
Landscaping Contract	1,000
Realty Taxes	6,800
Janitor's Salary (15,000 + 9,120)	24,120
Management (3% of 71,501)	2,145
Painting of Halls and Common Areas (1,500 ÷ 5)	300
Painting and Decorating (2,100 ÷ 3 x 8 = 5,600 ÷4)	1,400
Miscellaneous Sundry Expenses	300

Total Operating Expenses	**$46,893**
NET OPERATING INCOME	**$24,608**

$$I \div R = V$$
$$24,608 \div .0625 = \$393,728$$
Rounded to $394,000

Exercise 6

COMPARABLE #	SALE PRICE	EGI	NOI	GIM	RATE
1	535,000	82,308	50,022	6.50 (535,000 ÷ 82,308)	.093 (50,022 ÷ 535,000)
2	561,000	86,175	52,510	6.51 (561,000 ÷ 86,175)	.094 (52,510 ÷ 561,000)
3	495,000	76,154	46,282	6.50 (495,000 ÷ 76,154)	.093 (46,282 ÷ 495,000)

Overall capitalization rate: $I \div R = V$
$$49,088 \div .093 = \$527,828$$
Rounded to $528,000

GIM   EGI x GIM = Value
$$80,750 \times 6.5 = 524,875$$
Rounded to $525,000

Exercise 7

COMPARABLE #	SALE PRICE	EGI	NOI	GIM	RATE
1	700,000	133,080	53,200	5.26 (700,000 ÷ 133,080)	.076 (53,200 ÷ 700,000)
2	830,000	158,000	63,240	5.25 (830,000 ÷ 158,000)	.076 (63,240 ÷ 830,000)
3	640,000	123,560	49,429	5.18 (640,000 ÷ 123,560)	.077 (49,429 ÷ 640,000)

Overall capitalization rate: I/R = V

60,000 ÷ .076 = $789,474

Rounded to $789,000

GIM   EGI x GIM = Value

150,000 x 5.25 = 787,500

Rounded to $788,000

Exercise 8   Multiple Choice

Estimated Potential Annual Gross Income (1200 x 12 x 10) $144,000

    Additional Income (20 x 30 x 12)   7,200

Total Estimated Potential Annual Gross Income $151,200

    Vacancy & Bad Debt (151,200 x 3%) $4,536

Estimated Effective Gross Annual Income (EGI)   **$146,664**

Expenses:

    Utilities (Electricity, Water And Gas)   3,420

    Heating and Air Conditioning   4,100

    Insurance   1,680

    Repairs and Maintenance   4,350

    Realty Taxes (625,000 x 1.638%)   10,238

    Superintendent Salary (18,500 + 14,400 + 450)   33,350

    Painting Exterior (6,000 ÷ 6)   1,000

    Painting Suites (1,500 x 5 ÷ 2)   3,750

    Painting Halls And Common Areas (2,500/5)   500

    Cleaning Supplies   380

    Elevator Contract   1,000

    Landscaping and Snow Removal Contract   1,650

    Roof Repairs   320

    Management (Annual Contract)   3,750

Total Operating Expenses   **$69,488**

NET OPERATING INCOME   **$77,176**

NOTE: The NOI for each comparable needs to be calculated by deducting the operating expenses from the EGI.

CH10   EX8

COMPARABLE #	SALE PRICE	EGI	NOI	GIM	RATE
1	575,000	140,587	73,120	4.09 (575,000 ÷ 140,587)	12.72 (73,120 ÷ 575,000)
2	614,000	149,029	81,250	4.12 (614,000 ÷ 149,029)	13.23 (81,250 ÷ 614,000)
3	664,000	161,557	87,140	4.11 (664,000 ÷ 161,557)	13.12 (87,140 ÷ 664,000)

Overall capitalization rate: $I \div R = V$

$77,176 \div .13 = $593,662$

Rounded to $594,000

GIM   EGI x GIM = Value

$146,664 \times 4.1 = 601,322$

Rounded to $601,000

8.1 Calculate the effective gross income of the subject.

a. $151,200   ***Incorrect.*** Review the answer shown above. Check your math. Reminder—the Vacancy and Bad Debt needs to be deducted from the Total Estimated Potential Annual Gross Income.

b. $139,680   ***Incorrect.*** Review the answer shown above. Check your math. Reminder—there is additional income that needs to be added to the estimated Potential Annual Gross Income and the Vacancy and Bad Debt needs to be deducted from the Total Estimated Potential Annual Gross Income.

c. **$146,664** ✓ CORRECT. Review the answer shown above.

d. $155,736   ***Incorrect.*** Review the answer shown above. Check your math. Reminder—there is additional income that needs to be added to the estimated Potential Annual Gross Income and the Vacancy and Bad Debt needs to be deducted from the Total Estimated Potential Annual Gross Income.

8.2 Calculate the net operating income of the subject.

a. $66,426   ***Incorrect.*** Review the answer shown above. Check your math. Reminder—there are expenses that should have been excluded from and there are expenses that would need to have been added to the appraiser's reconstructed income and expense statement.

b. $72,176   ***Incorrect.*** Review the answer shown above. Check your math. Reminder—there are expenses that should have been excluded from and there are expenses that would need to have been added to the appraiser's reconstructed income and expense statement.

c. **$77,176** ✓ CORRECT. Review the answer shown above.

d. $77,626   ***Incorrect.*** Review the answer shown above. Check your math. Reminder—there are expenses that should have been excluded from and there are expenses that would need to have been added to the appraiser's reconstructed income and expense statement.

APPENDIX

8.3 Calculate Comparable #1's gross income multiplier.

a. 4.09   ✔ *CORRECT*. Review the answer shown above.

b. 8.52   *Incorrect*. Review the answer shown above. Check your math. Reminder—the comparable's sale price should be divided by its effective gross income.

c. 12.72   *Incorrect*. Review the answer shown above. Check your math. Reminder—the comparable's sale price should be divided by its effective gross income.

d. 7.86   *Incorrect*. Review the answer shown above. Check your math. Reminder—the comparable's sale price should be divided by its effective gross income.

8.4 Calculate Comparable #1's overall capitalization rate.

a. 11.73%   *Incorrect*. Review the answer shown above. Check your math. Reminder—the comparable's net operating income should be divided by its sale price.

b. 12.72%   ✔ *CORRECT*. Review the answer shown above.

c. 7.86%   *Incorrect*. Review the answer shown above. Check your math. Reminder—the comparable's net operating income should be divided by its sale price.

d. 4.13%   *Incorrect*. Review the answer shown above. Check your math. Reminder—the comparable's net operating income should be divided by its sale price.

8.5 Calculate Comparable #2's gross income multiplier.

a. 9.06   *Incorrect*. Review the answer shown above. Check your math. Reminder—the comparable's sale price should be divided by its effective gross income.

b. 13.23   *Incorrect*. Review the answer shown above. Check your math. Reminder—the comparable's sale price should be divided by its effective gross income.

c. 4.12   ✔ *CORRECT*. Review the answer shown above.

d. 7.56   *Incorrect*. Review the answer shown above. Check your math. Reminder—the comparable's sale price should be divided by its effective gross income.

8.6 Calculate Comparable #2's overall capitalization rate.

a. 11.04%   *Incorrect*. Review the answer shown above. Check your math. Reminder—the comparable's net operating income should be divided by its sale price.

b. 7.56%   *Incorrect*. Review the answer shown above. Check your math. Reminder—the comparable's net operating income should be divided by its sale price.

c. 4.17%   *Incorrect*. Review the answer shown above. Check your math. Reminder—the comparable's net operating income should be divided by its sale price.

d. 13.23%   ✔ *CORRECT*. Review the answer shown above.

APPENDIX

8.7 Calculate Comparable #3's gross income multiplier.

    a. 8.92   *Incorrect.* Review the answer shown above. Check your math. Reminder—the comparable's sale price should be divided by its effective gross income.

    b. 13.12   *Incorrect.* Review the answer shown above. Check your math. Reminder—the comparable's sale price should be divided by its effective gross income.

    c. 7.62   *Incorrect.* Review the answer shown above. Check your math. Reminder—the comparable's sale price should be divided by its effective gross income.

    d. 4.11   ✓ *CORRECT.* Review the answer shown above.

8.8 Calculate Comparable #3's overall capitalization rate.

    a. 13.12%   ✓ *CORRECT.* Review the answer shown above.

    b. 11.21%   *Incorrect.* Review the answer shown above. Check your math. Reminder—the comparable's net operating income should be divided by its sale price.

    c. 7.62%   *Incorrect.* Review the answer shown above. Check your math. Reminder—the comparable's net operating income should be divided by its sale price.

    d. 4.23%   *Incorrect.* Review the answer shown above. Check your math. Reminder—the comparable's net operating income should be divided by its sale price.

8.9 Calculate the value of the subject property using the gross income multiplier.

    a. $601,322 rounded to $601,000   ✓ *CORRECT.* Review the answer shown above.

    b. $694,584 rounded to $695,000   *Incorrect.* Review the answer shown above and check your math. Do you have the correct effective gross income for the subject? Did you select the correct GIM from the comparables? Reminder—you multiply the EGI (effective gross income) of the subject property by the GIM selected from the comparables.

    c. $1,003,288 rounded to $1,003,000   *Incorrect.* Review the answer shown above and check your math. Do you have the correct effective gross income for the subject? Did you select the correct GIM from the comparables? Reminder—you multiply the EGI (effective gross income) of the subject property by the GIM selected from the comparables.

    d. $567,114 rounded to $567,000   *Incorrect.* Review the answer shown above and check your math. Do you have the correct effective gross income for the subject? Did you select the correct GIM from the comparables? Reminder—you multiply the EGI (effective gross income) of the subject property by the GIM selected from the comparables.

8.10 Calculate the value of the subject property using the overall capitalization rate.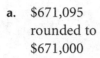

a. $671,095
rounded to
$671,000

Incorrect. Review the answer shown above and check your math. Do you have the correct net operating income for the subject? Did you select the correct overall capitalization rate from the comparables? Reminder—you divide the net operating income of the subject property by the overall capitalization rate selected from the comparables.

b. $735,010
rounded to
$735,000

Incorrect. Review the answer shown above and check your math. Do you have the correct net operating income for the subject? Did you select the correct overall capitalization rate from the comparables? Reminder—you divide the net operating income of the subject property by the overall capitalization rate selected from the comparables.

c. $981,679
rounded to
$982,000

Incorrect. Review the answer shown above and check your math. Do you have the correct net operating income for the subject? Did you select the correct overall capitalization rate from the comparables? Reminder—you divide the net operating income of the subject property by the overall capitalization rate selected from the comparables.

d. $593,662
rounded to
$594,000

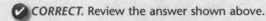 *CORRECT.* Review the answer shown above.